Dear Valued Customer,

We realize you're a busy professional with deadlines to hit. Whether your goal is to learn a new technology or solve a critical problem, we want to be there to lend you a hand. Our primary objective is to provide you with the insight and knowledge you need to stay atop the highly competitive and ever-changing technology industry.

Wiley Publishing, Inc., offers books on a wide variety of technical categories, including security, data warehousing, software development tools, and networking — everything you need to reach your peak. Regardless of your level of expertise, the Wiley family of books has you covered.

- For Dummies – The *fun* and *easy* way to learn
- The Weekend Crash Course –The *fastest* way to learn a new tool or technology
- Visual – For those who prefer to learn a new topic *visually*
- The Bible – The *100% comprehensive* tutorial and reference
- The Wiley Professional list – *Practical* and *reliable* resources for IT professionals

The book you hold now, *BEA Weblogic Workshop: Building Next Generation Web Services Visually* is your ultimate guide to creating Web services with BEA's new visual development tool — WebLogic Workshop. Whether you've never previously worked with Java and Web services or are an experienced Java and WebLogic Server maven, you'll find WebLogic Workshop to be a useful tool and this book to be a great guide to creating and deploying enterprise-quality Web services. The author team includes BEA insiders and an experienced field consultant who quickly guides you through the Workshop IDE, detailed asynchronous Web services, and explores using XML and other Web services with Workshop. With all this information, *BEA Weblogic Workshop: Building Next Generation Web Services Visually* offers something for everyone using this tool.

Our commitment to you does not end at the last page of this book. We'd want to open a dialog with you to see what other solutions we can provide. Please be sure to visit us at www.wiley.com/compbooks to review our complete title list and explore the other resources we offer. If you have a comment, suggestion, or any other inquiry, please locate the "contact us" link at www.wiley.com.

Thank you for your support and we look forward to hearing from you and serving your needs again in the future.

Sincerely,

Richard K. Swadley

Richard K. Swadley
Vice President & Executive Group Publisher
Wiley Technology Publishing

Wiley Publishing, Inc.

BEA WebLogic Workshop™: Building Next Generation Web Services Visually

Sean Christofferson, Srinivas Jayanthi,

Wira Pradjinata, and Steven Traut

Wiley Publishing, Inc.

BEA WebLogic Workshop™: Building Next Generation Web Services Visually

Published by
Wiley Publishing, Inc.
10475 Crosspoint Boulevard
Indianapolis, IN 46256
www.wiley.com

Copyright © 2003 by Wiley Publishing, Inc., Indianapolis, Indiana

Published by Wiley Publishing, Inc., Indianapolis, Indiana

Published simultaneously in Canada

Library of Congress Catalog Card Number: 2002111200

ISBN: 0-7645-1797-X

Manufactured in the United States of America

10 9 8 7 6 5 4 3 2 1

1B/SQ/QR/QT/IN

No part of this publication may be reproduced, stored in a retrieval system or transmitted in any form or by any means, electronic, mechanical, photocopying, recording, scanning or otherwise, except as permitted under Sections 107 or 108 of the 1976 United States Copyright Act, without either the prior written permission of the Publisher, or authorization through payment of the appropriate per@@hycopy fee to the Copyright Clearance Center, 222 Rosewood Drive, Danvers, MA 01923, (978) 750-8400, fax (978) 750-4744. Requests to the Publisher for permission should be addressed to the Legal Department, Wiley Publishing, Inc., 10475 Crosspoint Blvd., Indianapolis, IN 46256, (317) 572-3447, fax (317) 572-4447, E-Mail: permcoordinator@wiley.com.

LIMIT OF LIABILITY/DISCLAIMER OF WARRANTY: WHILE THE PUBLISHER AND AUTHOR HAVE USED THEIR BEST EFFORTS IN PREPARING THIS BOOK, THEY MAKE NO REPRESENTATIONS OR WARRANTIES WITH RESPECT TO THE ACCURACY OR COMPLETENESS OF THE CONTENTS OF THIS BOOK AND SPECIFICALLY DISCLAIM ANY IMPLIED WARRANTIES OF MERCHANTABILITY OR FITNESS FOR A PARTICULAR PURPOSE. NO WARRANTY MAY BE CREATED OR EXTENDED BY SALES REPRESENTATIVES OR WRITTEN SALES MATERIALS. THE ADVICE AND STRATEGIES CONTAINED HEREIN MAY NOT BE SUITABLE FOR YOUR SITUATION. YOU SHOULD CONSULT WITH A PROFESSIONAL WHERE APPROPRIATE. NEITHER THE PUBLISHER NOR AUTHOR SHALL BE LIABLE FOR ANY LOSS OF PROFIT OR ANY OTHER COMMERCIAL DAMAGES, INCLUDING BUT NOT LIMITED TO SPECIAL, INCIDENTAL, CONSEQUENTIAL, OR OTHER DAMAGES.

For general information on our other products and services or to obtain technical support, please contact our Customer Care Department within the U.S. at (800) 762-2974, outside the U.S. at (317) 572-3993 or fax (317) 572-4002.

Wiley also publishes its books in a variety of electronic formats. Some content that appears in print may not be available in electronic books.

Trademarks: Wiley, the Wiley Publishing logo and related trade dress are trademarks or registered trademarks of Wiley Publishing, Inc., in the United States and other countries, and may not be used without written permission. BEA WebLogic is a trademark of BEA Systems, Inc. All other trademarks are the property of their respective owners. Wiley Publishing, Inc., is not associated with any product or vendor mentioned in this book.

Wiley Publishing, Inc. is a trademark of Wiley Publishing, Inc.

Credits

ACQUISITIONS EDITORS
Grace Buechlein
Jim Minatel

PROJECT EDITOR
Chandani Thapa

TECHNICAL EDITOR
Kunal Mittal

COPY EDITOR
Elizabeth Kuball

EDITORIAL MANAGER
Mary Beth Wakefield

VICE PRESIDENT & EXECUTIVE GROUP PUBLISHER
Richard Swadley

VICE PRESIDENT AND EXECUTIVE PUBLISHER
Bob Ipsen

EXECUTIVE EDITORIAL DIRECTOR
Mary Bednarek

PROJECT COORDINATOR
Nancee Reeves

GRAPHICS AND PRODUCTION SPECIALISTS
Jennifer Click, Jackie Nicholas, Julie Trippetti

QUALITY CONTROL TECHNICIANS
John Tyler Connoley, Andy Hollandbeck, Angel Perez, Carl Pierce

About the Authors

Sean Christofferson was a Senior Software Engineer at BEA Systems, working on the design and development of WebLogic Workshop. Sean has written articles for BEA's developer network Dev2Dev. Sean graduated from the University of Washington with Bachelor's degrees in Biochemistry, Physics, and Mathematics.

Srinivas Jayanthi is a Senior Technologist with BEA Systems, Inc. He has over six years of experience in analysis, design, development, and testing of distributed systems using CORBA and J2EE. He is a Sun-Certified Architect for Java 2 Technologies and a BEA-Certified Technologist and Instructor for the WebLogic suite of products including WebLogic Server, Portal Server, and WebLogic Integration. He has also helped in authoring the course materials for various BEA products.

Wira Pradjinata is a SUN-Certified Architect for the J2EE Technology and a BEA Certified-Enterprise Developer. He is an independent System Architect/Integrator, focusing in J2EE and Web services development, with extensive experience with the entire BEA Platform stack.

Steven Traut is a member of the WebLogic Workshop documentation team at BEA. He has been a technical communicator in the software industry since 1995, contributing material for a variety of books for programming professionals.

To the Crossgain team
— Sean

Preface

This book is intended as an introduction to BEA's new Web services product, WebLogic Workshop. I had the opportunity to work on the first version of WebLogic Workshop team for most of the product cycle, and, as such, I had many opportunities to help shape the final product. When I was approached about doing a book on WebLogic Workshop, I was very excited by the prospect of being able to tell the world about a product I had put so much time and energy into.

My goal in writing this book was not to catalog every feature of WebLogic Workshop or to provide advice for advanced Web services developers. Instead, I kept most of the material oriented toward the beginning user who wants to get up and running with WebLogic Workshop in the minimum amount of time. I have included several chapters at the end of the book about more complicated features of WebLogic Workshop, but most of the book is focused on explaining those features that will permit developers to do start creating useful Web services as quickly as possible.

Although this book should be approachable if you don't have a great deal of experience with Java or Web services, you will be able to make more use of WebLogic Workshop and this book if you have some prior experience in those areas. The book is certainly geared toward programmers, but I make very few assumptions about your programming background. This book should be useful as much for the Visual Basic scripter as the fluent Java expert.

Likewise, I don't make too many assumptions about your understanding of Web services. The book takes a very hands-on approach to learning Web services. I don't spend a great deal of time in academic discussion of what a Web service is. Instead, I present examples of what can be done with WebLogic Workshop Web services in the hope that you'll be able to gain an intuitive understanding of Web services and from there see how you can apply Web services to your own problems.

How This Book Is Organized

The book is organized into four parts. The first part starts out with a quick overview of the field of Web services and frames the discussion of the rest of the book. After this, I embark on a chapter that walks through the steps needed to create a basic Web service. By necessity, many details are omitted, but by the end of the chapter, a fully functional Web service has been created. Finally, I give a more lengthy tour of the WebLogic Workshop IDE, talking about the various parts and discussing them in detail.

The second part introduces the core features of WebLogic Workshop. Conversations are discussed first, with some detailed explanation of this topic, which may be quite new to many people. I then embark on a discussion of asynchrony, one of the more powerful features of WebLogic Workshop. Finally, I discuss the basic controls, which allow Web services to access other services.

The third part of the book contains information on more advanced features. More advanced controls are included here, which allow access to services that most developers will probably not need for a while. Next there is a discussion of the protocols that are used by WebLogic Workshop and the control that can be exercised over these protocols.

The last part deals with JavaScript maps, very useful feature that everybody will probably end up wanting to use eventually.

A Java primer is included in an appendix at the end of the book. If you have only limited experience with Java, or you haven't worked with Java recently and are coming back to it with WebLogic Workshop, this appendix is a good reference for the basic Java language and its facilities that you could need a reminder on.

Conventions Used in This Book

Icons used in the book are described below:

This icon highlights an important point to take note of.

This icon provides a helpful hint or information.

This icon provides a reference to another chapter in the book or a resource where you can get further information on the topic under discussion.

This icon warns you of a potential problem or error.

Acknowledgments

First and foremost I would like to thank my three co-authors, Srinivas Jayanthi, Steven Traut, and Wira Pradjinata, without whom I don't know if I would have managed to complete this ambitious project.

I am very grateful to have been included in a project as interesting as WebLogic Workshop. For this I would like to thank everybody on the original Crossgain team. I would especially like to thank those who saw fit to include me in this project, including Adam Bosworth, Rod Chavez, Peter Horadan, and Stephen McMenamin. I would be remiss if I didn't mention those people with whom I worked so closely: Kevin Zatloukal, Mark Rafn, Roger Weber, and Terry Lucas.

In addition, I would like to thank the people at Wiley and Hungry Minds who kept me on track throughout this project: Jim Minatel and Chandani Thapa, as well as Grace Buechlein, who originally contacted me about doing this project.

— *Sean Christofferson*

Contents at a Glance

	Preface vii
	Acknowledgments.......................... ix
Part 1	**Getting Started**
Chapter 1	Introduction—WebLogic Workshop Web Services ... 3
Chapter 2	Getting Started with WebLogic Workshop 11
Chapter 3	A Tour of the WebLogic Workshop IDE 37
Part II	**Basic Concepts**
Chapter 4	Creating Conversational Web Services 75
Chapter 5	Creating Asynchronous Web Services 97
Chapter 6	Mapping from XML 115
Part III	**Advanced Concepts**
Chapter 7	Using the Core Controls 137
Chapter 8	Using the Advanced Controls 165
Chapter 9	Controlling the Web Service Protocols 209
Part IV	**Client Component**
Chapter 10	Calling Web Services from Outside WebLogic Workshop 237
Chapter 11	Using JavaScript in XML Maps 273
	Appendix A: What's on the CD-ROM? 311
	Appendix B: A Java Primer 315
	Index 371
	End-User License Agreement 389

Contents

Preface vii

Acknowledgments ix

Part 1	Getting Started
Chapter 1	**Introduction—WebLogic Workshop Web Services** . . . 3
	An Introduction to Web Services 3
	What are Web services? 4
	Some important standards 4
	Why are Web Services important? 6
	An Introduction to WebLogic Workshop 7
	The J2EE world 7
	WebLogic Workshop's place in the J2EE world 8
	What You Don't Need to Know to Use WebLogic Workshop . . . 8
	What You Do Need to Know to Use WebLogic Workshop 9
	JavaScript programming 9
	WebLogic Server configuration 9
	Summary 10
Chapter 2	**Getting Started with WebLogic Workshop** 11
	Introducing WebLogic Workshop 11
	Watching the First Web Service in Action 13
	Writing the First Web Service 15
	Creating Your First Web Service from Scratch 17
	Creating a new project 18
	Creating a new Web service 20
	Adding a method to your Web service 22
	Testing your Web service 26
	An Introduction to JWS 29
	Taking a closer look 29
	The Javadoc annotations 33
	Summary 36
Chapter 3	**A Tour of the WebLogic Workshop IDE** 37
	A Road Map to the IDE 37
	The Project Tree 42
	Managing projects 43
	Editing files in the project 48
	Other functions 48

Contents

The Source View	49
The text editor	49
Syntax coloring	49
Code completion	51
Error messages	54
The Structure Pane	55
The Navigation Bar	57
The Test View	59
Test View tabs	59
Getting directly at the Test View	66
The Debugger	66
Stepping through your Web services	67
The debugging interface	68
Summary	71

Part II   Basic Concepts

Chapter 4   **Creating Conversational Web Services**   **75**

The Conversational Phases	76
Starting a conversation	77
Continuing a conversation	77
Finishing a conversation	77
Working with Conversations in the Design View	78
Properties in the Source Code	81
A Conversational Example	83
What the example does	86
Using inner classes with conversations	87
Maintaining conversational state	88
Testing Conversational Web Services	89
Getting More Control Over Conversations	92
Conversational lifetimes	92
Using the Context object to control conversations	93
Summary	96

Chapter 5   **Creating Asynchronous Web Services**   **97**

Why You Need Asynchrony	97
WebLogic Workshop Asynchrony Mechanisms	98
Buffering	99
An example of a buffered service	99
Other attributes of the message-buffer tag	102
What buffering really does	103
Callbacks	103
Using callbacks	103
A callback example	106

		Viewing callbacks in the Test View 107
		Using the Context object to control callbacks 108
		Summary 113
Chapter 6		**Mapping from XML** **115**
		XML Messages 115
		Basic Maps 117
		Working with maps in the Design View 116
		XML map syntax 119
		Maps in the source code 122
		A mapping example 124
		More Mapping Constructs 126
		Dealing with repetitive elements 126
		Reusing maps 130
		Using JavaScript for mapping 132
		Summary 133

Part III		**Advanced Concepts**
Chapter 7		**Using the Core Controls** **137**
		An Introduction to WebLogic Workshop Controls 137
		The Service Control 139
		Adding Service controls 139
		How Service controls work 140
		The Timer Control 144
		The Database Control 152
		The Basics of the Database control 153
		Advanced Database control features 157
		A Database control example 159
		Summary 163
Chapter 8		**Using the Advanced Controls** **165**
		Leveraging J2EE from WebLogic Workshop 165
		The EJB Control 166
		Preparing to add an EJB control 167
		Adding an EJB control 168
		Using an EJB control 170
		The JMS Control 173
		A Java Message Service primer 173
		Adding a JMS control 177
		Using message types 181
		Adding methods to a JMS control 187
		Handling headers and properties with XML maps 188
		Correlating received messages 190
		Filtering messages using the receive-selector property 191
		Updated Online Store Example 192
		Using Control Factories 204
		Summary 208

Chapter 9	**Controlling the Web Service Protocols** 209	
	What Goes Down the Wire 209	
	Invoking a Web service using HTTP 209	
	Invoking a Web service using JMS 217	
	Understanding the Message Formats 224	
	Controlling SOAP Headers 227	
	Summary 234	
Part IV	**Client Component**	
Chapter 10	**Calling Web Services from Outside WebLogic Workshop** 237	
	Planning for Client Support 237	
	Providing an alternative to callbacks with a wrapper service ... 238	
	A wrapper for the OnlineStore service 239	
	Generating Proxies 242	
	Generating a Conversation ID 243	
	Sending a Conversation ID 245	
	Developing a JSP Client 245	
	A JavaServer Pages primer 246	
	Using the proxy from JSP code 249	
	Setting up for testing 250	
	Providing a place to log in 250	
	Starting the conversation 252	
	Developing a Swing Client 264	
	Summary 271	
Chapter 11	**Using JavaScript in XML Maps** 273	
	Enhancing XML Maps with Script 273	
	A JavaScript Primer 274	
	Variables 274	
	Objects and object hierarchies 275	
	Arrays 276	
	Declaring functions 277	
	if, else if, and else 278	
	for and for...in 279	
	JavaScript Tools for Handling XML 280	
	Creating XML variables 281	
	Working with hierarchies 282	
	Working with lists 286	
	Filtering by value 286	
	Combining, inserting, and deleting 288	
	Embedding expressions 290	
	Using loop structures with XML 291	
	Filtering by namespace 292	
	Importing Java classes 294	
	Debugging JavaScript 294	

Writing Script Functions for Mapping 295
   Connecting function names with function calls 295
   How translation through functions works 296
   Example: A FromXML function 300
   Example: A ToXML function 303
Summary of Extensions for Use with XML 307
Summary 310

Appendix A: What's on the CD-ROM? 311
System Requirements 311
Installing BEA WebLogic Platform Trial Edition
in Windows 312
What's on the CD 313
   Author-created materials 313
   Applications 313
   eBook version of BEA WebLogic Workshop: Building
   Next Generation Web Services Visually 314
Troubleshooting 314

Appendix B: A Java Primer 315
The Core Java Language 315
   A simple Java program 315
   Identifiers 317
   Variables 318
   Types 319
   Operators 324
   Expressions, statements, and blocks 329
   Control flow statements 331
The Java Libraries 341
   package java.io 341
   package java.lang 347
   package java.net 358
   package java.util 360
   package java.math 366
Summary 369

Index 371

End-User License Agreement 389

Part I

Getting Started

CHAPTER 1
Introduction: WebLogic Workshop Web Services

CHAPTER 2
Getting Started with WebLogic Workshop

CHAPTER 3
A Tour of the WebLogic Workshop IDE

Chapter 1

Introduction – WebLogic Workshop Web Services

IN THIS CHAPTER

- ◆ Introducing Web services
- ◆ Giving a basic outline of J2EE
- ◆ Explaining how WebLogic Workshop provides Web services in a J2EE environment
- ◆ Explaining what you do and don't need to know to use WebLogic Workshop

IN THIS CHAPTER, I begin the discussion of WebLogic Workshop by explaining the common usage of WebLogic Workshop in the Web Services arena.

I start the discussion by giving a brief explanation of what Web services are and a short discussion of the standards that have gained acceptance in the Web services community. After this, I talk about WebLogic Workshop and its relation to both Web services and the Java Enterprise standards known as J2EE. Finally, I discuss what you do and don't need to know in order to successfully understand this book and use WebLogic Workshop.

An Introduction to Web Services

Web services are becoming increasingly popular, and if you're reading this book, you're undoubtedly one of the many people who are interested in using them. I understand that people with many different backgrounds may pick up this book. However, even for those coming into this with a fair amount of knowledge about Web services, some common terminology and ideas can be helpful. If you have very little knowledge about Web services, this preliminary discussion should make the way a little clearer. Despite my best efforts to create a concise summary of the field of Web services, you shouldn't feel like you need to leave this chapter with a complete understanding of the material. Ultimately, the most effective way to learn about Web services is to start creating them – something I will show you how to do in Chapter 2.

What are Web services?

Web services are the next step in the evolution of providing services across a network. The moniker of *Web services* covers a set of standards that have been developed over the last few years in response to the classic difficulties that appear when creating services to be delivered over the network, such as trying to communicate with a different programming language running on a different operating system on the other side. In many cases, there are a number of competing standards. However, as Web services have begun to mature, several standards have come to dominate the field, namely SOAP, WSDL, and UDDI; which will be covered as you read this chapter further. However, beneath the standards, Web services provide a simple function: to provide services across a network.

The services that will be exposed to Web services are not new. Requesting stock quotes, submitting purchase orders, querying catalogs, services that already exist today are the types of services that will be exposed by Web services. The novelty of Web services is not in permitting services to be exposed on a network — there are many technologies available for doing that today. Instead, the main function of Web services is to provide a measure of standardization to these endeavors. In addition, WebLogic Workshop attempts to, and hopefully succeeds at, making the creation of Web services as easy as possible.

Those who spend their time attempting to divine the future of the computer industry do see several new developments being brought about by Web services. They envision large directories of services from which standardized descriptions of services can be retrieved. In addition, after a service is found, a standardized mechanism will be available to access the service. Whether this vision comes true, Web services are centered on providing standards for things that can already be done. The hope is that by providing such standards, Web services will become *the* medium for providing services across a network and will unify the many disparate technologies that exist today.

For example, let's say you have a bookstore. You want your computer to automatically notify your suppliers when you are running out of books. Traditionally this is a manual process, usually done via fax or e-mail. A human on the other side must receive the notification and send you a response, probably via the same media. Now, wouldn't it be nice if the process was fully automated, with no human intervention? Wouldn't it be nice if your computer and the suppliers' computers could talk to each other, giving responses to any request in a timely manner, or even real time? The solution to this problem, before Web Services arrive, is to define various APIs (Application Programming Interfaces) to accommodate different programming languages and various operating systems run by your suppliers. Web Services and the standards behind it enable us to leap forward and eliminate a lot of the traditional hurdles that we faced before.

Some important standards

The two standards you're most likely to make direct contact with using WebLogic Workshop are the Web Service Description Language (WSDL) and the Simple Object

Access Protocol (SOAP). WSDL is a language used to give a precise description of a Web service, and SOAP is the primary communications protocol used for Web services. If you want to publish your Web services in a common directory, you'll probably run into the Universal Description, Discovery, and Integration (UDDI) standards at some point.

SOAP (SIMPLE OBJECT ACCESS PROTOCOL)

SOAP is an XML messaging protocol that allows computers to pass around messages containing structured information. SOAP is a fairly flexible protocol, and it provides many facilities with an eye toward making it useful for many types of applications. In addition to XML, messages can contain arbitrary attachments allowing them to include binary data that isn't easily expressible in XML.

SOAP has been adopted by the Web services community as the standard messaging protocol for performing remote procedure calls (RPCs). RPC is one of the applications contemplated by the designers of SOAP, so much so that Section 7 of the SOAP standard has been devoted to considering how to use SOAP for RPC.

WebLogic Workshop uses SOAP to transmit and receive requests to access Web service methods. A Web service can be thought of as an object (in the object-oriented programming sense), which can contain a number of methods. The SOAP request is targeted at a particular object by using a particular URI, and the specific method to call is referenced by name. Any arguments to the method are passed as XML in the body of the request. Because the arguments are XML, very flexible information can be passed to the method.

WebLogic Workshop also includes facilities for making it easy to work with the XML in SOAP messages without having to use the programming APIs typically needed to decompose XML documents. Through a technology known as XML mapping, as well as an extended version of JavaScript (discussed later in this chapter), programmers can work with XML messages in WebLogic Workshop very easily.

The SOAP standard is maintained by the W3C and the text of the standard (really a note describing a proposal for a standard) can be found at the W3C Web site at www.w3.org/TR/SOAP.

WSDL

Back to the bookstore example described previously. Before your computer and the suppliers' computers can talk to each other, they have to agree on what topic to talk about and the format of that conversation. You need a standard that defines what kind of messages will be sent via SOAP. For your bookstore, you might need to define something like this: I will send you an out-of-stock notification with the book ISBN, title, and quantity needed, and you must respond with how many you can fulfill and at what price.

The standard that has been adopted by the Web services community for these descriptions is the Web Service Description Language (WSDL). WSDL is another XML standard that is a highly flexible language for describing network services. For any service, a WSDL can be produced that describes in painstaking detail the exact messages that can be passed to and from the service. WSDL files are frighteningly complex, mostly due to the fact that, like other standards that have been conscripted for duty in the Web service domain, WSDL was designed to be far more general than most current Web services that products require. Fortunately, the creation and processing of WSDL files is mostly a job for computers; there is rarely a need for people to examine these files.

WebLogic Workshop can produce WSDL files for any Web service it creates, and likewise, it can process WSDL files from other Web services. By this mechanism, WebLogic Workshop can easily interoperate with other Web services products.

As with SOAP, the standard describing WSDL is maintained by the W3C. If you're morbidly curious, you can read the standard at www.w3.org/TR/wsdl, but I don't necessarily recommend it. As I said before, WSDL is mostly used and processed by computers and there is very little need for people to scrutinize WSDL files.

UDDI

UDDI is basically electronic Yellow Pages for Web Services. UDDI is a standard being worked out by a number of important companies in the software industry. The principal aim of UDDI is to create a common directory format that can catalog services of just about every type. UDDI is very broad, and UDDI queries can be used to find everything from phone numbers to WSDL files for Web services. Although UDDI is not directly related to Web services, those who are looking forward to the future see a time when you'll find a Web service by examining a UDDI directory.

Some simple UDDI features are built into WebLogic Workshop, but UDDI is more an integrated feature of the WebLogic server itself; instead of the Workshop. If you want to learn more about UDDI, you can see their official Web site at http://uddi.org, where you can find all sorts of documents and information about this nascent standard.

Why are Web Services important?

Web services have received a great deal of hype in the press recently, and you could argue that a great deal of it is due to the fact that they solve (or at least are purported to solve) the problems I've listed above with the bookstore example. Of course, there are many gurus who offer many different reasons for the popularity of Web services, and some may put the emphasis on other issues.

Although these technical arguments are interesting, there are some more fundamental reasons for the popularity of Web services. Most fundamental is that, in some way or another, they're supposed to provide a lower-cost, higher-productivity mechanism for creating network-available services. This is something that every business is interested in because there are literally thousands of places where businesses would like their computers to interact with other computers within the business and to provide business services to the outside world. The HTML-centric Web has already made some inroads into this territory, making it easy to provide services to people, however; the Web doesn't solve the problems listed here. There are few organized directories (search engines aren't exactly the most organized of directories) and the services provided are not standard; they almost always rely on human comprehension to be effectively usable.

The most obvious disadvantage of HTML-based services is that they aren't amenable for computer-to-computer communications. HTML is useful for creating human-readable services, not computer-readable ones. One of the largest IT problems facing large companies today is the need to be able to integrate their computer systems together, so the disparate systems in various departments can talk to each other, further automating the humdrum aspects of business that add additional costs onto the real work that the business wants to perform. Web Services provide a reusable mechanism in the enterprise to connect various computer platforms from PC to mainframes (often built with a variety of programming languages and running numerous operating systems) with the same interface.

An Introduction to WebLogic Workshop

WebLogic Workshop is a tool for creating Web services. It is a Java-based tool, meaning that the code for Web services is written in the Java programming language. In addition, WebLogic Workshop sits on top of WebLogic Server, BEA's J2EE application server. WebLogic Workshop is unique in that it leverages J2EE in order to provide enterprise-quality Web services.

The J2EE world

You may or may not be familiar with Java 2 Enterprise Edition. If you aren't, don't get scared off by this complicated enterprise platform. The most amazing feature of WebLogic Workshop is that you can leverage the power of this platform without having to know all the arcane information usually required to program a J2EE application. However, despite the fact that you don't need to know anything about J2EE, sketching a basic outline of the platform can help you understand the world you'll be working in.

The central concept in J2EE is the application server. An application server allows a J2EE programmer to create an application in Java that provides fairly standardized access to typical facilities needed by enterprise applications: databases, messaging queues, security, and a network-transparent object model reminiscent of DCOM and CORBA. The application server made by BEA (and included with WebLogic Workshop) is WebLogic Server, a fully functional application server that is very popular in the enterprise world.

For in-depth discussion of the WebLogic Server, you might want to read the *BEA WebLogic Server Bible* by Joe Zuffoletto et al.

The applications created in an application server are made up of Enterprise Java Beans, a somewhat whimsical term for entities that appear somewhat like objects in an object-oriented programming language, but enhanced to add some special behavior. They are designed to be distributed components that can act as workflow coordinators, asynchronous processors, or persistence modelers.

If you want to learn more about J2EE in general, or BEA WebLogic Server specifically, plenty of books are available on the subject. WebLogic Workshop allows developers to leverage J2EE in creating Web services, without knowing too much about J2EE to get started. However, you need to be familiar with J2EE to be involved with any serious Web Services development using the Workshop.

WebLogic Workshop's place in the J2EE world

Web services aren't entirely new in J2EE. There are already some Web services solutions available. However, these solutions aren't entirely satisfactory; they are neither terribly easy to use nor incredibly well integrated with the rest of J2EE. WebLogic Workshop is designed to change the landscape somewhat, by providing a Web services solution that is both coupled to J2EE (WebLogic Workshop runs on top of WebLogic Server) and easy to use.

WebLogic Workshop provides an easy-to-use IDE that allows you to create Web services within WebLogic Server as well as a powerful run time, the actual J2EE application that provides the WebLogic Workshop facilities within WebLogic Server. With these tools, you can quickly create Web services that run on an enterprise-quality J2EE application server.

What You Don't Need to Know to Use WebLogic Workshop

You might be excited to use the Workshop right away at this point. There are some more topics you need to know prior to using the WebLogic Workshop.

The whole point of WebLogic Workshop is to permit developers to use J2EE without having to learn the complexities of the rather large J2EE standard. As a result, you can start using WebLogic Workshop knowing practically nothing about J2EE. In fact, the only thing you absolutely must understand is that WebLogic Workshop runs on top of WebLogic Server and that in order to run the Web services you create with WebLogic Workshop, you have to run WebLogic Server.

There is one thing that you cannot do with WebLogic Workshop, or at least that is not made easy by WebLogic Workshop, and that is to directly create Enterprise Java Beans. This is outside the scope of WebLogic Workshop, and if you want to start down that road, you'll need to start learning about J2EE. Fortunately, you'll find that the facilities provided by WebLogic Workshop will allow you to perform many of the tasks you want to do without resorting to the direct creation of Enterprise Java Beans.

What You Do Need to Know to Use WebLogic Workshop

WebLogic Workshop relieves you of the need to learn many things that would normally be needed to utilize J2EE. However, there are still some things you do need to know. The primary requirement is some knowledge of the Java programming language. I assume you are already familiar with Java. If not, you might want to refresh your memory by reading Java books first before continuing.

JavaScript programming

JavaScript is a scripting language that is loosely based on the Java language. It gained a great deal of popularity as an easy language to use when writing interactive Web pages, competing with VBScript as a scripting language for dynamic Web pages.

WebLogic Workshop includes a version of JavaScript that has been augmented with useful extensions for quickly and easily manipulating XML documents. Because XML figures so prominently in Web services, this scripting language has been made available for manipulating the XML documents that can be passed between various Web services and Web service clients.

Although it isn't strictly necessary to learn JavaScript in order to use WebLogic Workshop, using the advanced JavaScript features is very useful. If you want to use WebLogic Workshop for a complicated project, the time will undoubtedly come when you want to use JavaScript features. The discussion of how JavaScript is used in WebLogic Workshop is taken up in Chapter 11, and included with that discussion is a quick primer on JavaScript. However, it's somewhat out of the scope of this book to go over every possible aspect of JavaScript, and you may want to consult some external references because the primer isn't entirely self-contained and doesn't cover every aspect of the language.

WebLogic Server configuration

You do not have to understand all aspects about WebLogic server, but you need to be familiar with the configuration. This configuration is stored in a file called `config.xml`. You can use the WebLogic console or manually edit the XML file yourself. WebLogic console is much easier to use if you are not familiar with the application server. You can invoke the console by typing `http://localhost:7001/console` if you use the default installation. The configuration will be useful to customize the examples to your needs, such as to connect to your own database instead of the default that comes with the Workshop.

Summary

At this point, you may or may not feel that you actually have a firm grasp on exactly what Web services are and how you should use them. If the nature and use of Web services is fully familiar to you, this is certainly a good thing. However, you shouldn't despair if you feel a little lost at this point. Unlike user interfaces or Web pages, most of us don't make direct contact with Web services in our everyday work and life. As a result, it isn't a surprise if Web services still seem a little nebulous to you. They certainly did to me when I first heard about them. The best medicine for this is to simply dive in and start working with Web services. In a short while, you'll develop an intuitive understanding of what Web services are, and not long after that, possible uses of them will start becoming evident to you.

- Web services are a standardized mechanism for creating services available across a network.
- WebLogic Workshop Web services are created on top of J2EE, a well-established enterprise computing standard.
- You don't need to know J2EE programming or complicated object-oriented programming in order to get started with WebLogic Workshop. But eventually you need to know J2EE.
- You do need to know Java in order to use WebLogic Workshop.
- You need to be familiar with WebLogic configuration.

Chapter 2

Getting Started with WebLogic Workshop

IN THIS CHAPTER

- Creating a WebLogic Workshop Web service
- Using the test client for a WebLogic Workshop Web service
- Editing the source code of a WebLogic Workshop Web service
- Debugging a WebLogic Workshop Web service

In this chapter, I introduce you to WebLogic Workshop and get you up and running with your first WebLogic Workshop Web service. Most introductions to programming languages start with a simple example program that illustrates the basics of the particular language you're studying and helps you get your feet wet in the new programming environment. WebLogic Workshop doesn't really introduce a completely new language — for the most part, you create WebLogic Workshop Web services in Java. However, it certainly introduces a new programming environment, and you'll need a little time to become accustomed to working in this new environment.

Introducing WebLogic Workshop

So far in this book, I have covered a great deal of material that could be called theoretical. In Chapter 1, I gave a somewhat academic perspective on the utility of Web services and the role of WebLogic Workshop in this emerging technology. However, what I have said so far doesn't help you actually use WebLogic Workshop to create Web services. This chapter gives you some hands-on experience working with WebLogic Workshop.

In the spirit of making this a hands-on tutorial, I strongly suggest that you work through this chapter at your computer. The purpose of this chapter is to show you a little bit of what WebLogic Workshop can do and to help you begin to build a familiarity with the development environment. Just looking at screenshots and reading descriptions of how things are done is a poor substitute for actually pointing and clicking your way through each feature I introduce.

I assume you have already installed WebLogic Workshop or the entire WebLogic Platform 7 at this point. You do not need the whole Platform if you just want to use the Workshop, but you need WebLogic Server 7 to deploy applications built using the Workshop. For more information, you can check the WebLogic Workshop documentation site at http://edocs.bea.com/workshop/docs70/index.html.

Before you can begin developing Web services, you need to start up the WebLogic Workshop development environment. If WebLogic Workshop is set up normally on your computer, there should be an icon on the Start menu that allows you to start the development environment. Select Start⇨BEA WebLogic Platform 7.0⇨WebLogic Workshop This one stops at the Folder; there is no WebLogic Workshop executable after that. When you have done this, the splash screen will appear and in a few moments, WebLogic Workshop will start.

If this is the first time you've run WebLogic Workshop, it should look like Figure 2-1. By default, WebLogic Workshop starts up in the sample project, and opens the Hello Web service. The sample project contains some useful Web services that provide examples of a few of the important features of WebLogic Workshop. You can return to the sample project whenever you want by selecting File⇨Open Project and selecting *samples* from the project list that appears.

Chapter 2: Getting Started with WebLogic Workshop

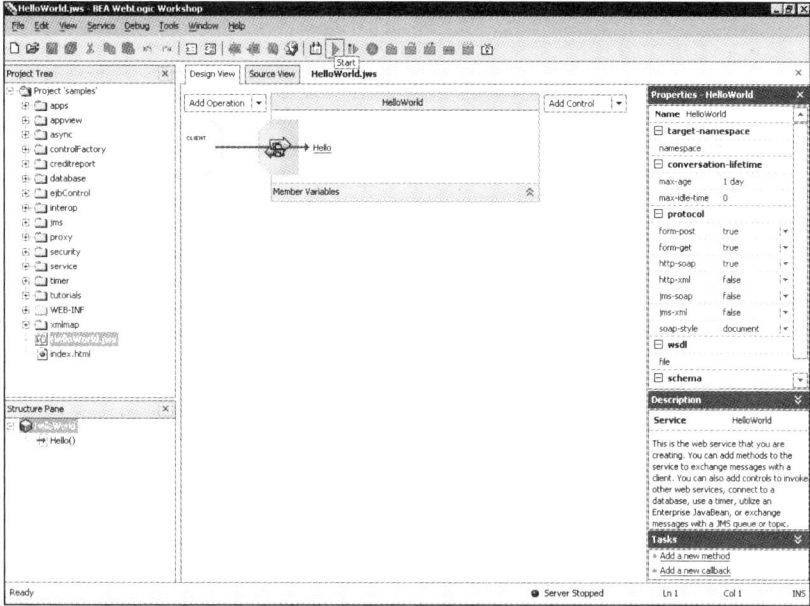

Figure 2-1: WebLogic Workshop the first time you open it.

Watching the First Web Service in Action

Let's take a look at the simplest Web Service you can possibly create, which is the Hello World sample you see when you start Workshop for the first time. To run this Web Service, you just need to click the green arrow ("Start") button at the top. Click OK if the Workshop asks you to start the WebLogic server. It will take about a minute or two to start the server (see Figure 2-2). More on starting WebLogic can be found later in this chapter.

A browser will be launched for you, with a URL that looks like the following:

http://localhost:7001/samples/HelloWorld.jws?.EXPLORE=.TEST

You will see a description of the Hello World Web Service (see Figure 2-3). It basically responds with "Hello, World!" when you invoke it. There is only one button on the screen to invoke it, and it is labeled "Hello". Click it. Voila! You just ran your very first Web Service! (See Figure 2-4.) Not bad for five minutes of work.

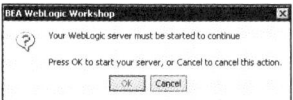

Figure 2-2: Starting the server.

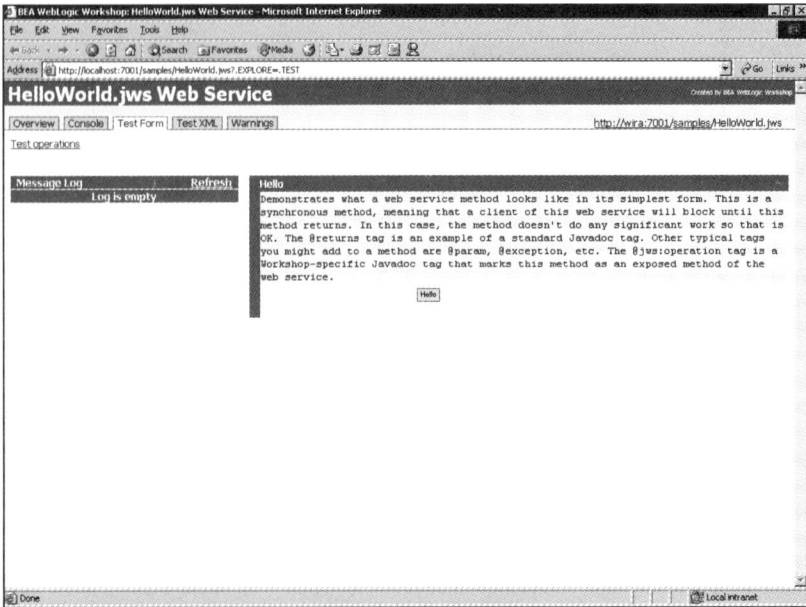

Figure 2-3: A description of the Hello World Web Service.

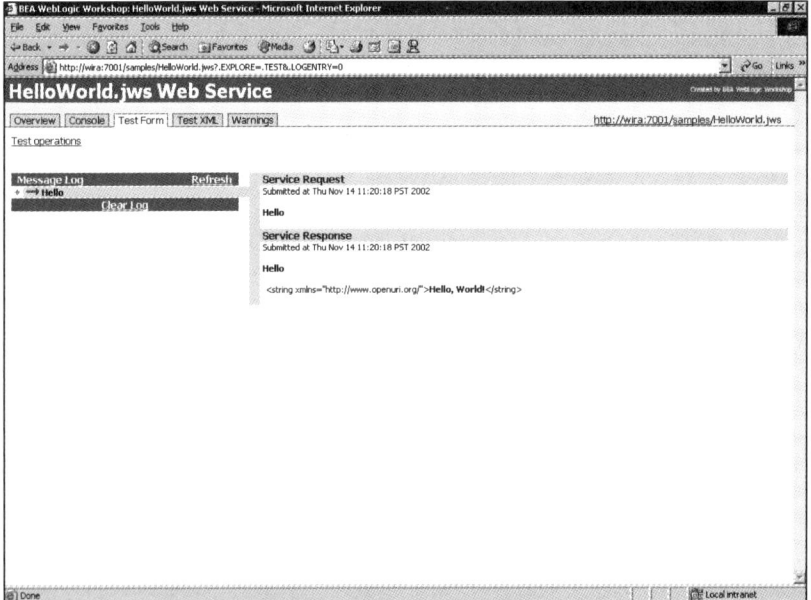

Figure 2-4: Your first Web service.

Writing the First Web Service

Let's try to modify this Web Service. Close your browser first. Click the "Source View" tab close to the "Design View" in the center top of the screen to see the source code (see Figure 2-5).

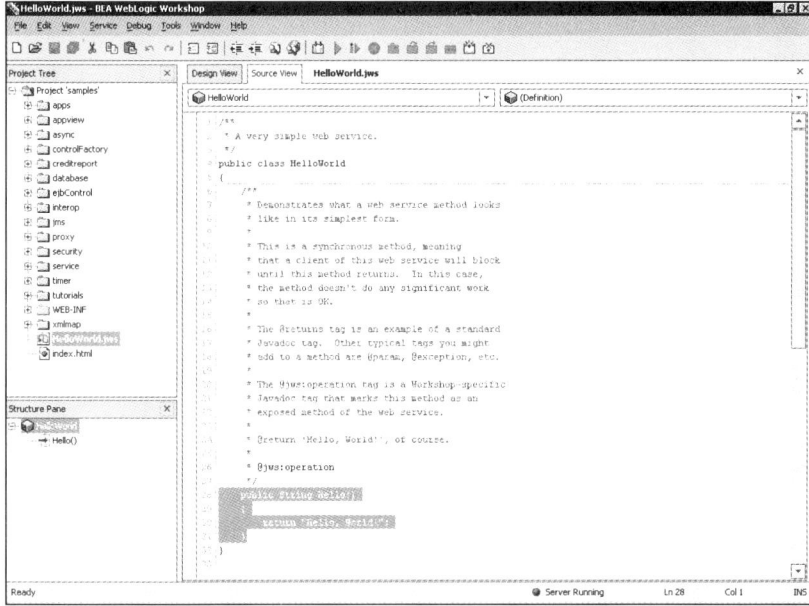

Figure 2-5: The source code.

The source code is surprisingly very simple and straightforward. There are actually a lot more comments than code in this sample. The comments are enclosed by the /** and */ pair, just like any other Java comments. In fact, the entire source code simply looks like a regular Java program.

```
public String Hello()
{
    return "Hello, World!";
}
```

We will modify this code so that the Web Service takes a name as a parameter and responds with "Hello, " plus the name that we enter.

```
public String Hello(String name)
{
    return "Hello, " + name;
}
```

Once you make the changes, run it again by clicking the same green arrow ("Start") button. This time you should notice that you do not have to start WebLogic server again. You should also see an additional text box where you can enter the name in the browser (Figure 2-6).

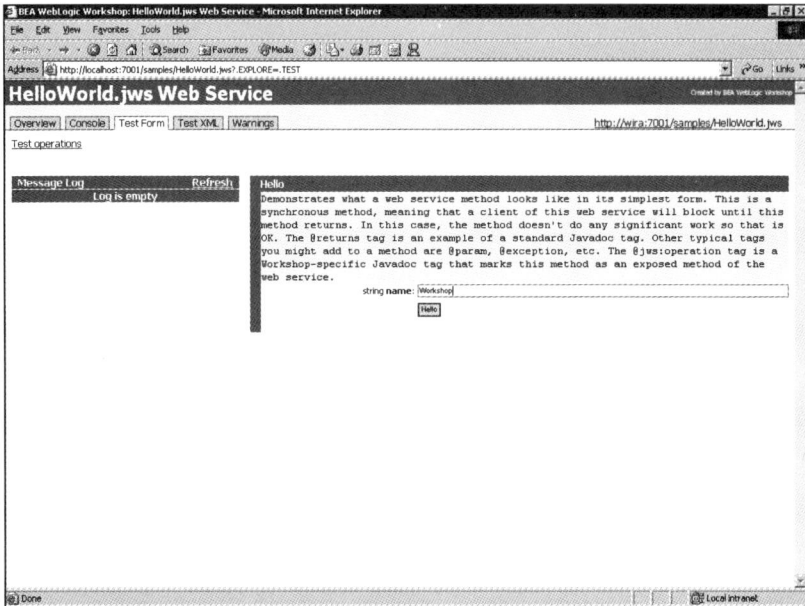

Figure 2-6: Entering the name of the browser.

Enter a name and then invoke the Hello Web Service. You should see the name displayed, instead of "World" (Figure 2-7).

Congratulations! You have just written your very first Web Service within a few minutes. This extremely simple Web Service used to take hours, if not days, to create, when you were not using the Workshop.

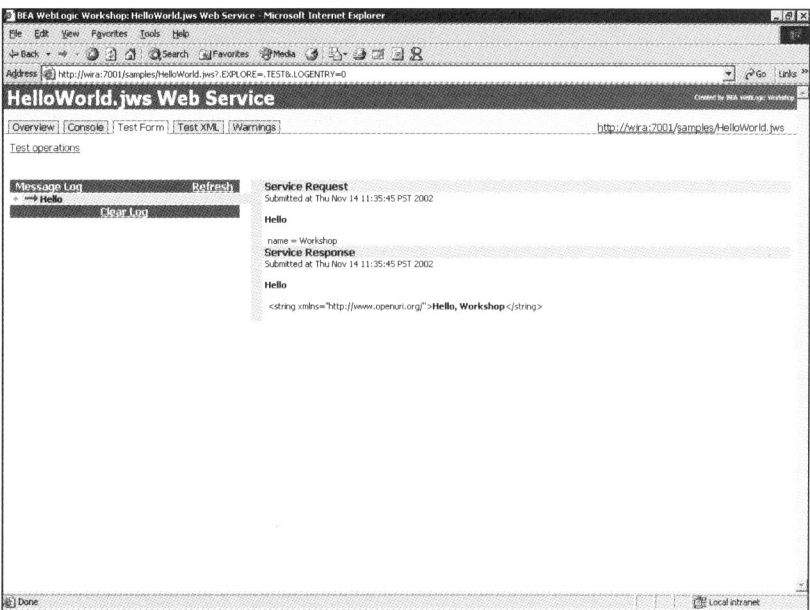

Figure 2-7: Modifying the Web Service.

Creating Your First Web Service from Scratch

Ready to move on? Good. Now let's try to write something more complicated from scratch. Imagine for a moment that you're working for a bank that has a service it wants to supply to the public. As a concrete example, let's assume the bank performs foreign exchange transactions. The bank would like to expose a conversion calculator to the public so anybody can translate a figure from one currency to another using the bank's present exchange rates. The bank may want to create a Web page where users can access this service, but it will also want to allow other clients to get at this service. Perhaps European online retailers would like to use this service to translate their prices into U.S. dollars, so their customers can see in real money how much their goods will cost. Or, a returning tourist may want to find out how much he can get for the money he's bringing back from whatever exotic land he just visited.

The bank has many options for creating this service. One very simple option is to provide the service through a Web page. Obviously, clients who are using a Web browser would have an easy time dealing with the service, however; creating other client code such as a Visual Basic program will be less pleasant. For instance, the client program would first have to perform a post or construct a possibly complicated URL in order to pass information to the Web page, and then it would have to decode the output of the page to locate the result. If the creator of the Web page decides to change the formatting of the page, which is not an uncommon occurrence, it's very possible that the Visual Basic client will break and have to be fixed. After all, Web page designers certainly don't see the form of the particular HTML code they use to make a page as an immutable contract that others will be depending on. All in all, providing services to general clients through Web pages is a very brittle solution.

As you may have guessed, this scenario is a setup to show how Web services can be used to solve the bank's problem. Web services were designed with just such a scenario in mind. They provide a powerful framework for exposing services on the network for clients who may be written in many different programming languages running on many different platforms. In addition, Web services do provide an explicit contract with their clients, in the form of a WSDL file. The Web service designers know the clients will be depending on that WSDL file, and the clients, therefore, can count on it not to change. If our fictitious bank exposes its currency calculator as a Web service, any other platform that provides support for Web services can use it. The number of platforms that provide Web service support is growing rapidly and includes such ubiquitous platforms as Microsoft Windows.

To get you started creating Web services, in the following sections I walk you through the process of creating a simple version of a currency calculator Web service. When we're finished, you should be able to appreciate how we could replace our somewhat simplified business logic with more realistic code. The point is, although you may not be creating a fully functional currency calculator, when you're done, you'll have created a fully functional Web service.

Creating a new project

When you start a new programming project in WebLogic Workshop, you'll probably want to create a new WebLogic Workshop project. The project is used in WebLogic Workshop to organize a collection of files, which include Web services. When you have a particular project open, you can manage the files in the project using the Project Browser. A WebLogic Workshop project can also contain folders, much like the file system of an operating system.

Figure 2-8 shows the WebLogic Workshop Project Browser. The Project Browser is the primary tool you'll use to work with your projects. The Project Browser is very similar in appearance to file system browsers, like Windows Explorer. The Project Browser has functionality similar to Windows Explorer and provides you with a fairly powerful tool to work with your projects.

Figure 2-8: The Project Browser.

 Your projects are not only organized like the file system, they are actually present on the file system. Assuming your installation directory is the default (which is c:\bea on a Windows system) you may find your project directories under c:\bea\weblogic700\samples\workshop\applications\. Being able to get directly at the project directory when you want to add files to the project or copy project files elsewhere is often very helpful.

The WebLogic Workshop project system is set up with Java projects in mind, and it is also designed to make the creation of deployable Web applications as straightforward as possible. As a result, the project structure closely mirrors the package structure of the Java files contained in it.

The Java package system allows you to organize your projects into units called packages. For instance, the standard Java libraries use many packages to sort out all the different classes they provide. For a refresher on the rules of Java packages, see the Java Primer in Appendix B. You can see in Figure 2-2 how locations in the sample project map to their respective Java packages.

You may have noticed that there is a slightly different looking folder, called WEB-INF, in the samples project. This folder is part of the WAR file, a concept that started with the Java Servlet standard. Later on in this chapter, I show you how this folder should be used and I explain what it means to put files in this folder. For now, all you need to know is that WEB-INF is a special WebLogic Workshop folder that is always part of your project.

All the Web services in this book are organized into a new project, which I have called "BookProject" on the CD. Before you start working on the example in this chapter, you need to create this new project. To create a new project, select File➪New Project from the menu.

Figure 2-9 shows the New Project dialog box. Enter the name "**BookProject**" in the text box and then click OK to create your new project.

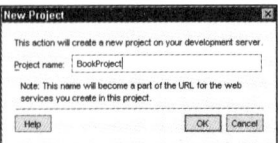

Figure 2-9: The New Project dialog box.

 You may have noticed that there is a button marked Help in the New Project dialog box. This button appears in nearly every dialog box in WebLogic Workshop and is linked to the Help system. The Help button activates the WebLogic Workshop Help system; when you click Help, you're taken to a Help page, which describes the dialog box you're working with. The WebLogic Workshop Help system runs in Internet Explorer, so pressing the Help button will never cancel, or interfere with, what you're trying to do.

Creating a new Web service

As soon as you create a new project, the New File dialog box appears, letting you create a new file to add to your project. Figure 2-10 shows the New File dialog box.

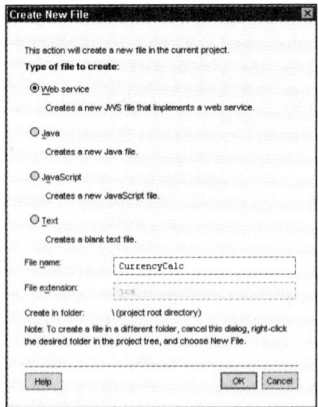

Figure 2-10: The New File dialog box.

The New File dialog box allows you to create several different file types; however, right now, we're only interested in creating a Web service. Make sure you have the Web service file type selected, and type the name **CurrencyCalc** into the File

Name text box. Because you've already selected the file type, you don't have to specify a file extension. Directly below the File Name text box, you'll see that the File Extension text box is disabled and contains the extension JWS (Java Web Services), which is the correct extension for a WebLogic Workshop Web service file. After you've entered the file name, click OK to create your new Web service.

JWS files contain Java codes with specific Javadoc tags. They are roughly similar to JSPs (Java Server Pages) in the following manner: when you put a JSP in the appropriate directory that is recognized by the application server, a class (i.e., Servlet) will be generated on the fly to process the request that is supposed to be handled by the JSP. Similarly, something will be generated on the fly when you put a JWS file in the same directory; but instead of a class, a complete J2EE deployment set () will be created.

When you first create a Web service, WebLogic Workshop opens it in the Design View. Figure 2-11 shows the Design View for your new Web service.

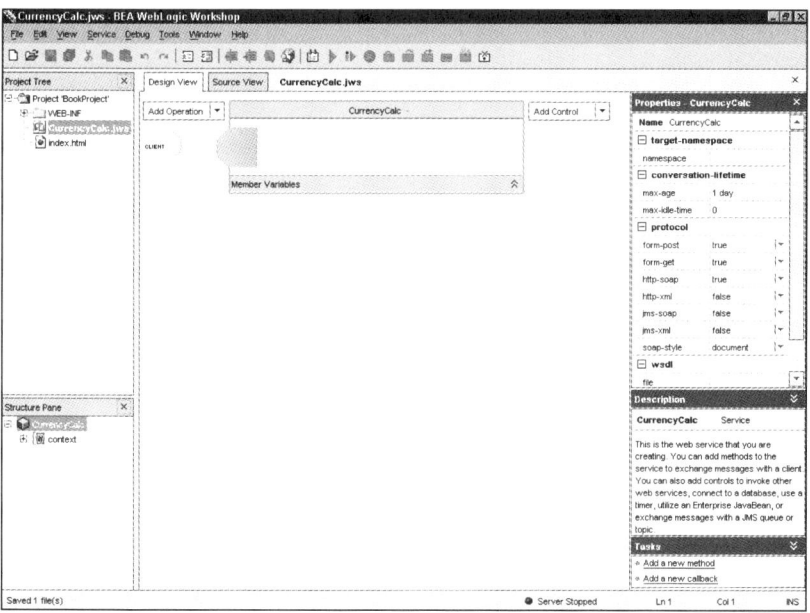

Figure 2-11: The Design View.

The Design View provides a graphical surface where you can view and edit your Web service without having to work directly with the source code. The box on the far left of the Design View depicts the Web service client. This client could be anything – perhaps another Web service, the WebLogic Workshop test client, or a client written in just about any programming language. The Web service you're creating is positioned in the center of the Design View. The Web service is completely empty right now, so there isn't anything much to see in this part of the Design View (although you may notice the name of your Web service at the top). Controls appear on the right-hand side of the Design View. Because you don't have any controls, this area is completely empty right now.

Adding a method to your Web service

You have now created a new Web service. There is only one problem: The Web service doesn't do anything! In order to make your Web service functional, you must add an operation to your Web service. Operations are the mechanism by which a WebLogic Workshop Web service communicates with the outside world. They allow your Web service to send and receive messages. WebLogic Workshop has two types of operations — methods and callbacks:

- **Methods:** Methods are what Web services expose to clients. A client can invoke a Web service method by sending an appropriate message to the Web service. Using the term *method* is a bit problematic, because it can be used to refer to a type of operation or a regular method in a Java class. Most of the time, the type of method I'm talking about will be clear; in situations where confusion could arise, I use the term *Java method* or *nonexposed method* to refer to normal methods in Java classes.

- **Callbacks:** These operations allow your Web services to send messages back to the client or the calling service. Callbacks are a feature of WebLogic Workshop that makes it easier to program asynchronous Web services.

I won't be saying anything more about callbacks in this chapter, but in Chapter 5 I will go into great detail about callbacks.

In order to allow the clients of your currency calculator to perform currency conversions, you need to add a `Convert` method to your Web service. The Design View makes adding new methods very simple.

Figure 2-12 shows the Add Operation drop-down list. Select Add Operation⇨Add Method. When you've done this, a new arrow appears on the Design View, which represents the new operation you've just added. To the right of the arrow, the name of the method is highlighted, so that you can edit it. Type **convert** and press Enter.

Figure 2-13 shows the Design View after you've added the `Convert` method. The method appears as an arrow pointing from the client, to the Web service you're developing. In order to call this method, the client sends a message to the Web service in the direction of this arrow. There is also a special icon of two large arrows, one pointing towards the Web service and another pointing away from it. You will see it once you add methods and callbacks. This icon represents the maps on this method. Maps can be used to intercept and transform messages sent from the client to the Web service and from the Web service back to the client.

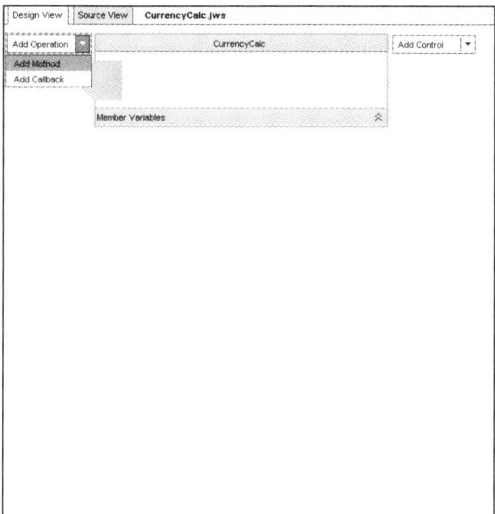

Figure 2-12: Adding an operation.

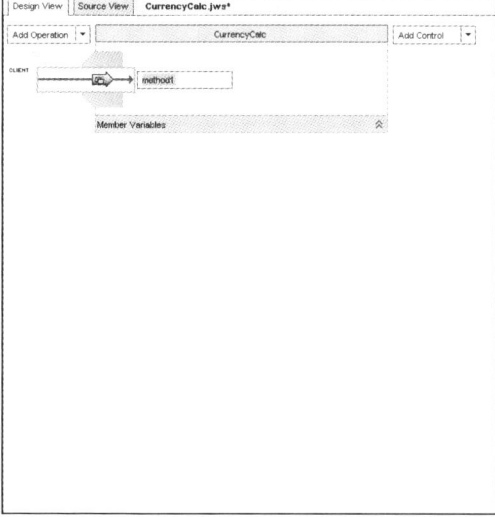

Figure 2-13: Your new method.

 You won't get to work with maps in this chapter, but I devote two whole chapters on them later in the book (Chapters 6 and 11).

Now that you've added the Convert method to your Web service, you need to write the business logic the method will implement. WebLogic Workshop doesn't include facilities for writing logic graphically, so to write the currency conversion logic, you need to edit the source code for your Web service.

Figure 2-14 shows the Convert method, after you finished renaming it. The name is now drawn blue and underlined, much like the hyperlinks on a Web page. These links connect the name of each method to the place in the source code where the method is defined. Move your mouse cursor over this link, and click to go to the source code for this method.

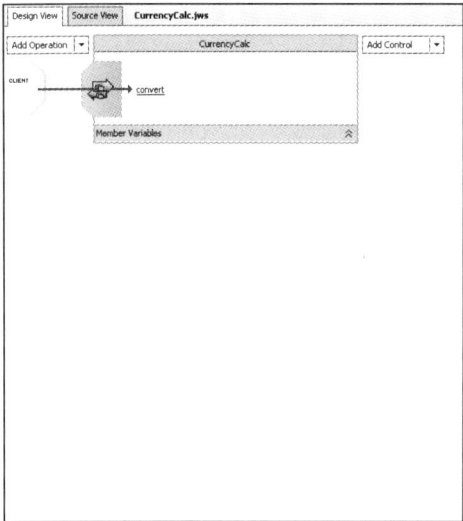

Figure 2-14: The Convert method.

Figure 2-15 shows the source code for the Convert method. Because the Source View displays the source code for your entire Web service, whenever you jump to a method, the method is highlighted in yellow and moved to the top of the screen.

In the source code, the Convert method appears as an empty Java method. Right now it takes no arguments and returns nothing. The only special thing about this method is the strange-looking comment above it (@jws:operation). This specially formatted comment tells WebLogic Workshop that this method is an operation and should be exposed to the network. If you remove this comment, the method will cease to be an operation and will become a normal Java method. Normal Java methods are not displayed in the Design View, so if you remove the comment, the arrow for the method will disappear as well.

 In reality, it is the special @jws:operation tag, and not the whole comment that WebLogic Workshop uses to determine that a method is an operation. Later in this chapter, I show you how these comments are formatted, so you can add to them and change them without fear of breaking your Web service.

Figure 2-15: The source code for Convert method.

In order to make the `Convert` method do something, you need to add some business logic that performs the currency conversion. In addition, you need to add parameters to the method so that arguments can be passed to it, and you need to add a return type so it can return results to the client.

Listing 2-1 shows a simple version of the `Convert` method. This method takes three-letter currency codes (defined by ISO 4217, if you're curious) for the currency to convert from and the currency to convert to and a double representing the amount to convert, and returns a double representing the converted amount. If the currency codes aren't recognized or the amount is negative, it will return -1.0.

Listing 2-1: The Edited Hello Operation

```
/**
 * @jws:operation
 */
public double convert(String from, String to, double amount)
{

    if (amount < 0)
        return -1.0;

    if (from.equals("USD") && to.equals("EUR"))
        return 1.11320 * amount;
    else if (from.equals("EUR") && to.equals("USD"))
        return 0.8983 * amount;
    else
        return -1.0;
}
```

This method has a couple of problems: It can only deal with U.S. dollars and Euros, and it won't recognize currency codes that aren't in all capital letters. Despite these shortcomings, it will serve for a first example. Soon enough, we'll improve this method to make it a little bit more interesting.

Testing your Web service

You've now created a Web service that can do currency conversion. The logical question to ask at this point is: Does it work? Several times I've mentioned the clients that will be accessing your Web service—in order to test the Web service you've just created, you're going to need your own client. Does this mean you now have to figure out how to write a Web service client before you can even test out your Web service? Fortunately, the answer is no.

WebLogic Workshop comes with its own client for any Web service you create. This client provides a rich interface you can use to test your Web services. You can access this interface directly through your Web browser, making it incredibly easy to test your Web services. However, before you can test your Web service, you must build it and deploy it to WebLogic Server, the application server that hosts WebLogic Workshop Web services. You have seen this client before when you run the Hello World Web Service.

Before you can deploy your new wWeb service, you need to start WebLogic Server. To start the server, select Tools⇨Start WebLogic Server.

As soon as you start up the server, you'll see a console window appear as well as the WebLogic Server Progress dialog box, as shown in Figure 2-16. The console window is associated with WebLogic Server, and if you close it, you will stop the server. The Server Progress window lets you know that the server is in the process of starting. Depending on the machine you're using, it may take a few minutes for WebLogic Server to start. If you're running on a slow machine, this may be a good time to go grab a cup of coffee.

Figure 2-16: Starting WebLogic Server.

After you've started the server, you can deploy your Web service and start the test client. To do this, you can click the "Start" green arrow button like you did before, or select Debug⇨Start. This will build your Web service and deploy it to the server. If there are any errors, WebLogic Workshop will not run the test client and you'll have to fix the errors before you proceed. Otherwise, after WebLogic Workshop has finished building and deploying the Web service, it will start the test client.

Figure 2-17 shows the test client for the CurrencyCalc Web service. Because the test client is a Web interface, WebLogic Workshop uses Internet Explorer by default to display it. The test client starts up showing you the list of methods (operations only, Java methods are not exposed) in your Web service. The CurrencyCalc Web service contains only one method, Convert, so this is the only method you'll see in the list.

Starting the Server

As you saw before, whenever you try to perform an operation that requires the server to be running, WebLogic Workshop will automatically prompt you to start the server, so you don't have to worry about whether you need the server running before you try to do something.

While you're starting the server, you don't have to stop working. If you click Close in the Server Progress dialog box, you can go back to work while the server starts in the background. You can tell if the server is running or stopped by looking at the status indicator in the lower-right corner of the screen. A little green dot means the server is running; a red dot means it is stopped.

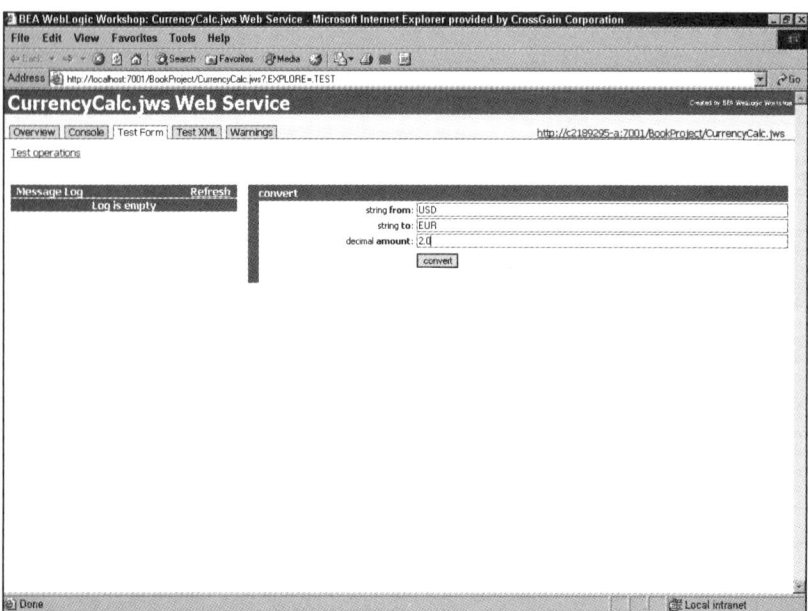

Figure 2-17: The test client for the CurrencyCalc Web service.

The test client provides text boxes for you to enter the three parameters to the Convert method and a button to click in order to invoke the method. Enter any values you want into these text boxes and click the Convert button to test this method.

Figure 2-18 shows the test client after you've invoked the Convert method. There are two important things to notice. First, the Message Log on the left side of the test client has changed to show that the Convert method has been called once. Each time you invoke a method of your Web service, the test client records this event in the Message Log.

Second, where the method list was before, there is now a record of the request you made to the Web service and the response from the Web service. The response contains an XML encoded form of the value returned from the Convert method. You can get back to the record for this method invocation at any time by clicking on the entry for this method invocation in the Message Log.

```
<double xmlns="http://www.openuri.org/">2.2264</double>
```

If you click the Back button on your browser (or click the Test operations link in the upper-left-hand corner of the page) you can get back to the list of your Web service's methods and try invoking Convert with other sets of arguments.

You've now created a complete, standards-compliant Web service. Clients on any platform in any programming language where Web services clients can be written — and that list is getting very big — could invoke this Web service across any network where your computer is visible. However, this Web service is pretty simple, so next let's make this service a little more interesting.

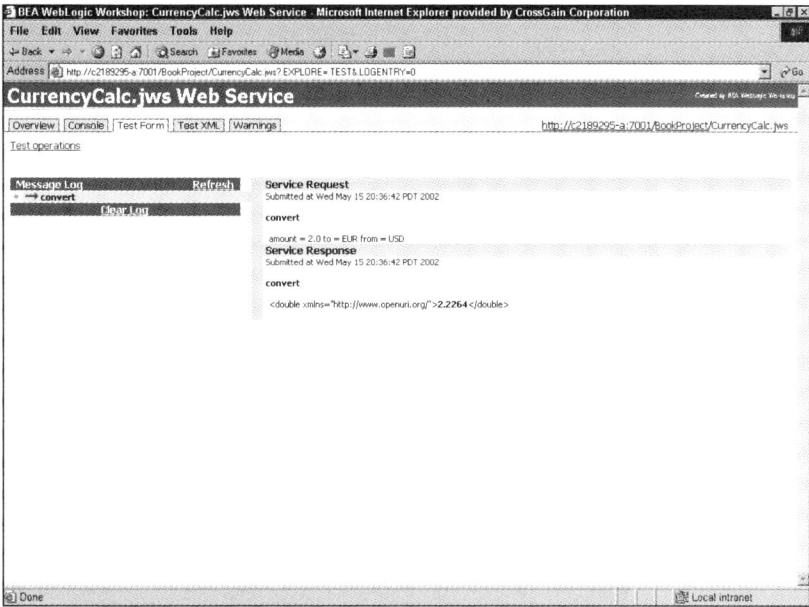

Figure 2-18: The test client after a method invocation.

An Introduction to JWS

When you're trying to get an overview of your Web service, or do certain operations like adding methods and callbacks, working in the Design View is very useful. However, when it's time to start writing your business logic, you'll need to work with the source code. Throughout this book, I present most of the examples as source code, without talking about how they could have been partially created in the Design View. As a result, understanding the source code representation of WebLogic Workshop Web services and being comfortable working in the Source View will be absolutely essential.

You may have already noticed that CurrencyCalc is not stored in a file with the JAVA extension, like most Java programs. Instead, it's located in a file with the JWS extension. This extension stands for Java Web Service, which refers to the format used for WebLogic Workshop Web services. The JWS format is very similar to Java; in fact, a JWS file always contains Java code that is completely legal. Extra information is stored in JWS files in the form of specially-formatted comments. Now, let's take a closer look at the source code for the CurrencyCalc Web service.

Taking a closer look

Earlier, you used the Design View to go the source code for the Convert method. If you were feeling adventurous, you may have scrolled around and noticed that the

Part I: Getting Started

Source View actually contains the complete source code for your Web service. In fact, the Source View is a fully-functional editing environment where you can edit JWS, Java, or plain text files.

You can switch between the Source View and the Design View at any time by using the view tabs shown in Figure 2-19 at the top of the WebLogic Workshop main window. If you switch to the Source View, you can see the source code for the entire CurrencyCalc Web service, which is also shown in Listing 2-2.

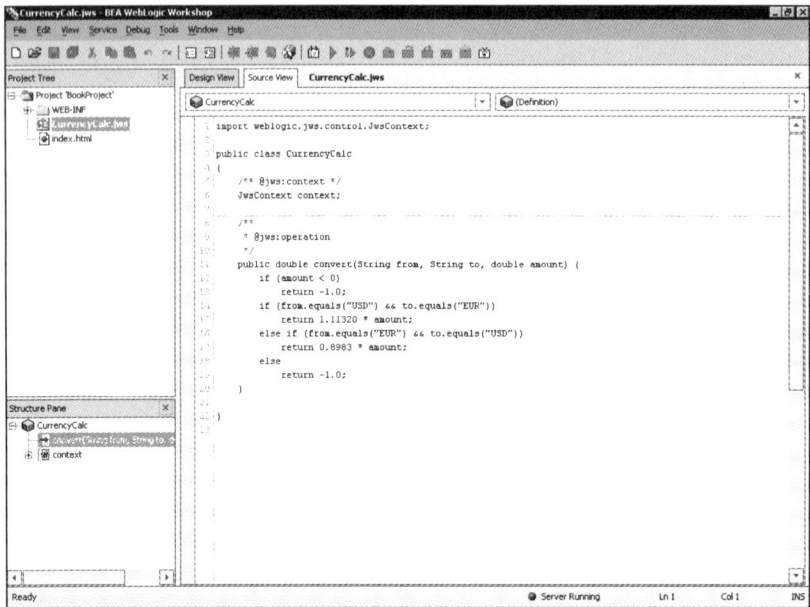

Figure 2-19: The Source and Design View tabs.

Listing 2-2: The CurrencyCalc Web Service

```
import weblogic.jws.control.JwsContext;

public class CurrencyCalc
{
    /** @jws:context */
    JwsContext context;

    /**
     * @jws:operation
     */
    public double convert(String from, String to, double amount)
    {
        if (amount < 0)
```

```
        return -1.0;

    if (from.equals("USD") && to.equals("EUR"))
        return 1.11320 * amount;
    else if (from.equals("EUR") && to.equals("USD"))
        return 0.8983 * amount;
    else
        return -1.0;
    }
}
```

Amazingly enough, all the source code needed to create the CurrencyCalc Web service can be fit into 23 lines, with room to spare. In fact, right now, there isn't much else besides the method you added. It bears repeating that the code in this listing is *all there is*. There are no extra files containing more information that is needed for WebLogic Workshop to use this Web service. You could have typed this code into a text editor, saved it directly into your project directory, and used it to create a fully functional Web service. The WebLogic Workshop runtime takes care of the (numerous!) details of transforming this code into a Web service.

THE IMPORT STATEMENT
The very first thing that appears in the CurrencyCalc source code is an import statement.

```
import weblogic.jws.control.JwsContext;
```

Because JWS files are just like normal Java files, you can import any class you want. When you create a new Web service in WebLogic Workshop, an import of the `JwsContext` class is automatically added. This object is very useful and the import is added so that it will be available to you as soon as you start working with the source code of your Web service

THE WEB SERVICE CLASS
The next thing you see in the source code is the declaration of the `CurrencyCalc` class.

```
public class CurrencyCalc
```

Every Web service you create in WebLogic Workshop becomes a Java class. This class is a completely normal Java class to which you can add any fields or methods you desire. The methods you declare can be operations, like `Convert` method in the `CurrencyCalc` class, or they can be normal Java methods. As I've mentioned earlier, the comments above the methods define exactly what those methods become in the Web service.

When you add a field — also known as a *member variable* — to a Java class, you can access it from any methods, whether or not they are operations. However, the values of fields aren't saved between calls to operation methods, unless the operations participate in conversations. We take a closer look at the details of conversations in Chapter 4.

THE CONTEXT OBJECT

The CurrencyCalc example contains one field, which declares an object called `Context` of the class `JwsContext`. As I mentioned in the preceding section, WebLogic Workshop automatically adds an import for the `JwsContext` class to every new Web service. Likewise, it automatically adds a `Context` field to every Web service.

```
/** @jws:context */
JwsContext context;
```

The comment above the `Context` object contains a special tag, `@jws:context`, just like the comment above the `Convert` method. These special tags are called *annotations*, and they are the principal means by which WebLogic Workshop adds extra information to JWS files. The annotation above the `Convert` method tells WebLogic Workshop that the method needs to be turned into an operation. The annotation above the `Context` fields tells WebLogic Workshop that this object is the `Context` object, a very special type of object that you'll learn much more about as you read the rest of the book. In fact, when WebLogic Workshop sees this tag, it automatically fills in this field with an instance of the `Context` object, so you never have to worry about initializing it.

THE CONVERT METHOD

I've already said a bit about the `Convert` method. However, there are a few extra points that can be made about it here.

```
/**
 * @jws:operation
 */
public double convert(String from, String to, double amount)

    if (amount < 0)
        return -1.0;

    if (from.equals("USD") && to.equals("EUR"))
        return 1.11320 * amount;
    else if (from.equals("EUR") && to.equals("USD"))
        return 0.8983 * amount;
    else
        return -1.0;
}
```

Like the `Context` object, the `Convert` method has an annotation above it. This annotation, `@jws:operation`, tells WebLogic Workshop to make this method into an operation. If you were to remove this annotation from the method, it would turn into a normal Java method, and the arrow in the Design View would disappear.

Aside from the annotation, this method is completely regular Java. To invoke this method, the client sends a message to the CurrencyCalc Web service. The arguments for the method are decoded from the message and then this method is called and run. When the method returns, the return value is encoded in a new message, which is sent back to the client. However, when you're writing the code for this method, you don't have to worry about any of this. You can work with normal Java types, almost totally oblivious to the messages that are being passed around, although later it will be very useful to think about the messages when you want to have more control over their format.

The Javadoc annotations

Thus far, I have provided very little detail about the annotations that appear in JWS files. You may have the impression that they're fragile things that you shouldn't touch, lest you break your Web service forever. On the contrary, editing the annotations by hand is very useful, and their syntax is simple enough that dealing with them is relatively easy. In addition, you may want to add some comments above your fields and methods, which can share a comment block with the annotations.

JAVADOC

The annotations that appear in JWS are not a new creation; they're an extension of an existing system known as Javadoc. Javadoc is a tool that allows programmers to write special comments that can be used to automatically generate documentation for their Java programming projects. If you've ever browsed the standard Java Development Kit documentation, you've seen documentation that has been generated by Javadoc. Javadoc outputs a nicely formatted set of HTML pages that allow you to easily navigate through your packages, classes, methods, and fields.

A Javadoc comment is a specially formatted comment that can be used by the Javadoc tool. These comments can appear anywhere in your source code, although the most common places to see Javadoc comments are above classes, fields, and methods. When you place a Javadoc comment directly above a class, method, or field, it's interpreted as documentation for that class, method, or field.

A Javadoc comment must start with the special sequence `/**`; that is, you must add an extra star to the normal comment sequence `/*`. Javadoc comments end with the standard `*/`. The first part of a Javadoc comment contains a plain-text or HTML-formatted description. The second part of the comment contains a list of *Javadoc tags,* which are started with an @ and are used as special directives to the Javadoc tool. Listing 2-3 shows a fairly typical Javadoc comment.

Listing 2-3: A Typical Javadoc Comment

```
/**
 * Computes the square root of the specified number.
 *
 * @author Sean Christofferson
 * @param num the number
 * @return the square root of the number
 */
public double squareRoot(double num)
```

This Javadoc comment appears above a method that takes the square root of a number. It documents the method, including giving specific details about the parameters to the method and the return value of the method. The first section is the general comment about the method; following this is the section containing the tags. When the Javadoc tool examines these comments, it will use them to create API documentation for this method, which will include all the information in the comment, formatted in a consistent manner.

Take special care not to intermix the text description of the method with the tags. The following code is erroneous, because the text description appears after the tags section has already started.

```
/**
 * @author Sean Christofferson
 *
 * Computes the square root of the specified number.
 *
 * @param num the number
 * @return the square root of the number
 */
```

Javadoc is an incredibly useful documentation tool. It can limit or eliminate the need to create external documentation, and you can use the Javadoc tool to generate your documentation in a nicely formatted set of Web pages. It's also very easy to keep Javadoc documentation in sync with your source code, because when you're changing your source code, the comment is right in front of you and easy to change.

If you haven't used Javadoc already, you should seriously consider trying it out. You can find out more about Javadoc at the official Java Web site (http://java.sun.com/j2se/javadoc).

WEBLOGIC WORKSHOP JAVADOC EXTENSIONS

WebLogic Workshop extends the standard Javadoc mechanism to create its annotations. The annotation on top of the `Convert` method contains the special tag `@jws:operation` to define the method as an operation. All WebLogic Workshop Javadoc tags have the prefix `jws` to distinguish them from the normal Javadoc tags.

```
/**
 * @jws:operation
 */
public String hello(String name)
{
    return "Hello, " + name;
}
```

The Javadoc comment above the `Convert` method is a normal Javadoc comment, except for the special WebLogic Workshop tag. You could fill out this comment with your own description and standard Javadoc without interfering with the operation of WebLogic Workshop. Listing 2-4 shows an example of the `Convert` method, augmented with a great deal of documentation.

Listing 2-4: A Commented Convert Method

```
/**
 * Converts the specified amount of from the currency type
 * specified by <code>from</code> to the currency specified
 * by the type <code>to</code>. The currency types are
 * specified using the ISO 7412 three-letter currency codes.
 *
 * @param from the currency type to convert from
 * @param to the currency type to convert to
 * @param amount the amount to be converted
 * @return the converted amount
 * @jws:operation
 */
public double convert(String from, String to, double amount)
{
)
    if (amount < 0)
        return -1.0;

    if (from.equals("USD") && to.equals("EUR"))
        return 1.11320 * amount;
    else if (from.equals("EUR") && to.equals("USD"))
        return 0.8983 * amount;
    else
        return -1.0;
}
```

I've used the standard Javadoc `@param` and `@return` tags, which are included with the `@jws:operation` tag in the tags section, and I have added a large documentation section above the tags. The special tag `<code>` is used by Javadoc to format a section of documentation in a monospace font, like source code is typically formatted.

Summary

In this chapter, I cover a great deal of material and little of it in any depth. This rapid tour was not intended to give you a full understanding of any feature in WebLogic Workshop, but rather, to give you some hands-on experience with WebLogic Workshop. You may be finishing this chapter with some unanswered questions. If that is the case hang on to them — you'll find many more answers in the chapters to come.

- All work in WebLogic Workshop is done in project. A project can contain many Web services as well as other types of files.
- WebLogic Workshop Web services are written in JWS files, which are essentially just normal Java files with special annotations.
- WebLogic Workshop annotations are written by extending the special commenting style known as Javadoc.
- WebLogic Workshop includes a powerful test client and debugger so you can test and debug your Web services as soon as you're finished writing them.

Chapter 3

A Tour of the WebLogic Workshop IDE

IN THIS CHAPTER

- Managing projects with the Project Tree
- Editing source code with the Source View
- Browsing and navigating the structure of files with the Structure Pane and Navigation Bar
- Using the WebLogic Workshop Test View
- Using the WebLogic Workshop debugger

AT THIS POINT, I will pause the presentation of WebLogic Workshop Web services to take up the topic of the WebLogic Workshop IDE. This chapter is not strictly necessary to understand Web services, but it serves as a useful place to collect a great deal of information about the IDE, which you'll very likely find useful as you develop your Web services.

If you're more interested in continuing to learn about Web services or if you prefer to learn how to use development environments by pointing and clicking, you can safely skim or even skip this chapter and refer back to it later if you want to know the details of any particular feature. This chapter is not meant to be an encyclopedia of IDE features, but rather a close look at those features you'll probably want to use frequently. The IDE provides an online Help system if you want to learn more about a particular feature, and you can access this Help system from the Help menu.

A Road Map to the IDE

The WebLogic Workshop IDE is a useful tool you can use to construct your Web services. Truthfully, you don't need the IDE to construct a Web service; a simple text editor will do. However, the IDE provides both a Java development environment as well as a Web services development environment, so it can make the job of constructing a Web service much easier.

If you have never experienced how hard it is to code Web Services manually by hand, here is a WSDL for describing the "Hello World" example that comes with the Workshop. It is a very simple Web Service that will respond with "Hello, World!" when invoked.

```xml
<?xml version="1.0" encoding="utf-8" ?>
<definitions xmlns="http://schemas.xmlsoap.org/wsdl/"
xmlns:conv="http://www.openuri.org/2002/04/soap/conversation/"
xmlns:cw="http://www.openuri.org/2002/04/wsdl/conversation/"
xmlns:http="http://schemas.xmlsoap.org/wsdl/http/"
xmlns:jms="http://www.openuri.org/2002/04/wsdl/jms/"
xmlns:mime="http://schemas.xmlsoap.org/wsdl/mime/"
xmlns:s="http://www.w3.org/2001/XMLSchema" xmlns:s0="http://www.openuri.org/"
xmlns:soap="http://schemas.xmlsoap.org/wsdl/soap/"
xmlns:soapenc="http://schemas.xmlsoap.org/soap/encoding/"
xmlns:xm="http://www.bea.com/2002/04/xmlmap/"
targetNamespace="http://www.openuri.org/">
 <types>
  <s:schema attributeFormDefault="qualified" elementFormDefault="qualified"
targetNamespace="http://www.openuri.org/">
    <s:element name="Hello">
      <s:complexType />
    </s:element>
    <s:element name="HelloResponse">
      <s:complexType>
        <s:sequence>
          <s:element minOccurs="0" maxOccurs="1" name="HelloResult"
type="s:string" />
        </s:sequence>
      </s:complexType>
    </s:element>
    <s:element nillable="true" name="string" type="s:string" />
  </s:schema>
 </types>
 <message name="HelloSoapIn">
  <part name="parameters" element="s0:Hello" />
 </message>
 <message name="HelloSoapOut">
  <part name="parameters" element="s0:HelloResponse" />
 </message>
 <message name="HelloHttpGetIn" />
 <message name="HelloHttpGetOut">
  <part name="Body" element="s0:string" />
 </message>
 <message name="HelloHttpPostIn" />
 <message name="HelloHttpPostOut">
```

```xml
    <part name="Body" element="s0:string" />
</message>
<portType name="HelloWorldSoap">
 <operation name="Hello">
    <documentation>Demonstrates what a web service method looks like in its simplest form. This is a synchronous method, meaning that a client of this web service will block until this method returns. In this case, the method doesn't do any significant work so that is OK. The @returns tag is an example of a standard Javadoc tag. Other typical tags you might add to a method are @param, @exception, etc. The @jws:operation tag is a Workshop-specific Javadoc tag that marks this method as an exposed method of the web service.</documentation>
    <input message="s0:HelloSoapIn" />
    <output message="s0:HelloSoapOut" />
 </operation>
</portType>
<portType name="HelloWorldHttpGet">
 <operation name="Hello">
    <documentation>Demonstrates what a web service method looks like in its simplest form. This is a synchronous method, meaning that a client of this web service will block until this method returns. In this case, the method doesn't do any significant work so that is OK. The @returns tag is an example of a standard Javadoc tag. Other typical tags you might add to a method are @param, @exception, etc. The @jws:operation tag is a Workshop-specific Javadoc tag that marks this method as an exposed method of the web service.</documentation>
    <input message="s0:HelloHttpGetIn" />
    <output message="s0:HelloHttpGetOut" />
 </operation>
</portType>
<portType name="HelloWorldHttpPost">
 <operation name="Hello">
    <documentation>Demonstrates what a web service method looks like in its simplest form. This is a synchronous method, meaning that a client of this web service will block until this method returns. In this case, the method doesn't do any significant work so that is OK. The @returns tag is an example of a standard Javadoc tag. Other typical tags you might add to a method are @param, @exception, etc. The @jws:operation tag is a Workshop-specific Javadoc tag that marks this method as an exposed method of the web service.</documentation>
    <input message="s0:HelloHttpPostIn" />
    <output message="s0:HelloHttpPostOut" />
 </operation>
</portType>
<binding name="HelloWorldSoap" type="s0:HelloWorldSoap">
  <soap:binding transport="http://schemas.xmlsoap.org/soap/http" style="document" />
   <operation name="Hello">
     <soap:operation soapAction="http://www.openuri.org/Hello" style="document" />
```

```xml
      <input>
        <soap:body use="literal" />
      </input>
      <output>
        <soap:body use="literal" />
      </output>
    </operation>
  </binding>
  <binding name="HelloWorldHttpGet" type="s0:HelloWorldHttpGet">
    <http:binding verb="GET" />
    <operation name="Hello">
      <http:operation location="/Hello" />
      <input>
        <http:urlEncoded />
      </input>
      <output>
        <mime:mimeXml part="Body" />
      </output>
    </operation>
  </binding>
  <binding name="HelloWorldHttpPost" type="s0:HelloWorldHttpPost">
    <http:binding verb="POST" />
    <operation name="Hello">
      <http:operation location="/Hello" />
      <input>
        <mime:content type="application/x-www-form-urlencoded" />
      </input>
      <output>
        <mime:mimeXml part="Body" />
      </output>
    </operation>
  </binding>
  <service name="HelloWorld">
    <documentation>A very simple web service.</documentation>
    <port name="HelloWorldSoap" binding="s0:HelloWorldSoap">
      <soap:address location="http://localhost:7001/samples/HelloWorld.jws" />
    </port>
    <port name="HelloWorldHttpGet" binding="s0:HelloWorldHttpGet">
      <http:address location="http://localhost:7001/samples/HelloWorld.jws" />
    </port>
    <port name="HelloWorldHttpPost" binding="s0:HelloWorldHttpPost">
      <http:address location="http://localhost:7001/samples/HelloWorld.jws" />
    </port>
  </service>
</definitions>
```

As you can see, a WSDL for such a simple Web Service is long and tedious. Imagine what you have to type manually if you have some really complicated Web Services interacting with each other!

Before I start discussing specific IDE features, I will begin by presenting an overall road map to the material I will present in this chapter. Figure 3-1 shows the IDE, and points out the various features I will be discussing in this chapter (with the exception of the Test View, which isn't pictured).

Table 3-1 provides a summary of the main features pictured in Figure 3-1.

TABLE 3-1 THE PRIMARY IDE FEATURES

Section	Description
Project Tree	Shows the structure of and allows you to manage the project.
Source View	Allows you to edit source files.
Structure Pane	Shows the class structure of the current file.
Navigation Bar	Shows a different view of the class structure of the current file.
Test View	Gives you an interface for testing your Web services.
Debugger	Gives you the ability to debug your Web services.

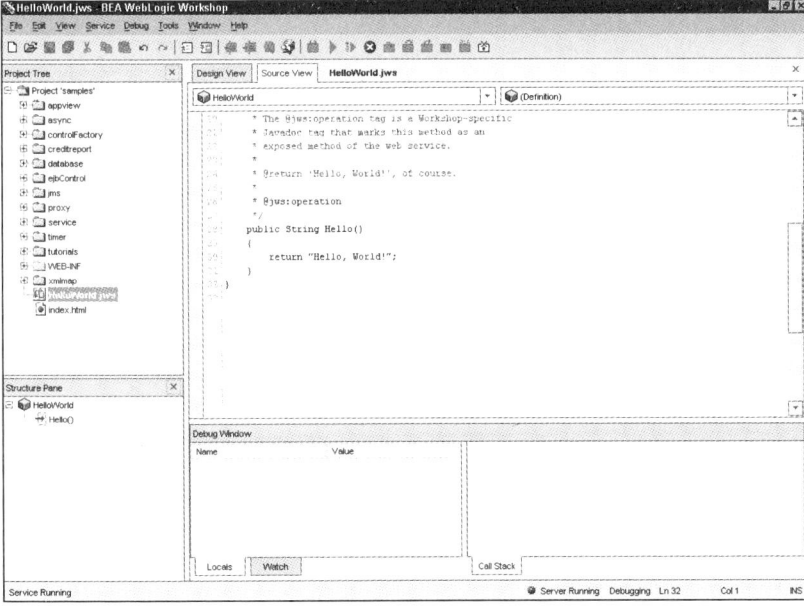

Figure 3-1: The IDE.

In Figure 3-1, the Source View is showing, so the Design View and the Property Editor, two other IDE features, are not pictured. These two features are also left out of the descriptions in Table 3-1. These two features are very Web-service specific and describing them right now wouldn't be very useful. Later on in the next few chapters, as I discuss more Web service features, I talk about the Design View and Property Editor in detail.

The Project Tree

The Project Tree allows you to view and manage your WebLogic Workshop projects. A Workshop project is essentially a set of files and other resources that makes up a Web Service or a group of related Web Services. It has a number of features commonly found in file system browsers, as well as some features useful for working with WebLogic Workshop projects in the Source View. Figure 3-2 shows the Project Tree for the samples project, included with WebLogic Workshop.

The Project Tree shows the exact structure of the files that are actually present in the file system. Each of the files shown in the Project Tree has a special icon next to it, which identifies its file type. The top-level folder, samples, is located on the file system in the applications folder, which holds all the top-level project folders. As I mentioned before, this folder can be found at:

`<installation directory>\weblogic700\samples\workshop\applications\`

By default, on a Windows system, the installation directory is `c:\bea`. If you look in this folder, you'll see directories for every project you've created, as well as any projects that were installed by default with WebLogic Workshop.

Figure 3-2: The Project Tree.

Managing projects

One of the primary functions of the Project Tree is to let you manage the files in your project. The Project Tree has a number of useful functions for organizing your project, some of which may be familiar from similar file-system browsers like the Windows Explorer. However, as you reorganize the files and folders in your project, the Project Tree does some work to make sure your Java files continue to follow the rules of package and class naming.

CREATING NEW FILES AND FOLDERS

When you created files in Chapter 1, you created them in the root directory of the project. At that point, the project contained no folders except the root folder (and the special WEB-INF folder), so you really weren't left with many other choices.

If you want to create new folders, you can use the Project Tree. To create a new folder, right-click on an existing folder and select New Folder. Figure 3-3 shows the New Folder dialog box, which is about as simple as it could be — so simple that it doesn't even have a Help button.

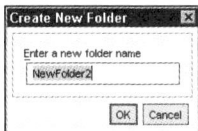

Figure 3-3: The New Folder dialog box.

Choose whatever name you want for your new folder and then click OK to create the new folder. When you click OK, WebLogic Workshop actually creates a new folder on the file system, which you can see if you go to the directory for your project in the applications directory.

You can also create new files anywhere in your project. To create a new file in a particular folder, right-click on that folder and select New File (if you use the File menu to create a new file, it's always created in the root folder of the project).

Figure 3-4 shows the New File dialog box. At the bottom of the dialog box, you can see the name of the folder where you're creating your new file. You can also choose to create several different files types, which are discussed in more detail below.

When you create a new Web service with a particular file name and in a particular folder, WebLogic Workshop automatically names a few elements in the file, according to the naming rules of Java.

 Here is the suggested naming rules and other Java conventions from SUN: `http://java.sun.com/docs/codeconv/html/CodeConvTOC.doc.html`.

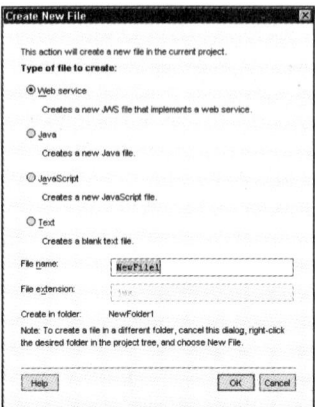

Figure 3-4: The New File dialog box.

Listing 3-1: A Brand-New File in a Folder

```
package NewFolder1;

import weblogic.jws.control.JwsContext;

public class NewFile1
{
    /** @jws:context */
    JwsContext context;
}
```

Listing 3-1 shows the source code for a new Web service; the Web service is named NewFile1, which matches the name of the file NewFile1.jws. This is the source code for a completely empty Web service, and you've seen everything in this file except perhaps the statement on the first line of the file:

```
package NewFolder1;
```

This package statement declares that the class NewFile1 is in the package NewFolder1 (in shorthand, the class is typically named as NewFolder1.NewFile1). Because WebLogic Workshop is a Java development environment, it tries to make the management of Java projects as simple as possible. The package naming rules require that the package of a particular file matches the directory structure in which that package is contained, relative to the root of the project.

WebLogic Workshop allows you to create other file types besides Web services. Table 3-2 shows the different file types you can create.

Chapter 3: A Tour of the WebLogic Workshop IDE

TABLE 3-2 WEBLOGIC WORKSHOP FILE TYPES

File Type	Extension	Description
Web service	JWS	WebLogic Workshop Web service files.
Java	JAVA	Plain Java files.
JavaScript	JSX	WebLogic Workshop extended JavaScript files.
Plain text	Anything	Any other file type you want to create. You're allowed to choose the extension for this file type.

MOVING AND COPYING FILES AND FOLDERS

When your projects start to get complicated, you can use the Project Tree to keep your files organized. To move files and folders around in the project, you can simply click and drag the file or folder to its new location. Let's look at some examples of this.

Figure 3-5 shows a simple project, which will serve as our example for talking about moving and copying files. Let's take a look at an example of what happens when NewFolder1 is moved into NewFolder2. In order to move a folder to a new location, you can simply click and drag the folder.

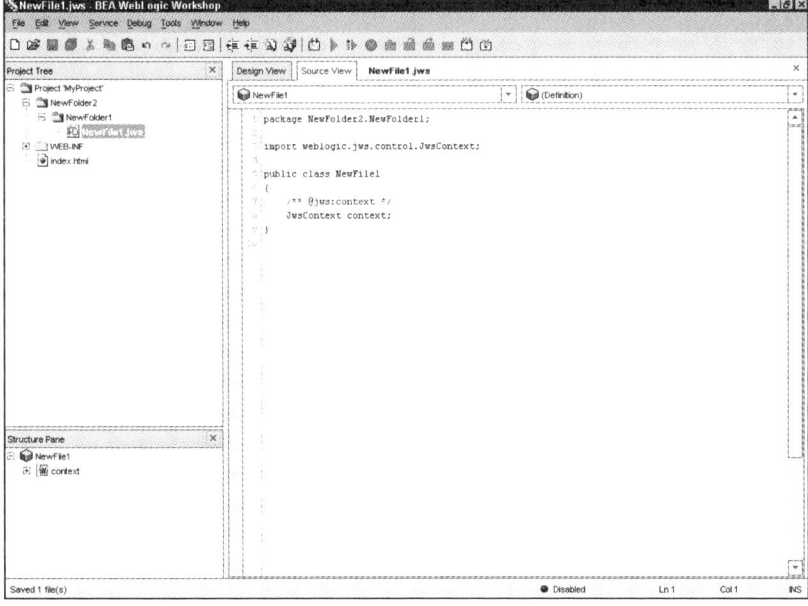

Figure 3-5: After the folder has been moved.

Because NewFolder1 has been moved into NewFolder2, NewFile1.jws also has been moved into the new package, NewFolder2.NewFolder1. If you open NewFile1, you will see that the package statement has changed to reflect the new location of the file. It now reads:

```
package NewFolder2.NewFolder1;
```

You can move files just like you move folders: by clicking and dragging the files to their new location. When you move a file, WebLogic Workshop changes to the package statement, so it matches its new location.

For a number of functions, the Project Tree will automatically change your class names and package statements, so that your files will always follow the rules of Java. However, WebLogic Workshop cannot fix references to classes in other files. For instance, if you have a class that is imported somewhere else in your project, and you move that class so that its package changes, any imports of that class in other files will now be broken.

Clicking and dragging files always moves them, it never makes copies of them. You can, however, create a copy of a file in the same directory (but with a different name) by right-clicking on the file and selecting Duplicate.

Figure 3-6 shows the Duplicate dialog box. You can choose any name you want for the file (except for the name of the original file) and then click OK to duplicate that file.

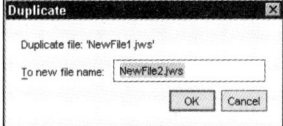

Figure 3-6: The Duplicate dialog box.

Listing 3-2 shows a duplicate of NewFile1.jws, which is identical to NewFile1 in all respects except for the class name. The class name in the duplicated file matches the new file name, with the .java extension removed. This feature of WebLogic Workshop is another one that attempts to make Java development a little easier. Because Java requires the class contained in a file to have the same name as the file, WebLogic Workshop automatically changes the class name to match the file name you selected.

Listing 3-2: A Duplicated File

```
package NewFolder1;

import weblogic.jws.control.JwsContext;

public class NewFile2
{
    /** @jws:context */
    JwsContext context;
}
```

RENAMING FILES AND FOLDERS

You can rename any file or folder by right-clicking on the file or folder in the Project Tree and selecting Rename. Figure 3-7 shows the Rename dialog box. You can type any name you want into the dialog box and click OK to cause the rename to occur. When you rename a file, WebLogic Workshop will rename the class inside the file to match the name of the file, as per the rules of Java.

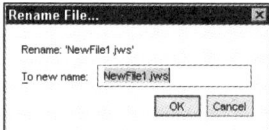

Figure 3-7: The Rename dialog box.

 You may have noticed that the Rename dialog box allows you to change the extension of a file as well as the name. If you change the extension of a file, you'll also change the file type. In particular, if you change the extension of a JWS file to anything else, it will no longer be treated as a Web service.

When you rename a folder, WebLogic Workshop also does some automatic renaming. Because the name of a folder will also be part of the package name for classes it contains, WebLogic Workshop will automatically change the package statement on each of these classes to reflect the new package they are now in.

DELETING FILES AND FOLDERS

If you decide you don't need a file or folder anymore, you can use the Project Tree to delete it by right-clicking on the file or folder and selecting Delete. You should be very careful when doing this, because WebLogic Workshop doesn't provide any way to undo this operation. When you delete something using the Project Tree, it's gone forever.

Editing files in the project

WebLogic Workshop allows you to have multiple files open for editing at a time, and the Project Tree has some functionality that allows you to see the current status of your files.

Figure 3-8 shows the Project Tree when some of the files in the project are being edited.

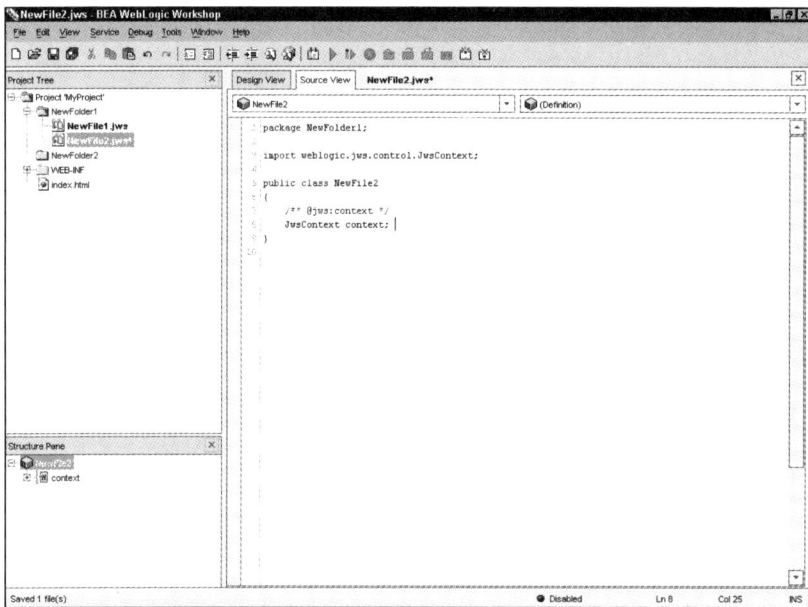

Figure 3-8: Using the Project Tree to see the status of files.

Two of the file names, NewFile1 and NewFile2 are in bold, which indicates that the files are presently open in the editor. NewFile2 has an asterisk next to its name, which indicates that the file is *dirty*. Dirty files contain changes that haven't yet been saved to disk.

Other functions

The Project Tree can do a few other things that I haven't yet mentioned. If you right-click on a JWS file, you will see the two menu items, "Generate WSDL from JWS" and "Generate CTRL from JWS." There are also some other generate options for other file types. All these options take the file in question and generate some other file type from it. I will discuss these new file types and the reasons you would want to generate them later in Chapters 7 and 8.

The Source View

The Source View provides a fully functional Java editing environment. It has a number of features that makes Java editing much easier than it would be in a plain text editor. In general, the Source View is set up to be familiar to users of common IDEs.

The text editor

First and foremost, the Source View is a text editor. It has a number of features that are common to most text editors, such as search & replace. The Edit menu contains a number of commands that should be familiar from any editor; Cut, Copy, and Paste are supported, as well as Undo. The key bindings in the editor are not customizable, but they were chosen to match those most people are used to.

Figure 3-9 shows the source editor. On the left-hand edge of the editor is a bar containing line numbers for the document that you're editing, which can be quite useful for quickly seeing which line you're on.

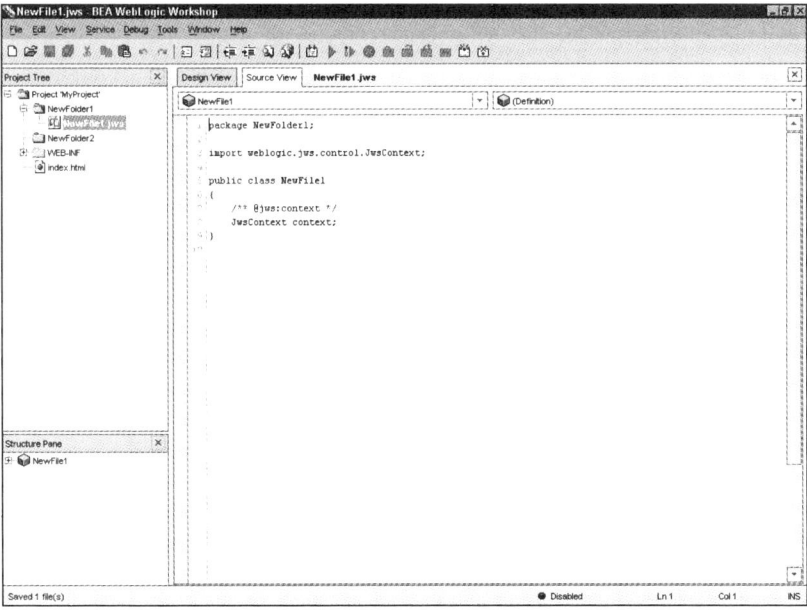

Figure 3-9: The Source Editor.

Syntax coloring

The first thing you probably noticed about the WebLogic Workshop source editor is that the text is *syntax colored*; different elements of the program text, such as keywords, are shown in special colors to set them apart from the rest of the text.

Syntax coloring helps you see the structure of your programs, and frankly, relieves some of the monotony of looking at source code in a plain text editor.

Many programmers have strong opinions about how they like their source code to look, and who could blame them? After all, programmers have to stare at source code for many hours of the day. WebLogic Workshop has a default set of colors, which were picked to match what most people are used to, but if you don't like these default colors, you can change them. To change the default colors, select Tools⇨Preferences. The Preferences dialog box will appear. Select the colors tab to see the list of colors you can customize.

Figure 3-10 shows the Color Preferences dialog box. The program elements you can customize are shown, and to the right of those a small square shows the current color for that element. Click on the square to invoke a Color Picker dialog box, shown in Figure 3-11, which will give you more options than you could possibly imagine.

Figure 3-10: The Color Preferences dialog box.

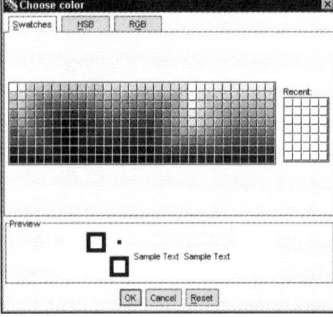

Figure 3-11: The Color Picker dialog box.

After you select a color and click OK, the color used for the particular element will be changed.

 The custom colors you chose for syntax coloring, as well as any other custom options you may set are stored in a special file named .Workshop (note the dot) in your home directory. On Windows, this home directory is found in:

`c:\Documents and Settings\<User Name>`

This file contains your preferences in the form of name=value pairs. You can copy this file to another computer if you want to use your preferences there. Don't change this file unless you make a backup, because improper entries in the .Workshop file can cause WebLogic Workshop to function incorrectly. If you want to restore your settings to the WebLogic Workshop default, you can delete your .Workshop file.

Code completion

Code completion is a relatively new feature of IDEs, but these days pretty much every IDE provides it. Code completion gives you extra information as you're typing, to help you write your source code. Instead of trying to provide you with an academic definition of what you can do with code completion, I'll illustrate this feature with some examples.

Listing 3-4 shows the source file I'll use to illustrate the features of code completion.

Listing 3-4: An Example File

```
import java.util.*;
public class Example
{
    private ArrayList a;

    public void method1()
    {
    }
}
```

A number of features are included with code completion. The first one I'll describe is the member list. To activate this feature type **a.** into the body of *method1*. The field *a* is an instance of one of the standard Java collection types, the *ArrayList*. After you press the . (period), wait a moment and the member list will appear.

Figure 3-12 shows the member list for the field *a*. Because *a* refers to an object, a number of members are defined on *a*. The member list shows you a list of these members and allows you to choose one to insert into the source code. The member list is very useful when you're working with the standard Java libraries — or any other objects that have a lot of members — because it makes remembering the exact field and method names a little easier. Use the up and down arrow keys to scroll through the list of members and press Enter or Tab to insert the name of a member into your source code.

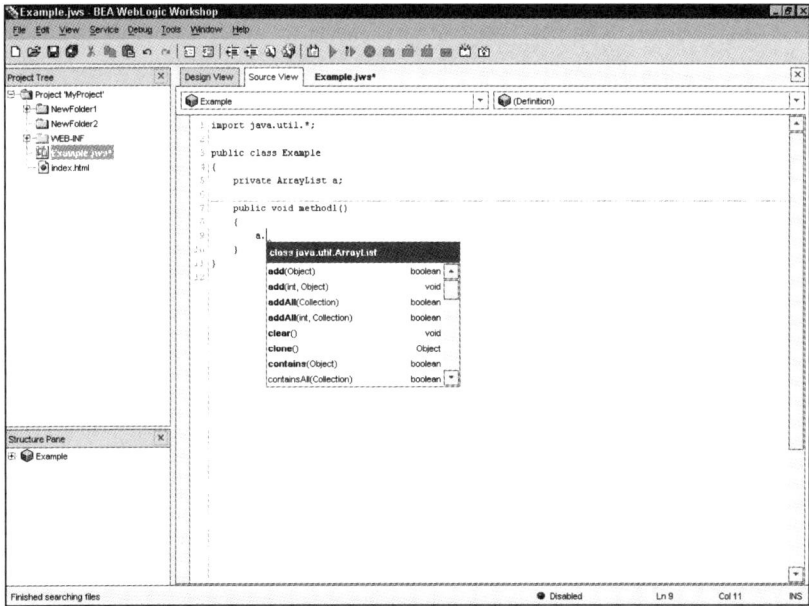

Figure 3-12: The member list.

 You may notice that some of the methods in the member list are bold, while others are not. Bold methods are the ones defined directly in the class you're referencing (that is, the class of the object right before the period) whereas the other methods are those that were inherited. Because every method inherits from java.lang.Object, there will also be a few methods that are not in bold in the method list, unless you're working with an instance of java.lang.Object.

There is another circumstance in which you can use the member list. If you have already partially typed a member name (or even if you haven't typed anything yet), you can always press Ctrl+Space to activate the member list. If the partially defined member prefix matches any one specific method, the member will be inserted into the source code and the member list will not be shown. As an example, type **a.f** and then press Ctrl+Space. The method name *finalize* will be inserted into the source code, because this is the only method that starts with the letter *f*, and the member list will not be shown.

If you decide to add a method to your source code, code completion can give you more help in filling out the arguments. To continue our example, choose the Add method from the member list and press Enter to insert it into the source code. When you've done this, you can type (to activate the parameter list.

Figure 3-13 shows the parameter list for the Add method. There are multiple versions of the Add method, all of which take different parameters, so the parameter list shows you all the possible versions. When the parameter list is first displayed, the first parameter in each method is drawn in bold. As you type additional method parameters, the bolding in the parameter list will track where you are so you can easily see which parameter you're currently working on. If you ever want to bring back the parameter list while you're typing the arguments of a method, you can press Ctrl+Shift+P.

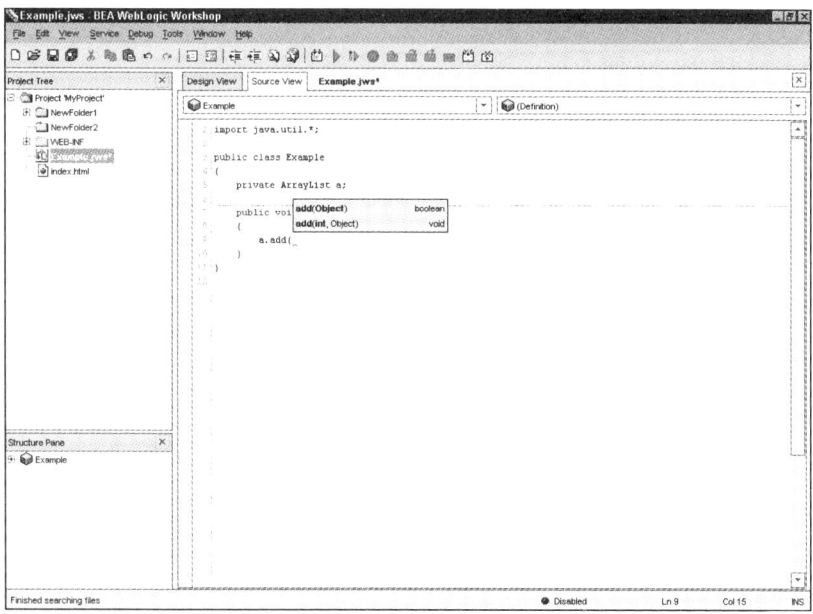

Figure 3-13: The parameter list.

The member list can also be used to complete packages in import statements. For instance, if you type **import java.** at the top of your source file, the member list will appear to show you the packages and classes in the Java package. This feature can be very useful for browsing through the complicated package structures, like the Java standard libraries.

Error messages

If you make errors in your Java code, you can discover them when you build, as is common with most development environments. However, the WebLogic Workshop IDE has the useful ability to show you your errors as you edit, so you don't have to wait until you build again to find out what you've done wrong.

Figure 3-14 shows the Source View in the midst of editing a file that contains an error. The error is underlined, and when the cursor is hovered over the error, the error message is displayed. The error highlighting is constantly updated as you type, so if you discover an error and correct it, the highlighting will go away after a small delay.

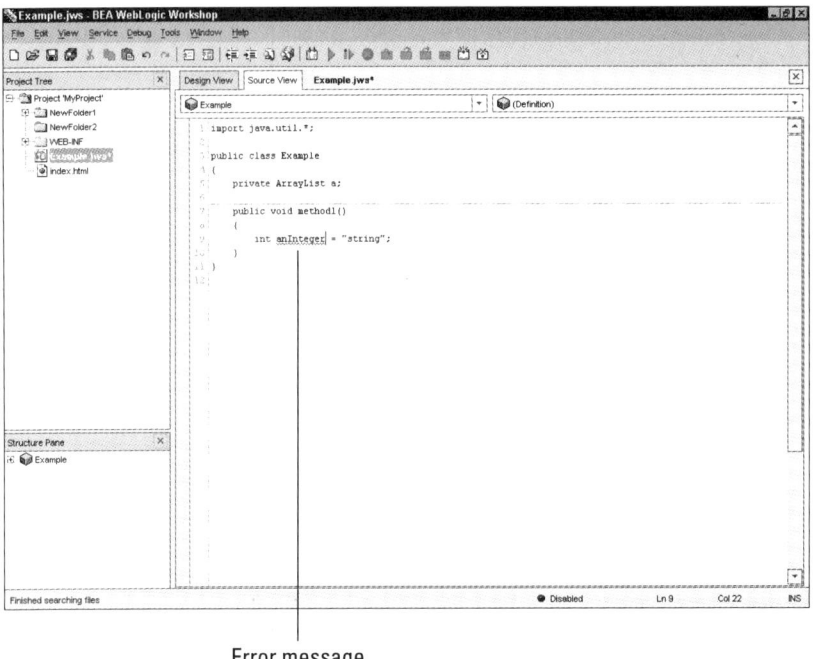

Figure 3-14: Error highlighting.

WebLogic Workshop will not highlight certain types of errors. You can discover these errors when you build your Web service. If you want to build your Web service without running, so you can see the current list of errors, select Debug⇨Build from the menu. This performs a build and shows you any errors in the Message window. Figure 3-15 shows the Message window displaying some errors.

I showed you the Message window earlier when I discussed the Find in Files feature. The same window (although a different tab) is used after a build to show you the errors and warnings for your current Web service. If you double-click on any error, you'll be taken to it in the source code.

Chapter 3: A Tour of the WebLogic Workshop IDE

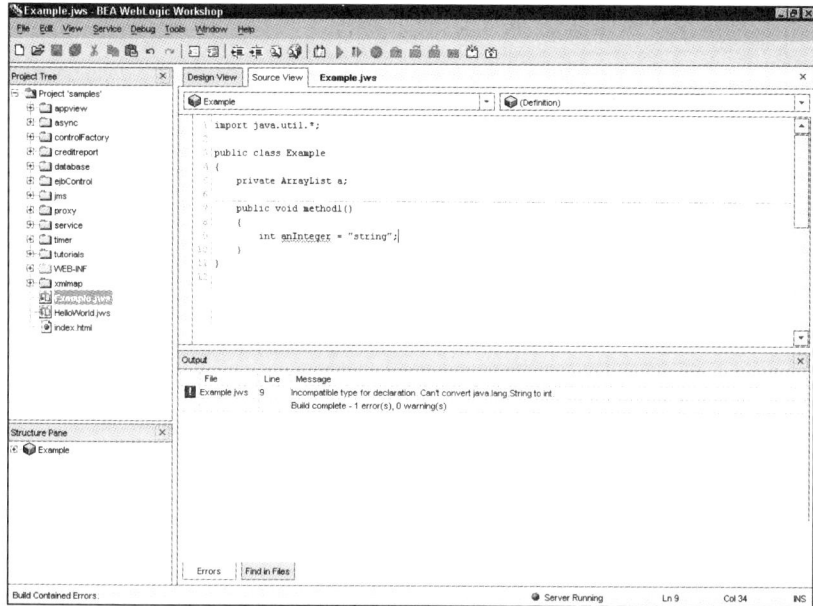

Figure 3-15: The Message window.

The Structure Pane

The Structure Pane displays the classes, methods, and fields in the currently open file. The Structure Pane is very helpful when you have large or complicated files and you want to get a quick view of their overall structure. Figure 3-16 shows the Structure Pane for the improved currency calculator from Chapter 1, the largest file I've shown you so far.

The Structure Pane for the improved currency calculator shows the fields and methods of the calculator. The two methods, getCurrencyName and Convert, have different icons than the method getCurrencyTypeCode, to indicate that they're operations and not normal Java methods like getCurrencyTypeCode.

You may also notice that the entry in the tree for Context can be expanded to show several normal Java methods as well as two methods, onFinish and onException, that have icons like no others in the Structure Pane. These two methods represent two callbacks provided by the Context object. The Context object gets this special treatment because it is a *control*, a special type of object that provides useful functions to your Web services. There are controls that allow access to databases, other Web services, queues, timers, Enterprise Java Beans, and even legacy systems. The Context control is a special type of control that provides you with all sorts of useful functionality, however, now is not the time to discuss it. Later, in Chapters 7 and 8 I discuss every type of control in excruciating detail.

56   Part I: Getting Started

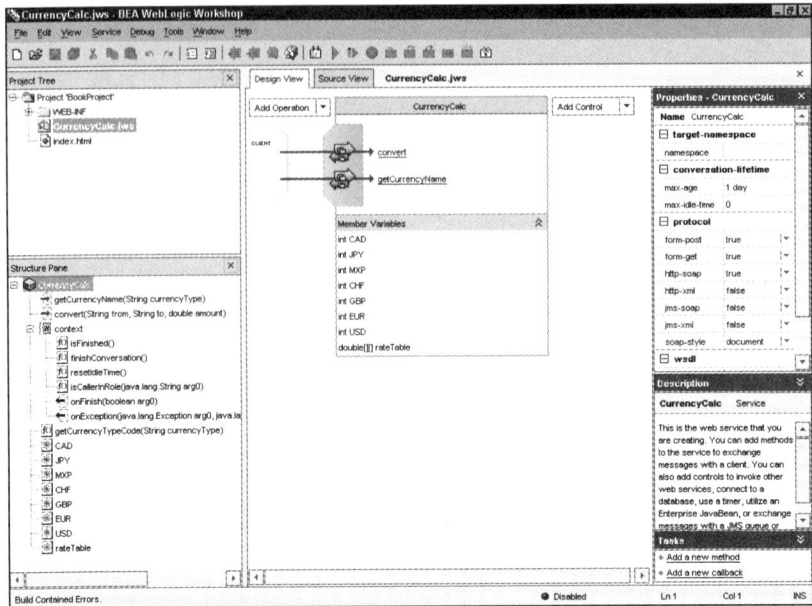

Figure 3-16: The Structure Pane.

In addition to displaying the structure of your Web service, the Structure Pane also allows you to quickly seek any method or field in your Web service. For example, if you double-click on the getCurrencyName method, you'll be taken directly to that method in the source code.

Figure 3-17 shows the result of seeking to the getCurrencyName method. The background of the method is highlighted in yellow and the background of the rest of the source code is made gray (if you don't like this, just move the caret outside the function and the highlighting will go away).

One last notable feature of the Structure Pane is the ordering of the elements inside it. In Figure 3-17, the elements are displayed in the same order as they appear in the source code. You can change this by selecting Tools⇨Preferences.

Figure 3-18 shows the options for the Structure Pane. There are two choices for the ordering of elements in the Structure Pane: code order, which places the elements in the order they appear in the source code, or alphabetical order, which, as you probably guessed, alphabetizes them. There is also a Group by Title option, which allows you to have all the elements aggregated according to type (for example, field, method, or operation). When the Structure Pane is set up to group by the type of element, the elements are ordered according to your preference within the group.

Chapter 3: A Tour of the WebLogic Workshop IDE

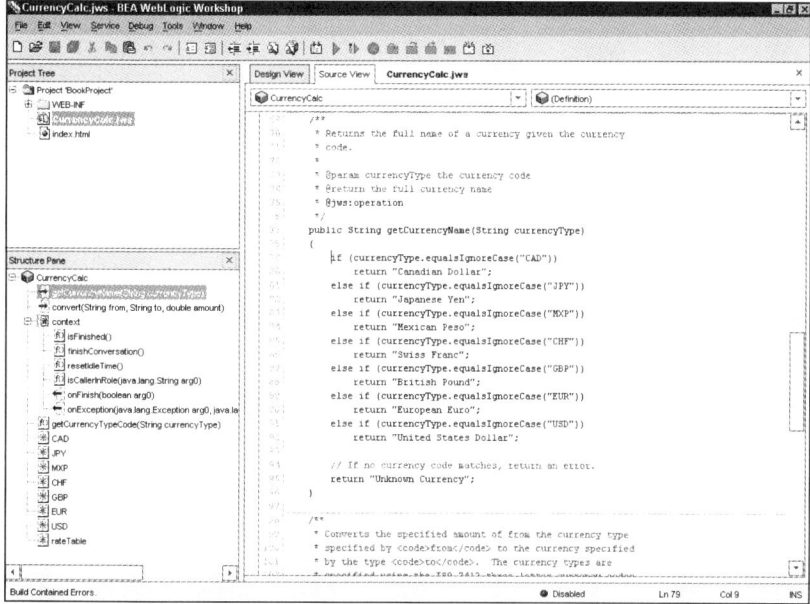

Figure 3-17: A highlighted method.

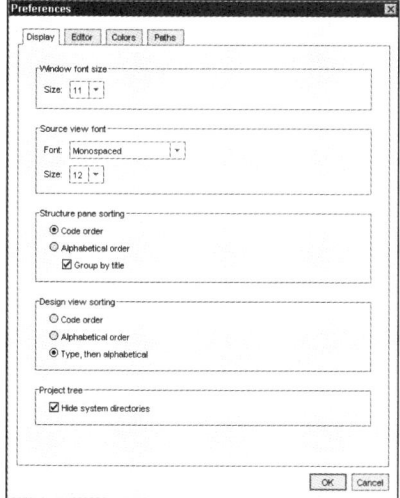

Figure 3-18: The Structure Pane Ordering dialog box.

The Navigation Bar

The Navigation Bar is very similar to the Structure Pane in function, but it presents the information in a somewhat different way and, thus, deserves some comment.

It's another tool that you can use to examine the structure of and navigate through the currently open file. The Navigation Bar can only be seen in the Source View and consists of two drop-down lists.

The list on the left shows the classes and controls in the current file. As a general rule, if it can be expanded (you can tell it can be expanded if it has a little plus icon by it) in the Structure Pane, it will show up in the left-hand list of the Navigation Bar.

Figure 3-19 shows the Navigation Bar with the left-hand list opened. Once again, I am using the improved currency calculator, because it is a file that is at least a little bit complicated. From the figure, you can see that the two items that were expandable in the Structure Pane, the CurrencyCalc class and the Context object, are both in this list.

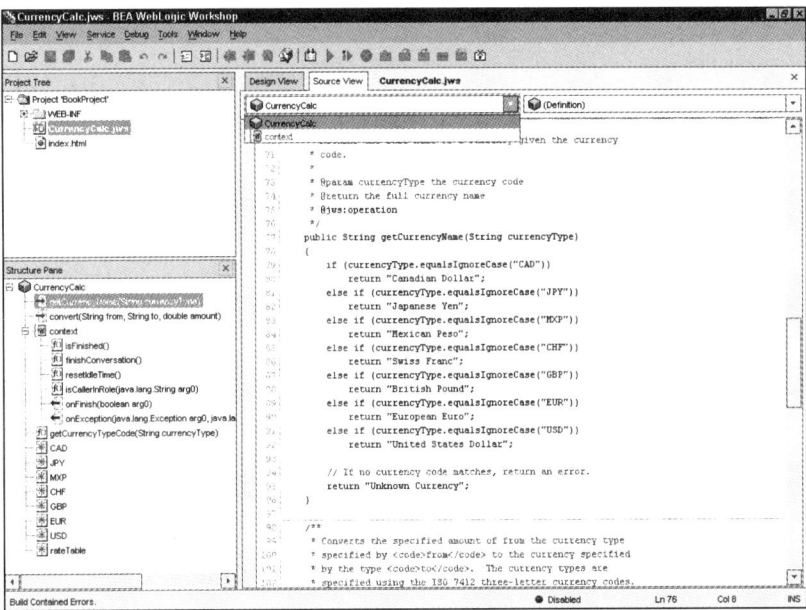

Figure 3-19: The Navigation Bar class list.

When you select an object from the left-hand drop-down list, the right-hand list is populated with its members. For instance, Figure 3-20 shows the right-hand list of the Navigation Bar, opened with the CurrencyCalc class selected in the left-hand list.

Only the methods are listed in the right-hand list of the Navigation Bar. If you select any of the methods, you'll be taken to that method in the source code. There is an additional member named "(Definition)" which refers to the code in the CurrencyCalc class that isn't inside the body of any method. If you now select the Context object from the left-hand list, you can see that only some of the methods are shown in the right-hand list. The only methods that get shown in this list are those that can actually appear in the source code.

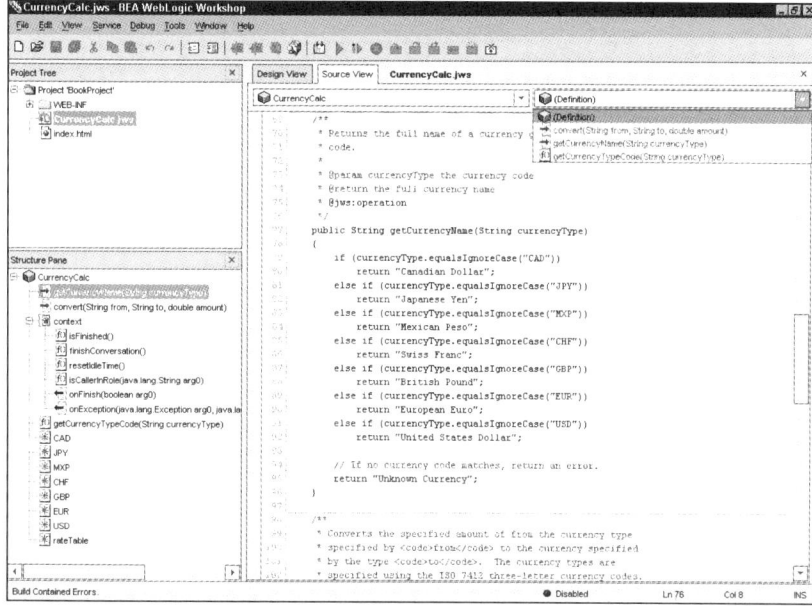

Figure 3-20: The Navigation Bar member list.

The Test View

The Test View is a generic WebLogic Workshop Web service client. You might recall that you get to this view by clicking the "Start" button in the Workshop (it looks like the "Play" symbol in VCRs). The Test View is hosted by WebLogic Workshop as a set of Web pages, which provide a rich set of features for testing your Web services. In order to access the Test View, WebLogic Server must be running and your Web service must be deployed. The Test View for a particular Web service is bound to a URL so you can access it from any Web browser.

Test View tabs

The functionality of the Test View is divided into a number of pages. There is a row of tabs across the top of the Test View, which you can use to switch between these pages.

Figure 3-21 shows the Test View tabs. In this section, I go through the various pages of the Test View and explain the functions provided by each of them. In order to change to a particular page, simply click on the corresponding tab.

THE OVERVIEW PAGE

Figure 3-21 shows the Overview page on the Test View. If you open the Test View directly from the browser, using a URL such as `http://localhost:7001/samples/HelloWorld.jws` for the HelloWorld sample, it will open to the Overview page. The

Overview page gives a summary of the Web service and some general information to help you use the Web service. Table 3-3 summarizes the context provided by each of these links.

TABLE 3-3 TEST VIEW OVERVIEW PAGE LINKS

Link	Description
Complete WSDL	Creates a Web Service Description Language (WSDL) file for this Web service. This allows you to create a platform-neutral description of your Web service that any standards-compliant Web service product should be able to use to access your Web service.
Workshop Control	Creates a WebLogic Workshop control (CTRL) file, which is the WebLogic Workshop-specific way of describing your Web service. Typically used by another JWS file in the Workshop. Controls are helpful in integrating with various back-end resources.
Java Proxy	Creates a Java class that can be used to call your Web service from normal Java code. Typically needed by a JSP or a standalone Java client to simplify Web Service calls.
Proxy Support JAR	A Java Archive (JAR) that is needed to use the Java proxy for this Web service. Only needed by a standalone Java client, in addition to the Java proxy.

In addition to these links, there are a few links at the bottom of the page to various Web services and XML standards documents. These documents don't make very exciting reading, but if you're looking for the full details of any of these standards, these standards documents are the place to look.

THE CONSOLE PAGE

The Console page allows you to set some options and perform some administrative functions on your Web service.

Figure 3-22 shows the Console page on the Test View. At the top of the page, you can find out how your Web service has been translated into Enterprise Java Beans; there is a link to the WebLogic Server console where you can see the details of the deployed beans. There are two sections in the Console page that allow you to set certain options controlling the behavior of the Test View and your Web services.

LOG SETTINGS The Log Settings area has two options that allow you to control the behavior of the Message Log, which records a history of the messages that have been sent to and from your Web service. Table 3-4 shows the logging options you can set.

Chapter 3: A Tour of the WebLogic Workshop IDE 61

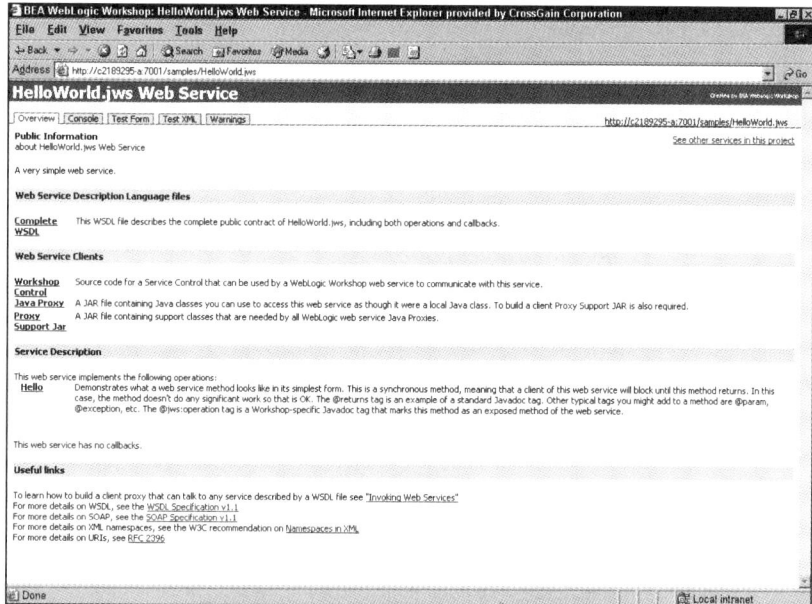

Figure 3-21: The Test View tabs.

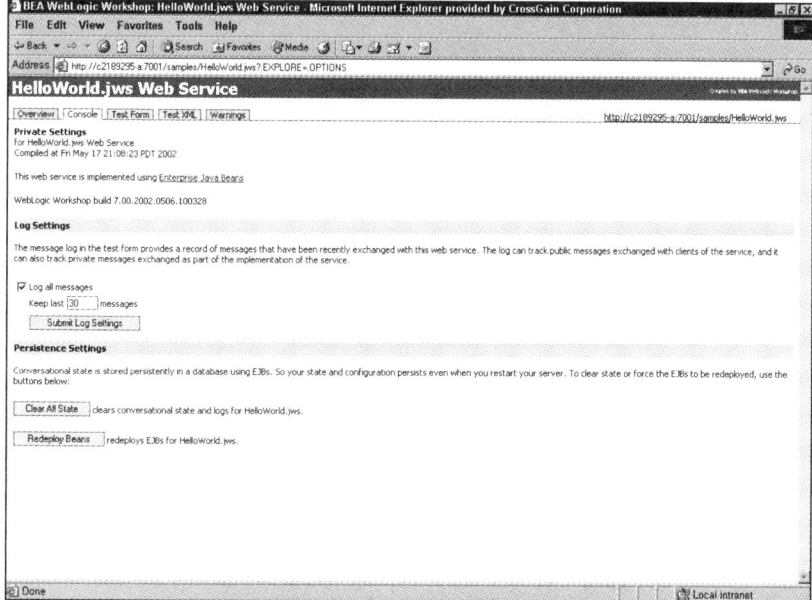

Figure 3-22: The Console page.

TABLE 3-4 THE LOGGING OPTIONS

Logging Option	Description
Log all messages	When selected, this option causes the Message Log to keep a record of all messages your Web service sends and receives. Normally, the Message Log only shows messages exchanged between your Web service and its clients. However, other messages can be sent and received by your Web service, such as the case where your Web service calls other Web services.
Keep Last *N* messages	Controls the number of messages that will be shown in the Message Log. When the log runs out of space, the oldest messages are thrown away first.

PERSISTENCE SETTINGS The Persistence Settings section allows you to reset the state of your Web services in various ways. Table 3-5 explains these two administrative functions.

TABLE 3-5 THE PERSISTENCE SETTINGS

Persistence Settings	Description
Clear All State	When you begin to use conversations, various states will be stored in the database that is associated with the conversations. When you click this button, this stored state is cleared.
Redeploy Beans	Your Web services are implemented as Enterprise Java Beans on WebLogic Server. When you click this button, the beans that make up your service will be removed from the server and redeployed.

THE TEST FORM PAGE

When you launch the Test View from WebLogic Workshop, as you did in Chapter 1, it opens to the Test Form page by default. This page shows you the list of operations defined by your Web service, and allows you to fill in the arguments and invoke any of these operations.

Figure 3-23 shows the Test Form page for the improved currency calculator Web service. For each operation on the Web service, there is a section on this page, which allows you to invoke the operation. In addition, for this Web service, there are descriptions at the top of each operation section. These descriptions are filled in using the Javadoc comment above the operation.

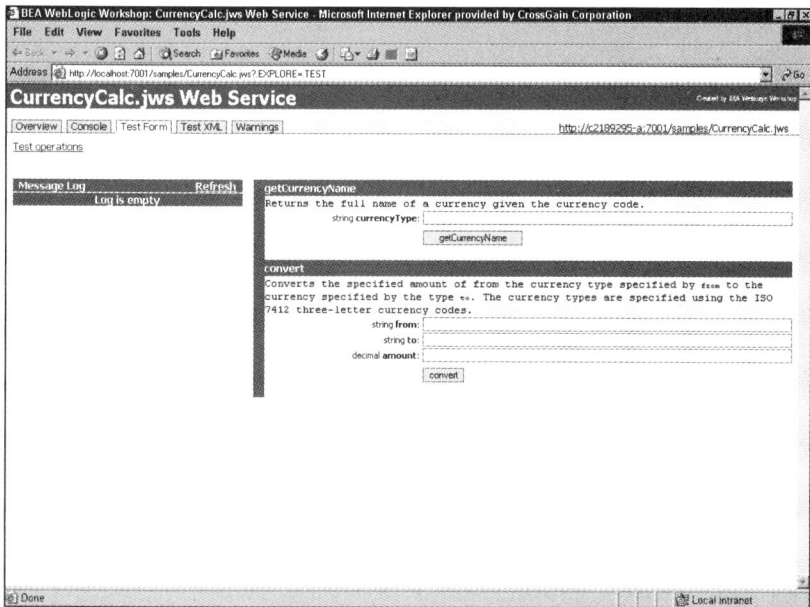

Figure 3-23: The Test Form page.

THE TEST XML PAGE

The Test XML page is very similar to the Test Form page. However, where you could enter each argument individually on the Test Form page, the Test XML page provides just one text box with the name *SOAP body* for each method. On the Test XML page, you enter the arguments to an operation by directly editing the XML message that will be sent to your Web service. Figure 3-24 shows the Test XML page for the improved currency calculator.

The SOAP body text box for the `Convert` method contains the following XML:

```
<convert xmlns="http://www.openuri.org/">
  <from>
    Value_from
  </from>
  <to>
    Value_to
  </to>
  <amount>
    Value_amount
  </amount>
</convert>
```

Part I: Getting Started

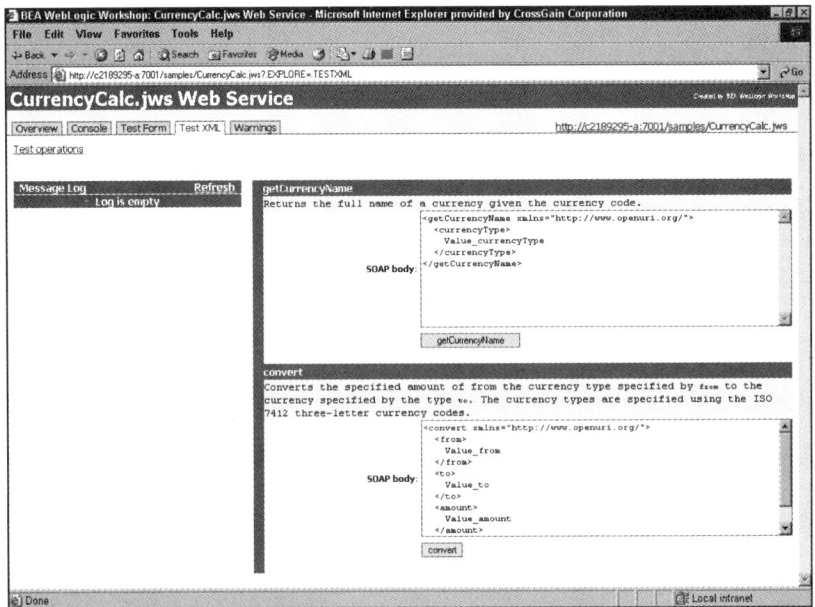

Figure 3-24: The Test XML page.

This XML represents the body of the SOAP message that will be used to call the currency calculator Web service. Each argument is wrapped with a set of tags that name the argument. There is a sample value for each argument, which you can replace with anything. As an example, you could use the following XML in order to convert two U.S. dollars to euros:

```
<convert xmlns="http://www.openuri.org/">
  <from>USD</from>
  <to>EUR</to>
  <amount>
    2.0
  </amount>
</convert>
```

 If you had entered the from parameter like the following:

```
<from>
  USD
</from>
```

you would have received an error, because the string USD would have ended up getting passed to your Web service (note the extra spaces). Be careful if you decide to use the Test XML form for normal methods.

When you're testing normal methods, you don't normally need to use the Test XML page. Later on, when you learn about XML maps, which are used to work directly with the XML messages passed to your Web services, the Test XML page will be very useful.

THE WARNINGS PAGE

The final page on the Test View is the Warnings page. This page shows any warnings generated by the compiler when your Web service is built. Warnings are potential problems with your Web service that are not serious enough to prevent it from being built. The serious problems will be flagged as errors — you have to fix them before Workshop allows you to test the Web Service.

Figure 3-25 shows the Warnings page, which contains only one warning in this case. By default, Web services created by WebLogic Workshop use the namespace http://www.openuri.org/. When you actually put a Web service into production, you'll probably want to give it a different namespace. As a result, WebLogic Workshop gives you a warning to remind you to change the namespace.

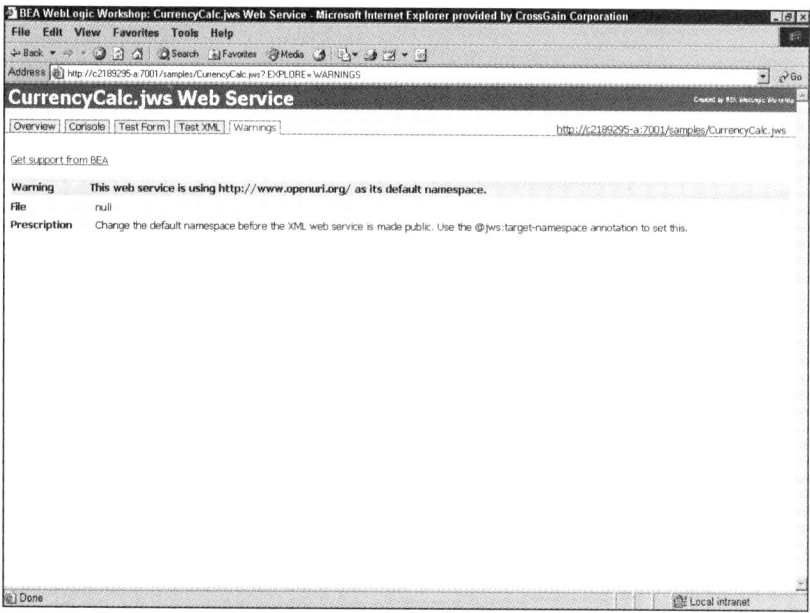

Figure 3-25: The Warnings page.

Other problems with your Web services can generate warnings. You can also see the warnings for your Web service if you build (but don't run) your Web service in the IDE.

Getting directly at the Test View

In Chapter 1, I showed you how you could use the Run command from the IDE in order to access the Test View for a Web service. However, you can also access the Test View directly, without using the IDE.

When a Web service is deployed on WebLogic Server, the Test View for that Web service is mapped to a special URL, which you can type into any browser (even on another machine) in order to access the Test View for that Web service. The URL has the following form:

```
http://<machine name>:<port number>/<project name>/<service name>
```

If you have WebLogic Server running on the local machine, you can use the machine name *localhost* to refer to your machine. Otherwise, you need the network name of the machine running WebLogic Server. The default port number is 7001. The project name is the name of the project directory located under the applications folder, and the service name is the name of the JWS file that contains your Web service.

As an example, to get at the *HelloWorld* Web service in the samples project on the local machine, you could use the following URL:

```
http://localhost:7001/samples/HelloWorld.jws
```

TEST VIEW AUTO-COMPILATION

In Chapter 1, I noted that before you can view the Test View for a Web service, you need to build and deploy the Web service to WebLogic Server. However, the startup script that WebLogic Workshop uses to start WebLogic Server puts the server into development mode, which causes it to automatically rebuild and deploy any changed Web service whenever you access it in the Test View. This means whenever WebLogic Server is running (in development mode) you could edit your Web services in Notepad, save your files to a project directory, and use a standalone instance of Internet Explorer (or Netscape) to build and test your Web services. This isn't the easiest way to build Web services, but some people do it this way.

The Debugger

The debugger is a useful tool for quickly finding bugs in programs. The WebLogic Workshop debugger allows you to step through your Web services, line-by-line, and see exactly what they're doing in real time. If you've used a debugger before, you should find the WebLogic Workshop debugger quite familiar. Although it doesn't provide the advanced functionality of the most sophisticated debuggers, it has most of the commonly useful features present in all debuggers.

Stepping through your Web services

The most powerful feature of the debugger is that it allows you to step through your Web services, line-by-line. In order to step through your Web services, you must first set a breakpoint in a source file. When the debugger has paused your Web service, you have several options about what you want to do next.

SETTING BREAKPOINTS

I discussed how to set breakpoints in Chapter 1, however, I will briefly review the procedure and add a few details I glossed over in Chapter 1.

In order to set a breakpoint, you can either click on the left gutter next to the Source View, as shown in Figure 3-26, or put the caret on the line where you want the breakpoint and press F9.

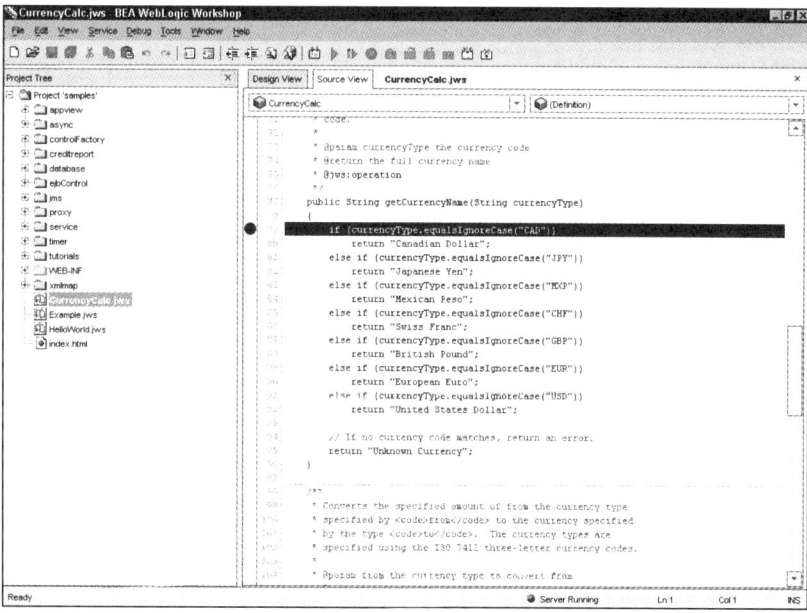

Figure 3-26: Setting a breakpoint.

When you set the breakpoint, the line will turn red and a red dot will appear in the gutter next to the line number. If you click on the red dot again, or press F9, the breakpoint will be cleared. You can also select Debug⇨Clear All Breakpoints (or press Ctrl+Shift+F9) to remove every breakpoint from every file in your project.

You can set a breakpoint in any open Java, JWS, or JSX file in your project. If you close the file, the breakpoint will be removed. When you're debugging and the program is about to execute the line on which the breakpoint is positioned, the program will be suspended on that line.

DEBUGGING COMMANDS

When the debugger has your Web service paused on a particular line, you have several choices about what you want to do. Table 3-6 shows the debugging commands available when the debugger is suspended at a breakpoint.

TABLE 3-6 DEBUGGING COMMANDS

Command	Description
Continue (F5)	Starts the Web service running again. The debugger will not suspend the Web service again until another breakpoint is reached.
Step Over (F10)	Runs the Web service until it reaches another line. Function calls will not be entered by the debugger.
Step Into (F11)	Runs the Web service until it reaches another line. If the current line is a function call, this command will enter the function.
Step Out (Shift+F11)	Runs the Web service until it executes a return statement. The net effect is to step out of the body of the current function.

The debugging interface

Most of your interaction with the WebLogic Workshop debugger occurs through the debugging interface, which appears at the bottom of the Source View when you select Debug⇨Start and Debug.

Figure 3-27 shows the debugging interface, which we took a look at before in Chapter 1. There are three panes in the debugging interface, each of which can be used to show different information.

THE LOCALS PANE

The Locals Pane and the Watch Pane are both located on the left of the debugging interface. You can switch between them using the tabs at the bottom of the debugging interface.

Figure 3-28 shows the Locals Pane, in the midst of a debugging session. As you step through your program, the Locals Pane shows you the current *in scope* variables and their values. Roughly speaking, a variable is in scope on a certain line of the program if you could access the variable from that line. In Java, the scoping rules are fairly simple: You can get to class member variables from anywhere in the class, and all other variables must be declared before you can access them.

You can also use the Locals Pane to change the values of local variables as the program is running. To change the value of the variable, start by double-clicking on the current value. The box containing the value will change to a text box where you can enter a new value. When you've entered the new value, press Enter.

Chapter 3: A Tour of the WebLogic Workshop IDE 69

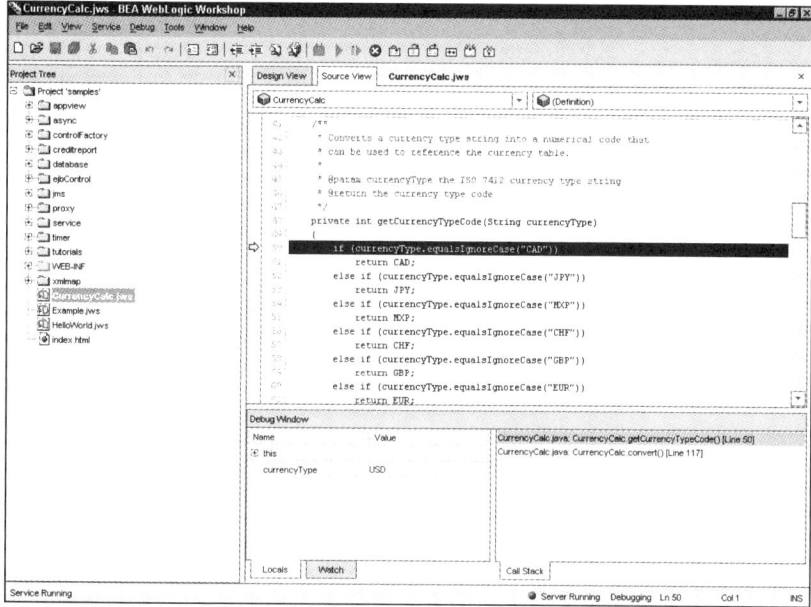

Figure 3-27: The debugging interface.

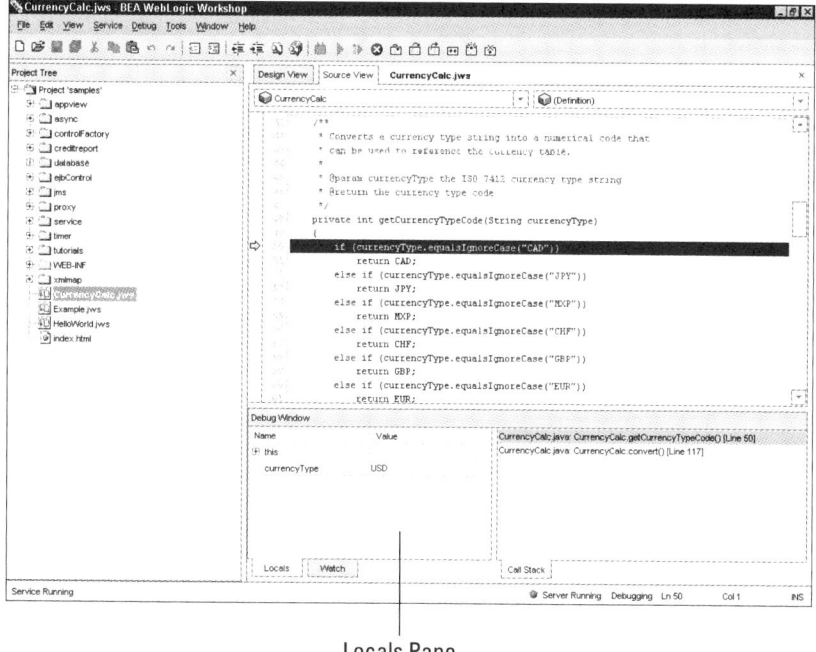

Locals Pane

Figure 3-28: The Locals Pane.

THE WATCH PANE

The Watch Pane is very similar to the Locals Pane in function. However, unlike the Locals Pane, which automatically decides which variables to show you, you may choose the set of variables you want to examine in the Watch Pane.

Figure 3-29 shows the Watch Pane, after a few variables have been added to it. The Watch Pane will show whatever variables you enter into it, whether or not they're presently in scope. If you enter the name of a variable that isn't in scope, the value of the variable will be set to "out of scope."

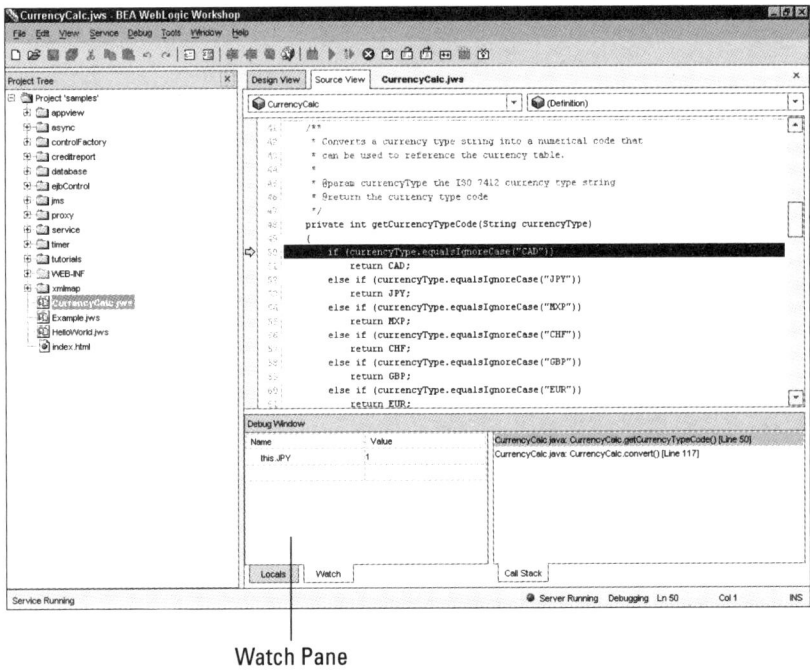

Figure 3-29: The Watch Pane.

In order to add a new variable to the Watch Pane, double-click on the Name column of the empty row at the end of the list of variables. A text box will appear, where you can enter the name of the variable. After you've entered a name, press Enter and the new value will be set.

THE CALL STACK PANE

The Call Stack Pane shows you the current stack frames in the program you're debugging. A *stack frame* is a record of the list of function calls you're currently inside. Every time you call a function, an additional frame is added to the list of stack frames, and every time you return from a function a stack frame is removed. In this way, you can see what series of function calls got you to your present location in the debugger.

Chapter 3: A Tour of the WebLogic Workshop IDE

Figure 3-30 shows the Call Stack Pane after a number of function calls. The top entry on the list shows the function you're presently in, the entry below that shows where the function you're presently in was called, and so forth. You can go to the source code for any stack frame entry by clicking on that stack frame. This doesn't affect the state of the program you're debugging.

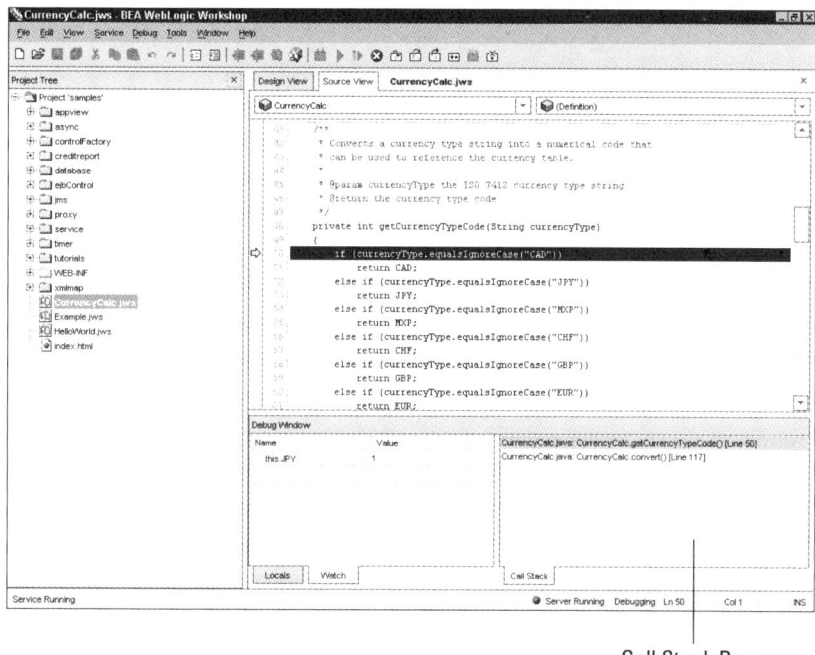

Figure 3-30: The Call Stack Pane.

Summary

This chapter has provided a fairly detailed tour of the core features of the WebLogic Workshop IDE. I didn't talk about everything; I focused on the features that you'll probably use frequently:

- ◆ The Project Tree is a useful tool for managing your WebLogic Workshop projects.

- ◆ The Source View is a powerful Java editing environment that contains many first-class editor features such as code completion and error highlighting.

- ◆ The Structure Pane and Navigation Bar are used to view and navigate the structure of source files.

- The Test View is a general test environment for your Web services.
- The Debugger allows you to watch your Web services run in real time.

Part II

Basic Concepts

CHAPTER 4
Creating Conversational Web Services

CHAPTER 5
Creating Asynchronous Web Services

CHAPTER 6
Mapping from XML

Chapter 4

Creating Conversational Web Services

IN THIS CHAPTER

- Understanding the basic theory of conversations
- Using the Property Editor to set conversational properties
- Writing conversational Web services
- Using the Test View to test conversational Web services

YOU HAVE SEEN HOW TO USE WebLogic Workshop to create basic Web services. Now it's time to discuss some of the special features of WebLogic Workshop that allow you to create more powerful Web services. In this chapter, I show you how to use WebLogic Workshop *conversations,* a feature that allows for the creation of Web services that maintain state. There is a good chance that a lot of the Web Services you build will use conversations to maintain sequence of events, hence it is important for you to master the concepts. In addition, this chapter provides an opportunity to introduce you to the Property Editor, a Web service–specific IDE feature I skipped over in Chapter 3.

Conversations are a feature unique to WebLogic Workshop in the Web services world. Conversations permit both the saving of state in Web services and specifying some rudimentary rules on the order in which Web service methods are called. Using conversational Web services can often provide a model that saves you a lot of work when writing certain types of Web services.

An example of a conversation is a loan application. The process is started when you fill an application and submit a loan request to an agency. The agency will forward your loan to a few loan providers and wait for their answers, which might take hours or even days. The agency might filter some responses and pick two loans for you. You will respond with the loan that you like, and the process is completed. Now, replace "you", "the agency", and "loan providers" with the corresponding Web Services, and you get a conversational Web Service application.

The conversation provides a mechanism for linking together a set of calls between a client and a Web service into a single logical interchange. As a conversation proceeds, a Web service may save information referred to as *conversational state,* which is correlated with the conversation and can be accessed throughout the conversation.

Conversations create a simple form of *workflow;* that is, they specify something about the sequence in which a set of Web service methods should be called. Although the types of workflows that can be created with conversations are very limited, a number of processes fit logically into the WebLogic Workshop conversation model, making it a very useful feature.

You can think of a WebLogic Workshop conversation as very similar to a conversation between two people (which is the source of the feature's name). When two people carry out a conversation, they exchange messages with each other in the form of spoken words. As these messages are exchanged, each party in the conversation remembers its state specific to the conversation. Each person in the conversation remembers at least some of what was said by the other person and uses that information later in the conversation.

Although human conversations do not have strict rules about who says what when, people normally obey a few informal rules. Conversations are typically started with some customary greetings, and they typically aren't ended without some sort of acknowledgement. In much the same way, WebLogic Workshop conversations have some rules about what methods must be used to start and finish a conversation.

The Conversational Phases

WebLogic Workshop organizes conversations into three distinct phases: the start phase, the continue phase, and the finish phase. Any Web service method that participates in a conversation may be part of one, and only one, of these phases. As the terminology should make somewhat clear, conversations begin in the start phase, are (most likely) conducted throughout the continue phase, and are ended in the finish phase (or it can go straight from start to finish).

After a conversation has been started by WebLogic Workshop, the state for the conversation — any information the web service needs to remember about the conversation — is stored in the database associated with WebLogic Server. As a result, the state of a conversation is very durable and can be persisted for a long time.

 If you're curious, conversational state is maintained on WebLogic Server by using J2EE Entity Beans, which allow the conversational state to be maintained in a database.

Documentation and articles about WebLogic Workshop use the terms *start method, continue method,* and *finish method* when talking about Web service methods that participate in the various phases of a conversation. To keep this discussion consistent with those sources, I will adopt this terminology as well. Figure 4-1 shows the lifecycle of a conversation as it proceeds through the start, continue, and finish phases. Each of these phases is discussed in more detail below.

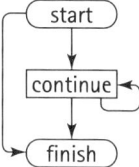

Figure 4-1: The lifecycle of a conversation.

Starting a conversation

A client can start a conversation by calling any of the start methods of a Web service. Only one start method may be called per conversation, although a Web service may have many start methods. After a conversation has been started, calling a second start method on that conversation is an error.

When the client calls a start method, WebLogic Workshop generates a *conversation key,* which is a unique identifier of the conversation. The client may use this key to correlate its future method calls with a particular conversation, and WebLogic Workshop uses this key to correlate a stored conversational state with a particular conversation.

The conversation key may be specified by the client, however; in normal usage, WebLogic Workshop will automatically generate the conversation key. In most cases, users of WebLogic Workshop Web services and clients will never have to worry about conversation keys. When accessing conversational WebLogic Workshop Web services from other platforms, such as .NET or Apache SOAP, you must do some extra work to make conversations function.

Continuing a conversation

After a conversation has been started, the client can continue the conversation by calling continue methods. The client must pass the conversation key to the continue method to identify the conversation to continue (when using WebLogic Workshop-generated clients this process is transparent). The client may call an unlimited number of continue methods, as long as the conversation has not been terminated. Conversations are designed to be long-running if necessary. Because conversational state is stored in a database, conversations can live for many days or even years.

A client cannot call any continue methods until a conversation has been started; attempting to do so is an error. After you call any start method, any continue method may be called as long as the conversation is extant.

Finishing a conversation

A client may terminate a conversation by calling a finish method. A Web service may have many finish methods, but when one of them is called for a particular conversation key, that conversation is over. No more continue or finish methods may be called for the conversation identified by that conversation key. Finishing a conversation frees the resources devoted to storing the conversational state and as a result, that state is destroyed.

Working with Conversations in the Design View

To manipulate the conversational phase of a method from the Design View, you must use the Property Editor, a feature I have conveniently ignored so far. The Property Editor is useful for some important Web service-specific features, so I will take a moment to describe its operation.

The Property Editor appears on the right-hand side of the Design View. It displays a list of *properties* for the presently selected object in the Design View. Although I didn't point it out earlier, you can select a number of objects in the Design View by clicking on them with the mouse. The presently selected object has a permanent orange border, and as you move the cursor over an object in the Design View, a temporary orange border appears around the object if it can be selected.

Figure 4-2 shows the Design View for a Web service where one of the Web service methods is selected. The Property Editor displays a list of properties for this method, which allow you to control many aspects of the object's behavior.

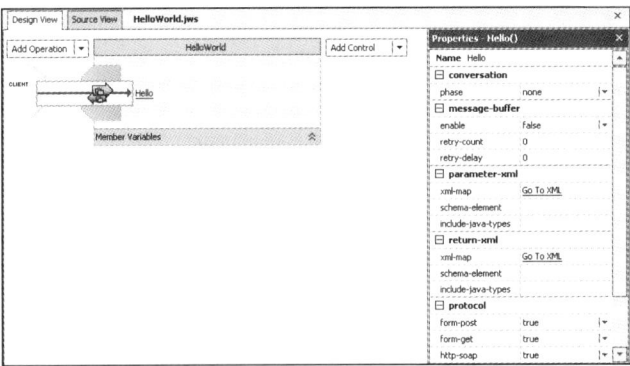

Figure 4-2: The Property Editor with a method selected.

The properties in the Property Editor have a very regular structure. Some of the properties are drawn in bold and have a little plus or minus sign next to them. These properties are called *tags* and do not have values you can set. However, tags do have child properties, called *attributes,* which are drawn in normal text and have an associated value. If you click on any of the plus signs for a tag, you can hide the attributes for that tag.

Chapter 4: Creating Conversational Web Services

Every attribute has a value, which can be changed by using the editor to the right of the attribute's name. Editors can be drop-down lists, text boxes, or links, depending on the attribute. Many WebLogic Workshop features are controlled by setting the values of attributes, and as I introduce those features I will point out the type of value that can be entered into the editor.

The selected method in Figure 4-2 has a number of tags and attributes, but for the moment I'll focus on the very first tag in the list. This tag, conversation, contains one attribute, phase. By setting the value of the phase attribute, you can control the conversational phase of the method.

Figure 4-3 shows the editor for the phase attribute, which is a drop-down box since there are a fixed set of conversational phases. There are five different entries in this drop-down: none, start, continue, finish, and default. You can select any of these values for the phase attribute. If you select start, continue, or finish, this will set the conversational phase of the method to the corresponding value. If you select the value none, the method will not be part of a conversation. The final value, default, appears in every drop-down attribute editor. Selecting this value will restore the attribute to its default value, which is none for the phase attribute.

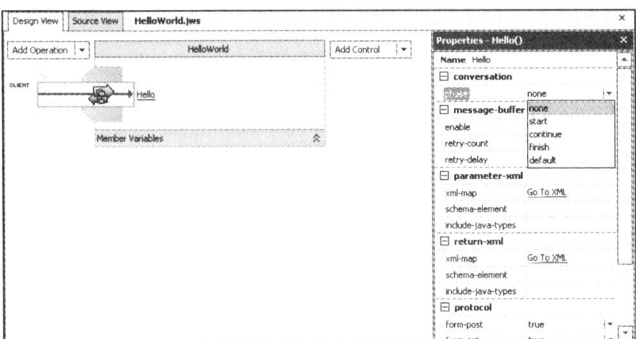

Figure 4-3: The conversation property.

When you set the conversational phase of a method to start, continue, or finish, an indicator appears on the arrow for the method. The indicator is a small circle containing an *s, c,* or *f* — I'm sure you can guess what these stand for.

Figure 4-4 shows a Web service with four methods, one in each conversational state. You can see the indicators on methods showing what state they're in (although I chose pretty obvious names for them as well).

In addition to the indicators, the methods on the Design View are sorted by their conversational phase: the non-conversational methods are first, the start methods are second, the continue methods are third, and the finish methods are fourth. If you prefer to have the methods sorted differently, you may choose between a few different options by selecting Tools⇨Preferences. Figure 4-5 shows the ordering choices for the Design View.

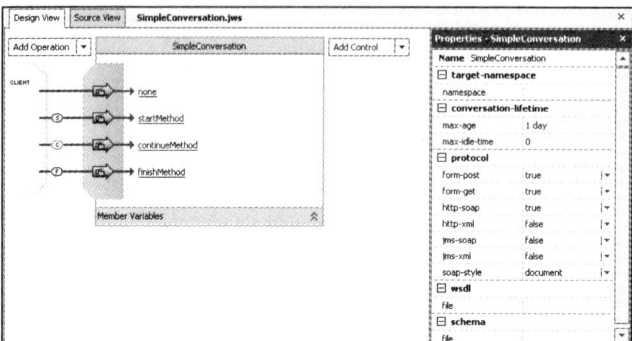

Figure 4-4: The Design View showing conversational phases.

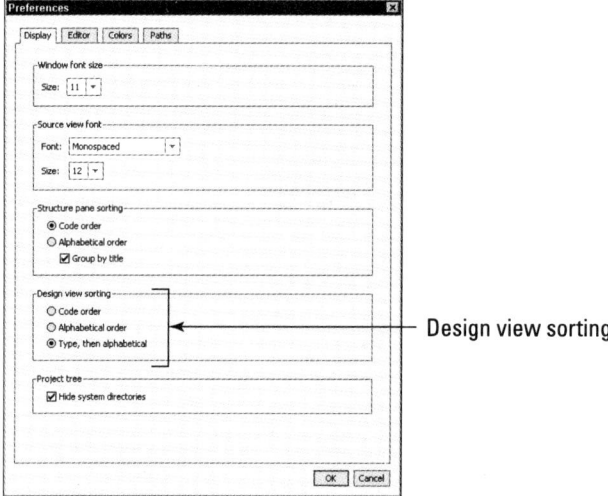

Figure 4-5: Design View display preferences.

Table 4-1 explains each of these choices in detail. The default ordering is the last one, which is intended to reveal the flow of the conversation by showing the methods in the order in which they should be called.

TABLE 4-1 SORTING OPTIONS FOR METHODS IN THE DESIGN VIEW

Sorting Options	Description
Code order	Show the methods in the same order as they appear in the source code.
Alphabetical order	Show the methods in alphabetical order.

Sorting Options	Description
Type, then alphabetical	Show the methods sorted first by conversational state and then in alphabetical order (default).

Properties in the Source Code

In Chapter 2, I made a fairly big deal out of the notion that WebLogic Workshop Web services are completely specified by the source code and that there was no hidden information squirreled away somewhere else that was needed in order for the Web service to run. Given this statement, you may wonder how the properties are represented in the source code.

From the terminology used earlier, you may have already guessed that properties in the Property Editor correspond to Javadoc annotations in the source code. This guess would be correct. In fact, the Property Editor is nothing more than a Javadoc annotation editor. Listing 4-1 shows the source code for the Web service exhibited in the previous section. This listing should make it rather clear how a conversational phase is specified in annotations.

Listing 4-1: A Conversational Web Service

```
package BookProject.Chapter4;

import weblogic.jws.control.JwsContext;

public class SimpleConversation
{
    /** @jws:context */
    JwsContext context;

    /**
     * @jws:operation
     */
    public void none()
    {}

    /**
     * @jws:operation
     * @jws:conversation phase="start"
     */
    public void startMethod()
```

Continued

Listing 4-1: A Conversational Web Service *(Continued)*

```
    {}

    /**
     * @jws:operation
     * @jws:conversation phase="continue"
     */
    public void continueMethod()
    {}

    /**
     * @jws:operation
     * @jws:conversation phase="finish"
     */
    public void finishMethod()
    {}
}
```

This source code shows the four methods that appeared earlier. The conversational phase for each method is specified by using the tag, `@jws:conversation`. This is the same as the name of the tag in the Property Editor, with the `jws` prefix added. The single attribute of this tag, `phase`, is also identical to the name of the attribute in the Property Editor.

The Property Editor shows every possible tag that can be placed above the selected object in the Design View. Looking at the Property Editor for the preceding example, you should be able to spot five different tags that can appear above a method: conversation, message-buffer, parameter-xml, return-xml, and protocol. When these tags appear in the source code, they must all be preceded by the jws prefix.

Many of the tags for a method have multiple attributes (the protocol tag being the winner with seven). When you add a tag into the source code, you may specify any subset of these attributes in any order.

When you use JWS tags with attributes, you must be very careful to include the quotes around the attribute values. If you don't, WebLogic Workshop won't recognize the value you entered. For instance,

`@jws:conversation phase=start`

will not be recognized by WebLogic Workshop as marking a start method.

You may have noticed that quite a number of the attributes that appear in the Property Editor contain values, yet there are no corresponding tags or attributes in the source code. If I was telling the truth when I said everything there can be found in the source code (and I was, I promise), where are these values coming from? If you don't specify the value of an attribute in the source code, WebLogic Workshop assigns it a default value. For instance, all the Web service methods you've seen in the previous chapters had no @jws:conversation tag and no phase attribute. As a result, WebLogic Workshop gave the phase attribute its default value, none, which means that these methods were not part of a conversation.

If you click on any tag or attribute in the Property Editor, you can see a short description of it in the Description Pane, which appears just below the Property Editor. The description often specifies the default value for an attribute.

A Conversational Example

Now that you've learned about the theory of conversations and the practical details of setting conversational phases, I'll show you how to use conversations by means of a simple example. In this example (Listing 4-2), I will create a very limited online store, which uses conversational state to manage a user's shopping cart.

Listing 4-2: The Online Store

```
packageChapter4;

import java.util.ArrayList;
import weblogic.jws.control.JwsContext;

public class OnlineStore
{
    /** @jws:context */
    JwsContext context;

    /** The name of the customer. */
    private String name;

    /** A list of items that represents the shopping cart. */
    private ArrayList shoppingCart;

    /**
     * Represents an item that can be stored in the shopping cart.
     */
    private static class Item implements java.io.Serializable
    {
        /** The name of the item. */
```

Continued

Listing 4-2: The Online Store *(Continued)*

```java
        public String name;

        /** The integer code for the item. */
        public int code;

        /** The price of this item. */
        public double price;

        public Item()
        {}

        public Item(String name, int code, double price)
        {
            this.name  = name;
            this.code  = code;
            this.price = price;
        }
    }

    /**
     * The catalog of available items.
     */
    private static Item[] catalog =    {
        new Item("Blue Widget", 0, 2.75),
        new Item("Red Widget", 1, 5.75),
        new Item("Green Widget", 2, 7.15),
        new Item("Yellow Widget", 3, 1.50),
        new Item("Orange Widget", 4, 3.25)
    };

    /**
     * @jws:operation
     * @jws:conversation phase="start"
     */
    public String startShopping(String name)
    {
        this.name         = name;
        this.shoppingCart = new ArrayList();

        return "Welcome, " + name;
    }

    /**
     * @jws:operation
```

```java
 */
public Item[] viewCatalog()
{
    return catalog;
}

/**
 * @jws:operation
 * @jws:conversation phase="continue"
 */
public void addItem(int code)
{
    shoppingCart.add(new Item(
        catalog[code].name, code, catalog[code].price));
}

/**
 * @jws:operation
 * @jws:conversation phase="continue"
 */
public void removeItem(int index)
{
    shoppingCart.remove(index);
}

/**
 * @jws:operation
 * @jws:conversation phase="continue"
 */
public Item[] viewCart()
{
    return (Item[])shoppingCart.toArray(new Item[0]);
}

/**
 * @jws:operation
 * @jws:conversation phase="finish"
 */
public double checkout()
{
    double total = 0.0;

    for (int i = 0; i < shoppingCart.size(); i++)
```

Continued

Listing 4-2: The Online Store *(Continued)*

```
            total += ((Item)shoppingCart.get(i)).price;

      return total;
   }
}
```

This example is obviously extremely limited. A real online store would have to deal with collecting information about payment; collecting more customer information, such as a mailing address; providing some sort of user interface; keeping a real catalog (probably in a database); setting up shipping; and doing other sundry work required to cause real, physical objects to be shipped and real money to be collected.

Despite all these limitations, this example does demonstrate the two most important features of conversations:

- The example provides a simple workflow for the online store. The customer must log in before he can shop or check out, and after the user has checked out he can't shop any more.

- The example uses conversational state to maintain a shopping cart for the user, a task that otherwise may have to be done explicitly by the Web service programmer using cookies or some other, more complicated, mechanism.

What the example does

Table 4-2 gives a summary of the conversational methods of this Web service detailed in Listing 4-2.

TABLE 4-2 THE METHODS OF THE ONLINE STORE

Method Name	Description
`void startShopping(String name)`	Starts a shopping session (and a conversation).
`void addItem(int code)`	Adds an item to the shopping cart with the specified code.
`void removeItem(int index)`	Removes the item at the specified index in the shopping cart.
`Item[] viewCart()`	Displays the current set of items in the shopping cart.

Method Name	Description
double checkout()	Terminates the conversation and returns the total price of the items in the shopping cart.

In addition to these methods, there is a *stateless* (another word for non-conversational) method that can be used to view the catalog for this online store. The catalog is represented by a static array of `Item` objects.

Using inner classes with conversations

This example defines an inner class to contain the data about items stored in the shopping cart and in the catalog. This inner class is named `Item` and is declared near the beginning of the file. If you're unfamiliar with the rules of inner classes in Java, you should consult the Java Primer in the appendix. An `Item` stores an item name, a code (used to reference the item in the catalog), and a price.

```
private static class Item implements java.io.Serializable
{
    /** The name of the item. */
    public String name;

    /** The integer code for the item. */
    public int code;

    /** The price of this item. */
    public double price;

    public Item()
    {}

    public Item(String name, int code, double price)
    {
        this.name  = name;
        this.code  = code;
        this.price = price;
    }
}
```

There are several important things to point out about this declaration. First, this class is declared to be static. When you're using inner classes in WebLogic Workshop, you almost always want them to be static. The precise reason has to do with how Java deals with inner classes and the "this" reference keyword. Suffice it to say, unless you have a really good reason for using non-static classes, and you know what you're doing, making your inner classes static is best.

Second, this class implements the interface `java.io.Serializable`. This interface is a very special interface that does not contain any methods but merely serves as a marker that *serialization* should be allowed for objects of the class. Serializing is a process by which an object is converted to a well-known data representation that can be stored away in a file or transmitted across the network and later used to re-create the object. Because `Item` objects will be stored in the database as part of this Web service's conversational state, these objects must be serializable.

Finally, although this class has a constructor that sets the values of all its fields, it also has a no-argument constructor (a *default constructor* in Java terminology) that does nothing. Furthermore, this constructor is not called anywhere in the Web service. However, WebLogic Workshop uses the empty constructor in conjunction with saving and restoring `Item` objects, so it needs to be there.

It may seem like the process of using inner classes is very complicated, with a set of strange rules. However, you really only need to remember three things:

- Make your inner classes static.
- Make your inner classes implement `java.io.Serializable`.
- Give your classes a default (that is, a no-argument) constructor. It can do anything you want it to do, just make sure it's there.

If you follow these rules when working with inner classes, you shouldn't encounter any problems. If you still don't like the idea of using inner classes, you can always define all your classes in separate Java files. In that case, you don't have to make them static, but the last two rules must still be followed.

Maintaining conversational state

The online store maintains two pieces of conversational state: the shopping cart and the user's name. This conversational state is created, very simply, by creating two (non-static) fields in the Web service, which are declared near the top.

```
/** The name of the customer. */
private String name;

/** A list of items that represents the shopping cart. */
private ArrayList shoppingCart;
```

Simply by virtue of creating these fields, they're added to the conversational state of the Web service—repetition of the line above the code. To gain better understanding of how these fields are made part of the conversational state of this Web service, I'll walk you through the life cycle of a conversation and talk about what happens to these fields.

The conversation is started when the `startShopping` method is called. At this point a conversation key is created. When the `startShopping` method returns, the values of `name` and `shoppingCart` are stored in the database, using the conversation key as the primary key. Later on, when a continue method, such as `addItem`, is called, the conversation key sent by the client is used to look up the conversational state that is loaded into the two fields. Throughout the continue method, these values can be used or changed; when the method returns, their values will be saved back into the database. This will go on until a finish method is called, when the conversational state is purged from the database.

This process is simple, but quite powerful. From the point of view of you, the Web service writer, the fields of the Web service always magically have the "right" value, and all without any work on your part (except for the typing of some simple annotations). You don't need to worry about the details of conversation keys or databases. You don't need to figure out how to serialize the values of the objects in question. It all just works.

To summarize, if you want to add some conversational state to a method, you must simply be aware of the following rules:

- Any fields of a Web service will be part of that Web service's conversational state.

- Conversational state is persisted to the database and recovered in a completely transparent way.

If you have a bunch of fields that don't need to be part of the conversational state, you probably don't want to waste space in the database storing them. You can exclude a field from the conversational state simply by marking it as transient. An example of this would be:

```
public transient int myNonConversationalInt;
```

The value of this field will be lost between method calls, because it isn't stored as part of the conversational state.

Testing Conversational Web Services

You've already seen how to test normal Web services using the Test View, but there are some additional features of the Test View that are used specifically when testing conversational Web services.

Figure 4-6 shows the Test View for the online store Web service before any methods have been invoked.

Part II: Basic Concepts

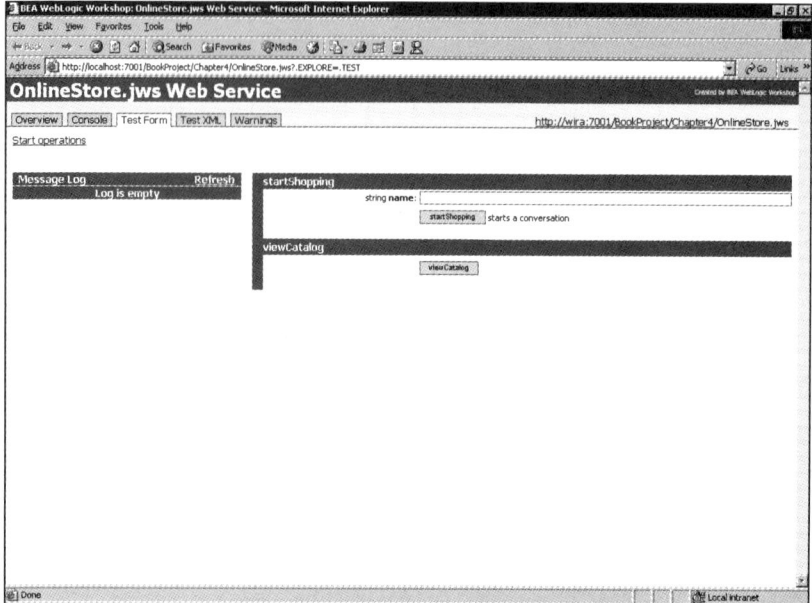

Figure 4-6: The Test View for a conversational Web service.

You will note that there are only two methods showing in the Test View. The stateless method viewCatalog and the start method startShopping are both present, but the continue and finish methods are not. There is some logic to this. You cannot call a continue method until you start a conversation, so it wouldn't make any sense to list the continue methods at this point.

When you invoke the startShopping method, the Message Log shows the method call, but it also shows the new conversation that has been started. Figure 4-7 shows the Test View after startShopping has been called.

Above the record for the call to startShopping there is another entry that contains a long number. This number is the conversation key for the new conversation you've created by calling the start method. If you click on this number, you'll be taken to the page for this conversation, which contains the continue and finish methods. As you invoke these methods, they'll appear in the message log under their conversations as shown in Figure 4-8. When you finish a conversation, this will be noted in the Message Log as well.

Chapter 4: Creating Conversational Web Services 91

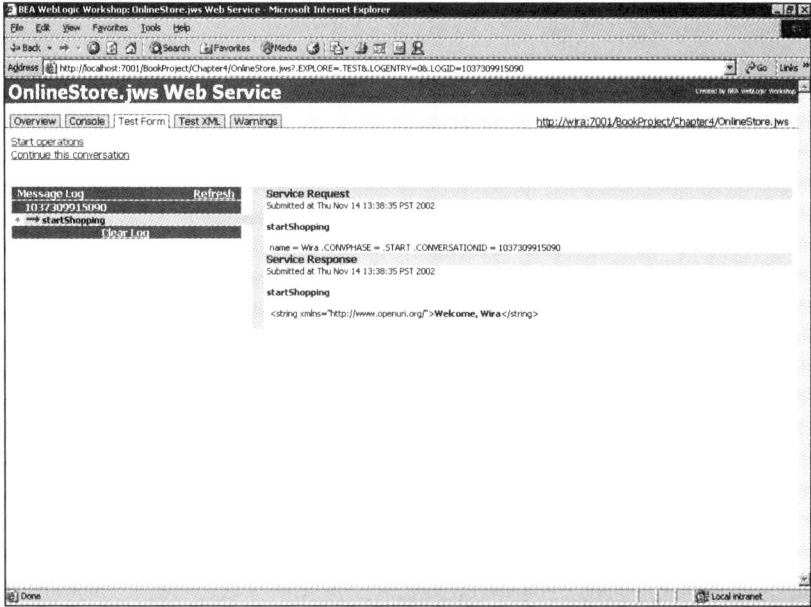

Figure 4-7: The Test View after calling a start method.

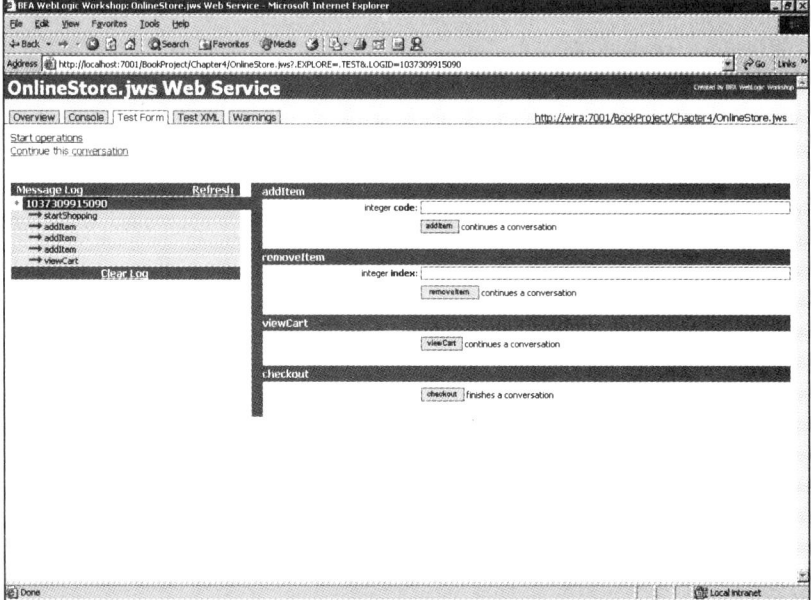

Figure 4-8: The continue and finish methods.

Getting More Control Over Conversations

So far I've shown you the fundamentals of how to use conversations, but there are additional features that you'll probably find useful eventually. These features allow you to control the lifetime of conversations as well as get detailed information about the conversation from within the Web service.

Conversational lifetimes

As I mentioned earlier, conversations maintain state in a database, which is cleaned up when a finish method is called to end the conversation. However, conversations can be very long in duration, potentially spanning years. A natural question to ask would be, "What if a client never calls a finish method? Will the resources associated with that conversation be retained forever?"

To solve this problem, WebLogic Workshop allows you to exercise fairly precise control over the lifetime of a conversation. These controls are accessible through the attributes of the conversation-lifetime tag, which is a property of the Web service (and hence will appear in the annotation above the Web service class).

Figure 4-9 shows the conversation-lifetime property in the Property Editor. Under the conversation-lifetime property, two attributes can be set: max-age and max-idle-time. The editors for both of these properties are text boxes. The values of these properties can be specified as durations, such as "1 hour 30 minutes" or "6 days 3 hours 5 minutes 12 seconds." If you enter an empty string into the editor (select the value, press Delete, and then press Enter), the attributes will be set to their default values.

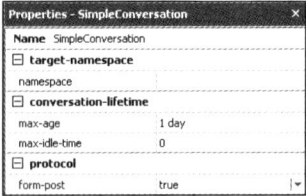

Figure 4-9: The conversation-lifetime property

Table 4-3 defines the two attributes that can be used to control conversation lifetime.

TABLE 4-3 THE CONVERSATION-LIFETIME ATTRIBUTES

Conversation Lifetime Attribute	Description
max-age	Specifies the longest possible duration of a conversation. After a conversation is created, WebLogic Workshop will wait max-age time before automatically terminating the conversation. A max-age of 0 allows the conversation to live forever. The default value is 1 day.
max-idle-time	Specifies the length of time a conversation must be idle (having no continue methods invoked) before the conversation is terminated. The default value is 0, which means idle conversations are never terminated.

Just like all other properties, the conversation lifetime tag appears in the source code as an annotation. You may specify the attributes in either order and you may omit either attribute, in which case it is set to its default value.

```
/**
 * @jws:conversation-lifetime max-age="3 days"
 *                            max idle-time="1 hour"
 */
public class MyWebService
```

The previous comment sets the conversation lifetime for `MyWebService`. It specifies a maximum conversation age of 3 days and a maximum idle time of 1 hour.

Using the Context object to control conversations

Earlier I told you the `Context` object provides useful functions to your Web service, but thus far I haven't talked about any of them. The `Context` object has quite a few methods, several of which can be used to find out information about conversations and conversation lifetimes. Some of the methods can also be used to perform useful functions, like forcing a conversation to finish.

There are a large number of methods on the `Context` object, and only some of them are useful for controlling conversations. Those that are related to conversations are listed in Table 4-4.

TABLE 4-4 CONVERSATION-RELATED METHODS ON THE CONTEXT OBJECT

Context Method	Description
`void finishConversation()`	Ends the current conversation.
`long getCurrentAge()`	Returns the age of the current conversation in seconds.
`long getCurrentIdleTime()`	Returns the idle time of the current conversation in seconds. When you call this method from within a conversational method, it returns the time between the current conversational method call and the last one.
`long getMaxAge()`	Returns the value of the max-age attribute for this conversation in seconds.
`long getMaxIdleTime()`	Returns the value of the max-idle-time attribute for this conversation in seconds.
`boolean isFinished()`	Returns true if the current conversation is finished.
`void resetIdleTime()`	Sets the current idle time — used in conjunction with the max-idle-time attribute — of this Web service to 0.
`void setMaxAge(Date)`	Sets the max-age property for this conversation to the value specified in by the Date.
`void setMaxAge(String)`	Sets the max-age property for this conversation to the value specified by the String. This string has the same format as the max-age attribute.
`void setMaxIdleTime(String)`	Sets the max-idle-time attribute for this conversation to the value specified in the String. This string has the same format as the max-idle-time attribute.
`void setMaxIdleTime(long)`	Sets the max-idle-time attribute for this conversation to the number of seconds specified in the long number parameter.

Assuming that you've left the declaration of the `Context` object in your Web service, you can call any of these methods from anywhere in your Web service. Listing 4-3 shows a simple Web service that allows you to start conversations and then query the age of the current Web service.

Listing 4-3: A Conversation Age Web Service

```
package BookProject.Chapter4;

import weblogic.jws.control.JwsContext;

public class ConversationAge
{
    /** @jws:context */
    JwsContext context;

    /**
     * @jws:operation
     * @jws:conversation phase="start"
     */
    public void startConversation()
    {}

    /**
     * @jws:operation
     * @jws:conversation phase="continue"
     */
    public Ages getConversationAges()
    {
        Ages ages = new Ages();
        ages.age = context.getCurrentAge();
        ages.idleTime = context.getCurrentIdleTime();

        return ages;
    }

    public static class Ages
    {
        public long age;
        public long idleTime;
    }
}
```

After you invoke `startConversation`, a conversation will be started on the server. Subsequent calls to `getConversationAge` will return an `Ages` object (declared as an inner class in the Web service), which is filled with the current age of the Web service (in seconds) and the current *idle time* (that is, the time between the current method call and the last call to a conversational method). For instance, if you call `startConversation`, wait 5 seconds and then call `getConversationAge`, you'll receive the following result:

```
<Ages xmlns="http://www.openuri.org/">
  <age>5</age>
  <idleTime>5</idleTime>
</Ages>
```

If you then wait another 15 seconds and then call `getConversationAge` again, you will receive the following result:

```
<Ages xmlns="http://www.openuri.org/">
<age>20</age>
<idleTime>15</idleTime>
</Ages>
```

Note that the age is now 20 seconds, because the conversation has been running for 20 seconds, but the idle time is 15 seconds, because it has been 15 seconds since the last method call.

There is one additional method, `context.getService()`, which returns a `ServiceHandle` object. The `ServiceHandle` object has one additional useful method `getConversationID`, which returns the conversation key for the current conversation.

Summary

Conversations are a very useful mechanism, and you may need a little time to figure out all the places where you can take advantage of them. A simple, but not universal, rule of thumb is that if your Web service has methods that should be called in the start, continue, and finish pattern, you should consider if conversations would be appropriate. However, you should also keep your eyes open for places where conversations may not be the obvious choice, but by applying them you could drastically simplify your Web service.

- ◆ Conversations are used to maintain state across Web service method calls.
- ◆ Conversations have three phases – start, continue, and finish – which should be traversed in order.
- ◆ You can gain additional control over conversations by using the `Context` object.
- ◆ The Test View has some facilities for helping you keep track of conversations.

Chapter 5

Creating Asynchronous Web Services

IN THIS CHAPTER

- Understanding asynchronous Web services
- Using buffering to queue requests to the Web service
- Using callbacks to send messages back to the client

CALLING YOUR FRIEND on the phone is a synchronous process; you dial a number and you hang on to your phone until you receive a response. An example of asynchronous process is sending email; once you click "send", you can move on to do other things – the mail program will notify you later on if a response is received. WebLogic Workshop attempts to make the programming of asynchronous Web services as easy as possible by providing a simple model for asynchrony. As a result, the amount of information you need to know in order to create asynchronous Web services is actually rather small. Despite this, you shouldn't take for granted the power and utility of asynchrony when you're creating Web services with WebLogic Workshop.

Why You Need Asynchrony

When one system wants to have another system perform a service, there are two general models that can be used: the synchronous model and the asynchronous model. To aid in describing these models, I'll call the system requesting the service the *client* and the system delivering the service the *server*.

In the synchronous model, the client makes a service request to the server and then waits for the server to complete the service. A good example of this would be an ATM. When you make a request for money from an ATM, you insert your card, press a bunch of buttons, and then wait for the server at the bank to either authorize the transaction and give you your money or reject the transaction and perhaps eat your card. Until you receive some response from the bank, you're completely occupied by waiting. You can't go off to the post office and send out some letters while your request is being processed (unless you want to lose your money). Fortunately, the servers at the bank are typically quick about their task and you don't have to wait very long.

In contrast, in the asynchronous model, after the client makes a request, it can go do something else — it doesn't need to wait for the server. When the server processes the request and performs the service, it notifies the client of service completion through some callback mechanism. The client can then do what it wants with the results of the service. Catalog shopping provides a simple example of an asynchronous service. When you order something from a catalog, you place a request for the delivery of some items and then you go on with your life. When the merchant has filled your order, your purchases are sent to you, and sometime later they appear on your doorstep. At that point you can respond appropriately to their arrival.

The important point in the asynchronous model is the client doesn't have to wait for the server to perform the service. When the client has submitted a service request, it can work on something else until the service is complete. When the server finally finishes processing the client's request, the client will be notified and the client can process the notification when it's appropriate. A nice asynchronous example is a loan processing Web Service. When you submit a loan application, the loan processor's computer will submit the application to a few loan providers' systems, which will respond in a few days (or maybe weeks) with an approved or rejected loan. Between the time you submit the application and the time you receive it, you want to free up your computer to do other things; you definitely don't want it to keep waiting and asking the other computers "Are we there yet?"

Synchronous systems are frequently very easy to program, but they aren't always an appropriate model for delivering a service. Synchronous systems become very disagreeable when the completion of the service takes a long time. Because synchronous systems require the client to wait for the completion of the service, the client is unable to do anything else until the service request is complete. This can lead to very poor system performance. Using the example from above, if the bank took 30 minutes to process an ATM request, you would undoubtedly find it very unsatisfying.

WebLogic Workshop Asynchrony Mechanisms

Web services provide a service model and WebLogic Workshop provides built-in facilities for making the creation of asynchronous Web service not only possible, but rather easy. Asynchronous systems don't have the best reputation for being easy to program. Asynchrony usually requires a lot of work, because it requires fairly reliable queuing facilities and some sort of callback mechanism that can inform a client of service completion. If this mechanism is not built into the operating environment (as it is with WebLogic Workshop), creating asynchronous systems can be rather difficult.

The WebLogic Workshop asynchrony model has two parts. First, there is a buffering mechanism that allows a Web service to have a queue of service requests, such that clients can quickly drop off a request without having to wait for the Web service to be available. Second, there is a callback mechanism, which allows a Web service to send messages back to its clients.

This chapter discusses these two asynchrony mechanisms and explains how they can be used together to create fully asynchronous Web services. Table 5-1 briefly summarizes both of these features.

TABLE 5-1 THE ASYNCHRONY FEATURES

Mechanism	Description
Buffering	Allows a Web service to enqueue incoming requests so clients don't have to wait synchronously for their requests to complete.
Callbacks	Allows a Web service to asynchronously send messages back to the client relieving the need for continuous polling.

Buffering

Buffering creates a queue for a Web service so that incoming Web service requests can be stored until the Web service is ready to handle them. A client that is submitting a request only has to wait as long as it takes to place a request into the queue, after which it does not need to wait for the Web service to actually process the request.

Buffering is not only helpful for creating asynchronous Web services, but it's also useful for buffering the Web service against heavy loads (hence, the name). A buffered Web service is much more tolerant in handling large numbers of requests, because Web service requests can be enqueued much faster than they can actually be processed.

An example of a buffered service

In WebLogic Workshop, buffering is controlled on a per-method basis. Any method on a Web service can be buffered by properly setting the attributes of the message-buffer tag. The attributes of the method buffer tag can be changed by using the Property Editor, or by adding the tag directly into the source code in an annotation above the method (remember that in the source code the tag will be @jws:message-buffer). The most important attribute of the message-buffer tag is the Enable attribute, which can have a value of either true or false. If the Enable attribute is set to true, the method will be buffered; if it is set to false, the method will not be buffered.

When you buffer a method, a spring icon appears on the arrow for the method, as is shown in Figure 5-1. This spring is intended to represent the "shock-absorbing" properties of buffering.

100 Part II: Basic Concepts

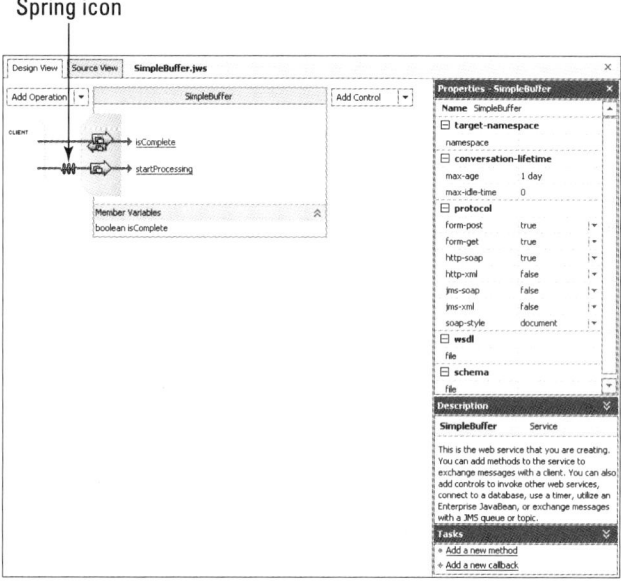

Figure 5-1: A buffered method.

Listing 5-1 shows an example of a simple Web service with a buffered method. By the two-part definition of asynchrony I gave previously, this service is only the first half of the Workshop's asynchronous features, because I have not yet shown you how to use callbacks to send messages back to the client. It uses buffering so clients don't have to wait while requests are being processed, but also relies on the client polling the service to find out when the processing is complete.

Listing 5-1: The SimpleBuffer Web Service

```
package Chapter5;

import weblogic.jws.control.JwsContext;

public class SimpleBuffer
{
    /** @jws:context */
    JwsContext context;

    /**
     * Set to true when the processing is complete.
     */
    private boolean complete = false;

    /**
     * Starts the "processing" which in this case is just a 10
```

```java
     * second sleep.
     *
     * @jws:operation
     * @jws:message-buffer enable="true"
     */
    public void startProcessing()
    {
        // Perform the "processing".
        try
        { Thread.sleep(10000); }
        catch (Exception e)
        {}

        // Set the flag once processing is complete.
        complete = true;
    }

    /**
     * Checks to see if the processing is complete.  If processing
     * is complete, this method will return true and reset the
     * <code>complete</code> flag so you can try out this example
     * multiple times.
     *
     * @jws:operation
     */
    public boolean isComplete()
    {
        if (complete)
    {
        complete = false;
        return true;
    }
    else
    {
         return false;
        }
    }
}
```

This Web service doesn't do much except illustrate how buffers work. When you invoke the startProcessing method, the Web service goes to sleep for ten seconds and then sets the complete flag to true to indicate that it has completed the "processing." There is a second method, isComplete, which returns the value of the complete flag so that the client can check to see if processing has been completed yet. If the processing has been completed when isComplete is called, the flag is set back to false so you can run the example more than one time.

 It is a common naming convention in Java to use the name *isX* for the "getter" method of - boolean – field named *x*. Also, if you have a "setter" method for the field, it is named *setX*. When the field is not a - boolean, the "getter" method is called *getX* instead of *isX*.

You can see buffering in action by running this Web service in the Test View. When you invoke the `startProcessing` method, the Test View immediately logs the call in the Message Log, signifying that the method has returned. However, if you invoke `isComplete` before ten seconds have passed, you'll see that the processing has not, in fact, completed. If you keep calling `isComplete`, it will eventually return true after ten seconds have passed.

The key point here is the client does not actually wait for `startProcessing` to complete. In fact, it doesn't even wait for it to be called. Instead, the call made by the client returns as soon as the request to call `startProcessing` is enqueued. The request may not be handled for quite a while, but it doesn't matter to the client, who is free to continue processing. Unfortunately, this example requires the client to poll the server in order to find out when the processing has completed. In just a few pages, I show you how to remedy this deficiency by using callbacks.

Because the client isn't actually calling the method itself, but rather is simply adding a request to a queue, the client doesn't actually interact with the method in the traditional sense. As a result, buffered methods must be void, because the client won't be waiting to receive the return value. If you want to return a value from a buffered method, you must use callbacks, which I discuss later in this chapter.

Other attributes of the message-buffer tag

The `message-buffer` tag has two other attributes, which are used to control the properties of the queue that holds the service requests. It is possible that the queue attempting to deliver service requests to the service will not be able to contact the service. Two additional properties on the `message-buffer` tag allow you to control the retry behavior of the queue when it is delivering requests to the Web service. These attributes are described in Table 5-2.

TABLE 5-2 THE RETRY ATTRIBUTES ON THE MESSAGE-BUFFER TAG

Retry Attribute	Description
retry-count	The number of times the queue will attempt to deliver service requests to the Web service. The default value is 0.
retry-delay	The amount of time in seconds that the queue should wait between delivery attempts to the Web service. The default value is 0 seconds.

What buffering really does

The queues WebLogic Workshop uses to implement buffering are part of J2EE and are provided through the Java Messaging Services (JMS) API in conjunction with Message Driven Beans. The JMS queues typically used with WebLogic Workshop are transactional, persistent queues, so they're a fairly safe place to store information. Although adding buffering may be easy, this feature, like all those provided by WebLogic Workshop is robust and reliable.

JMS queues (and the related JMS topics) are quite useful, and you may eventually want to use them for other asynchronous J2EE programming outside Web Services. If you want to work directly with JMS queues, you can use the JMS control, which I describe in Chapter 7.

Callbacks

The second half of creating an asynchronous Web service is the ability to get back to the client asynchronously. In WebLogic Workshop, the mechanism you use for this is the callback. Callbacks are the second type of operation, and just like methods they cause messages to be sent over the network. However, unlike methods, callbacks send messages from the Web service to the client.

Using callbacks

In the Design View, you can create callbacks using the same control you use to create methods. To create a callback, select Add Operation⇨Add Callback from the Design View. This will add a new arrow to the Design View, only this time, the arrow points from the Web service to the client, signifying that messages travel from the Web service to the client. Figure 5-2 shows a callback in the Design View.

Callbacks are created in the source code differently from anything I have shown you so far. Listing 5-2 shows the source code for the Web service pictured in Figure 5-2.

Listing 5-2: The CallbackExample Web Service

```
package Chapter5;

import weblogic.jws.control.JwsContext;

public class CallbackExample
{
    public Callback callback;

    public interface Callback
```

Continued

Listing 5-2 *(Continued)*

```
    {
        public void onCallback();
    }

    /** @jws:context */
    JwsContext context;
}
```

The first thing to notice about this Web service is that it contains no Java methods. Callbacks are not represented in a Web service by Java methods, because you don't need to write any code in the Web service for a callback. Callbacks cause code to be executed on the *client,* so the only thing you must do in the Web service is declare that the callbacks exist.

Although a Web service doesn't need to implement its callbacks, it must somehow declare what callbacks exist and what their shapes are. The normal way to do this in Java is to create an interface. An interface declares a set of methods, their return types and arguments, without specifying their implementation. You should note that while Web services are not responsible for implementing callbacks, the declaration of a Web service's callbacks is part of the definition of the Web service itself; it is part of the basic identity of the Web service. A Web service's "contract" with the outside world includes both the messages that can be sent to the Web service by methods and the messages that will be sent from the Web service by callbacks.

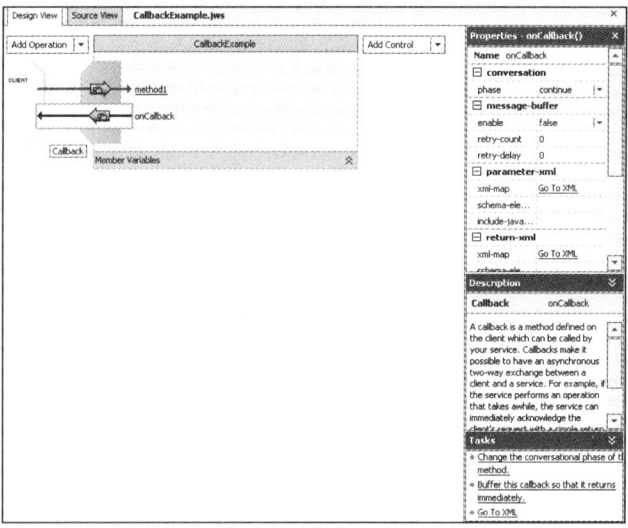

Figure 5-2: A callback.

Chapter 5: Creating Asynchronous Web Services

The interface in a Web service that contains the callbacks is identified by its name, `Callback`. In Listing 5-2, this interface is defined by the following code:

```
public interface Callback
{
    public void onCallback(); -
}
```

The `Callback` interface is an inner interface, an interface that is declared within another class, in this case, the Web service class. In this example, the interface contains one method `callback1`, which is the only callback for this Web service. As you add callbacks to the Design View, they'll be added to this interface. If you want to create callbacks directly in the source code, simply add the declarations to this interface yourself. Just make sure you remember to put the semicolon at the end of the declaration.

After the `Callback` interface has been declared, you must create an instance of this interface so you can call callbacks from the source code. Just like for classes, the declaration of an interface simply defines what the interface looks like. To use it, you must create an instance. In WebLogic Workshop, simply declaring a field of the `Callback` type creates an instance of the callback.

```
public Callback callback;
```

If you're familiar with Java, this may seem a little odd. Normally, simply declaring a variable is not enough to create an instance. Typically, you have to use the `new` operator to create a new instance of the class, like the following:

```
public ArrayList list = new ArrayList();
```

However, because the `Callback` interface is very special in the eyes of WebLogic Workshop, simply declaring the variable is enough. WebLogic Workshop takes care of initializing it. This may seem a little strange, but it is the same mechanism that is used to initialize the `Context` object as well as other controls that you will learn about in Chapters 6 and 7.

You may have noticed that callbacks follow a slightly different paradigm from everything else in WebLogic Workshop. Normally, WebLogic Workshop uses annotations to mark special objects, like the `JwsContext` object. However, no annotations are related to creating callbacks. Instead, the special name `Callback` is used to identify the callback interface. This mild inconsistency doesn't have any good explanation that I know of; it's just one of those things that happens in a programming project.

As a final note, callbacks, like methods, can participate in conversations. Callbacks cannot start conversations, but they can continue or finish them. If you want to make a callback participate in the conversation, you can set its conversational phase in the Property Editor. Listing 5-3 shows how this appears in the source code.

Listing 5-3: An Annotation on a Callback

```
public interface Callback
{
    /** @conversation phase="finish" */
    public void finishCallback();
}
```

A callback example

Listing 5-4 is a short example that uses callbacks. The example models a simple credit reporting service, where the user enqueues a request for a credit score (an operation which is assumed to take a long time) and the service returns the score at a later time in a callback. Unlike the earlier example, this service is entirely asynchronous. The client does not need to poll to find out when the credit score has been computed. Instead, the client is asynchronously notified via a callback.

Listing 5-4: The CreditReport Web Service

```
package Chapter5;

import weblogic.jws.control.JwsContext;

public class CreditReport
{
    public Callback callback;

    /**
     * An interface which defines the callback methods that
     * can be used to send message to the clients.
     */
    public interface Callback
    {
        /** Notifies the client of a completed score computation. */
        public void returnScore(int score);
    }

    /** @jws:context */
    JwsContext context;

    /**
```

```
 * Computes the credit score for a specific Social Security
 * number.
 *
 * @jws:operation
 * @jws:message-buffer enable="true"
 */
public void requestScore(String ssn)
{
    // Sleep for a random amount of time between 0 and 10
    // seconds.
    try
    { Thread.sleep((long)(Math.random() * 10000)); }
    catch (Exception e)
    {}

    // Return the "computed" score to the client.
    callback.returnScore((int)(Math.random() * 550) + 300);
}
}
```

This Web service has a single method, requestScore, which takes a Social Security number as an input. It then waits for a random period of time, up to ten seconds, and then calls the callback returnScore with the computed score. The score is passed to the callback as a parameter. Obviously, the method of computing the score isn't even remotely realistic (although the score range is correct). The method requestScore is buffered, so the client only has to wait as long as it takes to enqueue the request.

Viewing callbacks in the Test View

When you call the *requestScore* method using the Test View, the method returns immediately, because enqueuing the request takes only milliseconds. However, if you wait a few seconds and then click on the refresh link in the upper-right-hand corner of the Test View, you can see the call to the callback in the Message Log.

Figure 5-3 shows the Message Log, with a call to requestScore as well as a call to the returnScore callback. If you click on the log entry for the callback, you can see the details of the call, as shown in Figure 5-3.

This log entry shows the message that will be sent to the client. This message looks a lot like a message that is being sent to a Web service. In it you can see the credit score that will be passed to the callback. The Test View allows you to see callbacks (and even calls to other Web services) so you can get a better picture of what your Web service is doing.

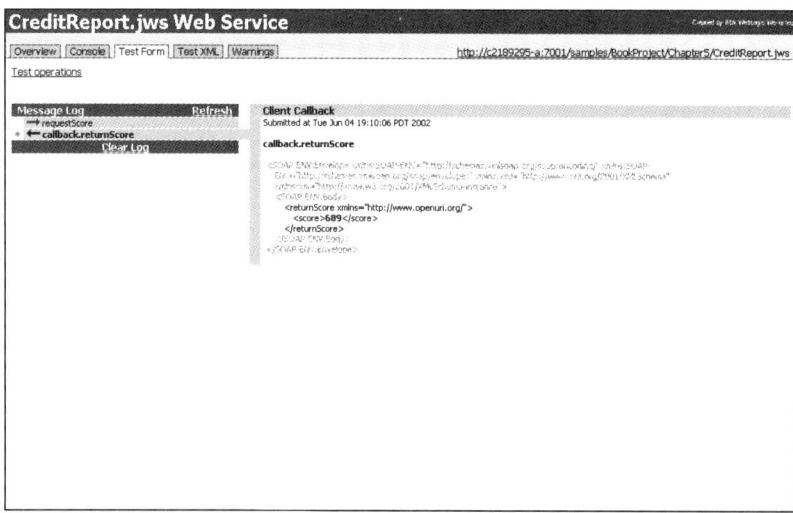

Figure 5-3: The Message Log for a callback.

Using the Context object to control callbacks

Just as for conversations, you can use the Context object to exercise some extra control over callbacks. In order to understand what you can do with the Context object to callbacks, you need to understand a little bit more about how callbacks work.

Along with a conversation key, another piece of WebLogic Workshop specific information can be passed around with the messages sent to and from the clients of your Web service. This information is the callback location, a URL that gives the location where callbacks are sent. Clients to WebLogic Workshop Web service that want to receive callbacks include their own URL for the callback location. When a WebLogic Workshop Web service calls a callback, this callback location is used to decide where to send the callback message. When you're writing WebLogic Workshop Web services, the management of callback locations is totally transparent, just like conversation keys, so normally you don't have to worry about it at all.

However, you may want to exercise more control over callbacks. The context object provides several functions that can be used to this end. These functions are summarized in Table 5-3.

Chapter 5: Creating Asynchronous Web Services

TABLE 5-3 CALLBACK-RELATED FUNCTIONS ON THE CONTEXT OBJECT

Context method	Description
`String getCallbackLocation()`	Returns the URL for the callback location as a string
`String getCallbackUsername()`	Returns the user name that will be used to access the callback location
`String getCallbackPassword()`	Returns the password that will be used to access the callback location
`void setCallbackLocation(String location)` `void setCallbackLocation(URL location)`	Sets the callback location to the specified string value or java.net.URL
`void setCallbackUsername(String name)`	Sets the callback user name to the specified value
`void setCallbackPassword(String password)`	Sets the callback password to the specified value

The most useful function in this list is `setCallbackLocation`. This function can be used to set the callback location that will be used to route callback messages. By changing the callback location, you can route callbacks wherever you want.

Listings 5-5 and 5-6 provide an example of how `setCallbackLocation` can be used to redirect callback messages to different locations. In the case of the example, the callbacks will be routed to another WebLogic Workshop Web service. Listing 5-5 defines a Web service named `Caller` that contains a callback that is redirected to a new location.

Listing 5-5: A Callback Redirecting Web Service

```
package Chapter5;

import weblogic.jws.control.JwsContext;

public class Caller
{
```

Continued

Listing 5-5 *(Continued)*

```
    public Callback callback;

    public interface Callback
    {
        public void sendCallback(String s);
    }
    /** @jws:context */
    JwsContext context;

    /**
     * @jws:operation
     * @jws:message-buffer enable="true"
     */
    public void callListener()
    {
        try
{
            context.setCallbackLocation(
            "http://localhost:7001" +
            "/ BookProject/Chapter5/Listener.jws");
        }
        catch (Exception e)
        {}

        callback.callback1("Hello");
    }
}
```

Listing 5-6 defines the Web service, `Listener`, that will receive the callbacks from the `Caller` Web service.

Listing 5-6: The Callback Listener

```
package Chapter5;

import weblogic.jws.control.JwsContext;

public class Listener
{
    /** @jws:context */
    JwsContext context;

    /** @jws:operation */
    public void callListener(String s)
```

{}
}

The Web service, `Caller`, has one method, `callListener`, which, when called, sets the callback location to the listener Web service and then calls the callback method. As a result, the callback ends up directing the callback to the `Listener` Web service. The new callback location is specified by a URL:

http://localhost:7001/ BookProject/Chapter5/Listener.jws

This is the URL used to locate the `Listener` Web service.

In order to test this Web service, it will be convenient to view both `Caller` and `Listener` in the Test View at once. Unfortunately, the WebLogic Workshop IDE doesn't have a way to do this, so you'll need to do it by hand. The easiest way to do this is to manually launch two instances of the browser, type the URL above into one and type

http://localhost:7001/ BookProject/Chapter5/Caller.jws

into the other. As I mentioned in Chapter 2, when WebLogic Server is run in development mode (the default when you launch WebLogic Server from WebLogic Workshop), WebLogic Workshop will auto-compile the Web services as soon as you hit them in the browser.

Switch to the Test View for the `Caller` Web service and invoke the method `callListener`. After you've invoked this method, you can press refresh and see that the callback has been sent, as shown in Figure 5-4.

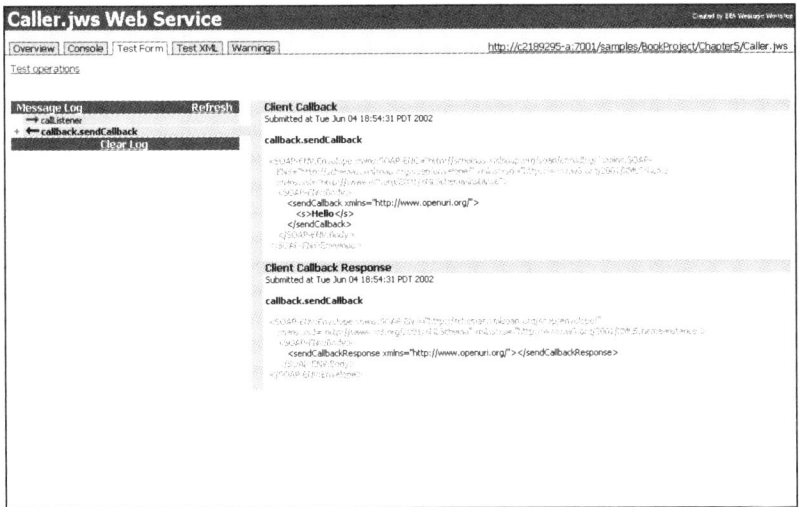

Figure 5-4: The Test View for `Caller`.

Now switch to the Test View for the `Listener` Web service. When you refresh the browser, you'll see that this Web service has received a call to `sendCallback`, shown in Figure 5-5, demonstrating that the `Caller` Web service has indeed been forced to send its callback to the `Listener` Web service, whereas normally the callback would have gone to the client (which is the WebLogic Workshop test client when using the Test View).

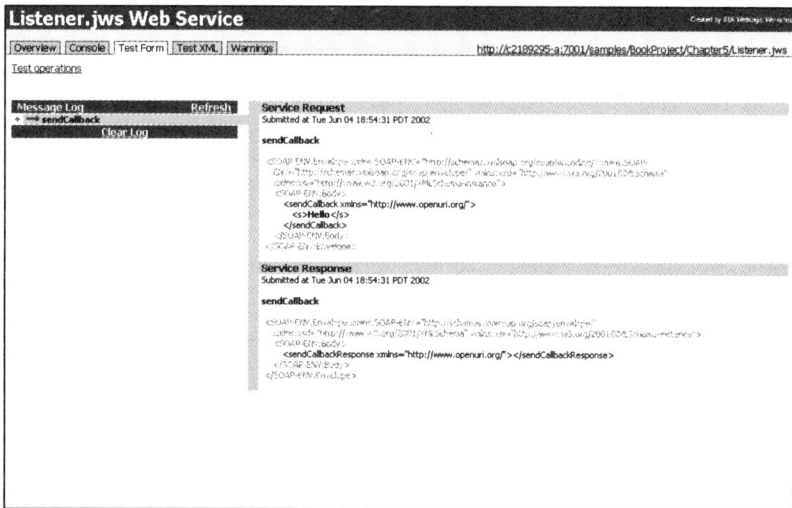

Figure 5-5: The Test View for `Listener`.

This has been a fairly simple example of how callbacks can be redirected by using methods on the `Context` object. You could do much more complicated things if you wanted to. For instance, there is no reason why you couldn't use this mechanism to cause a single method invocation to send a callback to many different listeners. The code in Listing 5-7 would allow you to send a callback to every listener in the `Listeners` array.

Listing 5-7: Sending Callbacks to Multiple Targets

```
for (int index = 0; index < listeners.length; index++)
{
    try
    { context.setCallbackLocation(listeners[index]); }
    catch (Exception e)
    {}

    callback.sendCallback();
}
```

There are several other methods on the `Context` object that have to do with callbacks. However, they're less useful than `setCallbackLocation`, so I won't get into the details of them here. Just keep in mind that they are there, in case you ever need them.

Summary

In the end, WebLogic Workshop asynchrony boils down to two facilities: buffering and callbacks. These facilities, when used together, permit the creation of asynchronous Web service of the sort I described in the beginning of this chapter. Even though creating an asynchronous Web service may seem rather simple, you shouldn't let that fool you. Asynchrony is a very powerful concept, and it's often the case that re-creating a system to be asynchronous can simplify its design and improve its performance. However, you should also recognize that asynchrony is a tool like any other, and it isn't necessarily always the right tool for the job at hand.

Here's a recap of the lessons learned in this chapter:

- Asynchronous Web services have two components: a mechanism for allowing the client to perform other tasks right after submitting a request (without waiting for the response) and a mechanism for the server to get back to the client later.
- WebLogic Workshop uses buffering to permit the client to enqueue Web service requests.
- WebLogic Workshop uses callbacks to permit the server to get back to the client asynchronously.
- The `Context` object can be used to gain control over where callback messages are sent.

Chapter 6

Mapping from XML

IN THIS CHAPTER

- Understanding the XML messages associated with Web service operations
- Using XML maps to work with complicated XML documents
- Using more complicated XML map features to deal with common mapping issues

Although methods and callbacks are represented as simple function calls within a WebLogic Workshop Web service, they actually involve the transmission of XML messages across the network. These messages can contain fairly arbitrary XML documents, allowing the transmission of complicated, structured documents. To allow the manipulation of these documents, WebLogic Workshop has a mapping facility, which permits XML documents to be mapped to Java data structures, and vice versa.

XML Messages

When you create a simple WebLogic Workshop service, you don't have to worry about the details of the XML messages that are being transmitted across the network. Instead, all the details of the process are hidden behind what appears to be a simple call to a Java method. However, behind the scenes, the process is far more complicated. When the client invokes even the simplest Web service method, XML messages are transmitted across the network. To understand how this process works, let us take a look at the messages generated by the simple Web service in Listing 6-1.

Listing 6-1: A Simple Method

```
public class Simple
{
    /** @jws:operation */
    public String makeName(String first, String last)
    {
        return first + " " + last;
    }
}
```

This very simple method takes two strings representing a first and last name and returns a string representing the full name. When the client "calls" `makeName`, the client actually sends a message over the network containing XML that is similar to the following:

```
<makeName xmlns="http://www.openuri.org/">
    <first>John</first>
    <last>Doe</last>
</makeName>
```

You should be able to correlate this XML to the original Java code in the JWS file, where the method makeName becomes the root node of the XML message, while each parameter (first, last) becomes a child note in the message. The xmlns is the XML naming space that you specify in the Property Editor to distinguish your "makeName" with somebody else's "makeName" method. The default XML namespace if you do not specify anything is `http://www.openuri.org`.

When WebLogic Workshop receives this message, it translates it into a method call, mapping the text for the `<first>` tag into the `first` parameter and the text for the `<second>` tag into the `second` parameter. After the method performs its simple operation, it wraps the return value into another XML message, which is of the following form:

```
<makeNameResponse xmlns="http://www.openuri.org/">
    <makeNameResult>John Doe</makeNameResult>
</makeNameResponse>
```

By default, WebLogic Workshop takes the method name and appends "Response" as the XML root node of the response (`makeNameResponse` in the example above). It also takes the method name and appends "Result" as the child node representing the result (`makeNameResult`). The Workshop understands that the return value, the string `John Doe`, should be mapped into the XML message by being inserted as the text of the `<makeNameResult>` tag. These two XML messages are very simple, representing a fairly direct mapping from Java to XML, however; WebLogic Workshop is capable of transmitting far more interesting messages.

Basic Maps

WebLogic Workshop has a default mapping mechanism that translates parameters and return types into XML; it also permits you to gain direct control over the mapping process. By using XML maps, your Web services can receive and transmit complicated XML documents, mapping them to and from Java in a very flexible way.

The fundamental WebLogic Workshop feature that permits this mapping process to occur is the XML map. An XML map (or simply map for short) looks very much like an XML document, except for some special directives that allow WebLogic Workshop to map Java objects to and from the XML.

Working with maps in the Design View

Every method on a Web service can contain two XML maps, which are depicted on the Design View. These XML maps are represented by the pair of arrows shown in Figure 6-1. The arrow pointing towards the Web service represents the map for messages entering the Web service, and the arrow pointing away represents the map for messages leaving the Web service.

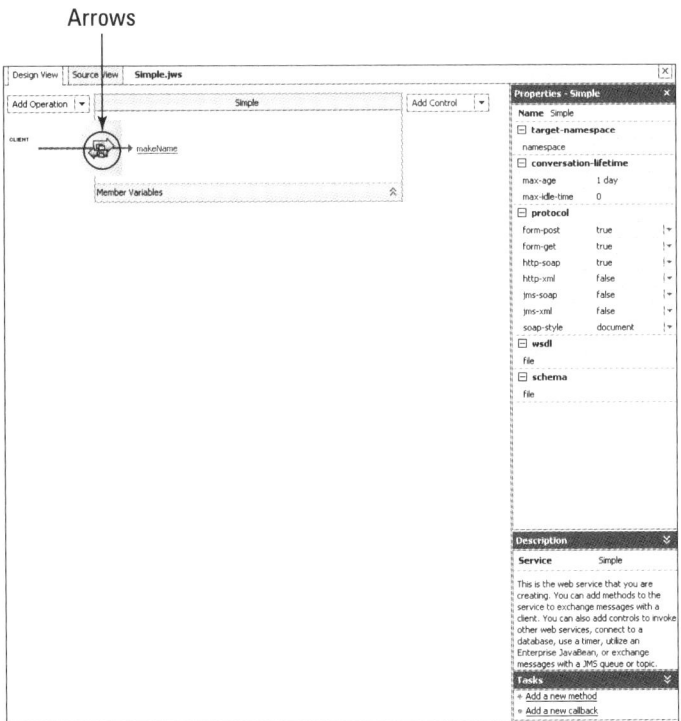

Figure 6-1: Maps in the Design View.

To view and edit these maps from the Design View, double-click on the icon representing the maps. This will invoke the map editor shown in Figure 6-2. If WebLogic Server isn't already running, you'll be prompted to start it, because some operations performed by the Map Editor require the server. When the Map Editor first appears it will be blank, but if you wait a second or two, it will be filled in with the *default map* for the method.

Figure 6-2: The Map Editor.

There are two text boxes in the Map Editor: the top text box contains the text of the XML map and the bottom box shows the signature of the method. The *signature* of a method includes the name, parameters, and return type, essentially everything about the method that isn't between the curly braces. For instance, the signature of the method defined above is the following:

```
public String makeName(String first, String last)
```

As part of defining an XML map, you may want to change either the map or the signature of the method, so both of them are editable from the Map Editor.

The Map Editor has two tabs, labeled Parameter XML and Return XML, which allow you to edit the two maps that are associated with each method. Both tabs show the same signature, but different maps, one for the incoming messages and the other for the outgoing messages.

- The Parameter XML tab shows the mapping from incoming XML messages to the parameters of the method.
- The Return XML tab shows the mapping from the return value of the method to the outgoing XML messages.

In the upper-right-hand corner of the Map Editor, there is a radio button labeled Map Type that has two options: Default and Custom. If you haven't yet changed an XML map, WebLogic Workshop will provide a default map, and the Map Type radio button will be set to Default, signifying that the default map is in use. After you make changes to a map, WebLogic Workshop will hand control of mapping over to you and the Map Type will be set to Custom. The Parameter map and Return map are separate, so you can choose to change one of them while leaving the other as the default. If you want to revert to the Default map, simply change the Map Type back to default, however; you should be careful, this operation cannot be undone and after you perform it, your custom map will be lost.

The Map Editor provides a great deal of editing help for the maps, just like the Source View. Error highlighting helps you find some of the problems with your map and there are various places where you can use code completion. However, any changes you make in the Map Editor are not applied to the actual source code until you click OK, and if you want to discard any changes you have made, press Cancel instead.

XML map syntax

Now that you know how to view maps, let us take a closer look at the maps for the simple Web service defined above. These maps are very similar to the XML messages that I showed you earlier, but they contain some special syntax that is used to perform the mapping. Listing 6-2 shows the default XML map for the `makeName` method.

Listing 6-2: The Default Map for makeName

```
<makeName xmlns="http://www.openuri.org/">
<first>{first}</first>
<last>{last}</last>
</makeName>
```

Where the data appears in the actual XML message, the maps contain the two special constructions {first} and {last}. These are *substitution directives* — they tell WebLogic Workshop to take the text found where the directive is located and place it into the parameters named in the directive. Comparing these two directives with the signature of `makeName` (which is very handily right below the map in the Map Editor), you can see that the names in the substitution directives match the names of the parameters for the method.

```
public String makeName(String first, String last)
```

By using these substitutions, the XML map instructs WebLogic Workshop to copy the appropriate text from the incoming XML message to the arguments of the `makeName` method when it is called. This default XML map represents a very sensible default scheme for mapping the incoming XML message into the parameters of the method.

If you make a simple change to the XML map for this method, you can see just how easy it is to change the mapping of the XML message. Listing 6-3 shows a slightly modified version of the Parameter map. This map reverses the mapping of the parameters, so the value contained within the `<first>` tag will be mapped to the parameter `last`, and the value contained within the `<last>` tag will be mapped to the parameter `first`.

Listing 6-3: A Custom Map for makeName

```
<makeName xmlns="http://www.openuri.org/">
<first>{last}</first>
<last>{first}</last>
</makeName>
```

Enter this map into the Map Editor and click OK. The icon for the Parameter map in the Design View will change to show you that you're now using a custom map.

When you invoke this new Web service in the Test View, you may notice the method invocation page no longer contains the text boxes for each of the parameters to the method. Instead, there is a single text box labeled XML Map, which contains a sample XML message that will be sent to the Web service, as shown in Figure 6-3. This allows you to send whatever XML you wish to the method and test out your newly created map.

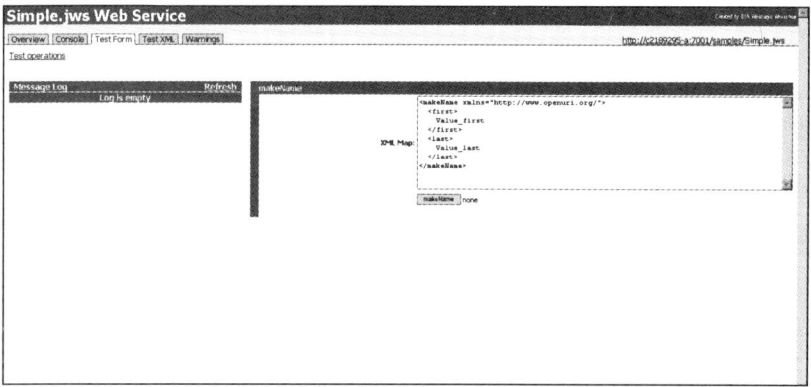

Figure 6-3: Using the Test View with a custom map.

The XML shown in the text box is very similar in shape to the XML map, and where the substitution directives appear in the map, there are placeholders named `Value_first` and `Value_last`. You can replace these with whatever text you want. When you've done so, invoke the method. The result is shown in Figure 6-4.

By examining the result, you can see that the parameters have indeed been reversed, such that the returned name is now in reverse order, the first name last and the last name first. This may not have been the most interesting thing to do, but it does illustrate the point. Soon enough you'll get to see some more interesting (and perhaps realistic) examples.

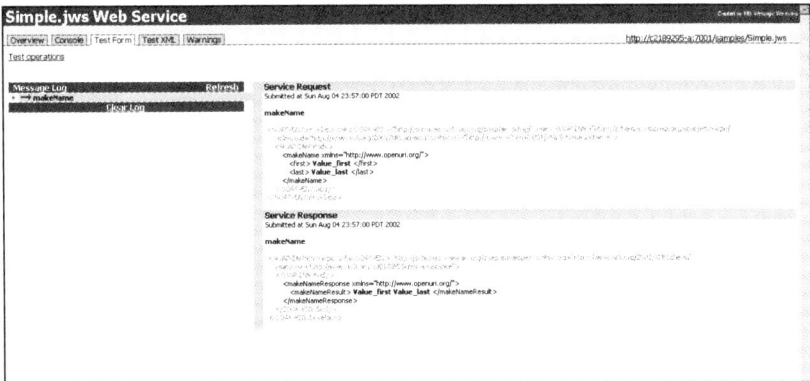

Figure 6-4: After the method invocation.

Now let us take a look at the Return map for the `makeName` method. You can get to this map by selecting the Return XML tab in the Map Editor. The Return map is shown in Listing 6-4.

Listing 6-4: The Return Map for makeName

```
<makeNameResponse xmlns="http://www.openuri.org/">
<makeNameResult>{return}</makeNameResult>
</makeNameResponse>
```

This map is fairly simple, containing a single substitution directive. Because there is no official name associated with the return value of a method, WebLogic Workshop uses the name `return` to refer to the return value in a Return map. As a result, the {return} directive will cause the return value to be inserted into the messages being sent from the Web service back to the client.

Substitution directives don't only have to appear between tags, they can also be used to map to and from attributes of tags. For instance, you could use a map like the following to return the name formed by the `makeName` method as an attribute of the `makeNameResult` tag (Listing 6-5).

Listing 6-5: Mapping into Attributes

```
<makeNameResponse xmlns="http://www.openuri.org/">
<makeNameResult value="{return}"/>
</makeNameResponse>
```

This will cause the message returned by `makeName` to look something like the following:

```
<makeNameResponse xmlns="http://www.openuri.org/">
<makeNameResult value="John Doe"></makeNameResult>
</makeNameResponse>
```

 Don't forget to include quotation marks around substitution directives that are used inside attributes. If you leave them off, you'll receive an error message that doesn't do a very good job of letting you know what you did wrong.

There is one last note I should make about substitution directives. When you use a substitution directive between tags (that is, not in the attribute case) you cannot use *mixed content,* consisting of some substitution directives and some text. For instance, the following is prohibited:

```
<aTag>Some text {param} more text</aTag>
```

Although you may be able to imagine some reasonable things mixed content could be used for, regrettably it cannot be done using normal maps. If you place a substitution directive between two tags, it must be the only thing there. If you're really interested in doing something like this, you can do it using JavaScript with maps, a topic that is discussed at the end of this chapter and in much more detail in Chapter 12.

Maps in the source code

Because you've seen the source code for a number of Web services, you've probably realized that the default maps for a method don't appear in the source code. However, as I've said before, a WebLogic Workshop Web service is totally specified by its source code, so when you customize a map, it must somehow be inserted into the source. WebLogic Workshop uses an annotation above a method to record any custom maps you may add to a method. Listing 6-6 shows the source code for the simple Web service we've been using as an example so far.

Listing 6-6: The Simple Web Service

```
package.Chapter6;

public class Simple
{
    /**
     * @jws:operation
     * @jws:parameter-xml xml-map::
     *      <makeName xmlns="http://www.openuri.org/">
     *          <first>{last}</first>
     *          <last>{first}</last>
     *      </makeName>
     * ::
```

```
    */
    public String makeName(String first, String last)
    {
        return first + " " + last;
    }
}
```

This code should be fairly familiar, except for the contents of the @jws:parameter-xml tag. Parameter maps are specified by using the @jws:parameter-xml tag and Return maps are specified by the @jws:return-xml tag.. The actual map is stored as the value of the xml-map attribute. If you look at these attributes in the Property Editor, shown in Figure 6-5, you will see an underlined link labeled "Go To XML." Clicking on this link is another way to invoke the Map Editor.

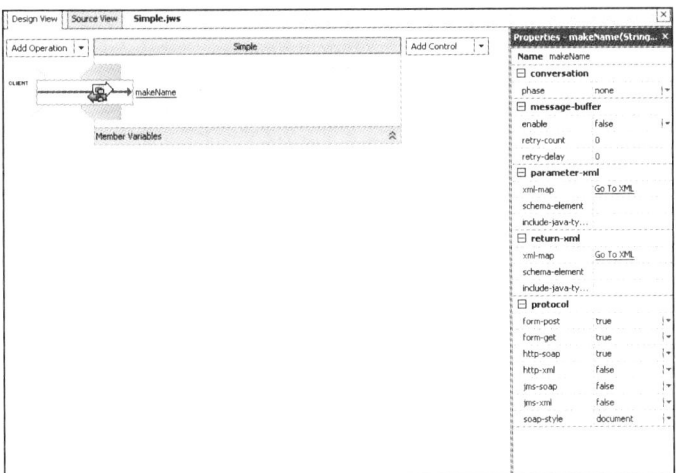

Figure 6-5: The editor for a map attribute.

The xml-map attribute is an example of a *multi-line attribute,* which is a type of attribute whose value can span multiple lines. The value of a multi-line attribute is started by the special delimiter ::, consisting of two colons. The value of the attribute may then continue across multiple lines until it is terminated by a second instance of the double colon. Everything between the double colons and to the right of the stars in the Javadoc comment is included as part of the value of the attribute. The stars are left out because they are part of the Javadoc comment itself.

You can add and remove maps directly from the source code, just as you can manipulate any other WebLogic Workshop feature directly from the source code. However, if you do this, be careful to keep the comments correctly formatted. Of course, if you use the Map Editor, WebLogic Workshop will automatically make sure the Javadoc comments stay well-formed.

A mapping example

Now that you've seen the basics of how maps work, a more complicated example is in order. This example will show how maps can be used to accept a complicated XML document and output a response that also contains an XML message. In this example, I will show you a Web service whose sole purpose is to translate a purchase order from one XML format to another (Listing 6-7).

Listing 6-7: A Purchase Order Translator

```
package Chapter6;

import weblogic.jws.control.JwsContext;

public class POTranslator
{
    /** @jws:context */
    JwsContext context;

    public static class PurchaseOrder
    {
        public PurchaseOrder() {}

        public int orderNumber;
        public Address shippingAddr;
        public Address billingAddr;
        public Item item;
    }

    public static class Address
    {
        public Address() {}

        public String name;
        public String street;
        public String city;
        public String state;
        public String zip;
    }

    public static class Item
    {
        public Item() {}

        public String name;
        public double price;
```

```
        public int quantity;
}

/**
 * @jws:operation
 * @jws:parameter-xml xml-map::
 * <purchaseOrder orderNo="{po.orderNumber}">
 *    <billingAddress>
 *       <name>{po.billingAddr.name}</name>
 *       <street>{po.billingAddr.street}</street>
 *       <city>{po.billingAddr.city}</city>
 *       <state>{po.billingAddr.state}</state>
 *       <zip>{po.billingAddr.zip}</zip>
 *    </billingAddress>
 *    <shippingAddress>
 *       <name>{po.shippingAddr.name}</name>
 *       <street>{po.shippingAddr.street}</street>
 *       <city>{po.shippingAddr.city}</city>
 *       <state>{po.shippingAddr.state}</state>
 *       <zip>{po.shippingAddr.zip}</zip>
 *    </shippingAddress>
 *    <item>
 *       <name>{po.item.name}</name>
 *       <price>{po.item.price}</price>
 *       <quantity>{po.item.quantity}</quantity>
 *    </item>
 * </purchaseOrder>
 * ::
 *
 * @jws:return-xml xml-map::
 * <Purchase-Order order-number="{return.orderNumber}">
 *    <Item>
 *       <name>{return.item.name}</name>
 *       <price>{return.item.price}</price>
 *       <quantity>{return.item.quantity}</quantity>
 *    </Item>
 *    <Shipping-Address>
 *       <name>{return.shippingAddr.name}</name>
 *       <street>{return.shippingAddr.street}</street>
 *       <city>{return.shippingAddr.city}</city>
 *       <state>{return.shippingAddr.state}</state>
 *       <zip>{return.shippingAddr.zip}</zip>
 *    </Shipping-Address>
 *    <Billing-Address>
 *       <Name>{return.billingAddr.name}</Name>
```

```
 *      <Street>{return.billingAddr.street}</Street>
 *      <City>{return.billingAddr.city}</City>
 *      <State>{return.billingAddr.state}</State>
 *      <Zip>{return.billingAddr.zip}</Zip>
 *    </Billing-Address>
 * </Purchase-Order>
 * ::
 */
public PurchaseOrder translate(PurchaseOrder po)
{
    return po;
}
}
```

This example maps an incoming XML purchase order into a Java object and then immediately returns that object using a different map to translate the XML into a different form. The differences between the incoming and outgoing documents are fairly superficial, the tag names are slightly different and the sections have a different order, but this example still illustrates how easy it is to perform manipulations of XML using maps.

This example consists of both a parameter map and a return map and serves as an illustration of mapping to more complicated Java objects. There are three Java classes defined at the top of the file, `PurchaseOrder`, `Address`, and `Item`. The functions of the objects are fairly obvious, and the example shows how a map can be used to fill out a more complicated, structured object with values taken from an XML document. Likewise, when the return XML is constructed, the values in the `PurchaseOrder` object are retrieved and placed back into an XML document.

More Mapping Constructs

There are some additional constructs that can be used in XML maps to solve certain common problems. These constructs help with problems such as specifying repetitive elements in XML, using JavaScript to help with mapping, and using maps that are specified in external files.

Dealing with repetitive elements

XML documents often specify certain constructs that can be repeated an indefinite number of times. For instance, a purchase order may include an arbitrary number of items to be purchased. The XML specifying an individual item will be repeated in the document many times; WebLogic Workshop permits you to map the repetitive elements to an array, with one entry for each element, which will be useful to count the number of elements or to enforce a certain data structure (i.e. array), among others.

Listing 6-8 shows an example of a Web service that can accept purchase orders that contain an arbitrary number of items.

Listing 6-8: The PurchaseOrder Web Service

```
package Chapter6;

import weblogic.jws.control.JwsContext;

public class PurchaseOrder
{
    /** @jws:context */
    JwsContext context;

    private static class Address
    {
        public String name;
        public String street;
        public String city;
        public String state;
        public int zip;
    }

    private static class Item
    {
        public String name;
        public double price;
        public int quantity;
    }

    /**
     * @jws:operation
     * @jws:parameter-xml xml-map::
     *   <purchaseOrder>
     *     <shippingAddress>
     *       <name>{addr.name}</name>
     *       <street>{addr.street}</street>
     *       <city>{addr.city}</city>
     *       <state>{addr.state}</state>
     *       <zip>{addr.zip}</zip>
     *     </shippingAddress>
     *     <item xm:multiple="Item item in items">
     *       <name>{item.name}</name>
     *       <price>{item.price}</price>
     *       <quantity>{item.quantity}</quantity>
     *     </item>
```

```
 *   </purchaseOrder>
 * ::
 */
public String submitOrder(Address addr, Item[] items)
{
    double price = 0.0;
    for (int i = 0; i < items.length; i++)
        price += items[i].price;

    return "Thank you for your order " + addr.name +
        ". Your total order price is " + price;
}
}
```

This Web service has a single method submitOrder, which takes a shipping address and an array of items. Each item contains an item name and a price. The input to this method is mapped from an XML document that contains a single shipping address section, followed by any number of item sections. As an example, the following document would be a valid input to this method:

```
<purchaseOrder>
  <shippingAddress>
    <name>Bob Smith</name>
    <street>1234 Somewhere Lane</street>
    <city>Someplace</city>
    <state>SW</state>
    <zip>12345</zip>
  </shippingAddress>
  <item>
    <name>Green Widget</name>
    <price>25.92</price>
    <quantity>3</quantity>
  </item>
  <item>
    <name>Blue Widget</name>
    <price>44.66</price>
    <quantity>6</quantity>
  </item>
  <item>
    <name>Yellow Widget</name>
    <price>22.16</price>
    <quantity>2</quantity>
  </item>
</purchaseOrder>
```

The map for the shipping address is just like the other maps you've already seen, but the map for the item tag contains a special attribute `xm:multiple`. This is a special WebLogic Workshop attribute, which specifies that this tag can appear multiple times and maps each occurrence of the tag to an entry in the items array. The key to the mapping is the value of the `xm:multiple` attribute.

```
xm:multiple="Item item in items"
```

This value has a very special syntax, which can be broken down according to the following pattern:

```
xm:multiple="Type Name in ParameterName"
```

The first element in the pattern, `Type`, is the type that each instance of the repeated tag will be mapped to. In the example, each item tag is mapped to an instance of the static inner class `Item`, which is defined at the top of the Web service.

The second element, `Name`, creates a name that can be used in the map for the repeated tag. You can think of this name as referring to an object of the class specified in `Type` that will be filled in and added to the array. In the example, the name defined is `Item`, which is then used as an instance of the `Item` class to map the name, price, and quantity of each item section to an `Item`.

The third element, `ParameterName`, gives the name of the parameter in the method that will contain all the item tags. This parameter must be either a Java array or a Java collection type, because it must be able to hold multiple copies of the same object. In the example, the parameter name is `Items`, which refers to an array of `Item` objects. As each item tag is found in the incoming XML document, it is mapped into an `Item` object, which is added to the `Items` array. When the mapping process is complete, `Items` contains an entry for every item that appeared in the original XML.

A single `xm:multiple` attribute can map to more than one variable at once. For instance, the following would have been a valid way to do the mapping for the previous example:

```
/**
 * @jws:operation
 * @jws:parameter-xml xml-map::
 *    <purchaseOrder>
 *      <shippingAddress>
 *        <name>{addr.name}</name>
 *        <street>{addr.street}</street>
 *        <city>{addr.city}</city>
 *        <state>{addr.state}</state>
 *        <zip>{addr.zip}</zip>
 *      </shippingAddress>
 *      <item xm:multiple="String name in names,
```

```
 *                          double price in prices,
 *                          int quantity in quantities">
 *        <name>{name}</name>
 *        <price>{price}</price>
 *        <quantity>{quantity}</quantity>
 *     </item>
 *   </purchaseOrder>
 * ::
 */
public String submitOrder(Address addr, ArrayList names,
                          double[] prices, int[] quantities)
```

In this example, the `xm:multiple` attribute is used to map each name, price, and quantity to separate parameters, called `names`, `prices`, and `quantities`, respectively. The parameters `prices` and `quantities` are still arrays, but `names` is an ArrayList, which can also be used with `xm:multiple`.

Reusing maps

Sometimes reusing XML maps can be very useful. For instance, you may have written a map that processes a certain type of XML document that is used throughout your system. Fortunately, WebLogic Workshop provides you with the ability to create an XML map in a separate file, and then to use that map everywhere you need it. In fact, an external map can be used to map just part of an XML document.

Listing 6-9 shows an example of a map defined in a separate file. This map is used to map addresses to Java data structures.

Listing 6-9: An External Address Map

```
<xm:map-file xmlns:xm="http://www.bea.com/2002/04/xmlmap/">
  <xm:java-import class=" Chapter6.Address"/>

  <xm:xml-map signature="mapAddress(Address address)">
    <name>{address.name}</name>
    <street>{address.street}</street>
    <city>{address.city}</city>
    <state>{address.state}</state>
    <zip>{address.zip}</zip>
  </xm:xml-map>
</xm:map>
```

This map file has a few elements that don't appear in normal maps. The first line specifies that this is an external map file, and specifies the XML namespace to use for the XML map specific tags. This tag `<xm:map-file>` must be the outermost tag in any external map file.

The second line specifies the import of a Java type into this XML map. This tag is analogous to a standard Java import statement. If you use any Java classes in your map that aren't accessible from the directory where the map file is located, you need to specify the import. The `import` tag in the example would be equivalent to the Java import:

```
import Chapter6.Address;
```

The class `Address` must, of course, be defined in the given location. Based on the shape of the map, the class declaration should look something like the following:

```
public class Address
{
    public Address() {}

    public String name;
    public String street;
    public String city;
    public String state;
    public String zip;
}
```

The body of the map, contained within the `xml-map` tag, should look familiar, except, of course, for the tag itself. The `xml-map` tag has a single attribute `signature`, which is used to specify how this map will be called from the external world. To show you how the `signature` attribute should be written, I'll show you a simple example of how this map could be used by a Web service in Listing 6-10.

Listing 6-10: Using an External Map

```
/**
 * @jws:operation
 * @jws:parameter-xml xml-map::
 * <addresses>
 *   <shippingAddress>
 *     {AddressMap.mapAddress(Address shippingAddr)}
 *   </shippingAddress>
 *   <billingAddress>
 *     {AddressMap.mapAddress(Address billingAddr)}
 *   </billingAddress>
 * </addresses>
 * ::
 */
public void processAddresses(Address shippingAddr,
                             Address billingAddr)
```

The external map is invoked in two places, by placing references to the map in between curly braces { }. The map is referenced by using the name of the map file, in this case AddressMap.xmlmap, followed by a reference to the signature that was defined in the external map. The arguments to this invocation refer to parameters of the method processAddress, which will actually have the addresses mapped to them.

Even in this simple example, some work has been saved by reusing the map to process an address. However, external maps can be taken much further, containing many xml-map sections. In this way, you could implement the mapping of an entire set of XML map documents in a single file that could be reused everywhere.

You may also need to use packages to refer to external map files. For instance, in the previous example, you could qualify the name of the map file with a package if the map isn't located in the same package as the JWS. For instance, you could invoke the previous external map by using the following: {BookProject.Chapter6.AddressMap.mapAddress(...)}

Using JavaScript for mapping

Because I'm discussing additional mapping facilities, it's worthwhile to mention another facility, which is the script map. The script map uses JavaScript, a scripting language that somewhat resembles Java, to perform the mapping in a procedural way, as opposed to the declarative way that you've seen in this chapter.

If you have a more complicated XML document that needs more hierarchical processing using XPath or something more than the simple maps I've shown you in this chapter, script maps may be what you need. I'm not going to talk about script maps in this chapter, because it's a somewhat advanced topic, but if you're interested, you can find out more about script maps in Chapter 11. Chapter 11 does not rely on anything you haven't seen already, so it's safe to read that chapter right now if you want to read everything this book has to say about script maps.

Script maps provide a powerful interface to deal with incoming XML, but if you really need to get at the raw XML, you can always take the incoming message as a Document Object Model (DOM). A DOM is a tree-like representation of an XML document that contains every last detail of the XML. Before you resort to directly implementing a DOM, you should make sure you can't do whatever it is you're trying to do through JavaScript.

Summary

XML messages are a big part of Web services, and in this chapter you've seen how to directly work with incoming and outgoing XML messages. Mapping is a very useful feature of WebLogic Workshop, and even more so when it's combined with the XML-enhanced version of JavaScript included with WebLogic Workshop. Using these tools you have the ability to create Web services that pass around arbitrary XML documents, significantly enhancing their power above and beyond a simple remote procedure call mechanism.

Part III

Advanced Concepts

CHAPTER 7
Using the Core Controls

CHAPTER 8
Using the Advanced Controls

CHAPTER 9
Controlling the Web Service Protocols

Chapter 7

Using the Core Controls

IN THIS CHAPTER

- Using the Service control
- Using the Timer control
- Using the Database control

So far the Web services model I've presented has been fairly simple. There is typically one Web service that is called by a number of clients. In a very real sense, this is only half the story. One of the most natural things you might want to do from a Web service is call out to other things besides your clients. These things might be other Web services, databases, queues, timers, or EJBs (Enterprise Java Beans). Now that you have spent a great deal of time reading about how to create a Web service, it's time to start thinking about how your Web service can become the client to other services.

An Introduction to WebLogic Workshop Controls

Controls are the mechanism WebLogic Workshop uses to expose services to Web services. These services may include other Web services, the discussion of which will consume most of this chapter, or other services common to the enterprise such as databases, queues, timers, EJBs, or legacy systems. At the present time, the set of controls used by WebLogic Workshop is fixed; however, in the future, controls will become one of the primary extensibility mechanisms of WebLogic Workshop.

You've already seen an example of a control in the `JwsContext` object since Chapter 4. Because you're somewhat familiar with this particular example of a control, it will make a suitable example of the basics of controls. As you may remember, the `Context` object is created when you create a new Web service by means of the following source code:

```
/** @jws:context */
public JwsContext context;
```

Two features of this declaration are noteworthy and common across all controls. First, the declaration is prefaced by an annotation. In this case, the annotation contains a single tag, @jws:context, although, in general, a control may have an arbitrary number of tags for identification and configuration. WebLogic Workshop uses these tags to identify these fields as controls, and treats them in a very special way.

The second thing to note about controls is that they're never explicitly initialized. Normal fields in a Java class must be initialized at some point before they're used, either when they're declared or somewhere else in the body of the class (often in the constructor). For instance, if you were to declare a new ArrayList in your Web service, you'd probably declare like this:

```
private ArrayList list = new ArrayList();
```

According to the rules of Java, a field that isn't initialized defaults to the special value null (unless it is a primitive type). If you try to use it when it's null, a NullPointerException will be thrown and your program will probably crash. However, you've already used an uninitialized Context object, and thus far none of these uses have caused a crash. In the case of controls, a little WebLogic Workshop magic is used to automatically initialize them at run time to a suitable value. As a result, you can use controls as soon as you enter the body of a method.

The Context object differs from the other controls in one very special way; it doesn't show up on the Design View. Every other control appears on the right-hand side of the Design View. Figure 7-1 depicts the Design View for a Web service that uses a number of controls.

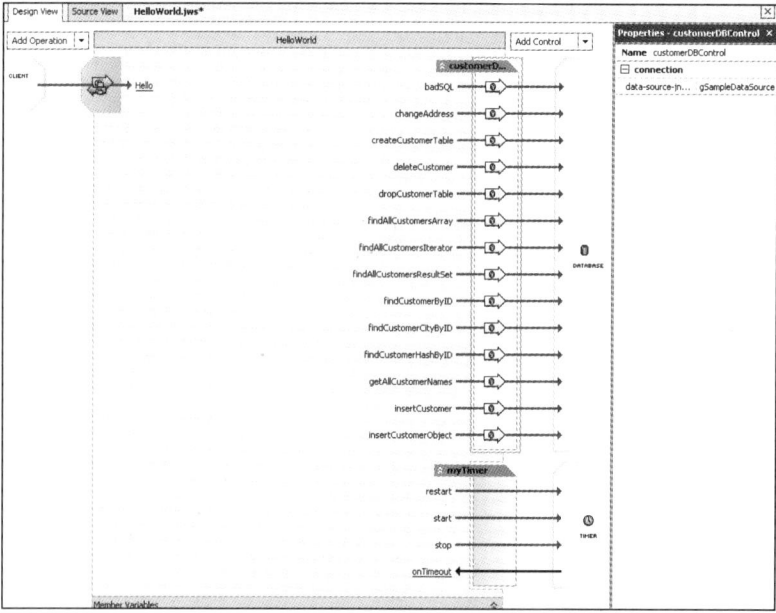

Figure 7-1: A Web service with controls.

The interactions between your Web services and its controls are depicted much like the interactions between your Web service and its clients. Arrows are drawn to show methods that are used to communicate between your Web service and controls. You can use buffers to provide asynchrony with some of the controls, and you can use maps if the control you're using communicates with XML messages.

The Service Control

The Service control represents another Web service whose methods you want to call. When you use a service control, you become the client sending requests and receiving responses from a foreign Web service. The Web service represented by the Service control can be another WebLogic Workshop Web service (in which case you can use all the facilities of WebLogic Workshop) or a Web service produced on another platform, such as .NET or Apache SOAP.

Adding Service controls

You can add a Service control to your Web service by selecting the Add Control drop-down from the right side of the Design View. This drop-down is shown in Figure 7-2.

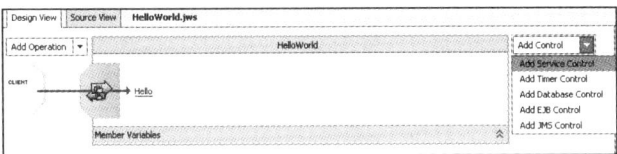

Figure 7-2: The Add Control drop-down.

Select Add Service Control from the drop-down to add a new Service control to your Web service. After you've done this, the dialog box shown in Figure 7-3 will appear, allowing you to configure your new Service control.

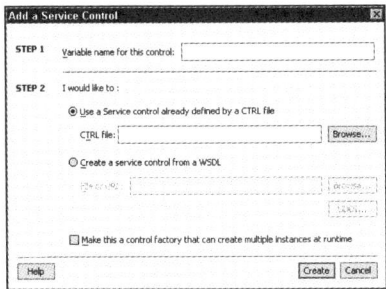

Figure 7-3: The Add Service Control dialog box.

This dialog has two steps you must complete before you can create your new control. First, you must choose a name for the control. This name will be the name of the field inserted into your class, which you will use to access the control from your source code.

Second, you must decide how you want the control to be created. When you create a new Service control, you must somehow specify what service this control will access. There are two methods for doing this, and you can make your choice by using the radio button and entering the requested information:

- ◆ **Use a Service control already defined by a CTRL file:** Nearly all WebLogic Workshop controls are specified with the CTRL (Control) file format. I will talk about this file format shortly in this chapter. For now, all you need to know is that if you have a CTRL file that specifies a Service control, you specify that file and the new Service control will use that file.

- ◆ **Create a Service control from a WSDL:** A Web Services Definition Language (WSDL) file is a standard format for specifying a Web service. When you create a Web service, you can publish a WSDL file so that it can be used by any platform that supports Web services. You can use a WSDL file located in your project directory, specify a URL to a WSDL file, or use the UDDI browser to locate a WSDL file.

You're also given the option to make the control you're creating a *control factory,* which can be used to create multiple instances of your control. I discuss control factories in Chapter 8, along with other advanced control topics. After you've specified all the information in the dialog box, click Create to add the control to your Web service.

How Service controls work

When you add a Service control to your Web service, it will appear on the right-hand side of the Design View. Figure 7-4 shows an example Web service that contains a Service control representing the currency calculator from Chapter 2.

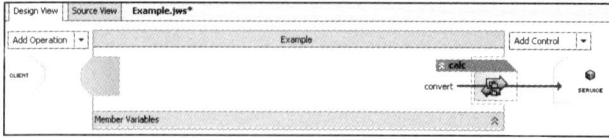

Figure 7-4: The currency calculator as a Service control.

The methods of the currency calculator appear as arrows pointing from the Web service to the Service control, signifying the fact that messages will be passed from the Web service to the service represented by the Service control when the control methods are called.

Now let's take a closer look at exactly what goes into creating a Service control and what a Service control looks like in the source code of a Web service. Listing 7-1 shows the source code for the example Web service depicted previously.

Listing 7-1: A Web Service with a Service Control

```
package Chapter7;

import weblogic.jws.control.JwsContext;
import Chapter2.CurrencyCalcControl;

public class Example
{
    /** @jws:context */
    JwsContext context;

    /**
     * @jws:control
     */
    private CurrencyCalcControl calc;
}
```

Most of what appears in this Web service should seem very familiar to you by now. So, I'll focus on the things that are new. First, there is an import of the Currency Calculator control.

```
importChapter2.CurrencyCalcControl;
```

This import is needed because the control exists in another package. In addition, this import is importing a class that has a different name than the Web service itself (which was `CurrencyCalc`). Shortly, I show you why this name is different and exactly what is being imported with this import statement.

The second thing to notice is the declaration of the field, which will be used to access the currency calculator:

```
/**
 * @jws:control
 */
private CurrencyCalcControl calc;
```

This declaration starts with the `@jws:control` annotation, which is used to mark every control (except the somewhat aberrant Context control). This declaration declares a new field named `calc`, which is an object of the type `CurrencyCalc` control. Like I mentioned in the previous discussion, this field is never initialized explicitly in the code; WebLogic Workshop takes care of making sure it references a valid object before you start using it.

The `calc` field refers to the type `CurrencyCalcControl`, and the natural question to ask is where this type is defined. This type is defined in a file named `CurrencyCalcControl.ctrl`, which serves as a definition of the `CurrencyCalc` Web service. Listing 7-2 shows the contents of `CurrencyCalcControl.ctrl`. Be aware that this file is very big, and you don't have to understand the whole thing in order to use CTRL files. However, you'll undoubtedly have many encounters with these files as you use WebLogic Workshop, and you should certainly have some familiarity with them.

Listing 7-2: The CTRL File for the CurrencyCalc Web Service

```java
/** @editor-info:link source="CurrencyCalc.jws" autogen="true" */
packageChapter2;

import weblogic.jws.control.ServiceControl;

/**
 * Performs exchange rate conversions between currencies.
 * @jws:location http-url="CurrencyCalc.jws" jms-url="CurrencyCalc.jws"
 * @jws:wsdl file="#CurrencyCalcWsdl"
 */
public interface CurrencyCalcControl extends ServiceControl
{
    /**
     * Returns the full name of a currency given the currency code.
     */
    public java.lang.String getCurrencyName (java.lang.String currencyType);

    /**
     * Converts the specified amount of from the currency type
     * specified by <code>from</code> to the currency specified
     * by the type <code>to</code>.  The currency types are
     * specified using the ISO 7412 three-letter currency codes.
     */
    public double convert (java.lang.String from,
                           java.lang.String to, double amount);
}

/** @jws:define name="CurrencyCalcWsdl" value::
 *  <?xml version="1.0" encoding="utf-8"?>
 *  The contents of the WSDL file go here.
 *  ::
 */
```

There are two major parts to this control file; the first is the definition of an interface, which represents the control. This interface has two methods, which are the same as the methods on the Currency Calculator Web service. In addition, the Javadoc comments from the Web service were copied over to provide documentation for this control.

The interface contains two annotations, which specify the location of this Web service and the location of the WSDL file that defines this Web service. Because this control was made for a Web service that resides on the local machine, both of these fields are fairly simple, but they could be replaced with URLs if the services were to reside on another computer.

The interface declaration is rather short (because this is a rather simple Web service); most of the bulk of this file is made up by a very large multi-line Javadoc attribute placed at the end of the file. This attribute is found on a @jws:define tag and actually consists of the entire WSDL file for the Web service. Surprisingly enough, even for a very short Web service, the WSDL file is quite long. This is a side effect of WSDL being a very general mechanism, which makes it very flexible but also very verbose. You don't need to understand the contents of a WSDL file to write a Web service, but you should recognize one and understand that it is an XML description of your Web service. When you finally reach the point where you want to expose your Web service publicly, you can do so by distributing its WSDL file, which contains all the information needed to locate the computer where your Web service is hosted and describe the methods provided by your Web service.

CTRL files like the preceding one can be generated for any JWS file in your project by right-clicking on the JWS in the Project Tree and selecting Generate CTRL from JWS. Likewise, you can generate a WSDL file from a JWS by selecting Generate WSDL from JWS. After you've done this, the new file appears in the Project Tree, as shown in Figure 7-5.

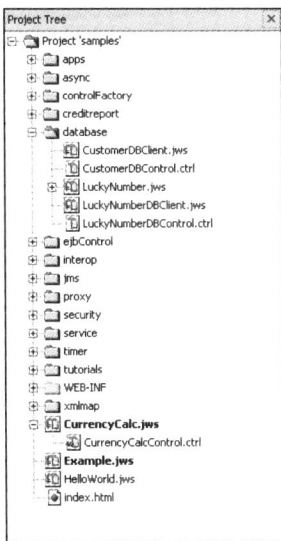

Figure 7-5: A generated CTRL file in the Project Tree.

The CTRL and WSDL files generated from a JWS are grouped in the Project Tree as children of the JWS. This grouping signifies the linkage between CTRL and WSDL files and their corresponding JWS files. After you generate a CTRL or WSDL file from a JWS file, WebLogic Workshop attempts to keep those files up to date with the JWS that generated them.

WebLogic Workshop has a special naming convention for CTRL files and WSDL files generated from a JWS. If you have a JWS named `Service.jws`, the WSDL will be named `ServiceContract.wsdl` and the CTRL will be named `ServiceControl.ctrl`. These names signify the respective roles of the WSDL and CTRL as a contract specifying the public behavior of the Web service and a control representing the Web service.

The Timer Control

The Timer control is probably one of the simplest controls. Its only function is to serve as a somewhat versatile timer that can be used by a Web service. Timer controls are a little different than Service controls; most notably, they don't require the creation of a CTRL file. Let's begin by looking at how you add a Timer control to your Web service.

To create a Timer control, select Add Control ⇨ Add Timer Control on the Design View. The Add Timer Control dialog box, which is pictured in Figure 7-6, will appear.

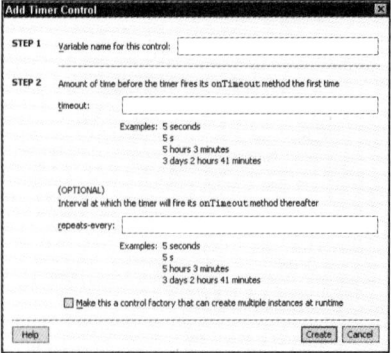

Figure 7-6: The Add Timer Control dialog box.

The first step in filling out the dialog box is to select the name of the variable that will represent the Timer control in the source code. This is the same thing you must do when you create any type of control.

When you've chosen a name, you have two choices to make about the timeout behavior of the Timer control. These choices determine how frequently timer events will be generated:

- **Timeout:** The amount of time before the timer fires its first event. If you want to create a *single-shot timer* (that is, a timer that waits for a particular interval, fires a single event, and doesn't do anything else), this is the only field you need to set. The value of this field is fairly versatile, it can contain values such as "1 hour 3 minutes 20 seconds" or "4 months 12 days 4 hours." There are a number of examples in the dialog box; if you follow their format, you probably won't go wrong. This field is a required to create a timer control.

- **Repeats-every:** The amount of time between successive timer events after the first. If you want to create a timer that repeats, you should set this field. The format of this field is the same as the timeout field, but unlike the timeout field, this field is not required.

The last option is similar to that on the Add Service Control dialog box and allows you to create a Timer control factory. I discuss in detail what this means in Chapter 8.

After you've filled out the dialog box, click Create to add the control to your Web service. The new Timer control will appear as shown in Figure 7-7.

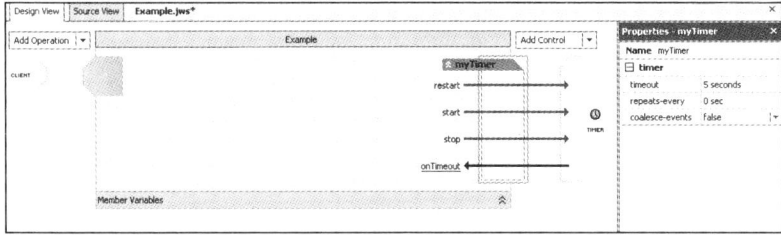

Figure 7-7: A new Timer control.

You'll notice that the new Timer control already has three methods and one callback. The methods and callbacks on a Timer control are always the same, unlike the methods and callbacks of a Service control, which are determined by the underlying Web service the control represents.

If you select the control in the Design View, you'll see the two properties you can specify in the Add Timer Control dialog box: Timeout and Repeats-every. In addition, there is one additional property that you can't set from that dialog box: Coalesce-events. If you set this property to true, the Timer control will *coalesce* successive timer events if you can handle them all. For example, if a number of timer events pile up on your Web service before it can handle them all, they will be delivered as a single event.

Although only three methods are shown on the Design View, the Timer control actually has a number of additional methods, which are not pictured. Taken together, these methods are used to set the various parameters of the Timer control. Table 7-1 describes the relevant Timer control methods, including the three that appear on the Design View.

TABLE 7-1 THE TIMER CONTROL METHODS

Method	Description
boolean getCoalesceEvents()	Returns the value of the Coalesce-events property on the Timer control.
String getRepeatsEvery()	Returns the value of the Repeats-every property as a string.
long getTimeout()	Returns the value of the Timeout property converted into seconds.
Date getTimeoutAt()	Returns the absolute time when the timer will time out (see below).
void restart()	Restarts the timer. This is equivalent to calling stop and then calling start.
void setCoalesceEvents(boolean)	Sets the value of the Coalesce-events property.
void setRepeatsEvery(long)	Sets the value of the Repeats-every property in seconds.
void setRepeatsEvery(String)	Sets the value of the Repeats-every property as a string.
void setTimeout(long)	Sets the value of the Timeout property in seconds.
void setTimeout(String)	Sets the value of the Timeout property as a string.

Method	Description
void setTimeoutAt (Date)	Sets the absolute time when the timer will time out (see below).
void start()	Starts the timer.
void stop()	Stops the timer.

Of the methods in Table 7-1, the two methods `setTimeoutAt()` and `getTimeoutAt()` deserve some mention. When you set the Timeout property, the Timeout-at property is automatically set to the absolute time at which the timer will time out. For instance, if it is 12:15:42 and you start a 10-second timer, the Timeout-at property will be set to 12:15:52. You can check this by calling `getTimeoutAt()`, which returns a Date. Additionally, if you want the timer to go off at a particular time, say 12:30 next Friday, you can use `setTimeoutAt(Date)` and set this value directly.

The last important thing to mention about the Timer control is how the timer events are actually delivered to your Web service. You may have noticed in Figure 7-7 that the name of the callback on the Timer control is drawn as a hyperlink. If you click this hyperlink, you'll be taken to the implementation of the callback in your Web service, as shown in Figure 7-8.

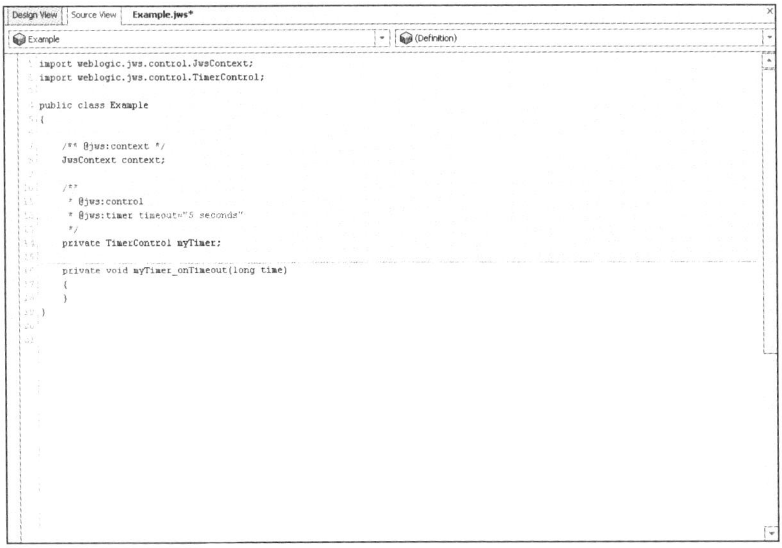

Figure 7-8: A Timer control callback.

If the callback doesn't already exist in your source code, WebLogic Workshop will automatically generate it when you click on the link in the Design View. Once again, the callback isn't identified by an annotation, but rather, it is given a special name,

```
private void TimerControlName_onTimeout(long time)
```

where `TimerControlName` is the name of the Timer control variable in your source code. If you want to work directly in the source code, you can add this method by hand. The callback is passed one parameter, which is the current time.

Listing 7-3 brings together the preceding discussion in an example that uses a Timer control, Service controls, maps, and conversations to create a simple news subscription service. This example brings together a number of concepts and serves as a nice review of a great deal of the material I've shown you so far.

Listing 7-3: A News Subscription Web Service

```
packageChapter7;

import java.util.ArrayList;
import weblogic.jws.control.*;

public class NewsSubService
{
    /**
     * @jws:control
     * @jws:timer timeout="1 day" repeats-every="1 day"
     */
    TimerControl sendTimer;


    /** @jws:control */
    private SportsNewsControl sportsNews;

    /** @jws:control */
    private FinNewsControl financeNews;

    /** @jws:context */
    JwsContext context;

    public interface Callback
    {
        /**
         * @jws:parameter-xml xml-map::
         * <articles>
         *    <article xm:multiple="Article a in articles">
```

```
 *        <headline>{a.headline}</headline>
 *        <author>{a.author}</author>
 *        <date>{a.date}</date>
 *        <text>{a.text}</text>
 *     </article>
 * </articles>
 * ::
 */
    public void sendNews(Article[] articles);
}

/** The callback interface. */
private Callback callback;

/** Set to true if the user has subscribed to sports news. */
private boolean sports;

/** Set to true if the user has subscribed to finance news. */
private boolean finance;

/**
 * @jws:operation
 * @jws:conversation phase="start"
 * @jws:parameter-xml xml-map::
 * <subscription>
 *    <finance>{finance}</finance>
 *    <sports>{sports}</sports>
 * </subscription>
 * ::
 */
public void subscribe(boolean finance, boolean sports)
{
    this.sports  = sports;
    this.finance = finance;

    sendTimer.start();
}

/**
 * @jws:operation
 * @jws:conversation phase="continue"
 * @jws:parameter-xml xml-map::
 * <subscription>
 *    <finance>{finance}</finance>
```

Continued

Listing 7-3 *(Continued)*

```
 *   <sports>{sports}</sports>
 * </subscription>
 * ::
 */
public void changeSubscription(boolean finance, boolean sports)
{
    this.finance = finance;
    this.sports  = sports;
}

/**
 * @jws:operation
 * @jws:conversation phase="continue"
 * @jws:return-xml xml-map::
 * <subscription>
 *   <finance>{return.finance}</finance>
 *   <sports>{return.sports}</sports>
 * </subscription>
 * ::
 */
public Preferences getSubscriptionStatus()
{
    Preferences p = new Preferences();
    p.sports  = this.sports;
    p.finance = this.finance;

    return p;
}

private static class Preferences
{
    public Preferences() {}

    public boolean sports;
    public boolean finance;
}

/**
 * @jws:conversation phase="continue"
 */
public void sendTimer_onTimeout(long time)
{
    ArrayList articles = new ArrayList();
```

```
        if (sports)
        {
            Article[] sportsArticles =
                sportsNews.getCurrentArticles();
            for (int i = 0; i < sportsArticles.length; i++)
                articles.add(sportsArticles[i]);
        }
        if (finance)
        {
            Article[] finArticles =
                financeNews.getCurrentArticles();
            for (int i = 0; i < finArticles.length; i++)
                articles.add(finArticles[i]);
        }

        callback.sendNews(
            (Article[])articles.toArray(new Article[0]));
    }

    /**
     * @jws:operation
     * @jws:conversation phase="finish"
     */
    public void unsubscribe()
    {
        sendTimer.stop();
    }
}
```

This example permits a user to choose the type of news he wants to subscribe to (here the choices are finance and sports) and then receive daily articles from his chosen topics. The financial and sports news stories are retrieved from two different Web services accessed using Service controls (the source code for the services is not shown here, but I'm sure you could invent something reasonable). The data between the service and its clients is passed around as XML, and the user preferences are stored by using conversations. Finally, a Timer control is used to invoke the daily news delivery. In short, there is a lot going on here. Let's look at it piece by piece.

A user starts out using this Web service by calling the Subscribe method, which is the only start method of the Web service. The user sends some XML to this method that looks something like the following:

```
<subscribe>
  <finance>true</finance>
  <sports>false</sports>
</subscribe>
```

This XML describes what type of news the user wants to receive, and it is translated by using a fairly simple XML map. In addition, the Timer control `sendTimer`, is started when this method is called.

After a user has subscribed, he can check the status of his subscription or change his subscription preferences at any time by using the methods `changeSubscription` and `getSubscriptionStatus`. These methods send and receive XML messages of the same form shown earlier.

Once the user has subscribed to his particular news choices, the timer callback, `sendTimer_onTimeout`, is responsible for retrieving and distributing the news. The first thing to note about this callback is that it is part of a conversation. The timer was started in the Start method and in order to use the conversational state set in the Start method, the callback must also participate in the conversation.

When the timer fires, some simple logic receives the requested articles using a couple of Service controls, and these articles are returned to the user through a callback. The articles are represented as `Article` objects, which are defined by the following class:

```
public class Article
{
    public Article() {}

    public String headline;
    public String author;
    public Date date;
    public String text;
}
```

In addition, you should notice that in this example there is a map on the callback method itself, which allows the message sent for the callback to be translated into arbitrary XML.

When the user no longer wants to receive any news, he can call the `Unsubscribe` method, which both terminates the conversation and stops the timer.

The Database Control

The final control I will discuss in this chapter is the Database control. The Database control provides a simple method to access a database through the somewhat familiar control interface. This section makes the assumption that you're somewhat familiar with Structured Query Language (SQL).

The methods of a Database control are each linked to a particular SQL query that is to be run when the method is called. The results of the query are returned as the return value of the method.

The Basics of the Database control

To add a Database control to your Web service, select Add Operation ⇨ Add Database Control. This will display the Add Database Control dialog box, which is pictured in Figure 7-9.

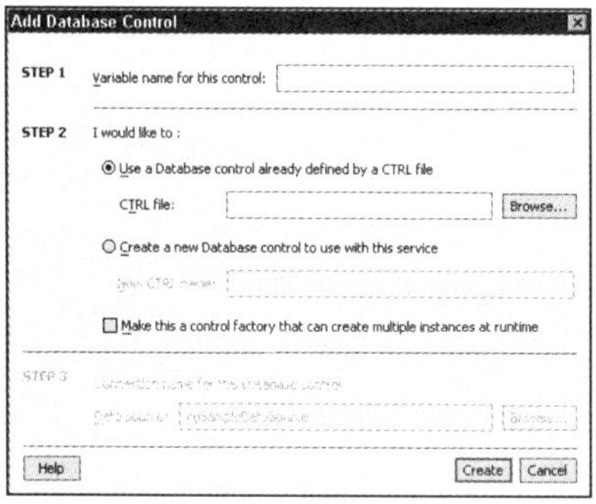

Figure 7-9: The Add Database Control dialog box.

There are two or three parts to the Add Database Control dialog box, depending on how you want to create the control. The first thing you must do is choose a name for the variable that will allow you to access the Database control. This is exactly the same as creating a Timer control or Service control.

In the second step, you must choose whether you want to create a new Database control, or use an existing CTRL file that defines a Database control. If you want to use an existing CTRL file, select this option in the dialog box and enter the name of the CTRL file. If you want to create a new Database control, there is a little more work to be done. First, you must pick a name for the CTRL file you will be creating.

Finally, if you're creating a new Database control, you must pick a *data source* for the control. The data source refers to the specific database connection you want to use for this database control. This field comes filled in with the default data source `cgSampleDataSource`. This data source will serve for our purposes; if you want to create another one, you should refer to the WebLogic Server documentation to find out how. When you've finished filling out the dialog box, click Create to add the control to your Web service.

For the subsequent discussion, I'll assume you want to create a new Database control. Figure 7-10 shows the new Database control, after it has been added.

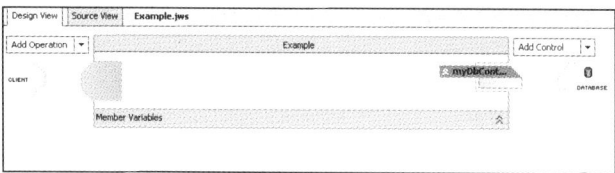

Figure 7-10: A new Database control.

The new Database control has no methods on it yet. However, WebLogic Workshop makes adding new methods quite easy. To add a new method, right-click on the Database Control in the Design View and select Add Method. A new method will be created, as shown in Figure 7-11. You can select a new name for the method just as you did in Chapter 2 when creating a new Web service method.

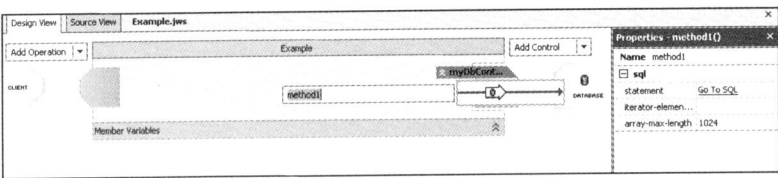

Figure 7-11: A new method on the Database Control.

Where the map icon appears on normal Web service methods, a slightly different icon appears on the Database Control method. There is a single large arrow in this area with a small cylinder (the universal symbol for a database) inside it. Double-click on this icon to activate the Query Editor. The Query Editor is very similar to the Map Editor and is shown in Figure 7-12.

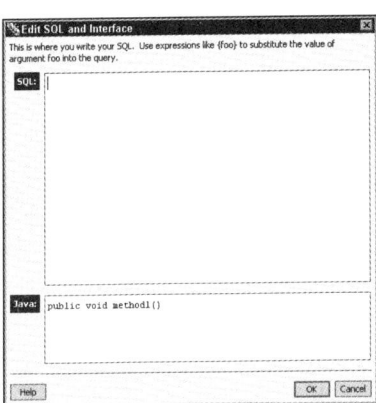

Figure 7-12: The Query Editor.

Like the Map Editor, the lower box in the Query Editor shows the signature of this method – the first line of the method before the opening curly brace of the body. The top box is where you type the SQL for the query you want to perform. For example, you could enter the following simple query to extract certain rows from the database:

```
SELECT exchange FROM currencies WHERE fromName="USD",toName="EUR"
```

 The sample here uses the default Data Source that comes with the WebLogic Workshop. To connect to your own database, you need to use WebLogic console or modify config.xml directly. You would first create a JDBC Connection Pool, and then create a Data Source. Here is an example of a database connection to Oracle in the config.xml.

```
<!-- JDBC pool -->

<JDBCConnectionPool Name="OracleConnectionPool"
DriverName="oracle.jdbc.driver.OracleDriver"
URL="jdbc:oracle:thin:@dbServer:1521:dbInstanceName"
InitialCapacity="1"
CapacityIncrement="1"
MaxCapacity="10"
ShrinkingEnabled="true"
Properties="user=developer;password=password"
Targets="cgServer"/>

<!-- Data Source -->

<JDBCDataSource Name="OracleDS"
    PoolName="OracleConnectionPool"
    JNDIName="OracleDS"
    Targets="cgServer"/>
```

In this example, I'm assuming that there is a table of exchange rates named Currencies, which contains three columns, fromName, toName, and exchange. These columns would correspond to the name of the currency to convert from, the name of the currency to convert to, and the exchange rate. This select statement retrieves the exchange rate from U.S. dollars to euros.

You don't want to make a different Database control method for every pair of currencies you can possibly convert between. In fact, what you'd really like is to pass the names of the currencies in and get the exchange rate back as a return value. By changing the query as follows, you can accomplish this task:

```
SELECT exchange FROM currencies WHERE
    fromName={fromName},toName={toName}
```

The signature must be changed as well to match the new query:

```
public double getExchangeRate(String fromName, String toName)
```

156 Part III: Advanced Concepts

Placing the parameter names `fromName` and `toName` within curly braces will cause the values of the parameters to be substituted into the query when the method is called. The return value will be set to the exchange rate returned by this query.

Now that you understand the basic theory of the Database control, I'll show you the body of the control file that generates this control. Fortunately, there is no WSDL file embedded in this CTRL file, so it's rather short and simple:

```
packageChapter7;

import weblogic.jws.*;
import weblogic.jws.control.*;
import java.sql.SQLException;

/**
 * Defines a new database control.
 *
 * The @jws:connection tag indicates which WebLogic data source will be used by
 * this database control. Please change this to suit your needs. You can see a
 * list of available data sources by going to the WebLogic console in a browser
 * (typically http://localhost:7001/console) and clicking Services, JDBC,
 * Data Sources.
 *
 * @jws:connection data-source-jndi-name="cgSampleDataSource"
 */
public interface MyDBControlControl extends DatabaseControl
{
    // Sample database function.  Uncomment to use

    // static public class Customer
    // {
    //    public int id;
    //    public String name;
    // }
    //
    // /**
    //  * @jws:sql statement="SELECT ID, NAME FROM CUSTOMERS WHERE ID = {id}"
    //  */
    // Customer findCustomer(int id);

    // Add "throws SQLException" to request that SQLExeptions be thrown on errors.

    /**
     * @jws:sql statement::
     *     SELECT exchange FROM currencies
```

```
 *           WHERE fromName={fromName},toName={toName}
 *
 * ::
 */
    public double getExchangeRate(String fromName, String toName);
}
```

The rather large comment (intended to provide some "quick and dirty" documentation) is inserted by WebLogic Workshop into every new Database control you create. It can provide a handy reference if you're trying to remember the exact syntax of a Database control. If you don't like it there, you can safely delete it.

You should notice that this CTRL file defines an interface, just like the Service control. There is a single annotation on this interface, which specifies the name of the data source you specified when creating the control.

The interface contains one method, which was the method created above. The signature of the method is terminated with a semicolon (you must do that in interfaces), but otherwise it's exactly the same as it appeared in the Query Editor. The SQL query has been embedded in an annotation, but it's also the same as it was in the Query Editor. The Query Editor provides a rather thin veneer over the contents of the CTRL file for the Database control. You could just as easily edit it by hand if you wanted.

Advanced Database control features

So far I've discussed how to use the Database control in the simplest instance. However, there are some more complicated features that are fairly useful. One of the most important issues is how to deal with queries that return whole rows instead of single values, as well as queries that return multiple rows.

USING QUERIES THAT RETURN A ROW

When a query returns a row, your Database control method needs to return a suitable object, because that's the best way to deal with composite values in Java. The following code demonstrates a simple Database control method that returns a whole row:

```
packageChapter7;

import weblogic.jws.*;
import weblogic.jws.control.*;
import java.sql.SQLException;

/**
 * @jws:connection data-source-jndi-name="cgSampleDataSource"
 */
```

```
public interface MyDBControl extends DatabaseControl
{
    static public class Customer
    {
        public int id;
        public String name;
    }

    /**
     * @jws:sql statement="SELECT ID, NAME FROM CUSTOMERS WHERE ID = {id}"
     */
    Customer findCustomer(int id);
}
```

This is actually the WebLogic Workshop example contained in the comments above every new Database control, reformatted a little bit. The `Customer` object declared in the CTRL file is what is returned from the method `findCustomer`. It's assumed that the customer table has two columns named `ID` and `NAME` (there may be more). The `SELECT` statement retrieves a row containing an `ID` and `NAME`, from the `CUSTOMERS` table, which has the ID equal to the value passed into the function.

The row returned by the query is mapped into the return value by the fairly simple process of name comparison. The value in a particular column is assigned to the field in the object of the same name, that is, `ID` from the table is mapped into `id` in the `Customer` object and likewise for the `NAME` column. The names are case-insensitive, so the names in the `Customer` object could have been called `Name`, `nAme`, `NAME`, or `name`.

USING QUERIES THAT RETURN MULTIPLE ROWS

There are a few different ways to return multiple rows from a Database control. The first and simplest is to have the Database control method return an array instead of a single object. For instance, the following example changes the method defined above to one that could plausibly return multiple rows and augments it to return an array:

```
/**
 * @jws:sql statement="SELECT ID, NAME FROM CUSTOMERS WHERE ID > {id}"
 *          array-max-length=500
 */
Customer[] findBiggerCustomers(int id);
```

There are two changes from the previous method. First, the return value has been changed from a single `Customer` object to an array of `Customer` objects. Second, a new attribute has been added to the `@jws:sql` tag, `array-max-length`, which constrains the maximum number of rows that can be returned by the method.

The second way to deal with multiple return values is to return an array of `java.util.HashMap` objects. These objects store a set of name-value pairs that can be quickly looked up by name. An example of using a `HashMap` would look like the following:

```
/**
 * @jws:sql statement="SELECT ID, NAME FROM CUSTOMERS WHERE ID > {id}"
 *          array-max-length=500
 */
HashMap[] findBiggerCustomers(int id);
```

Each returned row is represented by an entry in the `HashMap` array. You look up a particular column by using the name of the column as the key to the `HashMap`'s `get` method. When you use a HashMap, the extra `Customer` object is no longer necessary.

The third way to return multiple rows is to have the method return an `Iterator`. This is demonstrated by the following:

```
/**
 * @jws:sql statement="SELECT ID, NAME FROM CUSTOMERS WHERE ID > {id}"
 *          iterator-element-type="Customer"
 */
Iterator findBiggerCustomers(int id);
```

In this case, the method returns a `java.util.Iterator`, and the annotation on the `@jws:sql` statement is again changed, this time to include the `iterator-element-type` attribute. This attribute specifies the type of object that will be returned by the `Iterator`. In this case, `Customer` is specified, so the `Iterator` will return objects of the type `Customer`. The returned rows will be mapped to these objects exactly as described above.

A Database control example

I will use a simple example to demonstrate some of the features of the Database control. Listing 7-4 shows an example of a library catalog. This can be queried and updated through a Web service that employs a Database control. Listing 7-5 shows the source code for the Database control used in this example.

Listing 7-4: The LibraryCatalog Example

```
packageChapter7;

import java.util.ArrayList;
import java.util.HashMap;
import java.util.Iterator;
import weblogic.jws.control.JwsContext;
```

Continued

Listing 7-4 *(Continued)*

```java
public class LibraryCatalog
{
    /** @jws:context */
    JwsContext context;

    /** @jws:control */
    private CatalogDBControl catalog;

    /**
     * @jws:operation
     * @jws:return-xml xml-map::
     * <books>
     *   <book xm:multiple="CatalogDBControl.Book b in return">
     *     <author>{b.author}</author>
     *     <title>{b.title}</title>
     *     <ISBN>{b.ISBN}</ISBN>
     *   </book>
     * </books>
     * ::
     */
    public CatalogDBControl.Book[] lookupByAuthor(String author)
    {
        ArrayList list = new ArrayList();
        HashMap[] h = catalog.lookupByAuthor(author);
        for (int i = 0; i < h.length; i++)
        {
            CatalogDBControl.Book b = new CatalogDBControl.Book();
            b.author = (String)h[i].get("AUTHOR");
            b.title  = (String)h[i].get("TITLE");
            b.ISBN   = (String)h[i].get("ISBN");

            list.add(b);
        }

        return (CatalogDBControl.Book[])list.toArray(
            new CatalogDBControl.Book[0]);
    }

    /**
     * @jws:operation
     * @jws:return-xml xml-map::
     * <books>
     *   <book xm:multiple="CatalogDBControl.Book b in return">
     *     <author>{b.author}</author>
```

```
 *     <title>{b.title}</title>
 *     <ISBN>{b.ISBN}</ISBN>
 *   </book>
 * </books>
 * ::
 */
public CatalogDBControl.Book[] lookupByTitle(String title)
{
    Iterator i = catalog.lookupByTitle(title);

    ArrayList list = new ArrayList();
    while (i.hasNext())
        list.add(i.next());

    return (CatalogDBControl.Book[])list.toArray(
        new CatalogDBControl.Book[0]);
}

/**
 * @jws:operation
 * @jws:return-xml xml-map::
 * <books>
 *   <book xm:multiple="CatalogDBControl.Book b in return">
 *     <author>{b.author}</author>
 *     <title>{b.title}</title>
 *     <ISBN>{b.ISBN}</ISBN>
 *   </book>
 * </books>
 * ::
 */
public CatalogDBControl.Book[] lookupByISBN(String ISBN)
{
    return new CatalogDBControl.Book[]
        { catalog.lookupByISBN(ISBN) };
}

/** @jws:operation */
public void addRecord(String title, String author, String ISBN)
{ catalog.addRecord(title, author, ISBN); }

/** @jws:operation */
public void createTable()
{ catalog.createTable(); }
}
```

Listing 7-5: The Catalog Database Control

```java
packageChapter7;

import weblogic.jws.*;
import weblogic.jws.control.*;
import java.sql.SQLException;
import java.util.HashMap;
import java.util.Iterator;

/**
 * @jws:connection data-source-jndi-name="cgSampleDataSource"
 */
public interface CatalogDBControl extends DatabaseControl
{
    public static class Book
    {
        public Book() {}

        public String author;
        public String title;
        public String ISBN;
    }

    /**
     * @jws:sql statement::
     *    SELECT title, author, isbn FROM catalog
     *    WHERE author={author}
     * ::
     * max-array-length="100"
     */
    public HashMap[] lookupByAuthor(String author);

    /**
     * @jws:sql statement::
     *    SELECT title, author, isbn FROM catalog WHERE title={title}
     * ::
     * iterator-element-type="Book"
     */
    public Iterator lookupByTitle(String title);

    /**
     * @jws:sql statement::
     *    SELECT title, author, isbn FROM catalog WHERE isbn={ISBN}
     * ::
     */
```

```
    public Book lookupByISBN(String ISBN);


    /**
     * @jws:sql statement::
     *   INSERT INTO catalog VALUES ({author}, {title}, {ISBN})
     * ::
     */
    public void addRecord(String title, String author, String ISBN);

    /**
     * @jws:sql statement::
     *    CREATE TABLE catalog
     *    (
     *       author char(25),
     *       title char(50),
     *       isbn char(10),
     *       PRIMARY KEY (isbn)
     *    )
     * ::
     */
    public void createTable();
}
```

This example seems long; however, it would be much longer if not done using the Database controls. What you see essentially is an Object-to-Relational mapping that is easy to code, and you do not have to deal with other expensive tools to do it.

Summary

In this chapter, I've shown you the three "core" WebLogic Workshop controls: the Service control, the Timer control, and the Database control. Using these controls and the material presented up to this point, you can create very powerful, enterprise-class Web services. There are more controls, although these fall into the category of "advanced" controls. For the most part, you need to know J2EE in order to use those controls. Here is what you need to remember from this chapter:

- The Service control allows you to access other Web services and to expose your Web service to other WebLogic Workshop users.

- The Timer control gives you a somewhat versatile timer that can call back your Web service when certain timer events occur.

- The Database control provides a convenient wrapper around a database, allowing you to run SQL queries with very little work.

Chapter 8

Using the Advanced Controls

IN THIS CHAPTER

- Introducing J2EE and related tools from WebLogic Workshop
- Accessing Enterprise JavaBeans components with the EJB control
- Using the JMS control for access to the Java Message Service
- Expanding the Online Store example to incorporate the EJB and JMS controls
- Using multiple control instances with control factories

One of the areas where Web services offer the most promise is in providing a bridge between disparate parts of big applications. Where Chapter 7 showed you how you can build Web services that talk to other services and databases, this chapter describes how more advanced controls can connect your service's clients with parts of your company's application that may have been hard to access before. Where providing a bridge to components of a distributed Java 2, Enterprise Edition (J2EE) application may have previously required having a detailed knowledge of J2EE, WebLogic Workshop simplifies this work through the Enterprise Java Bean (EJB) and Java Message Service (JMS) controls.

Leveraging J2EE from WebLogic Workshop

Writing code that accesses Java enterprise components has traditionally required learning a fair amount about the infrastructure of the J2EE standard. Using the logic of an EJB has required writing code to navigate through the Java Naming and Directory Interface (JNDI) and the various interfaces implemented by EJBs.

The controls described in this chapter, the EJB control and the JMS control, are designed to make accessing J2EE components easier. As with the controls described in Chapter 7 – the Service control, Timer control, and Database control – the EJB and JMS controls provide greatly simplified access to resources outside your Web service. The most significant benefits of the EJB and JMS controls are essentially those of other controls: They reduce the amount of code you have to write before getting down to writing the logic of your application.

Because controls in WebLogic Workshop are designed so that you can use them in a consistent way, you add an EJB or JMS control to your Web service through the Add Control menu. When you use the menu to add a control, WebLogic Workshop presents a dialog box through which you can specify basic settings for the control. After you've added the control, you use it by calling its methods and handling its callbacks.

The J2EE specification defines a standard set of technologies on which to build distributed applications. These applications vary as widely as the businesses they're designed to support. They range from online shopping services to human resources infrastructure to banking transaction support and more. The J2EE specification defines a set of technologies, including Java Database Connectivity (JDBC), which is used by the Database control, and Enterprise JavaBeans (EJB) and the Java Message Service (JMS), which are used by the controls discussed in this chapter.

The EJB specification is a core part of J2EE. Components that encapsulate an application's business logic are typically written as EJBs and deployed to application servers such as WebLogic Server. The EJB specification supports an application design approach in which the application's components are said to *model* the processes the application is designed to support. An example often given is an online shopping application. There, one component might represent a customer, another an item that can be purchased, and still another the interaction of the two in the form of a shopping cart.

The resources used by a J2EE application are identified by their Java Naming and Directory Interface (JNDI) name. JNDI provides a way to give unique names to components deployed to a J2EE application. For example, cgSampleDataSource, the data source name used in Chapter 7, is the JNDI name for that data source. Likewise, when you add an EJB or JMS control to a Web service, you specify the JNDI name of the EJB or JMS queue or topic the control will represent. As with the data source, you select these JNDI names from a list when you add the control.

In the context of all of this, a Web service you build may have any of a variety of roles. For example, your service may receive requests from other businesses, then forward these requests to the appropriate J2EE components or services in the application. In effect, your service would be acting as an intermediary, kicking off your internal application's processing and possibly returning results as they are received from the application. The benefit for both your company and its client is that the service represents a single, usually asynchronous point of access that shields the underlying application.

The EJB Control

Although the EJB 2.0 specification defines three basic types of beans—session beans, entity beans, and message-driven beans—the EJB control itself is designed to access only the first two. Message-driven beans are available by using JMS as an intermediary, so you use the JMS control to access them. Entity and session beans, on the other hand, are accessed more or less directly through the EJB control.

Another difference arises through the interfaces that entity and session beans, according to the EJB specification, must implement. Each of these interfaces serves a different purpose, but together they make the bean accessible to the application server and to other components, including WebLogic Workshop.

Entity beans are typically designed to represent some *thing* in an application, such as a book in the bookseller application. In the online shopping application, an entity bean might represent a customer or a purchasable item. Also, an entity bean models a part of the application that has persistent characteristics (a customer has a name, address, credit card number, and so on, that may be stored from one purchase to the next). An instance of an entity bean represents a row in a database table.

Unlike an entity bean, a session bean typically represents a business *process*. Session beans are usually created and used for a specific action, then discarded when that action finishes. In the online shopping application, a shopping cart may be modeled as a session bean. The shopping cart bean is created with data about the customer and their purchases and it need only exist until the purchase is finished.

EJBs communicate with each other and their client synchronously, typically through Remote Method Invocation (RMI). An EJB control you add to your Web service will list the methods for the bean it represents, and you call the EJB's methods by calling the control's. Through WebLogic Workshop's control model, calling an EJB's methods is as simple as adding the control, then calling the methods it provides.

For more information on EJB, you can look up *Mastering Enterprise Java Beans, 2nd Edition* by Ed Roman, Scott Ambler, and Tyler Jewell.

Preparing to add an EJB control

As you would when developing other components that are clients of an EJB, you must ensure that your code has access to client versions of the EJB's interfaces.

WebLogic Workshop uses this information to access the bean. Because this information is used when you add an EJB control to your service, you must add the information to your project *before* you add the control. You do this by copying the required interfaces to the WEB-INF/lib folder of your WebLogic Workshop project.

As it turns out, this is fairly simple to do: If the EJB is deployed in a JAR file, you can copy the EJB's JAR file to your project. You can also copy what is known as a *client-jar*. For EJBs configured to generate one, a client-jar is a by-product of the EJB deployment process. It contains only the parts of the bean that are needed by clients to access it.

In the end, it doesn't matter whether you use the client-jar or the bean's complete JAR file; either will do for WebLogic Workshop. However, given that the client-jar is likely to be smaller, and all WebLogic Workshop really needs, it's probably a better choice. Also, keep in mind that an EJB may be deployed in other package forms, such as an EAR (Enterprise archive) file, which may be quite large because it can contain many files. In this case, it is more practical to use a client-jar than to use the much larger archive file.

Finally, you need to know the JNDI name of the EJB your Web service will be accessing. You'll use the JNDI name to specify which EJB on the system the control will represent.

Adding an EJB control

Once you've added the required interfaces to your project, you're ready to add an EJB control for access to the bean. You reach the EJB control from the Add Control menu through which you add a Service, Timer, or Database control. As it is when adding other controls, the Add EJB Control dialog box prompts you to enter a name for the control variable. You can also specify whether to use an existing control or to create a new one.

If you decide to create a new control, you'll be prompted to provide a name for the new CTRL file. Also, if you're creating a new control, Step 3 provides a place for you to specify the EJB's JNDI name. Specifying the JNDI name here is similar to adding a Database control, as described in Chapter 7. The JNDI name is the name by which WebLogic Server knows the EJB. When you click the first Browse button in Step 3, WebLogic Workshop asks WebLogic Server for the JNDI names of EJBs in the current domain, as shown in Figure 8-1. Choose the bean you want to access from the list and click OK. Back in the Add EJB Control dialog box, you'll see that WebLogic Workshop has used the JNDI name to add interface names to complete the dialog box.

Figure 8-1: A list of the EJBs on the server.

Chapter 8: Using the Advanced Controls 169

If you were adding the ValidateCredit EJB that is installed with WebLogic Workshop, you might end up with a completed dialog box that looks something like what you see in Figure 8-2.

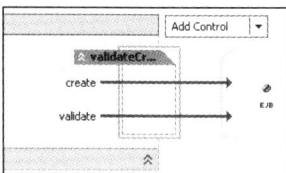

Figure 8-2: The Add EJB Control dialog box.

After you clicked Create, WebLogic Workshop would add a control to your design such as the one shown in Figure 8-3.

Figure 8-3: An EJB control in Design View.

Listing 8-1 shows you what the code for such a control would look like. As with the CTRL source code you saw in Listing 7-2, in Chapter 7, this code contains annotations that help to define the control's behavior. Note that the annotation values here are the values used in the Add EJB Control dialog box.

Listing 8-1: An EJB Control

```
package Chapter08;

import weblogic.jws.*;
import weblogic.jws.control.*;

/**
 *    @jws:ejb home-jndi-name="financial.ValidateCredit"
```

Continued

Listing 8-1 *(Continued)*
```
 *   @editor-info:ejb home="ValidateCreditBean.jar"
 *       bean="ValidateCreditBean.jar"
 */
public interface ValidateCreditControl
    // home interface
    extends financial.ValidateCreditHome,
    // bean interface
    financial.ValidateCredit,
    // control interface
    weblogic.jws.control.SessionEJBControl
{
}
```

You may immediately notice one aspect of this CTRL code that is different from other controls. This code does not define the `create` and `validate` methods that you see on the control in Design View. These methods appear in Design View because WebLogic Workshop discovered them in the EJB's interface. Finally, take care not to edit the source code of an EJB control's CTRL file. The code here was created based on information WebLogic Workshop collected from the EJB to which the control points. Only changes in the EJB itself should provoke changes to the EJB control.

Using an EJB control

EJB controls are remarkably simple to use. Like the Service control, the EJB control arrives in your service design with a set of methods defined by the component the control will be accessing. There is no need to add or remove methods because its method list must be the same as that exposed by the bean itself.

As I mentioned in "The EJB Control," earlier in this chapter, entity and session beans differ in the roles they play in an application. Even if you weren't party to designing or developing the EJBs you will be accessing from a web service, you still need an understanding of how the bean works in order to use it. This will differ from bean to bean, although there are design conventions common to entity beans and conventions common to session beans.

USING SESSION BEANS

Session beans exist to execute on behalf of a particular client. If you're using an EJB control to access a session bean, that client is your web service. A session bean typically exists to do things on your behalf. Depending on the bean, this may include calling on other beans, interacting with a database, and so on. For example, a shopping cart session bean might check a customer's credit and merchandise inventory before proceeding with the customer's purchase. Session beans are usually designed to be short-lived. In fact, once your web service is finished with it, the session bean may be said to go away.

A few basics to keep in mind about using session beans:

- You can use a session bean's `create` method to create a new instance, but it's not necessary. The EJB control gets an instance when you call one of the bean's other methods, too.

- The EJB control caches a reference to the session bean it creates, and uses this reference for subsequent calls made within the same web service method. The reference is released after the method is finished executing.

USING ENTITY BEANS

Entity beans exist to represent application data. That data might pertain to a customer, a piece of merchandise, an employee — in short, anything the application keeps track of over time. As a result, you create or find a *particular* entity bean instance — not just *any* one, as with session beans. For example, you might use a Widget bean (if your application had them) by calling a method such as `findByWidgetID`. WebLogic Server would give you a Widget bean whose data corresponded to the widget whose ID you specified. With such a bean, you could get or set that widget's price, color, and so on.

A few basics to keep in mind about entity beans:

- You create an entity bean by calling a `create` method it provides.

- You find a specific entity bean by calling a `find` method it provides.

- To call other methods of an EJB via the EJB control, you must already have a reference to a particular bean obtained by creating or finding one. For example, if you try to call setWidgetColor before you've created or found a particular widget, the EJB control will throw an exception.

- The EJB control caches a reference to a bean it creates or finds, and uses that for subsequent calls to the bean. This cached reference is useful for the life of the service's conversation (if any), or until the service method has finished executing.

- If a bean's `find` method returns data about multiple entities (such as multiple widgets), it might return an `Enumeration` or `Collection` object. Because the EJB control doesn't cache this data, you should store it in a member variable.

ACCESSING AN EJB THROUGH THE EJB CONTROL

Take a look again at the ValidateCredit bean I mentioned in "Adding an EJB Control." The bean only exposes two methods — `create` and `validate` — so these are the only methods on the control. Yet unlike the Service control (and more like the Timer control), methods of an EJB control do not require or support special annotations for communicating with their targets. In other words, you don't add an XML map to a method of an EJB control, nor do the methods expose properties.

What you see in Design View after adding an EJB control should seem a little recognizable now, even if you haven't written EJBs or client code to access them. The ValidateCredit bean's `create` method lets you create new instances of it. If ValidateCredit were an entity bean (it's a session bean), you might also see the `findByPrimaryKey` or other `find` methods that entity beans expose so that clients can gain access to the particular application entity the bean represents, such as a particular customer.

In the case of the ValidateCredit bean, the bean also exposes a `validate` method through which you can obtain a credit assessment (here, a statement about the creditworthiness of an applicant) based on a credit score. Listing 8-2 illustrates code you could write in your Web service to call the ValidateCredit bean's `validate` method by calling the same method exposed by the EJB control.

Listing 8-2: Accessing an EJB Control

```
/**
 * @jws:operation
 */
public String getCreditAssessment(int creditScore)
{
    String assessment = new String();
    try
    {
        assessment = validateCreditEJB.validate(creditScore);
    } catch (java.rmi.RemoteException re)
    {
        System.out.println("Exception using the EJB control: "
            + re);
    }
    return assessment;
}
```

If you're EJB-literate, this code may bewilder you because it's so simple. There are several lines of client code that you didn't have to write. Under the covers, the EJB control simplifies client code by doing typical EJB-related things like finding the EJB on the system using JNDI. You helped make this possible when you specified the EJB's JNDI name while creating the control.

A little experimentation with source code that calls methods of an EJB control will show you that you can access the functionality of an Enterprise JavaBean as you might from another kind of Java client. By typing the control variable name (in this case, `validateCreditEJB`) in your code, you can view and access the bean's methods in the member list – that is, by typing a dot after the variable name. In other words, you can use the functionality of the bean just as you might from other client code.

The JMS Control

The JMS control provides a way for you to conveniently access a messaging system through the Java Message Service (JMS). The JMS control makes using JMS easier by handling much of the plumbing associated with using the API. In fact, you'll find that, in many cases, using the JMS control makes it possible for you to avoid writing any code that directly involves the JMS API.

JMS is one of the most powerful aspects of J2EE, but messaging systems can be bewildering at first glance. In this section, I introduce messaging and JMS, describing the key concepts that find their way into your use of the control. If you aren't already familiar with JMS, the following section should help you make the kinds of decisions that using the control requires.

A Java Message Service primer

In this section, I introduce the basic concepts behind messaging systems, and JMS in particular. As with other J2EE technologies, WebLogic Workshop goes a long way toward making JMS easy to use. In other words, you don't have to have a detailed grasp of its nuances. However, as you will see, messaging systems provide their benefits in part through indirectness that makes asynchrony possible. Because of this, you should understand JMS fundamentals in order to make the most of the JMS control.

JMS is a widely used API for accessing messaging systems, also known as Message-Oriented Middleware (MOM) systems. Messaging systems are essentially a means for components to communicate with each other, in the way that Remote Method Invocation (RMI) is such a system for entity and session EJBs. The primary difference is that communication through messaging systems is asynchronous and loosely coupled.

As you might remember from Chapter 5, asynchrony enables one component to request a service from another without requiring the first component to wait for a response. On the client side of your Web service design, you might support asynchrony by providing a method for clients to use when making requests, and by providing a callback to return the response. In this way, the client can return to its own business after making the request, relying on the callback for a response.

UNDERSTANDING QUEUES AND TOPICS

Messaging systems accomplish asynchrony by providing a kind of waypoint for exchanges. In messaging, one component sends a message to the waypoint, and the message is forwarded by the system to one or more other components that are recipients. In JMS, there are two kinds of waypoints (known as *destinations*): queues and topics. Each of these is designed to support a different communication model. Also, in JMS both the sender and the recipient are considered *clients* of the messaging system.

You send a message to a *queue* when you expect only one other client to receive it. This is known as *point-to-point* messaging. A message sent to a queue will be delivered by the system to a client that has expressed an interest in the queue. If multiple clients are listening on the queue, only one will receive the message. For example, you might send a message containing credit information for evaluation to a queue so that only the accounting department's credit evaluator component will receive it. You want the credit information to be evaluated only once, and you want it to be seen by only the accounting department. This process is illustrated in Figure 8-4.

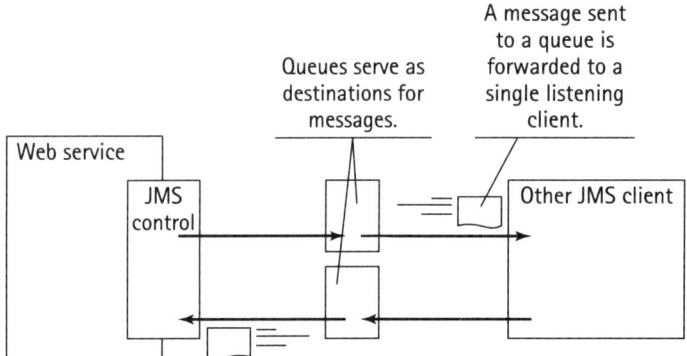

Figure 8-4: Point-to-point messaging with queues.

You send a message to a *topic* in order for potentially many clients to receive it. This model is known as the *publish-and-subscribe model*. Clients register an interest in a topic by *subscribing* to it, then receive any messages that are *published* to the topic. You might send a message requesting bids on a project to a topic, while potential bidders might subscribe to the topic to find out about available projects. Your Web service can also subscribe to a topic using the JMS control and receive messages sent after it subscribes. Figure 8-5 illustrates the publish-and-subscribe model.

The two messaging models, publish-and-subscribe (or pub/sub) and point-to-point (or p2p), are known in JMS as messaging *domains*. When you build a Web service using the JMS control, you select "Queue" or "Topic" as a JMS destination type, then specify which queue or topic the control should use for sending and receiving messages. I describe this in more detail later in the section, "Adding a JMS control."

UNDERSTANDING MESSAGES

Within the context of a messaging domain, the message itself is the focus. You may find that most of the code you write associated with JMS is designed to put data into messages you send and to extract data from messages you receive. As you will see, for many messages the JMS control greatly simplifies this process.

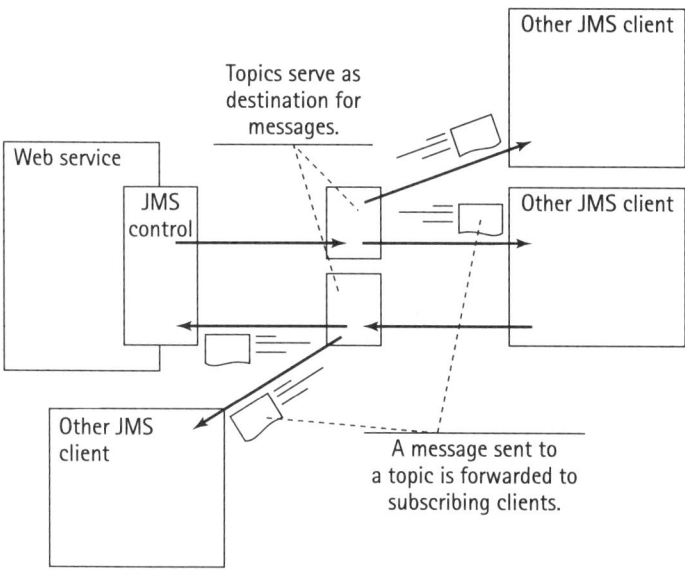

Figure 8-5: Publish-and-subscribe messaging with topics.

Messages are made up of three parts: a message payload, properties, and headers. Message properties and headers are similar in that they're designed to contain data *about* the message. In general, the difference is that headers are defined by the system for its own use, while properties are defined by JMS client developers who have agreed that certain properties are needed. JMS defines a set of headers that all messages support and which are typically used to route the message to the correct place. For example, by default, a message's JMSCorrelationID header is used by WebLogic Workshop to ensure that a message sent in response to a request is routed to the Web service that made the initial request (I describe this in more detail later in the section, "Correlating Received Messages"). In contrast, you may define whatever properties you like in keeping with the needs of clients interested in the message. The only real constraint is that properties must be one of the eight types supported by JMS: `boolean`, `byte`, `short`, `int`, `long`, `float`, `double`, and `String`.

In typical JMS code, you use get/set pairs to store and retrieve header and property values. However, for some messages, the JMS control provides a greatly simplified means to work with these values using XML maps, as described in "Handling headers and properties with XML maps."

The message payload contains the data that clients are most interested in, the data that application logic acts on. Clients can exchange several different types of messages depending on the kind of data needed by clients. JMS defines interfaces for six message types, each with its own set of methods for putting data in and taking it out. These types are described in Table 8-1.

TABLE 8-1 MESSAGE TYPES DEFINED BY JMS

Message type	Description
`Message`	The base interface for message types. The other five types extend Message.
`TextMessage`	Used to contain a String.
`ObjectMessage`	Used to contain Java objects.
`BytesMessage`	Used to contain an array of primitive bytes.
`StreamMessage`	Used to contain a stream of primitive Java types.
`MapMessage`	Used to contain name-value pairs.

When you add a JMS control to your Web service, you're prompted to specify a message type. As I describe later in "Using message types," the options you're given support all of the JMS types listed in Table 8-1, but they also reflect the JMS control's simplified support for two of the JMS types, `TextMessage` and `ObjectMessage`. Later in this chapter, I describe in general how you might use the other types in your Web service, but I focus on the specific benefits provided by the JMS control for certain types.

I've introduced quite a few new terms in this section. The following list should provide a quick review of them:

- **Client:** A component that is sending or receiving messages using JMS.
- **Queue:** A destination used when a message must be delivered to only one client.
- **Topic:** A destination used when multiple clients may receive a message.
- **Publish-and-subscribe:** A messaging model in which clients publish messages to topics for potentially many clients to receive, and subscribe to topics to receive messages sent by other clients.
- **Point-to-point:** A messaging model in which a client sends messages to a queue, and the message is delivered to one other client.
- **Producer:** A client that sends a message.
- **Consumer:** A client that receives a message.

Earlier I mentioned that, although there are three types of EJBs, the EJB control does not support communication with message-driven beans. Now that you know a little about messaging systems, you can probably begin to understand why.

Message-driven beans (MDBs) are JMS clients, just as your Web service is when you use the JMS control. Session and entity beans, on the other hand, typically communicate using direct, synchronous means such as RMI. You don't call methods of an MDB — you send messages that it is designed to receive, and receive messages it sends.

The next section takes the JMS abstractions I've introduced and describes how they apply to your use of the JMS control.

Adding a JMS control

Unlike the EJB control, you don't need to prepare in advance by adding client JAR files to your WebLogic Workshop project before adding a JMS control. However, adding a JMS control requires making a few decisions that you haven't had to make before. As with other controls that access external resources, your decisions are driven by what you know about the resource.

To start, you click the Add Control menu in Design View, then click Add JMS Control. The Add JMS Control dialog box will appear, providing a place for you to define characteristics of the control. Figure 8-6 reflects settings you might have used if you worked through the tutorial provided with WebLogic Workshop.

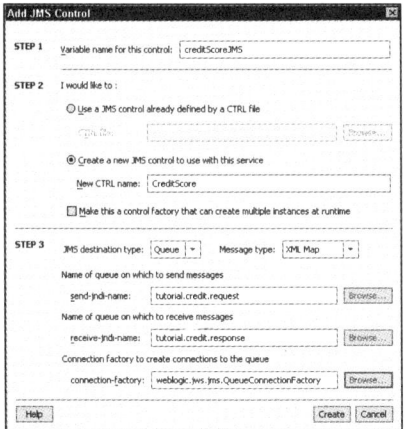

Figure 8-6: The Add JMS Control dialog box.

As you can see, Step 1 and Step 2 of the Add JMS Control dialog box are nearly identical to the same steps for adding an EJB control and a Database control. As with those controls, it is through Step 3 that you provide information specific to the control. Ideally, when you create a JMS control, you'll be working with a predefined list of values and simply entering those values in the dialog box.

Note that, with one exception, all the values you specify in Step 3 are also available as properties of the JMS control. In other words, you can edit them after you add the control. The one exception is the message type, which I discuss in "Using message types."

As you can probably tell from the Step 3 options, a JMS control is designed to represent a single JMS queue or topic combination. Methods on the control will send messages to that destination, while the control's callback will receive messages from it. Four of the options in this dialog box are fairly straightforward in that they directly echo aspects of JMS itself. The fifth, Message type, deserves a little more explanation so I describe it separately later in the chapter.

- **JMS destination type:** You can choose Queue or Topic here, depending on the needs of the application. If you choose Queue, the send-jndi-name and receive-jndi-name boxes must contain, when they have values, the JNDI name of JMS queues registered on the server. The same is true for Topic, in which case the contents of send-jndi-name and receive-jndi-name must be the JNDI name of a registered topic.

- **send-jndi-name:** This property specifies the JNDI name of the queue or topic to which the control will be sending messages. You only need a value here if your control will have methods – that is, if it will send messages. Click the Browse button to view a list of the queues or topics (depending on your choice for destination type) available for the server on which you're building the service.

  Needless to say, the value you enter here will depend on aspects of the application. For example, if you're creating a JMS control that will connect to a queue for sending messages in point-to-point messaging, then you need the JNDI name of the queue here. In the point-to-point scenario, this assumes that there is another component listening on that queue, waiting to receive your message.

- **receive-jndi-name:** Specifies the JNDI name of the queue or topic from which the control will receive messages. As you might imagine, you need only put a value here if your control will have a callback handler – that is, if it will receive messages.

  Note that if the send and receive value are the same JNDI name, your Web service will send messages to itself.

- **connection-factory:** The connection factory provides connections to the queue or topic you specified in send-jndi-name and receive-jndi-name. If you click Browse, you should see a list of the connection factories available on the server.

The values you give to these four options provide the control with the information it needs to send and receive messages. If you've previously written code that accesses the JMS API directly, you'll realize that making these settings saves you a bit of trouble for most needs.

I'd like to describe the message type setting in more depth, but first I want to show you what the CTRL file for a JMS control looks like. It begins in a manner similar to other controls, with the package name and import statements needed to support the control.

```
package Chapter08;

import weblogic.jws.control.JMSControl;
import java.io.Serializable;
```

The @jws:jms annotation specifies that this is a JMS control. The annotation's attributes contain values you used when filling out the Add JMS Control dialog box. If you make changes to these in the Property Editor, they will change here as well. The annotations are applied to the control's interface name.

```
/**
 *   @jws:jms type="queue" send-jndi-name="tutorial.credit.request"
 *       receive-jndi-name="tutorial.credit.response"
 *       connection-factory-jndi-name=
 *       "weblogic.jws.jms.QueueConnectionFactory"
 */
public interface CreditScoreControl extends JMSControl
{
```

Because this control was defined using the XML map message type, its default method and callback (`sendMessage` and `receiveMessage`, respectively) are given sample XML maps that you can modify to suit your needs (Listing 8-3).

I describe XML maps as they apply to the JMS control in "Using message types that contain XML" and "Handling headers and properties with XML maps."

Listing 8-3: A JMS Control's Default Method and Callback with XML Maps Applied

```
    /**
     * If you would like to use XML maps to give the body of the
     * outgoing message a specific XML shape, you may define a
     * method in this file and annotate it with an XML map. For
     * example, if you want the payload to look like this:
     *
     * <YourOuterTag>
     *    <SampleParameter1>Param1</SampleParameter1>
     *    <SampleParameter2>Param2</SampleParameter2>
     * </YourOuterTag>
```

Continued

Listing 8-3 *(Continued)*

```
 *
 * Then define a "sendMessage" method as follows:
 *
 * @jws:jms-message xml-map::
 * <YourOuterTag>
 *   <SampleParameter1>{param1}</SampleParameter1>
 *   <SampleParameter2>{param2}</SampleParameter2>
 * </YourOuterTag>
 * ::
 */
public void sendMessage(String param1, String param2);

/*
 * NOTE: if you do not want to use XML map to shape the outgoing
 * message you do not need to define any "publishing" methods
 * here. In your JWS, simply use one of the methods defined in
 * JMSControl. For example, publishText(String)
 */

/**
 * If your control specifies receive-jndi-name, that is your JWS
 * expects to receive messages from this control, you will need
 * to implement callback handlers. There are 2 ways to do this.
 * If the incoming message is in the form of XML, and you would
 * like to use XML maps to extract values from it, you need to
 * define a Callback interface in this file as follows.
 */

interface Callback extends JMSControl.Callback
{
    /**
     * Define only 1 callback method here.
     *
     * For example, if your incoming message looks like
     * <YourOuterTag>
     *   <SampleParameter1>Param1</SampleParameter1>
     *   <SampleParameter2>Param2</SampleParameter2>
     * </YourOuterTag>
     *
     * Then define the method like this:
     *
     * @jws:jms-message xml-map::
     * <YourOuterTag>
     *   <SampleParameter1>{param1}</SampleParameter1>
```

```
 *     <SampleParameter2>{param2}</SampleParameter2>
 *    </YourOuterTag>
 *    ::
 */
    public void receiveMessage(String param1, String param2);
}

/*
 * NOTE: if you do not need to use XML maps to parse the values
 * from the incoming message, then you don't need to define any
 * Callback interface in this file. In this case, in your JWS
 * file, implement a handler for one callback from
 * JMSControl.Callback. You may only implement one handler; this
 * handler will be called for all incoming methods.
 */
}
```

Many of the guidelines offered in the comments of this source code (and other code generated by WebLogic Workshop) describe actions you can take within the code itself. However, remember that you can accomplish most of these actions by editing the *design* of your Web service — by setting properties in the Property Editor, adding XML maps through the Edit Maps and Interface dialog box, adding and removing methods in Design View, and so on.

Using message types

As I mentioned, the Message Type option in the Add JMS Control dialog box deserves a little more attention (Figure 8-7). The message type options offered by the dialog box will result in JMS message types I introduced earlier in this chapter, and all the JMS types are supported by the JMS control. Still, although the Text and Object options seem clear, at first glance it's not particularly easy to understand why there is also a JMS message option (since `TextMessage` and `ObjectMessage` are JMS message types) and what the XML map option is for.

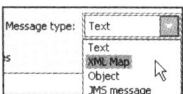

Figure 8-7: Selecting a message type option.

To help make all of this clear, I'll describe message use from two angles. First, I'll describe each of the options presented by the dialog box, along with how they relate to the JMS message types I introduced earlier. Then I'll describe how you might go about using the particular message type your application requires in the particular way that WebLogic Workshop supports it.

UNDERSTANDING THE MESSAGE TYPES EXPOSED BY THE JMS CONTROL

The Message Type box in the Add JMS Control dialog box is designed to provide an easy path to creating JMS message types you might commonly use, such as `TextMessage` and `ObjectMessage`. When you create a JMS control, WebLogic Workshop gives the control one method and one callback, both of which are customizable according to your needs, and you can add new methods if you like. The Message Type option you select dictates what arguments the default method and callback will have. In other words, if you choose Object, the default method and callback will each have an `Object` parameter.

This is the key point to remember about the message type options. The purpose of the options is to collect information needed to add the default method and callback and import types to support them. For example, you can create a new control whose "message type" is Text and receive the default method and callback, each with a single `String` parameter. Left unchanged, the default method will create and send a JMS `TextMessage` when you call it by passing a `String` value. But you can also change the method's parameter type to another type, such as `Object`. If you do, the method will create and send a JMS `ObjectMessage` when you call it by passing a Java object as its argument.

The following summarizes each of the options:

- **Text:** Choose this option when you want to use JMS `TextMessage`. With this type selected, the parameters for the control's default method and callback will be simply a single `String`.

  Benefit: When you specify a single `String` parameter in any JMS control method, the JMS control automatically constructs and sends a JMS `TextMessage`. Also, you can use XML maps to specify properties and headers for outgoing messages, and to handle properties and headers of incoming messages. Both of these conveniences can help to eliminate several lines of JMS code.

- **XML map:** This option is useful when you want to send a JMS `TextMessage` whose payload is structured as XML. The parameters for the default method and callback will be typed as `String`, but you can replace them with other types in keeping with the requirements of the XML. In addition, the default method and callback come with example XML maps that you can modify to suit your needs.

  Benefit: As with the Text option, this option prompts the JMS control to create a JMS `TextMessage` automatically, inserting the XML as the message's payload. XML maps here provide the same sort of benefit as they do other places, translating types in a method declaration into XML without your having to write XML API-related code. As with the Text option, you can use XML maps to specify properties and headers for outgoing messages, and to handle properties and headers of incoming messages.

 Chapter 6 covers XML maps in detail.

Note that the actual message type sent by the default method is a `TextMessage`, not the `XMLMessage` provided by WebLogic Server.

- **Object:** This option is designed for sending and receiving a JMS `ObjectMessage`. The default method and callback will each have a single `Object` parameter.

   Benefit: Like Text and XML map, a method for a control of the Object type creates the message for you and sets the payload as the object you specify. The `ObjectMessage` created is given the control's send method parameter as a payload.

- **JMS message:** Use this option when the control must send and receive any JMS message type other than `TextMessage` or `ObjectMessage`, including `BytesMessage`, `StreamMessage`, `MapMessage`, or other extended message types supported by WebLogic Server, such as `XMLMessage`.

   Benefit: This option is for those cases when the only way to accomplish the task at hand is to go about it in something like the traditional JMS way. To send any JMS message type but `TextMessage` and `ObjectMessage`, you construct the message using the JMS API, then send the message as a Message parameter of the send method. You do not need to change the parameter's type to the specific JMS message type you're sending.

You can probably see now why there is no "message type" property for the JMS control once you add it to your Web service. The meaning of such a property is ambiguous when in many cases you can specify the actual message type simply by changing a method's parameter.

Now that you have an understanding of what the message type options mean, I'll describe how you can approach the task of building messages based on the kind of message you actually want to send or receive.

USING THE JMS TEXTMESSAGE TYPE

The JMS `TextMessage` type is probably the simplest to use through the JMS control. If a `TextMessage` meets your needs, you can easily avoid writing the JMS code typically needed to construct a `TextMessage`, set its payload, and set its properties and headers (if any).

If you're sending a `TextMessage` and need to set the values of its message headers or properties, you can do it with XML maps rather than using the JMS API. The same is true for extracting the properties and headers of a TextMessage your service receives.

For more on using XML maps with TextMessage properties and headers, see "Handling headers and properties with XML maps," later in this chapter.

USING TEXT MESSAGES THAT CONTAIN XML When you need a TextMessage whose payload is structured as XML, you can use an XML map. As you may recall from Chapter 6, XML maps provide a way to translate Java types into an XML structure. They work by using an XML-like syntax that specifies where Java values correspond to parts of an XML structure. As with other methods and callbacks that support XML maps, you can add a map through the Edit Maps and Interface dialog box. To view the dialog box, double-click the arrow corresponding to the JMS method or callback you want to map.

Figure 8-8 shows the Edit Maps and Interface dialog box for a sendMessage method. In it, the method's parameters widgetName and quantity are set as values of the <name> and <total> elements. When this method is called, the XML shown in the top pane will be sent as the payload of the outgoing JMS TextMessage.

Figure 8-8: An XML map on a sendMessage method.

You can apply similar kinds of maps to a JMS control's callback as well. Keep in mind that applying a map to the payload of a callback assumes that the incoming message is a String in the shape of XML — in other words, it has < and > symbols delimiting element names, and so on. When the message arrives, WebLogic Workshop will examine the payload and parse its contents as XML.

In Figure 8-9, a `receiveMessage` map takes the value of the `<response>` element in the incoming message and passes it to the callback as the `orderResponse` parameter.

Figure 8-9: An XML map on a receiveMessage callback handler.

If you've worked with XML in JMS messages before, you should keep in mind that the message type generated when you use an XML map is a JMS `TextMessage`, *not* the `XMLMessage` type provided by WebLogic Server. The similarity in the message type names suggests a connection between the two, but it's merely a coincidence. To use an XML map message's payload as XML, the component receiving the message must parse the text into XML. Of course, if the other component is a WebLogic Workshop Web service, an XML map on its JMS control `receiveMessage` callback handler will do the trick.

USING THE JMS OBJECTMESSAGE TYPE

The JMS `ObjectMessage` type provides a way to set a Java object as a message's payload. The JMS control makes handling this type a little easier by creating and sending an `ObjectMessage` automatically if the method's parameter is a Java object (other than `String` or one of the JMS message types, which result in other types of messages). The object you pass to the method will be used as the message's payload.

At this writing, to set or retrieve property or header values of an `ObjectMessage`, you should use the JMS API to create the message. To send and receive the message, send it with a method whose parameter is a JMS `Message`, and receive it with a callback that has a `Message` parameter. Note that this is pretty much the same as creating a new JMS control by setting the JMS message option in the message type box.

USING THE OTHER JMS MESSAGE TYPES

You use the JMS API to create a `BytesMessage`, `StreamMessage`, or `MapMessage`. Also, as I've mentioned, WebLogic Server provides an `XMLMessage` type that extends `TextMessage`. If your needs require one of these types, you write the JMS code needed to create the message, then pass the message to a JMS control send method that takes a `Message` parameter. Also, you use the JMS API to set and retrieve property and header values.

Details about creating and using each of the JMS message types is an integral part of the JMS API, and beyond the scope of this book. However, the following (Listing 8-4) is an example of how you might create a `MapMessage` to carry widget order values.

Listing 8-4: Create a MapMessage Using the JMS API

```
/*
 * Declare a variable to hold the JNDI name of the
 * queue connection factory through which you will connect
 * to the queue. Note that this value is a property
 * of the JMS control itself. You need it here simply so that
 * you can create the message you will be sending.
 */
public final static String QUEUE_CONNECTION_FACTORY =
    "weblogic.jws.jms.QueueConnectionFactory";

/*
 * Declare an InitialContext instance through which you can
 * create a connection to a queue. The queue will be the destination
 * to which you send the message.
 */
MessageDrivenContext ejbContext;
Context jndiContext;
jndiContext = new InitialContext();
QueueConnectionFactory factory =
(QueueConnectionFactory)jndiContext.lookup
    (QUEUE_CONNECTION_FACTORY);

/*
 * Connect to the queue to create a session through which
 * you can create the message.
 */
QueueConnection connect = factory.createQueueConnection();
QueueSession session = connect.createQueueSession(true, 0);

/* Create the message as a MapMessage. */
MapMessage orderMessage = session.createMapMessage();

/*
 * Give the message an orderNumber property and give the
 * property a value.
 */
```

```
String orderNumber = "123-654-79-6";
orderMessage.setStringProperty("orderNumber", orderNumber);

/* Give the message two values for its payload. */
String widgetName = "Blue Widget";
int quantity = 43;
orderMessage.setString("name", widgetName);
orderMessage.setInt("total", quantity);

/*
 * Send the message using a sendOrderMessage on the
 * JMS control.
 */
orderJMS.sendOrderMessage(orderMessage);
```

The `sendOrderMessage` method would be declared something like this:

```
public void sendOrderMessage(Message msg);
```

JMS code to create other kinds of JMS message types would be similar.

Adding methods to a JMS control

As I've mentioned, the default method and callback provided when you create a JMS control are in a sense just examples. They're a convenient start based on the message type option you selected in the Add JMS Control dialog box. You can delete them, rename them, and add more methods as you like (as shown in Figure 8-10). For example, you might create a control designed to send a particular type of message, but define multiple methods that send the message's data in different forms, with different properties set, and so on.

When adding methods, keep in mind the rules by which the control creates messages. When the message type the method will send is one of the types that the JMS control makes convenient to use, you can design the new method to support the convenience. For example, adding a method that takes a `Date` parameter will result in a JMS `ObjectMessage`. Adding a method that takes a single `String` (or uses XML maps) will result in a `TextMessage`.

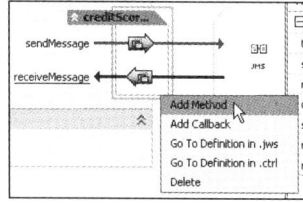

Figure 8-10: Add a method to a JMS control.

While you can add more methods, adding callbacks will yield unpredictable results. This is because WebLogic Workshop has no way of knowing which callback should receive the incoming message. You can rename the callback, and you can delete it if you don't expect the control to receive messages.

Handling headers and properties with XML maps

For the JMS `TextMessage` message type, specified as Text or XML Map message, WebLogic Workshop provides simple access to message header and property values through XML maps. As in working with a message payload in XML shape, you can use maps to indicate how portions of a method or callback declaration correspond to header and property values.

USING XML MAPS WITH TEXTMESSAGE HEADERS

As you may recall from the JMS primer earlier in this chapter, message headers typically store information about a message. JMS itself defines several headers containing information about how the message should be routed, who created it, its expiration time, and so on. Typically the values of these headers are set by the messaging system.

With the `TextMessage` type, you can use XML maps to work with headers. Figure 8-11 illustrates how you might use an XML map to extract the value of a message's JMSExpiration header. JMSExpiration is set by a message's producer, typically to indicate the amount of time after which a message is considered invalid. Set as a number of milliseconds, the expiration time prevents a message from being delivered after a certain amount of time has passed.

In source code, the header XML map and method declaration from Figure 8-12 look like this:

```
/**
 * @jws:jms-header xml-map::
 * <header>
 *    <JMSExpiration>{expireTime}</JMSExpiration>
 * </header>::
 */
public void receivePriceQuote(double quote, long expireTime);
```

In this example, the JMSExpiration header value indicates that the price quote is good only for a certain time.

USING XML MAPS WITH TEXTMESSAGE PROPERTIES

Message properties are like customizable headers. Where headers are typically used by the messaging system, properties are used by developers to include additional information about a message. You can define your own properties depending on what is required for the application. JMS does specify that property values can be only certain types, including `String`, `int`, `boolean`, `byte`, `short`, `long`, `float`, and `double`.

Chapter 8: Using the Advanced Controls   189

Figure 8-11: An XML map to extract the JMSExpiration header value.

With a `TextMessage` (specified with WebLogic Workshop's Text or XML Map message types), you can use XML maps to set and retrieve property values without using the JMS API. In Figure 8-12, the order number for an order message is stored as the value of the `order_id` property.

Figure 8-12: An XML map to set the order_id property value.

In source code, the property XML map and method declaration from Figure 8-12 look like this:

```
/**
 * @jws:jms-property xml-map::
 * <property>
 *    <order_id>{orderNumber}</order_id>
 * </property>::
 */
```

```
public void sendWidgetOrder(String widgetName, int quantity,
                       String orderNumber);
```

You may set properties through XML maps or through the JMS API, but not both. If you specify both, only the values set with an XML map will be used for the actual message.

Correlating received messages

When you have a JMS control that sends a message and expects to receive a related response, the system needs a way to find your service when it's time to deliver the response message. For example, imagine that there are two instances of the same Web service sending widget orders via a JMS control. The order details are different for each, and they each expect to separate confirmations, also via their JMS control. It wouldn't do for the first service to receive the second service's confirmation, and vice versa. To keep things straight, WebLogic Workshop uses unique identifier to correlate messages. This is similar to conversations, where the conversation ID serves to make sure that requests and responses are correctly correlated.

Fortunately, there is automatic support for this. When a JMS control in your service sends a message, WebLogic Workshop inserts your service's conversation ID into the message's JMSCorrelationID header. To make sure that your service receives the properly correlated response, the client at the other end of the exchange returns the same conversation ID in the JMSCorrelationID header of the response message. All of this means that you must keep the following in mind when using a JMS control that sends messages for which it expects to receive a related response:

♦ Your Web service must be conversational. If it isn't, there won't be a conversation ID to use for correlating messages.

♦ The component or application with which your service is exchanging messages must extract the conversation ID from the JMSCorrelationID header in the message your service sends, then put the same value into the message it sends back. Although making this happen is a fairly trivial bit of programming, it is a requirement on the *other* component.

It's possible that the component with which your service is exchanging messages already uses the JMSCorrelationID header for some other purpose. For example, this header is often used to correlate messages using another value, the message's ID. If this is the case, you can specify another message property to contain the conversation ID. Here, too, the other component must extract the conversation ID from the specified message property and insert it into the same property on the message it sends back.

You can tell WebLogic Workshop to use another message property for correlating messages with the conversation ID. You do this by entering the message property's name in the Property Editor, among the properties for the JMS control. Use the `send-correlation-property` attribute to specify the correlation property for the outgoing message; use the `receive-correlation-property` attribute to specify the correlation property that will be in the message returned to your service. Figure 8-13 shows a property called "convID" set for both.

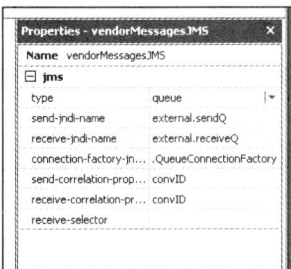

Figure 8-13: A message's convID property used to correlate incoming response messages with outgoing request messages.

All of this must be done in cooperation with the other component's author, of course. Based on this example, the developer of the other component must extract the conversation ID from the convID property in the message received from your service. The message sent back to your service must have a convID property containing the same conversation ID. Different properties may be used for sending and receiving as long as you and the other component's developer are in agreement.

WebLogic Workshop takes care of the rest at your end. You don't need to write JMS code to set or get the correlation property's value.

Filtering messages using the receive-selector property

You can filter incoming messages so that only those with certain property values will actually be received by your Web service. For example, imagine that you've added a JMS control that subscribes to a topic to receive announcements about products offered by other vendors. Knowing in advance that your company will be interested in buying only products of a certain type, you could filter incoming messages to receive only those that are potential buys. Reducing the number of messages your service receives can help to ease network traffic.

In JMS, you filter messages through what are known as *message selectors*. The JMS control exposes this ability through its receive-selector property. The value of the receive-selector property is an expression that evaluates to true or false by examining property or header values in the incoming message. If the expression evaluates to true, then the message is delivered to your service; if the result of the expression is false, your service won't see it. The syntax for the expression itself is based on the rules governing expressions in the `WHERE` clause of a SQL `SELECT` statement.

For example, consider the vendor message scenario I just mentioned and imagine that your company is a hardware chain. You know that incoming messages will be about a particular item that a vendor wants to sell. The message's payload will have details about the item, such as its name, the quantity available, its cost, and so on. The message will also feature a Department property that can contain standard values, such as "Garden," "Heavy Tools," and "Appliances." Your company's stores don't sell appliances, so you filter out messages offering merchandise in that category with a statement such as the following:

```
Department NOT LIKE 'Appliances'
```

In the Property Editor, the value would look like as shown in Figure 8-14:

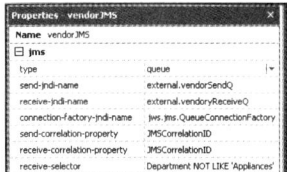

Figure 8-14: The receive-selector property set to filter messages.

This expression would evaluate to true if the Department message property did not contain the value "Appliances," and would not be delivered to your Web service.

Updated Online Store Example

I'd like to pull together a bit of what you've read in this chapter about the EJB and JMS controls. To illustrate, I'll modify the online shopping example introduced in the chapter so that it gets information about items for sale from an EJB, and requests a credit rating from another application via the JMS control.

Remember that the original online store offered just the sort of methods you might expect. Through this service, clients could request a list of the items in the catalog, maintain a shopping cart, and check out when they were finished. Figure 8-15 shows the design for the original service.

As it is pictured in Figure 8-15, OnlineStore stores the list of items that may be purchased by defining an inner class for the items, then setting the values of the items through a catalog variable. The first modification to make is to replace this by getting the list of items from a stateless session bean called Inventory. The EJB will always have the current list of items, even as it's updated.

After putting the client JAR for the inventory EJB into the WEB-INF\lib folder of the project, the control can be added. The EJB control to access the inventory bean is defined as shown in Figure 8-16.

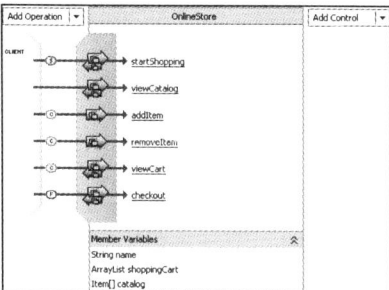

Figure 8-15: The existing OnlineStore Web service design.

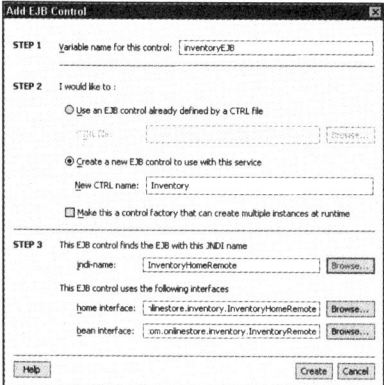

Figure 8-16: Adding an EJB control to access the Inventory bean.

This should look familiar from the EJB control section earlier in this chapter. After picking the EJB's JNDI name from the list of available EJBs, WebLogic Workshop added the home and bean interface names. Clicking Create changes the service's design so that it looks like Figure 8-17.

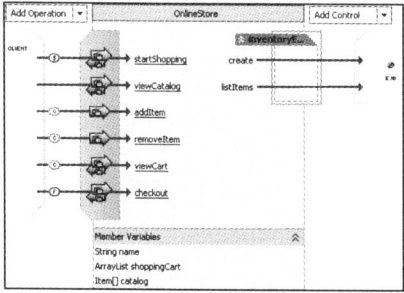

Figure 8-17: The Inventory EJB control included in the design.

Notice that the EJB exposes two methods, `create` and `listItems`. As you may recall, the `create` method is standard for session beans, providing a way to create an instance of the bean on the server when it is needed. It won't be necessary to call this method from the Web service code because WebLogic Workshop takes care of creating the bean. It's the `listItems` method that we're interested in. This method returns an array of `Item` objects. In the new design, the `Item` class is a helper class included in the same package that contains the bean itself; its definition is pretty much the same as the `Item` class defined in the original OnlineStore service. In other words, the class defined in the original service will no longer be needed, so it will eventually be deleted.

Let's add another control while we're at it, and to get all the new components in place before updating the service's code. As I mentioned, another change to OnlineStore will be adding the ability to ensure that shoppers have the right credit to make the purchases in their cart. This feature will be supported by an internal application that is accessible through JMS. We'll make it possible for the Web service to send the total cost of items in the customer's cart to the credit application, then receive a `boolean` response indicating whether the purchase should be allowed.

The new JMS control is defined as in Figure 8-18.

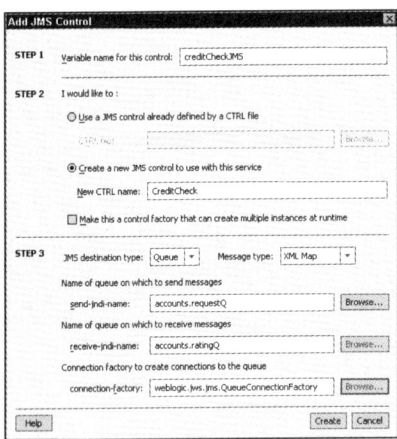

Figure 8-18: Adding a JMS control to access the CreditCheck application.

The CreditCheck JMS control will exchange messages as JMS `TextMessages`. The payload for these messages will be text in the shape of XML. Although the format is defined by the credit application itself, it also illustrates how easy it is to create a TextMessage that contains XML with data from the Web service. All of this means that the control's method and callback will need XML maps that handle message shapes required by the credit application. In addition, we'll use an XML map to send the customer's ID number as a property of the outgoing message (another requirement of the credit application).

Figure 8-19 sums up changes to the send method and the message body.

Figure 8-19: The CreditCheck JMS control's send method
with an XML map applied to compose the message payload.

As you can see from the XML map in the top pane of the dialog box in Figure 8-19, the value of the `getApproval` method's `total` parameter will become the `<purchase_total>` element's value in the outgoing message. In other words, if the parameter's value was 15, the payload of the outgoing `TextMessage` will look something like this:

```
<rating_request>
    <purchase_total>15</purchase_total>
</rating_request>
```

The credit application will extract the value in whatever way it is implemented to do so. For example, it might first convert the message payload to an XML document using an XML DOM API such as Xerces.

Figure 8-20 illustrates how the customer ID will be included as a message property by using the dialog's Property XML tab. The property name is applicantID, and it can be accessed by the message's recipient just as if it had been set using the JMS API. In other words, unlike the message payload, the property XML map you see here does not arrive as text in XML form; this is merely a convenient way to specify a property and set its value.

Finally, notice that we have changed the name of the `send` method to something more intuitive.

The new callback handler will look like Figure 8-21.

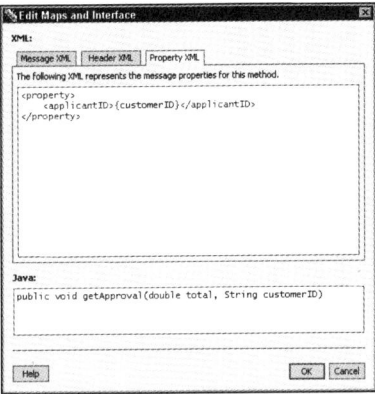

Figure 8-20: A CreditCheck JMS control send method
with an XML map applied to set a property value.

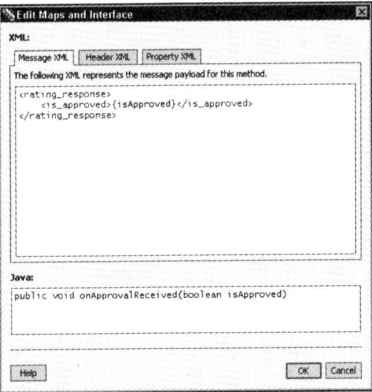

Figure 8-21: A CreditCheck JMS control callback handler
with an XML map applied to extract a value from the message payload.

Here, of course, the XML map is used to translate in the opposite direction – to Java from the message's payload. The `<is_approved>` element's value will be passed to the isApproved callback parameter. In the callback handler's code, we'll test for a true value and respond to the client accordingly. Note that there is no need for you to write XML-oriented code to retrieve a value from the `<is_approved>` element. Simply having an XML map takes care of that for you.

Finally, before we move on to updating the code, we need to make one more design change. We'll add a callback to the design, and through it we'll send back a response based on the outcome of the purchase and credit check. The onPurchaseAppoved callback will notify the client if their purchase request was approved. The new callback's declaration looks like this:

```
public void onPurchaseApproved(String message,
    Item[] itemsPurchased)
```

We'll use the message parameter to send a message that either confirms the success of the purchase or notifies the client of an unsuccessful credit check. If the purchase was successful, we'll send a list of the items they bought. Otherwise, we'll pass `null` in the `itemsPurchased` parameter.

Our final *design* change will be to update OnlineStore's conversation behavior to support the callback we added. In the new design, `startShopping` will still start the conversation, but it will not finish with the checkout method. Instead, the callback's execution will finish the conversation. All other methods will continue it, as shown in Figure 8-22, showing the updated design.

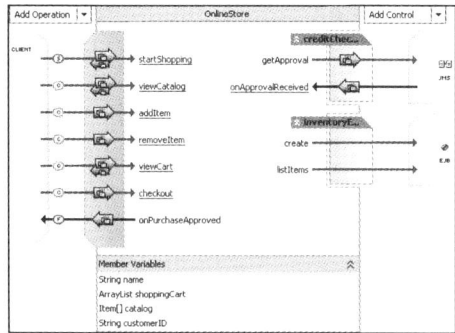

Figure 8-22: The updated OnlineStore design.

Now, on to the code changes. I'll include the code of the newly revised service in its entirety here, then point out the highlights afterward (Listing 8-5).

Listing 8-5: Revised Code for the OnlineStore Web Service

```
package Chapter08;

import weblogic.jws.control.JwsContext;
import java.util.ArrayList;
import com.onlinestore.item.Item;

public class OnlineStore
{

    public Callback callback;

    public interface Callback
    {
        /**
```

Continued

Listing 8-5 *(Continued)*

```
     * @jws:conversation phase="finish"
     */
    public void onPurchaseApproved(String message,
        Item[] itemsPurchased);
}

/**
 * @jws:control
 */
private CreditCheckControl creditCheckJMS;

/**
 * @jws:control
 */
private InventoryControl inventoryEJB;

/** @jws:context */
JwsContext context;

/** The name of the customer. */
private String name;

/* The customer's ID, to be used when requesting
 * credit approval. */
private String customerID;

/* A list of items that represents the shopping
 * cart. */
private ArrayList shoppingCart;

/* A variable to hold the item list received from
 * the inventory bean. */
private Item[] catalog;

/**
 * @jws:operation
 * @jws:conversation phase="start"
 */
public String startShopping(String name, String customerNumber)
{
    customerID       = customerNumber;
    this.name        = name;
    this.shoppingCart = new ArrayList();

    return "Welcome, " + name;
```

```java
    }

    /**
     * @jws:operation
     * @jws:conversation phase="continue"
     */
    public Item[] viewCatalog() throws Exception
    {
        /*
         * Handle RemoteException, which is thrown by EJB methods.
         * If the exception is caught, send it, along with a
         * message, to the client for handling. Also,
         * RemoteRuntimeException must be caught for calls to
         * EJB control methods.
         */
        try{
            /*
             * Retrieve the list of available items from the
             * inventory bean, then assign the list to a member
             * variable.
             */
            catalog = inventoryEJB.listItems();
        } catch (java.rmi.RemoteException re){
            throw new Exception("OnlineStore: There was a " +
            "problem getting the list of items.");
        } catch (weblogic.rmi.extensions.RemoteRuntimeException rre)
        {
            throw new Exception("OnlineStore: There was a " +
            "problem getting the list of items.");
        }
        /* Return the retrieved list to the client. */
        return catalog;
    }

    /**
     * @jws:operation
     * @jws:conversation phase="continue"
     */
    public void addItem(Integer code)
    {
        /*
         * Use the list of items in the catalog to find and add a
         * new item to the shopping cart.
         */
        shoppingCart.add(new Item(
```

Continued

Listing 8-5 *(Continued)*

```
            catalog[code.intValue()].getName(),
            code, catalog[code.intValue()].getPrice())
    );
}

/**
 * @jws:operation
 * @jws:conversation phase="continue"
 */
public void removeItem(int index)
{
    /*
     * Use the list of items in the catalog to find and
     * remove an item from the shopping cart.
     */
    shoppingCart.remove(index);
}

/**
 * @jws:operation
 * @jws:conversation phase="continue"
 */
public Item[] viewCart()
{
    /*
     * Convert the ArrayList that is the shopping cart into
     * an array of Item objects for return to the client.
     */
    return (Item[])shoppingCart.toArray(new Item[0]);
}

/**
 * @jws:operation
 * @jws:conversation phase="continue"
 */
public void checkout()
{
    /* Add the prices of items in the shopping cart. */
    double total = 0.00;

    for (int i = 0; i < shoppingCart.size(); i++) {
        total += (
        (Item)shoppingCart.get(i)).getPrice().doubleValue();
    }
    /*
```

```
     * Send the total price and the customer's ID to the credit
     * application for approval. The response will be received
     * in the JMS control callback.
     */
    creditCheckJMS.getApproval(total, customerID);
}

private void creditCheckJMS_onApprovalReceived(
    boolean isApproved)
{
    /*
     * If the customer's purchase is not approved, respond with
     * a polite message through the onPurchaseApproved callback.
     * Otherwise, respond with a "Thank you" message and the
     * list of items they purchased.
     */
    if (isApproved == false) {
        callback.onPurchaseApproved("We're sorry, but credit " +
        "was declined for your account number: " +
        customerID, null);
    } else {
        callback.onPurchaseApproved("Thanks! Here's a list " +
        "of your purchases.",
            (Item[])shoppingCart.toArray(new Item[0]));
    }
}
}
```

I'll call out the major changes with code. Here is a list of some of the more minor supporting changes:

- We imported the `Item` helper class from the package containing the Inventory EJB.

    `import com.onlinestore.item.Item;`

- WebLogic Workshop inserted code for the callback we added.
- WebLogic Workshop inserted declarations for the new controls.
- We added a variable to hold the customerID value sent by the client.
- We reduced the `catalog` variable to an unitialized array of `Item` objects. This variable will now get its value from a call to the Inventory bean.
- We added a `customerID` parameter to the `startShopping` method to provide a place for client's to submit that information.

The viewCatalog method has changed quite a bit, as you can see. Where it used to simply return an array of Item objects initialized with values from within the service itself, it now gets those values from the Inventory bean via the EJB control. In particular, notice that the code needed to make the actual call to the bean is quite a bit smaller than what would be needed by a typical EJB client. Aside from handling exceptions, that code is really just the line that assigns the listItems return value to the catalog member variable.

As for exceptions, note that two are caught here. The RemoteException is a standard exception thrown by EJBs. The RemoteRuntimeException, on the other hand, is needed to catch any other exceptions thrown by the bean. This particular bean doesn't throw any, but if it did you would have access to that exception nested within RemoteRuntimeException. I have put the code here as a reminder (Listing 8-6). (Of course, the way you handle exceptions depends on the sort of client you expect to have. The messages here are simple for the purposes of this illustration.)

Listing 8-6: The viewCatalog Method Updated to Use the Inventory Bean

```
/**
 * @jws:operation
 * @jws:conversation phase="continue"
 */
public Item[] viewCatalog() throws Exception
{
    /*
     * Handle RemoteException, which is thrown by EJB methods.
     * If the exception is caught, send it, along with a
     * message, to the client for handling. Also,
     * RemoteRuntimeException must be caught for calls to
     * EJB control methods.
     */
    try{
        /*
         * Retrieve the list of available items from the
         * inventory bean, then assign the list to a member
         * variable.
         */
        catalog = inventoryEJB.listItems();
    } catch (java.rmi.RemoteException re){
        throw new Exception("OnlineStore: There was a " +
        "problem getting the list of items.");
    } catch (weblogic.rmi.extensions.RemoteRuntimeException rre)
    {
        throw new Exception("OnlineStore: There was a " +
        "problem getting the list of items.");
    }
    /* Return the retrieved list to the client. */
```

Chapter 8: Using the Advanced Controls   203

```
        return catalog;
    }
```

Methods that handle Item members — such as add and remove — have been updated to account for the fact that the new Item class uses primitive wrapper types.

The new checkout method has changed a bit, too. Now, instead of simply returning a total, it first passes the purchase information to the credit application through the JMS control. The returned message will arrive via the control's callback handler (Listing 8-7).

Listing 8-7: The Checkout Method Updated to Use the Credit Application

```
    /**
     * @jws:operation
     * @jws:conversation phase="continue"
     */
    public void checkout()
    {
        /* Add the prices of items in the shopping cart. */
        double total = 0.00;

        for (int i = 0; i < shoppingCart.size(); i++) {
            total += (
            (Item)shoppingCart.get(i)).getPrice().doubleValue();
        }
        /*
         * Send the total price and the customer's ID to the credit
         * application for approval. The response will be received
         * in the JMS control callback.
         */
        creditCheckJMS.getApproval(total, customerID);
    }
```

For the last change, we use the CreditCheck JMS control's callback handler to return an appropriate response based on whether the customer's credit checked out (Listing 8-8).

Listing 8-8: The CreditCheck JMS Control's Callback Handler

```
    private void creditCheckJMS_onApprovalReceived(
        boolean isApproved)
    {
        /*
         * If the customer's purchase is not approved, respond with
         * a polite message through the onPurchaseApproved callback.
         * Otherwise, respond with a "Thank you" message and the
         * list of items they purchased.
```

Continued

Listing 8-8 (Continued)

```
        */
        if (isApproved == false) {
            callback.onPurchaseApproved("We're sorry, but credit " +
            "was declined for your account number: " +
            customerID, null);
        } else {
            callback.onPurchaseApproved("Thanks! Here's a list " +
            "of your purchases.",
                (Item[])shoppingCart.toArray(new Item[0]));
        }
    }
```

Using Control Factories

Finally, I want to tell you a little bit about that Control Factory check box you've been passing over in the various Add Control dialog boxes (Figure 8-23). WebLogic Workshop provides a way for you to use multiple instances of the same control. Through control factories, you can add a control to your Web service, then create multiple instances of it and have them run all at the same time. For example, imagine you were building a Web service that processes internal purchase orders for office supplies. It's designed to receive large orders for (potentially) several departments at once, and to keep each set of items separate by department as it requests the supplies from an office supply vendor.

To do this, your Web service might have a Service control that communicates with the office supply vendor. The service submits each department's request separately using the Service control, and responds separately when the responses arrive. For each department's set of items, your code creates a new instance of the same Service control and submits the request.

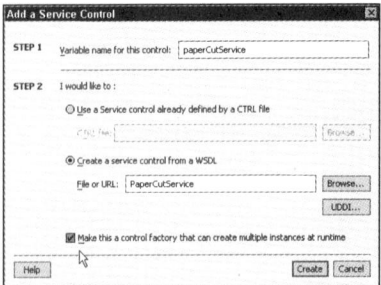

Figure 8-23: A Service control created as a control factory.

Chapter 8: Using the Advanced Controls

The office supply vendor in this case is Paper Cut Office Supplies. The following example is code from a Web service designed to handle this sort of scenario. In the example, look for the Paper Cut Web service Service control variable. The variable, `paperCutService`, is declared with a type whose name ends with "Factory." This is WebLogic Workshop's shorthand for indicating that the control should be used as a control factory.

Other variables declared in this service support using the control as a factory by providing counters (`m_numOrders`) to keep track of how many control instances the service creates, and of the instances themselves (`serviceMap`) (Listing 8-9).

Listing 8-9: Declaring Variables to Support a Control Factory

```
package purchasing;

import weblogic.jws.control.JwsContext;
import java.util.*;

/**
 * @jws:protocol http-xml="false"
 */
public class supplyDepot
{
    /**
     * @jws:control
     */
    private paperCutOfficeSuppliesControlFactory paperCutService;

    public int m_numOrders;
    public int m_numConfirmed;
    HashMap serviceMap = new HashMap();
    ArrayList confirmedOrders = new ArrayList();

    public static class Order implements java.io.Serializable{
        public Order(){}
        public String widgetName;
        public int quantity;
        public String poNumber;
    }

    public Callback callback;
```

Declare a callback that returns the number of orders received and confirmed by Paper Cut Office Supplies.

```
    public interface Callback
    {
        /**
```

```
 * @jws:conversation phase="finish"
 */
public void respond(ArrayList confirmedOrders);
}

/** @jws:context */
JwsContext context;
```

The following code for the service's request method illustrates how you might create a new instance for each purchase order the service receives. In particular, notice that a new instance of paperCutOfficeSuppliesControl is created using the control's create method, which is available for control factories. The method then uses the HashMap declared earlier to store the instance along with the purchase order number received with the order itself. This pairs the two — the control instance and the purchase order number — so that as each order response is received, the corresponding purchase order can be identified and stored for response back to the client (Listing 8-10).

Listing 8-10: A Method That Creates New Instances of a Service Control from a Control Factory

```
/**
 * @jws:operation
 * @jws:conversation phase="start"
 */
public void request(Order[] orders)
{
    for (int i = 0; i < orders.length; i++){
        m_numOrders++;

        /*
         * Create a new instance of the control for each
         * purchase order received.
         */
        paperCutOfficeSuppliesControl thisPaperCut =
            paperCutService.create();
        /*
         * Pair the new control instance with the PO number
         * it contains.
         */
        serviceMap.put(thisPaperCut, orders[i].poNumber);

        /* Use the new instance to request widgets. */
        thisPaperCut.requestGoods(orders[i].widgetName,
            orders[i].quantity);
    }
}
```

Even though several Service control instances are created, only one callback is needed to handle their responses because the callback itself provides a place for WebLogic Workshop to specify which control instance is calling back. In this way, the callback handler code in Listing 8-11 differs a little from handlers you may have seen so far: its parameter list includes the control instance itself. This is how control factories enable you to use a single handler for multiple instances. You can use the instance returned in the callback (in the paperCutService parameter below, for instance) to find out which control instance is calling back.

Remember that earlier code associated each control instance created with the purchase order number through a HashMap called serviceMap. The following code extracts the purchase order number associated with the incoming control instance. It then adds the number to the ArrayList that will be returned to the client. Finally, each time this callback handler executes (that is, for each control instance), the code compares the number of instances with the number of times the control callback has executed. When they are the same, the respond callback sends the confirmed purchase order numbers back to the client.

Listing 8-11: A Conversational Web Service

```
private void paperCutService_confirmOrder(
    paperCutOfficeSuppliesControl paperCutService, int quantity)
{
    /* Increment the number of orders that have returned. */
    m_numConfirmed++;
    /*
     * Extract the PO number for the order instance that has
     * been returned. Add the number to an array containing
     * all that have been returned.
     */
    String poReturned = (String)serviceMap.get(paperCutService);
    confirmedOrders.add(poReturned);

    /*
     * When the number of returned orders equals the number of
     * requests submitted, return the response to the client.
     */
    if (m_numOrders == m_numConfirmed){
        callback.respond(confirmedOrders);
    }
}
}
```

Summary

WebLogic Workshop simplifies one of the most difficult tasks for developers working with server-side Java: accessing J2EE technologies such as Enterprise Java Beans and the Java Message Service. The EJB and JMS controls provide access to these components while at the same time remaining consistent with other WebLogic Workshop controls.

- Applications built on J2EE are built largely of Enterprise JavaBeans (EJBs) that model the application by representing its abstractions as components.

- The EJB control provides access to two different kinds of Enterprise JavaBeans: entity and session beans. The JMS control provides access to a third kind of bean: message-driven beans.

- The EJB control simplifies access to entity and session beans by exposing a bean's interface while removing the need to write traditional J2EE client-side code.

- Components use the Java Message Service (JMS) to communicate asynchronously through intermediate message destinations such as queues and topics.

- JMS supports several message types to choose from, depending on the data that will be exchanged.

- By automatically creating JMS messages based on parameter values, and through a user interface that provides declarative access to properties and headers, the JMS control eases the work of accessing components via the Java Message Service.

- For its Text and XML Map message types, WebLogic Workshop makes setting and retrieving property and header values more convenient through XML maps.

- You can use a control factory to create multiple instances of the same control.

Chapter 9

Controlling the Web Service Protocols

IN THIS CHAPTER

- Understanding the format of messages exchanged between a Web service and its client
- Using the Test View to watch these messages
- Controlling the Web service protocols over which these messages are exchanged
- Controlling the SOAP headers

Web services built using WebLogic Workshop can send and receive data using different protocols and message formats. WebLogic Workshop currently supports two protocols: Hypertext Transport Protocol (HTTP) and Java Messaging Service (JMS). In this chapter, I'll show you how to control these protocols. I'll also use the Test View to monitor the messages that are sent and received by the Web service.

What Goes Down the Wire

If a client needs to invoke a method on a Web service, it has to send a message to the Web service. This message can be sent using a protocol. A protocol is a set of rules that govern the way in which different systems can communicate with each other. In this chapter, we shall discuss a couple of these protocols and how messages can be sent over them to invoke a Web service.

Invoking a Web service using HTTP

The most common protocol over which Web services can be invoked is the Hypertext Transport Protocol (HTTP). Web clients and web servers use this protocol to communicate with each other. I'll discuss JMS, the other protocol supported by Web services, later, in the section "Invoking a Web service using JMS."

HTTP is a useful protocol for Web services that require synchronous, two-way communication. Typically, Web clients invoke a Web service by sending an HTTP request. The Web service sends an HTTP response in return. But the HTTP response that is sent back by the Web service is not necessarily an HTML page; instead it is typically an XML message. Similarly, the HTTP request that was originally sent by the client can include an XML message as well.

So, if the Web service and its client are exchanging XML messages, they could come to an agreement as to the XML message structure. This means that every Web service-client pair would have its own protocol, which would lead to probably zillions of such message structures or protocols. Simple Object Access Protocol (SOAP) standardizes this XML message structure. It provides a framework for XML messaging and allows methods to be invoked over HTTP.

The HTTP request consists of an HTTP header and an HTTP body. To send a SOAP message, you should specify a specific HTTP header called SOAPAction that indicates the Web service method being called. The following is a sample SOAP HTTP header:

```
POST /someApp HTTP/1.1
Host: www.something.com
SOAPAction: someWebService#someMethod
Content-Type: text/xml
Content-Length: xyz
```

This HTTP header indicates that a method named someMethod (from the Web service represented by the urn:foo-com:MyWebService namespace) should be invoked against the URI identified by http://www.something.com/someApp.

The HTTP body of a SOAP method request is an XML document that contains the information needed to invoke the request. SOAP's messaging framework allows SOAP messages to be composed of an outer envelope that can contain a header and a body. The header portion of the message holds metadata about the message and the body contains the actual request. Figure 9-1 illustrates this.

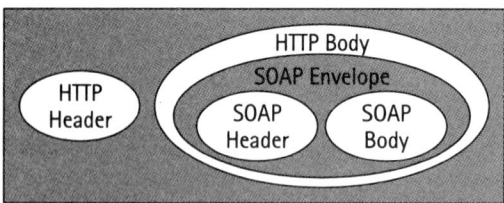

Figure 9-1: SOAP message over HTTP.

The following is a sample of a SOAP message:

```
<SOAP-ENV:Envelope xmlns:SOAP-
ENC="http://schemas.xmlsoap.org/soap/encoding/">
    <SOAP-ENV:Header>
```

```
    <-- Headers go here -->

  </SOAP-ENV:Header>
  <SOAP-ENV:Body>

    <-- Request goes here -->

  </SOAP-ENV:Body>
</SOAP-ENV:Envelope>
```

Now that you've seen the composition of an HTTP request that invokes a method on a Web service, let's take an example and see the structure of the SOAP message.

Let's assume that there is a Web service, which takes a dollar amount as input and gives the corresponding euro value. The HTTP payload of the request would look something like this:

HTTP Request Header:

```
POST /financialApplications HTTP/1.1
Host: www.mybank.com
SOAPAction: CurrencyService#convertfromDollarToEuro
Content-Type: text/xml
Content-Length: 617
```

HTTP Request Body:

```
<?xml version='1.0'?>
<SOAP-ENV:Envelope xmlns:SOAP-
ENC="http://schemas.xmlsoap.org/soap/encoding/">
  <SOAP-ENV:Body>
    <convertfromDollarToEuro xmlns="CurrencyService">
      <dollaramount>100</dollaramount>
    </convertfromDollarToEuro>
  </SOAP-ENV:Body>
</SOAP-ENV:Envelope>
```

The root element of the `SOAP-ENV:Body` element matches the `SOAPAction` HTTP header. This is to allow the HTTP-based infrastructure (proxies, firewalls, web server software) to process the call without parsing XML, while also allowing the XML payload to stand independent of the surrounding HTTP message.

Upon receiving this request, the `convertDollarToEuro` method of the Web service is executed. An HTTP response message will then be returned to the client containing the results of the execution. There are no SOAP-specific HTTP response headers. However, the HTTP body will contain an XML document that contains the results of the Web service method execution. Here's a sample response message:

HTTP Response Header:

```
200 OK
Content-Type: text/xml
Content-Length: xyz
```

HTTP Response Header:

```
<?xml version='1.0'?>
<SOAP-ENV:Envelope xmlns:SOAP-
ENC="http://schemas.xmlsoap.org/soap/encoding/">
   <SOAP-ENV:Body>
      <convertDollarToEuroResponse xmlns="CurrencyService">
         <convertDollarToEuroResult>89.32</convertDollarToEuroResult>
      </convertCurrencyResponse>
   </SOAP-ENV:Body>
</SOAP-ENV:Envelope>
```

As you've already seen, WebLogic Workshop provides a Test Environment for the Web services you develop and deploy using WebLogic Workshop on a WebLogic Server. This environment is called the Test View, which is a browser-based application. The Test View provides a way for you to see these messages that are passed to and from a Web service and its client.

The Test View also maintains a log of all the activity that takes place between the Web service and its client, so that you can see the details of an interaction between a Web service and a client at any point. For example, consider a conversation going on between a Web service and its client. Let's assume that this conversation spans multiple calls (method invocations by the client on the Web service). The Test View logs all this activity. So, if you're interested, let's say, in the details of a particular step at any point in time after execution, you can see this information in the Test View.

Let's now make use of this Test View to watch the messages that flow between the Web service and its client. Figure 9-2 depicts a simple Web service named currencyService. As you can see, it has a single method called convert DollarToEuro.

Let's start the Test View by clicking the Start button, shown by the green arrow on the top menu. Figure 9-3 shows the resulting Test View.

Chapter 9: Controlling the Web Service Protocols 213

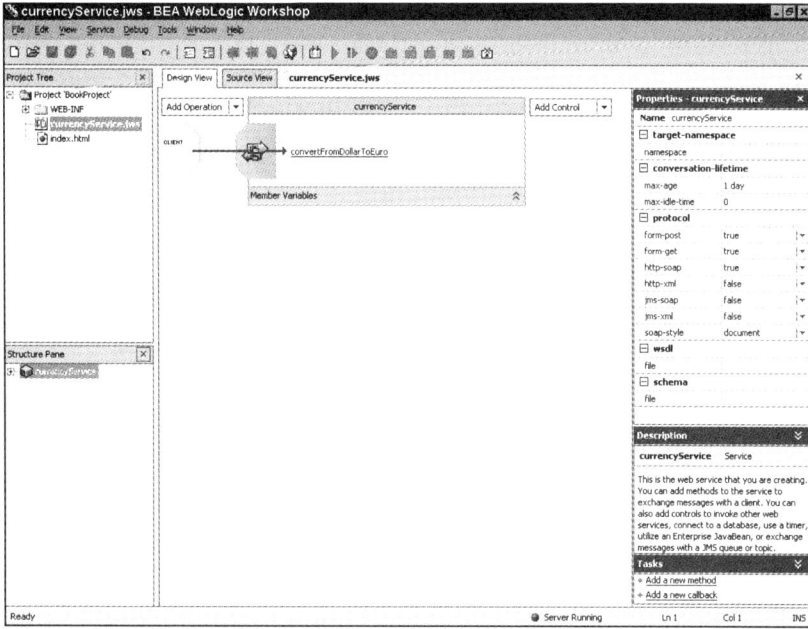

Figure 9-2: The currencyService Web service.

Figure 9-3: Test View for currencyService.

Part III: Advanced Concepts

On the left-hand side, you can see a Message Log, which is currently empty. The Message Log is where a separate entry is listed for every test call that the client makes on a Web service method. As you've already seen, the Test Form page provides a way by which you can test the Web service method by passing values. So, enter a value for the `dollarAmount` and click on the convertFromDollarToEuro button. A summary of the messages exchanged by the Web service and the client is then displayed, as shown in Figure 9-4.

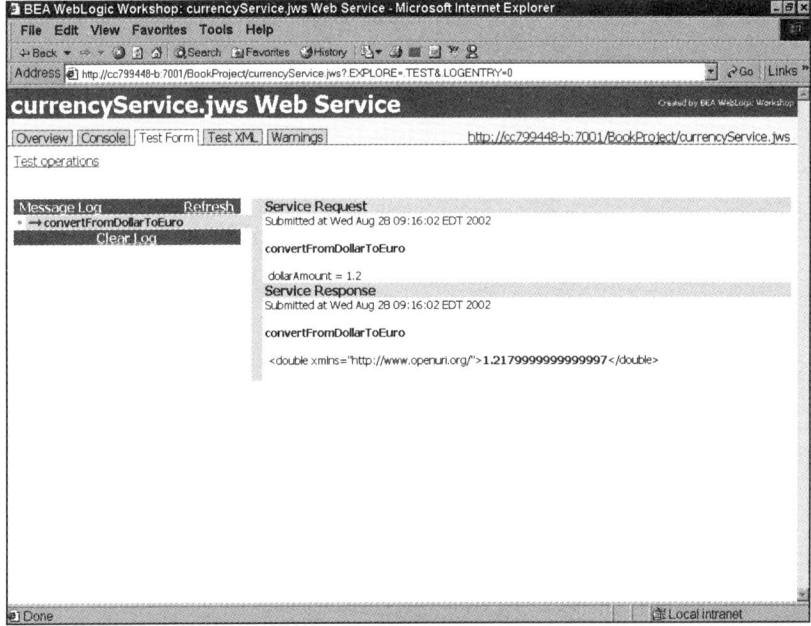

Figure 9-4: Summary of the test.

Under the Message Log area, you can see that there is a new entry, which corresponds to the test that you executed now. If you're interested in a more detailed message, then click on the Test XML tab to see the sample SOAP message that would be sent by the client to the Web service in the HTTP payload. Figure 9-5 shows this XML message.

Now, let's specify a value of 100 in place of `Value_dollarAmount` and then click on the convertFromDollarToEuro button. The resulting HTTP response sent by the Web service to the client is as shown in Figure 9-6.

Chapter 9: Controlling the Web Service Protocols   215

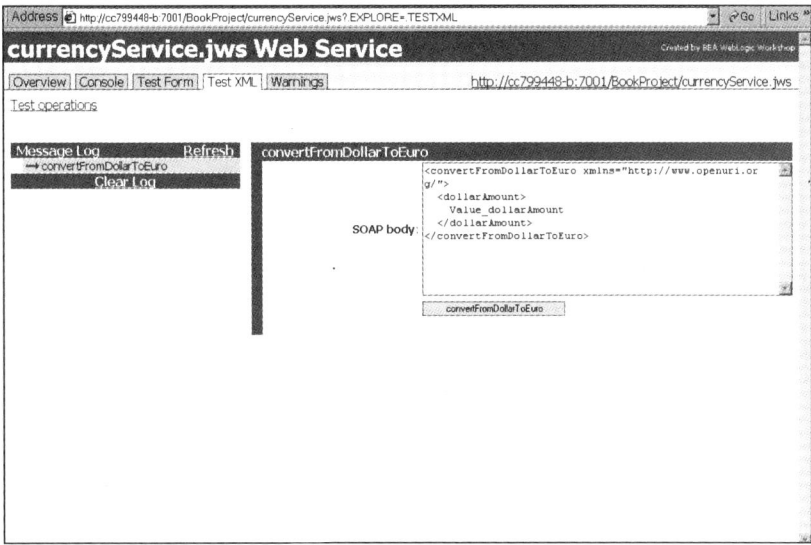

Figure 9-5: The sample XML message.

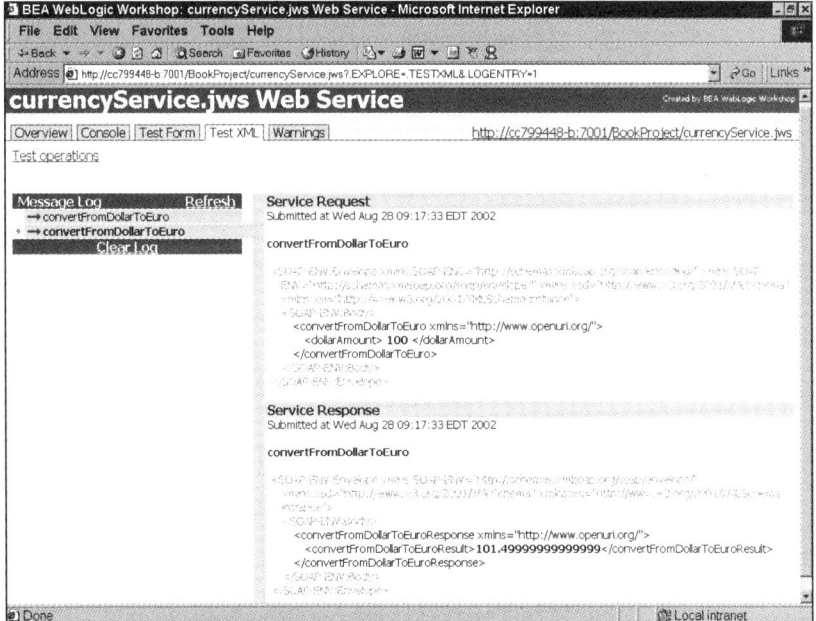

Figure 9-6: The resulting XML message.

Note that on the left-hand side Message Log, we have a new entry, which corresponds to the messages that were exchanged in this Test for a dollarAmount of 100. You can click on either entry to go back and forth between the summary pages for every single test that you perform against this Web service.

Let me now show you how to use the Test View to monitor messages that are sent back and forth in a Conversation. Let's add a new method called getExpenditureForQuarter to our Web service. When a client calls this method, assume that this method does some background processing (say, it calls a control as explained in Chapter 8) to get the quarterly expenditure for a particular company. The background processing could take a while. So, let's add a callback method called onExpenseReportDone, which the Web service will execute after finishing the background processing. As you may expect, there would be a small time delay between these calls. Figure 9-7 shows you this Web service with the new methods.

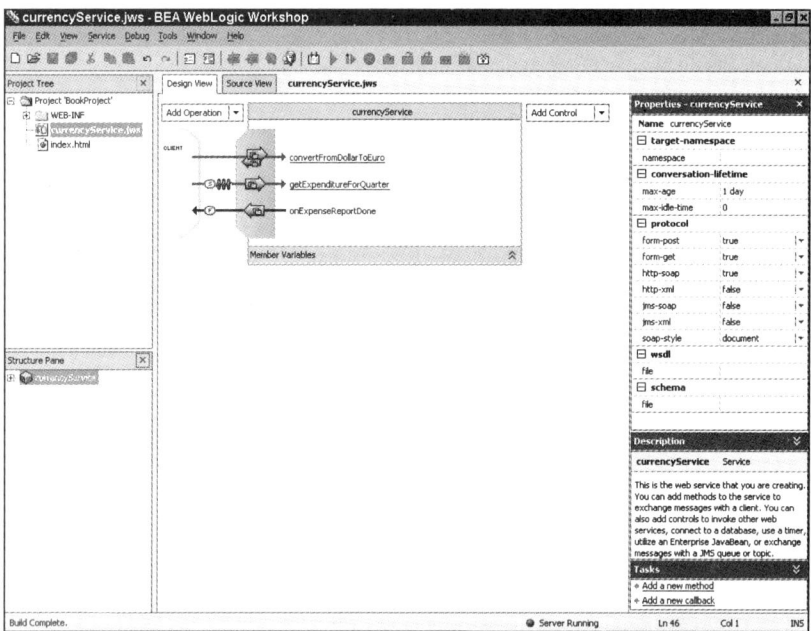

Figure 9-7: A Web service with new method.

Let's bring up the Test View as shown in Figure 9-8. As you can see, there is a new Test Form for the getExpenditureForQuarter method. Click on the Test XML tab and enter a value of 1 for the quarter in the SOAP body of the getExpenditureForQuarter method. Click on the button to start the conversation.

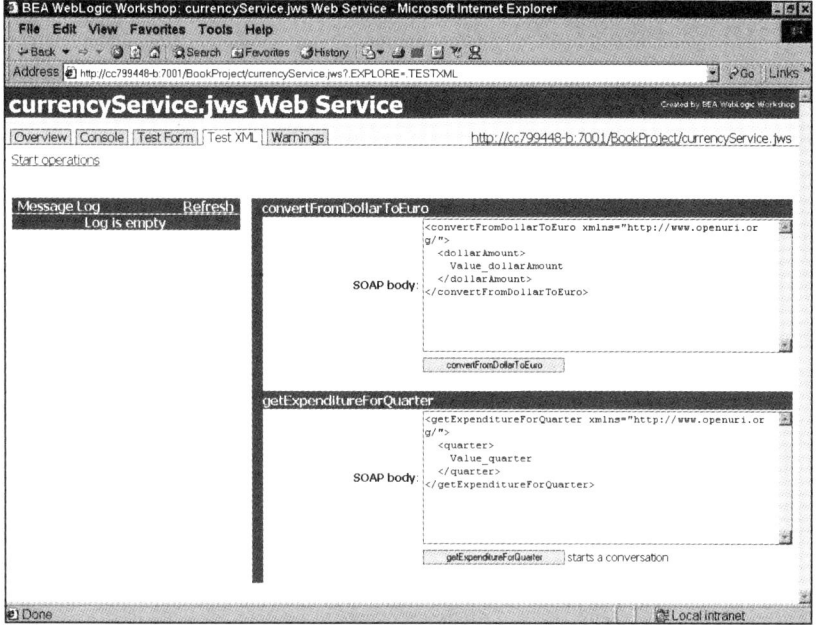

Figure 9-8: The XML message in the Test View.

Watch the Message Log area for new messages. As you can see, there is a new message with a conversation Id. Refresh the Message Logs and you can see that there is a new callback message from the Web service and that the conversation has finished. Figure 9-9 shows this.

Note that the messages that you saw for the earlier tests are also shown. You can click on any of the messages to see the corresponding details.

Invoking a Web service using JMS

In the previous section, you saw how to invoke a Web service over the HTTP protocol. Although HTTP protocol is useful for invoking Web services, which require synchronous two-way communication, it doesn't have enough features to support asynchronous messaging. Asynchronous messaging provides a lot of advantages to systems as described in Chapter 5. Some of them include the following:

♦ Clients can continue processing other tasks while waiting for a call to return.

♦ Clients can send messages to systems that are not active at that time.

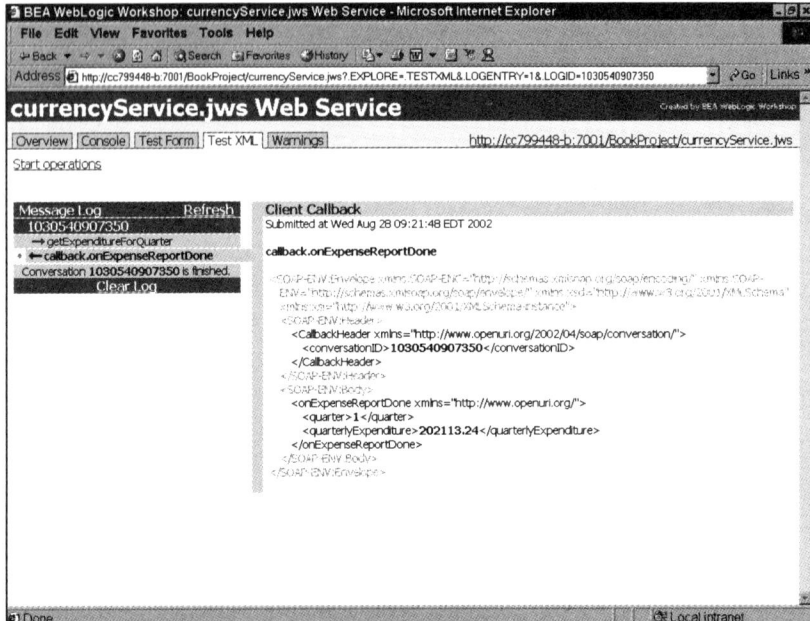

Figure 9-9: The Message Log area in the Test View.

This is where Java Message Service (JMS) comes into the picture. JMS is a messaging protocol that is defined by the Java 2 Enterprise Edition (J2EE) standard. It is a specification for passing messages and related operations among distributed systems in a reliable manner. There are three elements involved in a JMS system:

- Message Sender
- Message-Oriented Middleware (MOM) Server
- Message Receiver

JMS provides a set of APIs to help write a Java client that can send messages to the MOM server. These clients are the message sender and the message receiver. The messages are JMS messages as defined by the JMS specification. A JMS message is composed of three main sections:

- JMS Header
- Properties
- Body

Every JMS message must contain ten JMS headers, which are standard name-value pairs. Table 9-1 illustrates these ten headers.

TABLE 9-1 THE JMS HEADERS

HeadingJMS Header	Description
JMSDestination	Destination to which message is being sent.
JMSDeliveryMode	Delivery mode for the message. It could be either Persistent or Non-persistent.
JMSMessageID	Unique identifier for the message.
JMSTimeStamp	Time when a message was handed over to the server.
JMSExpiration	Sum of time to live and the current GMT.
JMSPriority	Priority of the Message. It can have a value between 0 (lowest) and 9 (highest).
JMSCorrelationID	Identifier used to correlate one message with another. For example, a response with a request.
JMSReplyTo	Destination where a reply to the message should be sent.
JMSType	Identifier that references a message definition stored on the server.
JMSRedelivered	Indicates that the message was probably delivered to the client earlier, for which the client did not acknowledge.

The properties section of a JMS message is optional. It is also a set of name-value pairs, which could be specific to an application, standard, or vendor.

The body of the JMS message holds the actual message that has to be sent. The JMS specification defines five different message types, as discussed in Chapter 8.

Now, that I have introduced you to the concept of JMS, let me show you how to write a simple JMS client. This involves the following steps:

1. Use JNDI to get the JMS `ConnectionFactory` object.

2. Use the `ConnectionFactory` object to create a JMS connection.

3. Use the connection to create one or more session objects.

4. Use JNDI to get a destination (queue or topic).

5. Use the session and the destination to create a `MessageProducer` or a `MessageConsumer`.

6. Use the `MessageProducer` to send JMS messages or the `MessageConsumer` to receive JMS messages.

Listing 9-1 illustrates this. In this example, I show you how to write a simple JMS client that sends a JMS TextMessage to a queue called BookProjectQueue on the Weblogic Server running on the localhost and listening on port 7001.

Listing 9-1: SendXMLMessage.java

```java
package BookProject.Chapter9;

import javax.naming.Context;
import javax.naming.InitialContext;
import javax.naming.NamingException;
import java.util.Hashtable;
import javax.jms.*;

public class SendXMLMessage
{
    private static String QUEUE_NAME = "BookProjectQueue";
    private QueueConnection qc = null;
    private QueueConnectionFactory qcf = null;
    private Queue q = null;
    private QueueSession qs = null;
    private QueueSender qsen = null;

    private static InitialContext ctx = null;

    public SendXMLMessage()
    {
        try
        {
            Hashtable env = new Hashtable();
            env.put(Context.INITIAL_CONTEXT_FACTORY,
                        "weblogic.jndi.WLInitialContextFactory");
            env.put(Context.PROVIDER_URL, "t3://localhost:7001");
            env.put(Context.SECURITY_PRINCIPAL,
                                        "installadministrator");
            env.put(Context.SECURITY_CREDENTIALS,
                                        "installadministrator");
            ctx = new InitialContext(env);

            // lookup the QueueConnectionFactory
            qcf = (QueueConnectionFactory)
                    ctx.lookup("javax.jms.QueueConnectionFactory");

            // create a QueueConnection
            qc = qcf.createQueueConnection();
```

```java
            // start the Connection
            qc.start();

            // create a QueueSession
            qs = qc.createQueueSession(false, 1);

            // lookup the Queue
            q = (Queue) ctx.lookup(QUEUE_NAME);

            // create a QueueSender
            qsen = qs.createSender(q);

            // create a JMS message
            TextMessage tm = qs.createTextMessage();
            tm.setText("Hello JMS World");

            //send the JMS message
            qsen.send(tm);
        }
        catch (NamingException ne)
        {
            ne.printStackTrace();
        }
        catch (JMSException je)
        {
            je.printStackTrace();
        }
    }

    public static void main(String[] args)
    {
        SendXMLMessage msg = new SendXMLMessage();
    }
}
```

Now, let's make this JMS client invoke a Web service. For this, we need to send a SOAP message through a JMS TextMessage as shown in Figure 9-10.

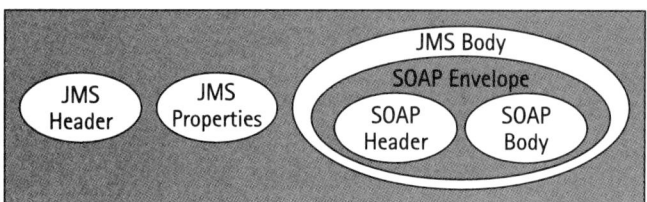

Figure 9-10: SOAP message over JMS TextMessage.

First, let's create a new method called doSomething on the Web service. This is as shown in Figure 9-11. A Web service method that is invoked over JMS should not have a return value, because it's asynchronous.

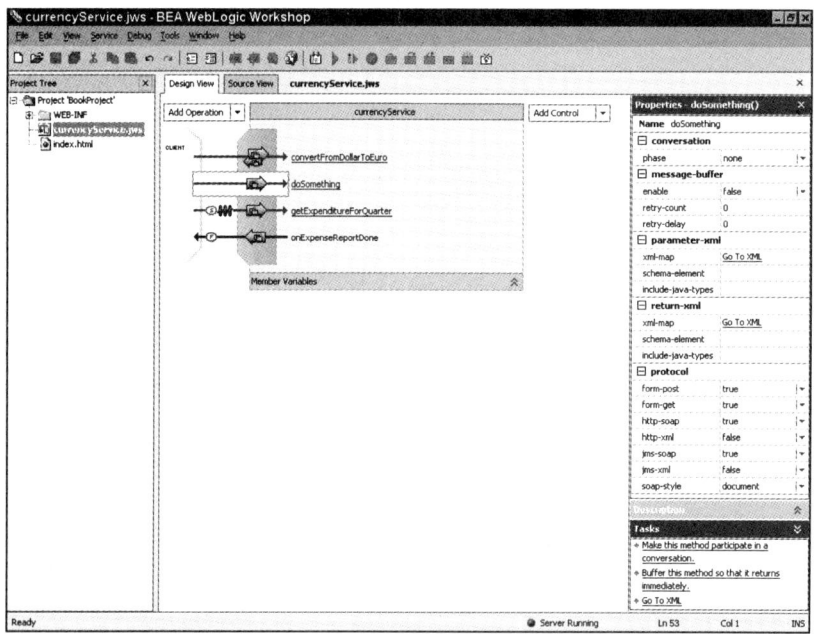

Figure 9-11: The doSomething method in the Web service.

The message should then be sent to the queue with the JNDI name as jws.queue.

```
private static String QUEUE_NAME = "jws.queue";
```

Next, specify a String Property called URI, which has a value that corresponds to the name of the Web service. In our example, we invoked the Web service with the following URL:

Chapter 9: Controlling the Web Service Protocols   223

```
http://localhost:7001/BookProject/currencyService.jws
```

So, the URI will have a value of `BookProject/currencyService.jws`. So, the code would look like this:

```
TextMessage tm = qs.createTextMessage();
tm.setStringProperty("URI", "BookProject/currencyService.jws");
```

Then, let's add the SOAP message to the body of the JMS TextMessage:

```
String soapXMLMessage = "<SOAP-ENV:Envelope xmlns:SOAP-
ENC=\"http://schemas.xmlsoap.org/soap/encoding/\" xmlns:SOAP-
ENV=\"http://schemas.xmlsoap.org/soap/envelope/\"
xmlns:xsd=\"http://www.w3.org/2001/XMLSchema\"
xmlns:xsi=\"http://www.w3.org/2001/XMLSchema-instance\">
<SOAP-ENV:Body> <doSomething
xmlns=\"http://www.openuri.org/\"> </doSomething>        </SOAP-
ENV:Body> </SOAP-ENV:Envelope>";
tm.setText(soapXMLMessage);
```

When enclosing a double quote (") inside a String, make sure you escape it with a back slash (\ ). This is because in Java double quotes are used as delimiters for a String. For example, if you want to assign: He said "Hello" to a String, it would look like this: `String str = "He said \"Hello\"";`

In this example, note that the JMS client is invoking the `doSomething` method.
Finally, make sure that the Web service method supports the jms-soap protocol. I'll discuss more about this and other message formats in the next section. You're now ready to run the JMS client. So, compile the SendXMLMessage.java file and execute it as follows:

```
java BookProject.Chapter9.SendXMLMessage
```

This will invoke the `doSomething` method on the Web service. Let's check the Message Log area and see if we have any new messages. Figure 9-12 illustrates this.

224 Part III: Advanced Concepts

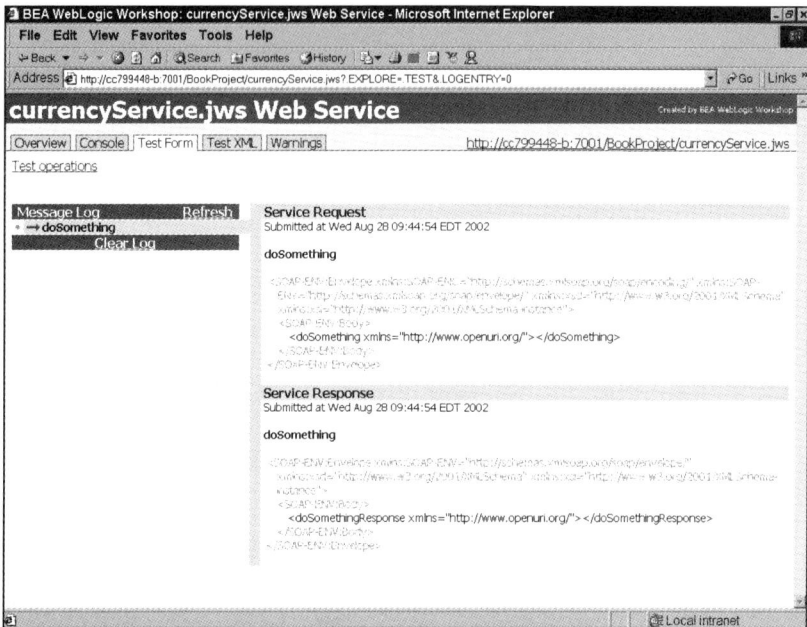

Figure 9-12: Message Log area in the Test View.

Understanding the Message Formats

In the previous section, I showed you how messages were exchanged between a Web service and a client. The messages could be in different formats. For example, they could be either SOAP messages or raw XML messages. In fact, these messages could be sent over HTTP or JMS. Now, I'll show you how to control the format for these messages. This can be done either for the Web service or for every single method in the Web service.

The property window on the right-hand side lets you choose the appropriate message format, as shown in Figure 9-13.

In the Design View, choose the Web service or method for which you want to set the message format. Then, on the right-hand side, expand the protocol property and set the appropriate attributes. You can set six different message formats:

- ◆ `form-post:` If this attribute is set to true, then the Web service is capable of receiving data from a client in an HTTP-POST request. Data is sent as name-value pairs in the body of the HTTP request. In this case the MIME type is set to "application/x-url-formencoded." This attribute is set to true by default. No SOAP headers are sent with form-post.

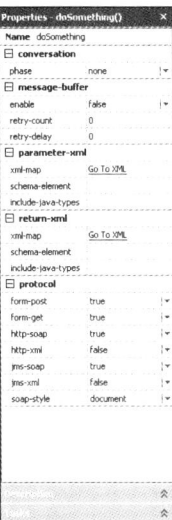

Figure 9-13: Property window
to set message formats.

- `form-get`: If this attribute is set to true, then the Web service is capable of receiving data from a client in an HTTP-GET request. Data is sent as name-value pairs in the URL of the HTTP request. This attribute is set to true by default. No SOAP headers are sent with form-post.

- `http-soap`: If this attribute is set to true, then the Web service is capable of receiving messages that are SOAP-formatted and delivered over HTTP. This is the most common protocol and message format for Web services. If this attribute is set to true, you can also specify the soap-style. This attribute is set to true by default.

- `http-xml`: If this attribute is set to true, then the Web service is capable of receiving messages as raw XML over HTTP without any SOAP Headers. The XML message is sent over an HTTP POST. The MIME type in this case is set to "text/xml." This attribute is set to false by default.

- `jms-soap`: If this attribute is set to true, then the Web service is capable of receiving SOAP messages in the body of a JMS TextMessage over a JMS queue. You can specify the soap-style for the soap message as well. This attribute is set to false by default.

- `jms-xml`: If this attribute is set to true, then the Web service is capable of receiving raw XML messages in the body of a JMS TextMessage without any SOAP headers over a JMS queue. This attribute is set to false by default.

The soap-style attribute can be used in conjunction with the http-soap and jms-soap attributes as discussed above. SOAP messages can be encoded in two styles – either as document or as RPC. If this attribute is set to document, then the developer can determine the shape of the XML data and how it maps to Java data structures. If it is set to RPC, it doesn't allow the developer to configure XML data. This attribute is set to document by default.

Alternatively, these attributes can be set in the Source View as well. This can be done using the @jws:protocol tag. The syntax for this tag is as follows:

```
@jws:protocol
        form-get="true | false"
        form-post="true | false"
        http-soap="true | false"
        http-xml="true | false"
        jms-soap="true | false"
        jms-xml="true | false"
        soap-style="document | rpc"
```

For this select the Source View. You can specify the @jws:protocol tag for the entire Web service or for every method or callback or control. You can find an example in Listing 9-2.

Listing 9-2: Setting the @jws:protocol Tag in the Source View

```
/**
 * @jws:protocol jms-soap="true" jms-xml="false"
 */
public class currencyService
{
    /**
     * @jws:operation
     */
    public double convertFromDollarToEuro(double dollarAmount)
    {
        return dollarAmount * 1.015;
    }
}
```

In this example, the Web service called currencyService has the @jws:protocol tag with the jms-soap attribute set to true and the jms-xml attribute set to false. As I discussed earlier, form-get, form-post, and http-soap attributes are set to true by default. Hence, you don't need to specify them here unless you don't want the Web service to support these message formats. So, in this case, the Web service is capable of accepting messages over form-get, form-post, http-soap, and jms-soap.

You can also specify these attributes for every single method in the Web service. If you have any callbacks or controls defined in your Web service, you can specify these attributes for them as well.

Controlling SOAP Headers

Earlier in this chapter, you saw that the header portion of the SOAP message holds metadata about the message and the body contains the actual request. Now, let's see what kind of metadata can be specified in the header section.

You could force the WebLogic Server to process a SOAP header block by specifying the `mustUnderstand` header attribute in the SOAP message that the client sends to the Web service. The value of the `mustUnderstand` attribute can be either a boolean "true" or 1 or a boolean "false" or 0. If it is set to "true" or 1, then the server must process the header, and if it does not then it should fail and return a `fault` message to the client. If the value of the attribute is "false" or 0, then it is optional for the server to process that block. If this attribute is not present, then it is considered as "false" or 0 as defined by the SOAP specification. Listing 9-3 illustrates how to use the `mustUnderstand` attribute.

Listing 9-3: The mustUnderstand SOAP Header Attribute

```
<SOAP-ENV:Header>
    <InvoiceID xmlns="some-URI" SOAP-ENV:mustUnderstand="1">
        2011
    </InvoiceID>
</SOAP-ENV:Header>
<SOAP-ENV:Body>

    <-- body of the SOAP message -->

</SOAP-ENV:Body>
```

When the server receives the preceding SOAP message, it tries to process the header, which has the `InvoiceID` element. If it succeeds, then it continues processing the body. If it fails, it sends an error message back to the client, as shown in Listing 9-4.

Listing 9-4: The Error Message Sent Back to the Client

```
<SOAP-ENV:Envelope xmlns:SOAP-ENV=
"http://schemas.xmlsoap.org/soap/envelope/">
  <SOAP-ENV:Body>
    <SOAP-ENV:Fault>
      <faultcode>SOAP-ENV:MustUnderstand</faultcode>
      <faultstring>SOAP Must Understand Error</faultstring>
```

Continued

Listing 9-4 *(Continued)*

```
    </SOAP-ENV:Fault>
  </SOAP-ENV:Body>
</SOAP-ENV:Envelope>
```

In Chapter 4, you saw how to build Web services, which support a conversation. There are three phases in a conversation: start, continue, and finish. In WebLogic Workshop, you can specify these phases in the Property pane of the Design View. The messages exchanged between the Web service and the client should have the conversational phase information as part of the SOAP header.

If you're using WebLogic Workshop to generate the client code (Test View), then it already has all this coded. But if you want to write your own client or in general a non-Workshop client, then it is your responsibility to send the appropriate header information.

There are three SOAP headers associated with conversations.

- `<StartHeader>`
- `<ContinueHeader>`
- `<CallbackHeader>`

To illustrate this, here is an example. Consider a Web service called `HeaderTest`. This Web service has three methods: `beginProcess`, `continueProcess`, and `endProcess`. Figure 9-14 shows this.

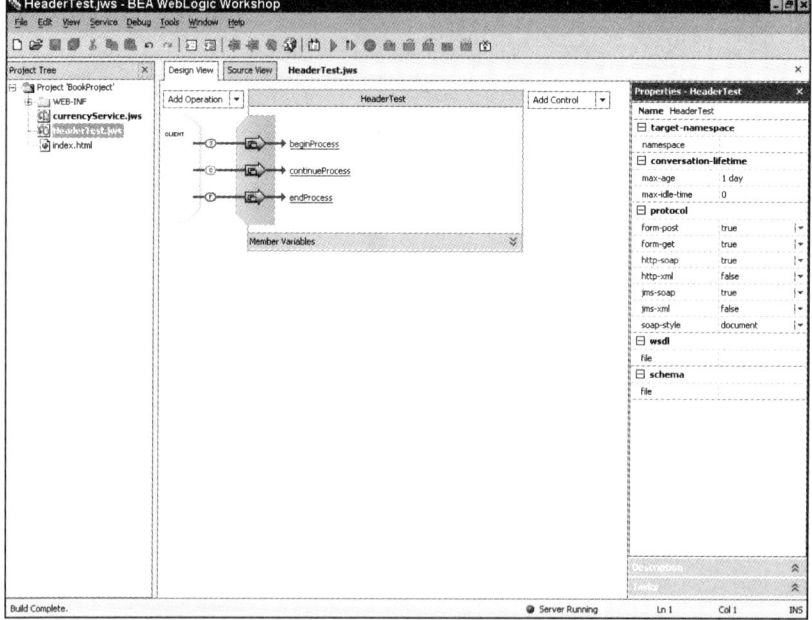

Figure 9-14: HeaderTest Web service.

As named, `beginProcess` starts a conversation, `continueProcess` continues the conversation, and `endProcess` completes the process. As you can see, the `jms-soap` message format has been enabled for this Web service. So, let's write a JMS client, which sends a SOAP message with the required headers.

First, in order to start the conversation, the client has to call the `beginProcess` method. For this, it has to send a JMS TextMessage with a SOAP message:

```
TextMessage tm = qs.createTextMessage();
tm.setStringProperty("URI", "BookProject/HeaderTest.jws");
```

Then, let's add the SOAP message to the body of the JMS TextMessage. This SOAP message should have a `<startHeader>` SOAP header:

```
String soapXMLMessage = "<SOAP-ENV:Envelope
   xmlns:SOAP-ENC="http://schemas.xmlsoap.org/soap/encoding/"
   xmlns:SOAP-ENV="http://schemas.xmlsoap.org/soap/envelope/"
   xmlns:xsd="http://www.w3.org/2001/XMLSchema"
   xmlns:xsi="http://www.w3.org/2001/XMLSchema-instance">
  <SOAP-ENV:Header>
    <StartHeader
xmlns="http://www.openuri.org/2002/04/soap/conversation/">
            <conversationID>12345</conversationID>
    </StartHeader>
  </SOAP-ENV:Header>
  <SOAP-ENV:Body>
    <beginProcess xmlns="http://www.openuri.org/"></beginProcess>
  </SOAP-ENV:Body>
</SOAP-ENV:Envelope>";
tm.setText(soapXMLMessage);
```

The `conversationID` element within the `StartHeader` element specifies a unique ID, which identifies a conversation. The `conversationID` is optional. If the client doesn't specify this, then the Web service will provide one for use locally. In such a case, the client will have no way of finding the `conversationID` and, hence, will not be able to correlate any responses for the original request. This approach is acceptable only when the client is not expecting any callbacks or responses from the Web service. The SOAP body has an element `beginProcess`, which indicates the method to be invoked. Now, let's execute this sample code. Then, let's take a look at the message area in the Test View (Figure 9-15).

Figure 9-15: The message area for the HeaderTest Web service when beginProcess is invoked.

As you can see, the `beginProcess` method has been started, and the conversation has been assigned an ID of `12345`. Now, let's continue the conversation by invoking the `continueProcess` method. For this we need to provide another SOAP header called `ContinueHeader` with the same `conversationID`, which we specified while invoking the `beginProcess` method.

```
String soapXMLMessage = "<SOAP-ENV:Envelope
    xmlns:SOAP-ENC="http://schemas.xmlsoap.org/soap/encoding/"
    xmlns:SOAP-ENV="http://schemas.xmlsoap.org/soap/envelope/"
    xmlns:xsd="http://www.w3.org/2001/XMLSchema"
    xmlns:xsi="http://www.w3.org/2001/XMLSchema-instance">
    <SOAP-ENV:Header>
       <ContinueHeader
xmlns="http://www.openuri.org/2002/04/soap/conversation/">
            <conversationID>12345</conversationID>
       </ContinueHeader>
    </SOAP-ENV:Header>
    <SOAP-ENV:Body>
       <continueProcess xmlns="http://www.openuri.org/">
       </continueProcess>
    </SOAP-ENV:Body>
  </SOAP-ENV:Envelope>";
tm.setText(soapXMLMessage);
```

Chapter 9: Controlling the Web Service Protocols

Now, let's execute this JMS client and then watch the Message area in the Test View. Figure 9-16 illustrates this.

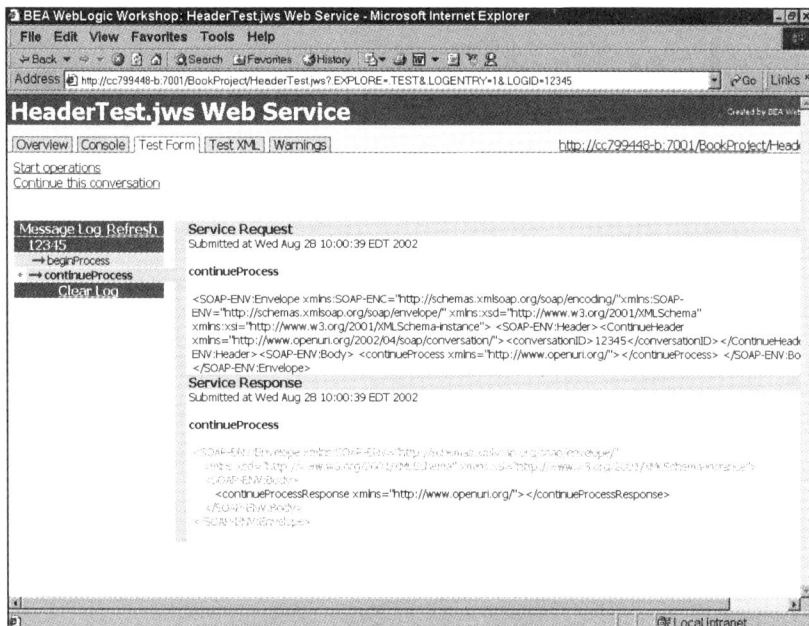

Figure 9-16: The message area for the HeaderTest Web service when continueProcess is invoked.

Because we had provided the same `conversationID` in the `ContinueHeader`, the Web service associated this invocation to the `continueProcess` method with the previous invocation to the `beginProcess` method. Finally, let's end the conversation by invoking the `endProcess` method. As in the earlier invocation, we need to provide the same SOAP header called `ContinueHeader` with the same `conversationID`.

```
String soapXMLMessage = "<SOAP-ENV:Envelope
   xmlns:SOAP-ENC="http://schemas.xmlsoap.org/soap/encoding/"
   xmlns:SOAP-ENV="http://schemas.xmlsoap.org/soap/envelope/"
   xmlns:xsd="http://www.w3.org/2001/XMLSchema"
   xmlns:xsi="http://www.w3.org/2001/XMLSchema-instance">
   <SOAP-ENV:Header>
     <ContinueHeader
xmlns="http://www.openuri.org/2002/04/soap/conversation/">
            <conversationID>12345</conversationID>
     </ContinueHeader>
   </SOAP-ENV:Header>
```

```
    <SOAP-ENV:Body>
      <endProcess xmlns="http://www.openuri.org/">
      </endProcess>
    </SOAP-ENV:Body>
  </SOAP-ENV:Envelope>";
tm.setText(soapXMLMessage);
```

 To begin a conversation, the SOAP message should have a `StartHeader`. To either continue or to finish a conversation, the SOAP message should have the `ContinueHeader`.

Now, let's execute this JMS client and then watch the Message area in the Test View. Figure 9-17 illustrates this.

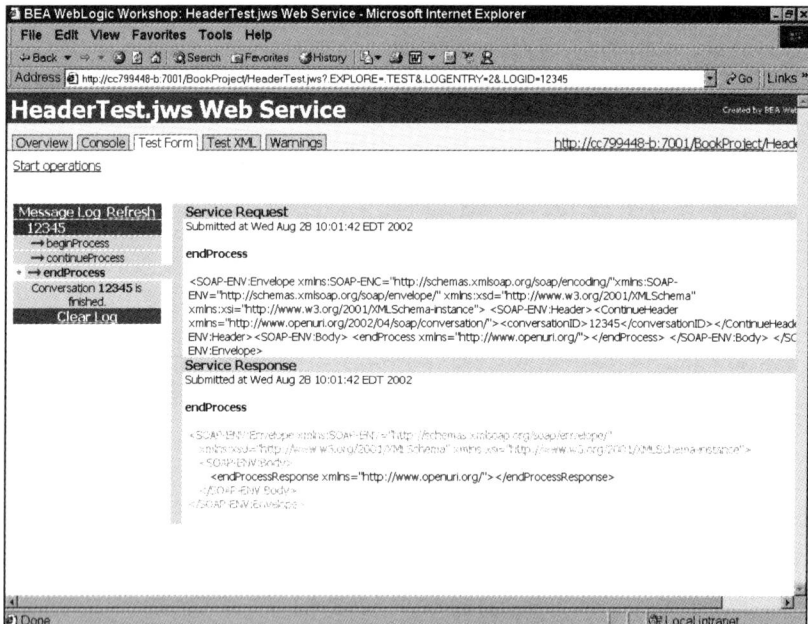

Figure 9-17: Message area for HeaderTest Web service.

Now you can see that the conversation with ID 12345 is finished. Sometimes, the client could be built in such a way that it could receive callbacks from the Web service. In such cases, the client should provide another element in the Start Header, call the callbackLocation. This element specifies the URI, where the client wants the Web service to call back the client.

```
<SOAP-ENV:Envelope
   xmlns:SOAP-ENC="http://schemas.xmlsoap.org/soap/encoding/"
   xmlns:SOAP-ENV="http://schemas.xmlsoap.org/soap/envelope/"
   xmlns:xsd="http://www.w3.org/2001/XMLSchema"
   xmlns:xsi="http://www.w3.org/2001/XMLSchema-instance">
   <SOAP-ENV:Header>
     <StartHeader
xmlns="http://www.openuri.org/2002/04/soap/conversation/">
            <conversationID>12345</conversationID>
            <callbackLocation>Client URI</callbackLocation>
     </StartHeader>
   </SOAP-ENV:Header>
   <SOAP-ENV:Body>
     <beginProcess xmlns="http://www.openuri.org/"></beginProcess>
   </SOAP-ENV:Body>
</SOAP-ENV:Envelope>
```

When the Web service sends a callback message to the client, it contains a header in the SOAP message called the CallbackHeader. The CallbackHeader includes the conversationID, which the client sent in the first invocation. Using this conversationID, the client can correlate the response with the request, which it sent originally.

```
<SOAP-ENV:Envelope
   xmlns:SOAP-ENC="http://schemas.xmlsoap.org/soap/encoding/"
   xmlns:SOAP-ENV="http://schemas.xmlsoap.org/soap/envelope/"
   xmlns:xsd="http://www.w3.org/2001/XMLSchema"
   xmlns:xsi="http://www.w3.org/2001/XMLSchema-instance">
   <SOAP-ENV:Header>
     <CallbackHeader
xmlns="http://www.openuri.org/2002/04/soap/conversation/">
            <conversationID>12345</conversationID>
     </CallbackHeader>
   </SOAP-ENV:Header>
   <SOAP-ENV:Body>
     <beginProcess xmlns="http://www.openuri.org/"></beginProcess>
   </SOAP-ENV:Body>
</SOAP-ENV:Envelope>
```

Summary

Web services and clients talk to each other by exchanging messages. In this chapter, I discussed the format of these messages. These messages could be either XML messages or SOAP messages, which could be sent over HTTP or JMS. I also dealt with how to use the Test View to watch these messages.

This chapter covered how to control the format of the messages using the property pane in the Design View and by using the @jws:protocol tag in the Source View. Finally, you saw the structure of a SOAP header and how to control it by specifying the various header elements (StartHeader, ContinueHeader, CallbackHeader) and the mustUnderstand attribute.

Part IV

Client Component

CHAPTER 10
Calling Web Services from Outside WebLogic Workshop

CHAPTER 11
Using JavaScript in XML Maps

Chapter 10

Calling Web Services from Outside WebLogic Workshop

IN THIS CHAPTER

- Thinking about the client before you actually have one
- Generating Web service proxies
- Generating unique identifiers to use as conversation IDs
- Building a JSP client for a Web service
- Building a Swing client for a Web service

IN THE CHAPTERS leading up to this one, you've been learning about the server side of Web services. This chapter focuses on the client's point of view. This chapter is important because the needs of potential clients will undoubtedly influence your service's design.

WebLogic Workshop provides proxy components you can use to call Web services you build. Through a proxy, your client code can access a Web service as if it were calling a method of a JavaBean or other component. The proxy does the work of turning client calls into the message format the service requires, and of converting the service's response into types the client can use. This chapter introduces how to use the proxy to build clients with two popular Java technologies: JavaServer Pages and Swing.

Planning for Client Support

Although this chapter comes relatively late in the book, it probably goes without saying that the time to plan for client access is when you're planning your Web service's design. Design questions related to asynchrony and conversations, types used in your service, and so on need to be answered with clients in mind.

For example, if you're planning an asynchronous Web service that relies on a conversation to correlate calls and keep track of state, then obviously the needs of the client play a role. In most cases, the client will be responsible for generating a new conversation ID whenever it uses the Web service. Also, you'll need to provide a polling interface for those clients that do not support callbacks.

In the following sections, I describe a few approaches for addressing these design questions.

Providing an alternative to callbacks with a wrapper service

Clients that aren't WebLogic Workshop Web services aren't typically capable of receiving callbacks. If a Web service exposes callbacks as part of a conversational interface, then you (or the service's designer) must provide some way for the client to explicitly ask for what the callback would have given it. You can handle this sort of thing by including code in the Web service that tests for the client's callback support — for example, by checking to see if the client sent a callback URL with its first request. However, it's probably simpler just to "wrap" the Web service within a service that exposes an interface the client can use for polling.

In a polling interface, the Web service provides a synchronous method that the client can call to retrieve the results of a request. In the earlier OnlineStore example, the Web service uses a callback to send back purchase confirmation. In a polling interface alternative, the Web service would simply store the confirmation information in a member variable and wait for the client to come and get it.

You can provide this alternative pretty easily by using a wrapper service. A wrapper service provides all the methods the original service provides (omitting any callbacks, of course) but delegates processing for most of these methods to the original service. In other words, for most methods, the client calls the wrapper service and the wrapper service in turns calls the original service. Responses are passed back out in the same way. The client only ever interacts with the wrapper service that is, for the most part, a hollow shell.

But the wrapper service also exposes additional methods that may be needed to replace callbacks. In the OnlineStore service example, a wrapper service with a `getResults` method would serve this purpose. Because the wrapper is actually the original service's client, it receives the callback and stores the value in a member variable. When the client calls the `getResults` method, the wrapper sends what it received from OnlineStore.

While we're redesigning the OnlineStore example to support a polling interface, we should account for one more of its quirks. Because it uses other resources (an Enterprise JavaBean and an application it accesses via Java Message Service), there may be some delay before the results are ready for the client to pick up. In other words, if the resource accessed via JMS is busy, the client could repeatedly ask for its results for quite a while before actually getting them. To handle this, the wrapper service could also provide a method that simply indicates whether the results are ready. The client polls *that* method until it receives a true value, then calls the `getResults` method.

A wrapper for the OnlineStore service

The examples in this chapter use a wrapper service for the OnlineStore Web service (you just knew this was coming, didn't you?). Here's an overview of the process I used when creating the wrapper service, called OnlineStorePoll:

1. *Create a duplicate of the OnlineStore Web service.*

   You can easily do this in WebLogic Workshop by right-clicking the JWS file in the Project Tree, and then clicking Duplicate.

2. *Add a Service control to communicate with the original Web service.*

3. *Rename the duplicate to something that suggests it's an alternative for polling (in this case, simply by appending "Poll" to the service's name).*

4. *Replace all implementation code in the duplicate's methods with calls to the original Web service's methods.*

5. *Remove original callback handlers.*

   These are used by the original service but not needed in the wrapper.

6. *Add variables needed to store values that support the polling interface.*

   In OnlineStore, these include variables to hold the callback response and a boolean to indicate whether the response has been received.

7. *Add a callback handler for the original Web service's callback.*

   Code in this handler will store the response in a member variable for later retrieval by the client.

8. *Add a new method the client can call to find out if results are ready.*

9. *Add a new method the client can call to retrieve the results.*

10. *Edit the Service control's CTRL file so that it used the same Item class as the one used by the original Web service.*

    Typically, a Service control will declare its own version of custom types such as the Item class. However, the Item class used is actually defined by the EJB the original service uses. Simply importing that type into the Service control and removing its own definition allows all parties – original service, wrapper, and client – to be in agreement about the type needed.

The code for the wrapper service is shown in Listing 10-1.

Listing 10-1: A Wrapper for the OnlineStore Web Service

```
package Chapter10;

import weblogic.jws.control.JwsContext;
import java.util.ArrayList;
import java.util.HashMap;
import com.onlinestore.item.Item;
import weblogic.jws.control.TimerControl;

public class OnlineStorePoll
{
    /**
     * @jws:control
     */
    private OnlineStoreControl onlineStoreControl;

    /** @jws:context */
    JwsContext context;

    /**
     * A string to store the message that will
     * be sent back to the client.
     */
    private String m_message;

    /*
     * The list of items that the client was approved
     * to purchase
     */
    private Item[] m_itemsPurchased;

    /*
     * A flag to set when the transaction is finished.
     */
    private boolean m_isComplete = false;

    /**
     * @jws:operation
     * @jws:conversation phase="start"
     */
    public String startShopping(String name, String customerNumber)
    {
        return onlineStoreControl.startShopping(name,
            customerNumber);
    }
```

Chapter 10: Calling Web Services from Outside WebLogic Workshop

```java
/**
 * @jws:operation
 * @jws:conversation phase="continue"
 */
public Item[] viewCatalog() throws Exception
{
    return onlineStoreControl.viewCatalog();
}

/**
 * @jws:operation
 * @jws:conversation phase="continue"
 */
public void addItem(Integer code)
{
    onlineStoreControl.addItem(code.intValue());
}

/**
 * @jws:operation
 * @jws:conversation phase="continue"
 */
public void removeItem(int index)
{
    onlineStoreControl.removeItem(index);
}

/**
 * @jws:operation
 * @jws:conversation phase="continue"
 */
public Item[] viewCart()
{
    return onlineStoreControl.viewCart();
}

/**
 * @jws:operation
 * @jws:conversation phase="continue"
 */
public void checkout()
{
    onlineStoreControl.checkout();
```

Continued

Listing 10-1 *(Continued)*

```
    }

    private void onlineStoreControl_onPurchaseApproved(
        java.lang.String message, Item[] itemsPurchased)
    {
        m_message = message;
        m_itemsPurchased = itemsPurchased;

        m_isComplete = true;
    }

    /**
     * @jws:operation
     * @jws:conversation phase="continue"
     */
    public boolean isPurchaseComplete()
    {
        return m_isComplete;
    }

    /**
     * @jws:operation
     * @jws:conversation phase="finish"
     */
    public Item[] getResults()
    {
        return m_itemsPurchased;
    }
}
```

Finally, note that with a wrapper service, you have two alternatives to access the same functionality. Both the wrapper and the original service remain useful, but for different kinds of clients.

Generating Proxies

Client software accesses Web services you build with WebLogic Workshop by using a proxy. A proxy is a software component that represents the Web service to the client. Through a proxy, a client can call the Web service's methods as if it were calling them directly. The proxy is responsible for packaging the client's requests and sending them in the appropriate form to the Web service.

Getting a proxy for a Web service is pretty simple. The Test View Web page you've been using to test and develop your Web service has several other uses, including providing access to supporting files. The JAR file containing the proxy component is available there. You can get to the Test View page with access to the proxy either by running your Web service in WebLogic Workshop (as if you were testing it), or by using the test page's URL directly. The URL looks something like the following:

```
http://localhost:7001/bookproject/Chapter10/OnlineStore.jws
```

A URL like this one is displayed in the Test View address box when you test a Web service. Of course, you should replace this URL with one that points to your own Web service.

When you're looking at Test View, click the Overview tab. There you'll see several links that provide access to files generated to support your Web service and its use by clients. About halfway down the page, under Web Service Clients, you'll see a Java Proxy link, as shown in Figure 10-1.

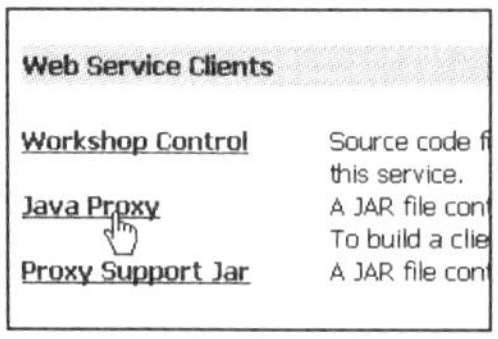

Figure 10-1: Test View provides a link for generating a proxy JAR file.

Click the link to display a dialog box prompting you to download the proxy JAR file. Click Save, then select a location to save the JAR file. As with other JAR files containing classes you'll use in Java code, this one will need to end up in a location known to your client code. If you're developing JSP pages to provide UI, and the pages are in the same project as your Web service, you could save the JAR file to the project's `web-inf/lib` folder.

Notice that there is also a Proxy Support Jar link. Although the Java Proxy link produces a JAR file with classes specific to your Web service, the Proxy Support Jar link produces other classes that are needed to support client access. You should make the support JAR file available to clients as well, particularly when the client code will be deployed on a computer where WebLogic Workshop or its server components are not available.

After you have client and supporting JAR files on the client's class path, you can begin writing and debugging code that accesses your Web service.

Generating a Conversation ID

When you're developing a client that will access a conversational Web service, you'll need a way to generate a globally unique identifier (GUID) to use as a conversation ID. Remember that Web services use conversation IDs to correlate related calls. If there were several running instances of the OnlineStore Web service on the server, and your client called once to make a request and again to get its results, the server needs a way to know which service instance to direct the second call to.

To ensure the client gets the right data, you need to generate a new unique identifier for each initial request your client sends, then include that ID in subsequent requests. Your client must send the conversation ID as a value in a header of the SOAP message it sends with each request. However, as it turns out, WebLogic Workshop provides a fairly painless way to accomplish this. I describe this method in more detail in a moment.

The client sends the conversation ID when it calls the Web service's "start" method — the method marked with a `start` attribute in the Property Editor — and then sends it with each subsequent call to other methods. The Web service uses the identifier to know that subsequent calls belong with the first.

There are various ways to generate a GUID. I'll suggest one here and then use it in examples of client code. The string generated here is made up of a UID (which is itself made up of values such as an identifier for the local copy of the Java virtual machine and a time value) and a value representing the local machine. Listing 10-2 contains code for a method you can use to generate conversation IDs.

Listing 10-2: A Method to Generate a GUID

```
public void generateConvID()
{
    java.rmi.server.UID uid = new java.rmi.server.UID();
    String iastr = null;
    try
    {
        java.net.InetAddress ia =
            java.net.InetAddress.getLocalHost();
        iastr = ia.getHostAddress();
    }
    catch(java.net.UnknownHostException uhe)
    {
        iastr = "uknownhost";
    }

    String guid = iastr + "-" + uid.toString();

    /*
     * Colons won't be accepted by the WebLogic
     * Workshop run-time components.
     */
    guid = guid.replace(':', '.');
    guid = guid.replace('[', '(');
    guid = guid.replace(']', ')');
    convID = guid;
}
```

Sending a Conversation ID

Proxy components include a means for you to send the generated GUID as a value in the request's SOAP header. Through `StartHeader` and `ContinueHeader` classes included with the proxy, you can specify the conversation ID and a URL that points to the component that should receive callbacks the Web service sends. For example, to create a conversation ID, then add it to Start and Continue headers, you might have code such as in Listing 10-3.

Listing 10-3: Create Start and Continue Headers

```
// Receive a GUID from a function that generates one.
String convID = generateConvID();

/*
 * Create a start header with the GUID and a URL to a web service
 * that can receive callbacks.
 */
StartHeader sh = new StartHeader(convID,
    "http://localhost:7001/OnlineStorePoll.jws");

// Create a continue header with the GUID.
ContinueHeader ch = new ContinueHeader(convID);
```

You use the header instances you've created by passing them as the last parameter of a conversational method — even though the methods themselves don't define a parameter for the header class. For example, the OnlineStore Web service described in this book exposes a `startShopping` method that you could call with a conversation header object as an argument. In this example, the `storeProxy` variable represents a proxy class I describe in more detail later.

```
String greeting = storeProxy.startShopping(userName,
    customerNumber, sh);
```

Calling a method that otherwise takes no parameters would look like the following call to an OnlineStore service's "continue" method (a method marked with the `continue` attribute in the Property Editor).

```
Item[] itemsInCart = storeProxy.viewCart(ch);
```

Developing a JSP Client

JavaServer Pages (JSP) technology is a natural choice for the client side of Web applications. Through a combination of HTML, client-side script, and server-side script, they can provide both a professional-looking user interface and powerful request-specific customization. HTML provides a way to display your application's user interface as Web pages. Through client-side script, you can specify the user interface's behavior within the user's browser, including visual effects or, as with the OnlineStore client, behavior behind the scenes such as polling. Server-side script is the most powerful aspect of JSP in that it enables your user interface to behave dynamically, changing with request-specific data.

I'll begin this section with a JSP overview. If you're already familiar with JSP, you may want to skip to the section, "Using the proxy from JSP code."

A JavaServer Pages primer

Like Web services, JSP is designed to be a technology for building Web applications. JSP pages are typically a mix of HTML and JSP elements (special tags and Java code) that are processed by the server in order to send request-specific results to the client. You can think of a JSP page as a kind of template in which the JSP elements fill in information that may be known only when the page is requested. Through their non-HTML parts, JSP pages can incorporate other parts of a J2EE application, including Web services you build with WebLogic Workshop. For example, you can call methods of a Web service from a JSP page, then incorporate the return value into the HTML sent to the client's browser.

In this section, I introduce JavaServer Pages, giving you a bit of background on what they're made up of and how they work. In particular, I focus on the pieces you'll need to know in order to incorporate the functionality of WebLogic Workshop Web services into JSP pages.

 Although JSP supports languages other than Java, the Java language is by far the most frequently used. For that reason, this section uses Java in all code examples.

As I mentioned, JSP pages are typically a mix of HTML and JSP-specific elements (although a JSP page can legally include one without the other). The parts specific to JSP are known as *JSP elements,* while the rest is called *template text.* When a JSP page is requested by a browser, its JSP elements are processed by the server and the results are merged with the template text and sent to the client. You set JSP elements apart from template text (including script designed to execute within the client's browser) by enclosing the JSP elements in special ways.

DIRECTIVES

For example, you use <%@ to begin an element that will be a JSP *directive.* A directive typically specifies something that applies for the entire page. So just as you would use the `import` statement in a Java class (including a Web service) to make a particular class available to your code, you would do the same in a JSP page with the `page` directive.

```
<%@ page import="java.util.HashMap" %>
```

You'll use this sort of directive to import classes exposed by Web service proxy code. Other directives specify the language to be used on the page (such as Java), where other pages should be included inline with the current page, which page to use (if any) for handling errors on the current page, and so on.

DECLARATIONS

You declare instance variables and methods by beginning a JSP element with the <%! symbol.

```
<%! HashMap myMap = new HashMap(); %>
```

Variables and methods you declare this way are available from anywhere on the page. You can also declare variables elsewhere, such as in scriptlets. Variables declared in scriptlets are local to the scriptlets; in contrast, variables declared with <%! are available to all script on the page. Also, because variables declared with <%! are instance variables, you need to be aware of threading implications when you use declaration elements.

SCRIPTLETS

Blocks of Java code inside JSP elements are referred to as *script* or *scriptlets* because they don't require all the contextual constraints of other Java code. For example, you don't enclose JSP Java code in a class definition, nor do you need to include a package definition.

A scriptlet can be a long batch of code or it can be a single line. The following example and the JSP example later in this chapter illustrate how you can mix scriptlets and HTML.

EXPRESSIONS

Through expressions you can sprinkle HTML with values that are resolved separately for each request. Through expression elements, for example, you can insert data that has been retrieved from a Web service.

The following example simply repeats three values until there aren't any more values to repeat.

```
<% Products[] productList = widgetService.getProducts();
for (int i = 0; i < productList.length; i++; ) {
%>
    <p><%= productList.getName(); %></p>
    <p><%= productList.getDescription(); %></p>
    <p><%= productList.getPrice(); %></p>
<%
}
%>
```

 Notice that this example uses the <% and %> symbols to set off the scriptlet code. Mixing scriptlets and HTML in this way can make the code hard to visually parse. With large batches of code, it can be hard to follow what the code does — particularly if you're new to it or haven't looked at it in a while. If you're new to JSP, I suggest you find a convention for formatting your markup so that you can read it easily. In the examples I use in this chapter, I try to place <% and %> symbols at the far left of the page in an effort to make long passages of code easier to scan.

ACTIONS

Another piece of JSP markup is the *action* element, sometimes called a JSP tag. The JSP specification defines several actions you can use to do things like forward processing to another page. Action elements begin with a prefix that, in effect, specifies their namespace (so that other tags with the same names won't conflict), and you use the element tags as you would use XML tags.

One commonly used JSP action element declares a variable for a JavaBean. The `<jsp:useBean>` action specifies which bean to use and gives it a name that you can use in scriptlets. In the following example, the action declares an `Item` bean variable:

```
<jsp:useBean id="item" class="com.myco.onlinestore.Item" />
```

The `id` attribute specifies the variable name that you'd use in code to refer to the bean. For example, you might put the value of the bean's price property in a paragraph tag:

```
<p><%=item.getPrice() %></p>
```

IMPLICIT OBJECTS

For scriptlets in a JSP page, a few objects are always available. In other words, you don't need to declare and initialize variables for them. The most commonly used of these are (listed by their variable names):

- `request`: Provides access to information that came with the current request, such as information in an HTML form sent from the client's browser.

- `response`: Provides methods you can use to track the user's current session (the context of a particular use of the application), to add cookies to the user's computer, and so on.

- `session`: Provides a way to access information specific to the user's current use of the application. For example, for a JSP application spanning multiple JSP pages, you might store information in the `session` object from one page for later retrieval from another page.

- `application`: Provides a way to access information that may pertain to the application's use by multiple users.

- `out`: Provides one way to write text, such as text that you want to appear when the client receives the resulting page. As you may have noticed from the description of expressions in this section, however, sending text as template text is usually easier and more intuitive.

- `exception`: Provides a way to access run-time error information from an error page.

Using the proxy from JSP code

JavaServer Pages is a popular choice for building user interfaces these days. It allows the amount of software actually deployed to the client to remain small while still offering a great deal of processing power through server-side script. Because the Java code that executes within a JSP page never reaches the client, it's not necessary for client computers to receive any of your Web service proxy code.

A complex application that uses JSP as its front end can get to be pretty large, with pages both for user interface and providing logic that controls how processing flows from one page to another. Consider a JSP-based front end for the OnlineStore Web service discussed in this book. JSP pages for that application might have a login page, a page to display the catalog contents, a page to display the shopping cart contents, and a page to display purchase confirmation. In addition, there may be pages whose sole purpose is to provide continuity — say, to add an item to the shopping cart, then forward the user to the page that displays cart contents.

I'll use the OnlineStore Web service to illustrate how you can use the proxy provided by WebLogic Workshop to call Web service methods from JSP pages. The examples I'll be giving assume that the proxy was generated from a *wrapper service*, a Web service whose sole purpose is to provide an interface to clients that don't support callbacks. The example JSP pages used in this section will get the results of the transaction by polling the wrapper service for results.

Setting up for testing

Before getting started, you need to get the proxy JAR file for the Web service as described earlier in this chapter. The classes in the JAR file must be available to the JSP pages, so the JAR file must be on the class path for the Web application of which the JSP pages are a part. If the JSP pages will be part of the same Web application as the Web service, this is easily accomplished by putting the JAR file in the `web-inf/lib` folder of the WebLogic Workshop project. Developing JSPs in your WebLogic Workshop project is also a convenient way to get the code in the JSP pages working before handing the pages off to a designer.

Remember that you'll need to regenerate the proxy JAR file each time you make a change to the Web service's interface. In particular, if you change the names or parameter lists of any exposed methods or callbacks (those marked as operations), you'll need to get a new proxy JAR and put it in the `web-inf/lib` folder. (If you forget, look for an error message when you next try to access the Web service from a JSP page.)

Providing a place to log in

The OnlineStore is designed to be conversational and its logic requires getting information about items in the catalog before anything else can be done (like adding items to the cart or checking out). As a result, the login page is a good place to start. Starting in the middle somewhere — say, a JSP page to view the cart contents — would be difficult without having first populated the catalog.

From a visible interface point of view, the login page needs to send a user name and customer number to the Web service. This will call the `startShopping` method and get the purchase process going. At the same time, however, it will be necessary to send a conversation ID. Although WebLogic Workshop creates a conversation ID when you're testing and debugging the Web service, this is really just for the sake of convenience. In practice, the client must send a conversation ID that will be used for all exchanges. If the Web service simply created one when the first method was called, the JSP page would have no way of knowing what the ID was. As a result, the JSP page wouldn't have a key with which to tell the Web service during subsequent requests that those requests were associated with the first.

As it turns out, however, the login page has no Java code whatsoever. It merely provides a way to collect information from the shopper and pass it along to another page. The code for the login page currently doesn't have any of the extras, including script to ensure that the user actually filled out both boxes before clicking the Start Shopping button. Still, it will do for the purpose of putting into place the pieces necessary to connect the pages together, and to connect them with the Web service. Figure 10-2 displays a rudimentary login page. (Incidentally, the pages in this example also lack, as you may have noticed, good design. That sort of thing is best left to those who know how to do it well!)

Figure 10-2: Displaying a login page.

This page is pretty unremarkable, but there are a few things to notice in its code in Listing 10-4. Take a look at the page directive that defines an error page. This tells the JSP engine which JSP page to use if an error occurs that was not accounted for. Also, the call to the setAttribute method of the request object places the URI of the current request where it can be fetched later. For example, the error page may have code that puts the URI into a log file. A JavaScript function on this page places the cursor conveniently in the first box of the form. Finally, the action attribute of the form tag specifies that clicking the submit button (here, labeled "Start Shopping!") will send the user name and customer number to the startShopping.jsp page.

Listing 10-4: A Login Page

```
<%@ page contentType="text/html; charset=iso-8859-1" %>
<%@ page errorPage="errorPage.jsp?debug=log" %>
<% request.setAttribute("sourcePage", request.getRequestURI()); %>

<html>
<head>
<link rel="stylesheet" href="onlinestore.css" type="text/css">
<title>Widgets R Us Login</title>
<script language="JavaScript">
    function setFocus(){
        document.requestInfoForm.userName.focus();
    }
</script>
</head>
<body bgcolor="white" onLoad="setFocus()">
<form method="get" action="startShopping.jsp"
                  name="requestInfoForm">
```

Continued

Listing 10-4 *(Continued)*

```html
    <table width="100%">
      <tr>
        <td>
          <h1>Widgets R Us Online Store</h1>
          <h4>Please sign in to start shopping!</h4>
        </td>
      </tr>
      <tr>
        <td colspan="5">
          <p>Enter your user name: <br>
            <input tabindex="1" type="text" name="userName" size="30">
          </p>
        </td>
      </tr>
      <tr>
        <td colspan="5">
          <p>Enter your customer number: <br>
            <input tabindex="2" type="text" name="customerNumber"
              size="30">
          </p>
        </td>
      </tr>
      <tr>
        <td colspan="6">
          <p><input tabindex="3" type="submit" value="Start Shopping!"
            name="Submit"></p>
        </td>
      </tr>
    </table>
  </form>
  </body>
</html>
```

Starting the conversation

Having collected a user name and customer number from the user, the login page redirects processing to the startShopping.jsp page, whose code is shown in Listing 10-5. This page has no user interface. Its sole purpose is to get the conversation started and create an instance of the Web service proxy that can be used in subsequent pages. The page begins by importing the necessary classes and packages. Note that the `weblogic.jws.proxies` package is required to support the proxy. The `org.openuri.www.x2002.x04.soap.conversation` package provides header classes that will be used to send conversation information with requests to the Web service.

Chapter 10: Calling Web Services from Outside WebLogic Workshop

Comments in this example describe what each portion of the code is for.

Listing 10-5: A startShopping.jsp Page

```jsp
<%@ page contentType="text/html; charset=iso-8859-1" %>
<%@ page import="javax.servlet.* %>
<%@ page import="javax.servlet.http.* %>
<%@ page import="java.util.* %>
<%@ page import="weblogic.jws.proxies.*" %>
<%@ page import="org.openuri.www.x2002.x04.soap.conversation.*" %>
<%@ page errorPage="errorPage.jsp?debug=log" %>
<% request.setAttribute("sourcePage", request.getRequestURI()); %>

<%
try {
    /*
     * Grab the user name and customer number from the URL, where
     * it was placed by the login form.
     */
    String userName = request.getParameter("userName");
    String customerNumber = request.getParameter("customerNumber");

    /*
     * Create a variable to hold the web service proxy. This
     * code follows a predictable format. For example, the
     * generated proxy name is the name of the service
     * with "_Impl" appended. The name of the SOAP proxy is
     * the name of the service with "Soap" appended (because it
     * communicate via SOAP over http). This is the
     * component that does the actual work of translating requests
     * and responses to and from SOAP-style XML messages. To make
     * the code easier to understand, we'll use "storeProxy" as the
     * variable name in each page.
     */
    String serviceURL =
"http://localhost:7001/bookproject/Chapter08/OnlineStorePoll.jws?WSDL";
    OnlineStorePoll_Impl storeImpl =
        new OnlineStorePoll_Impl(serviceURL);
    OnlineStorePollSoap storeProxy =
        storeImpl.getOnlineStorePollSoap();

    /*
     * Store the newly created proxy object in the Session object.
     * There, it will be available to other pages in the
```

```java
 * application, so that it won't need to be created for each new
 * page that communicates with the web service.
 */
session.setAttribute("proxy", storeProxy);

/*
 * Create a GUID that may be used as a conversation
 * ID throughout the course of this purchase.
 */
java.rmi.server.UID uid = new java.rmi.server.UID();
String iastr = null;
try
{
    java.net.InetAddress ia =
        java.net.InetAddress.getLocalHost();
    iastr = ia.getHostAddress();
}
catch(java.net.UnknownHostException uhe)
{
    iastr = "uknownhost";
}

String guid = iastr + "-" + uid.toString();

/*
 * Colons won't be accepted by the WebLogic
 * Workshop runtime.
 */
guid = guid.replace(':', '.');
guid = guid.replace('[', '(');
guid = guid.replace(']', ')');

/* Store the conversation ID in the Session object. */
session.setAttribute("convID", guid);

/*
 * Create an instance of the StartHeader class.
 * The start header will carry the conversation ID
 * to start this conversation. It will also carry the
 * callback URL, the URL to which the OnlineStore web
 * service will send its callback containing the outcome
 * of the transaction. Notice that the callback URL
 * points to the wrapper web service. The results will
 * be stored there, then retrieved by a JSP page designed
 * to poll until results are available.
```

Chapter 10: Calling Web Services from Outside WebLogic Workshop 255

```
      */
      StartHeader sh = new StartHeader(convID,
         "http://localhost:7001/OnlineStorePoll.jws");

      /*
       * Call the "start" method of the web service, officially
       * starting a conversation. Along with parameters specified
       * by the method itself, pass the start header so that the
       * service can begin a conversation with the conversation
       * ID specified here.
       */
      String greeting = storeProxy.startShopping(userName,
         customerNumber, sh);

      /*
       * After starting the conversation, move to the
       * displayCatalog.jsp page, which is designed to display
       * a list of items.
       */
      response.sendRedirect( "displayCatalog.jsp" );

   } catch ( java.rmi.RemoteException re )
   {
      /*
       * Catch an exception that may be thrown by the web service.
       * Note that the exception arrives as a RemoteException. From
       * this, you can extract the actual exception stored inside.
       * This code stores the contents of the exception in an "errMsg"
       * attribute where it will be accessible from the error page.
       * This isn't the best way to handle exceptions in production,
       * but it can be useful while you're debugging.
       */
      session.setAttribute( "errMsg", re.detail.getMessage() );
      response.sendRedirect( "errorPage.jsp" );
   }
%>
```

When this page has finished its work, it redirects processing to the display Catalog.jsp page whose code is in Listing 10-6. Now that the Web service's catalog variable has been filled with items that can be displayed, the displayCatalog.jsp page can retrieve the items in the catalog and display them for the user as shown in Figure 10-3.

In terms of its Java code, this page doesn't do much that you didn't see in startShopping.jsp. One difference that's worth pointing out is that the code creates a Continue header. This header is sent with a call to the Web service's `viewCatalog` method.

Figure 10-3: Displaying a list of items.

Listing 10-6: A displayCatalog.jsp Page

```jsp
<%@ page contentType="text/html; charset=iso-8859-1" %>
<%@ page import="weblogic.jws.proxies.*" %>
<%@ page import="org.openuri.www.Item" %>
<%@ page import="org.openuri.www.x2002.x04.soap.conversation.*" %>

<%
try {
    /*
     * Retrieve the web service proxy from the Session object, where
     * it was placed by the startShopping.jsp page.
     */
    OnlineStorePollSoap storeProxy =
        (OnlineStorePollSoap)session.getAttribute("proxy");

    /*
     * Prepare a continue header. This will be sent with new
     * requests to the web service. Notice that it contains the same
     * conversation ID that was created and used to start the
     * conversation.
     */
    ContinueHeader ch =
        new ContinueHeader((String)session.getAttribute("convID"));
%>
    <html>
        <head>
            <link rel="stylesheet" href="onlinestore.css"
                type="text/css">
            <title>Widgets R Us Catalog</title>
```

```
            </head>
            <body>
            <h1>Widgets R Us Online Store</h1>
            <h4>Our Current Catalog</h4>
<%
            /*
             * Get a list of the catalog items by calling the
             * web service's viewCatalog method. Note that the method
             * call passes in the conversation header even though the
             * method (as defined by the web service) doesn't include
             * this parameter. This is a convenience offered by the
             * proxy, enabling you to send a conversation ID without
             * having had to account for it in your service interface.
             * the header parameter is automatically made the last
             * parameter of each conversational method.
             */
            Item[] catalogItems = storeProxy.viewCatalog(ch);

            /*
             * Use the returned array of items to build a table that
             * displays their names. The table also displays a button
             * that users can click to purchase the item. Notice that
             * expressions are used to insert values from the Item
             * class. Finally, notice that the entire table is contained
             * by a form whose action is the addItem.jsp page. This
             * provides a way to respond to the user's request to
             * buy a particular item by passing the code of the
             * item to the addItem.jsp page. The addItem page has code
             * that can request that the item be added to the shopping
             * cart managed by the web service.
             */
            if (catalogItems.length > 0){
%>
                        name="catalogList">
                    <table width="401">
                      <tr>
                        <td width="80">
                          <div align="left">
                          </div>
                        </td>
                        <td width="120">
                          <div align="left"><b>Item Name</b></div>
                        </td>
                        <td width="80"><b>Item Price</b>
```

Continued

Listing 10-6 *(Continued)*

```
                            <div align="left"></div>
                        </td>
                        <td width="100">
                            <div align="left"><b>Item Code</b></div>
                        </td>
                    </tr>
                    <tr><td colspan=4><hr noshade
                        size="1"/></td></tr>
<%
        for (int i = 0; i < catalogItems.length; i++){
            Item currentItem = catalogItems[i];
%>
                    <form method="get" action="addItem.jsp"
                    <tr>
                        <td width="80">
                            <div align="left">
                                <input type="submit" value="Buy Me"/>
                            </div>
                        </td>
                        <td width="120">
                            <div align="left"><%=
                                currentItem.getName() %></div>
                        </td>
                        <td width="80"> <%= currentItem.getPrice() %>
                            <div align="left"></div>
                        </td>
                        <td width="100">
                            <div align="left">Code:
                                <%= currentItem.getCode() %></div>
                        </td>
                        <input type="hidden" name="code"
                            value="<%= currentItem.getCode() %>"/>
                    </tr>
                    </form>
<%
        }
%>
                </table>
<%
    } else {
%>
        <p>Looks like we're sold out for now! Please check back
            later.</p>
<%
```

Chapter 10: Calling Web Services from Outside WebLogic Workshop

```
        }
    } catch ( java.rmi.RemoteException re )
    {
        session.setAttribute( "errMsg", re.detail.getMessage() );
        response.sendRedirect( "errorPage.jsp" );
    }
%>
        </body>
</html>
```

The for loop on this page is designed to create a new form for each item in the list. Each form has its own "Buy Me" submit button, its own action attribute specifying the addItem.jsp page, and its own hidden <input> element containing the item's code number. When the user clicks an item's "Buy Me" button, the code number is forwarded to the addItem.jsp page. Listing 10-7 shows the resulting HTML for one of the items.

Listing 10-7: HTML Output of displayCatalog.jsp

```
<form method="get" action="addItem.jsp" name="catalogList">
    <tr>
        <td width="80">
            <div align="left">
                <input type="submit" value="Buy Me"/>
            </div>
        </td>
        <td width="120">
            <div align="left">Blue Widget</div>
        </td>
        <td width="80"> 2.75
            <div align="left"></div>
        </td>
        <td width="100">
            <div align="left">Code: 0</div>
        </td>
        <input type="hidden" name="code" value="0"/>
    </tr>
</form>
```

The addItem.jsp page that receives the "buy" request is very similar to what you've seen so far. It retrieves the code number of the item passed to it, then calls the Web service's addItem method, continuing the conversation with a Continue header parameter. The page then redirects the user to a viewCart.jsp page that displays the current contents of their shopping cart (based on a call to the Web service's viewCart method). When the user has finished shopping, they can click a checkout link. The link redirects to another JSP that, like the addItem.jsp page, is designed simply to call a method of the Web service. The page then redirects again to the viewResults.jsp page, which polls the web service (if necessary) until the Web service's `isPurchaseComplete` method returns true. Figure 10-4 shows the page as it is polling and Figure 10-5 shows the page after it has received results.

Figure 10-4: The viewResults.jsp page is designed to display a message while polling for completion of the transaction.

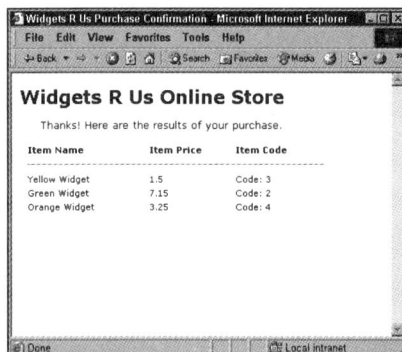

Figure 10-5: The viewResults.jsp page displays results when they become available.

Listing 10-8 shows the code for viewResults.jsp. Notice that JavaScript does the actual polling work. Client-side script such as this is placed between `<script>` tags to set it off.

Listing 10-8: A viewResults.jsp Page

```
<%@ page contentType="text/html; charset=iso-8859-1" %>
<%@ page import="org.openuri.www.Item" %>
<%@ page import="weblogic.jws.proxies.*" %>
<%@ page import="org.openuri.www.x2002.x04.soap.conversation.*" %>
```

```
<%
try {
    OnlineStorePollSoap storeProxy =
        (OnlineStorePollSoap)session.getAttribute("proxy");

    ContinueHeader ch =
        new ContinueHeader((String)session.getAttribute("convID"));
%>
<html>
    <head>
        <link rel="stylesheet" href="onlinestore.css"
            type="text/css">
        <title>Widgets R Us Purchase Confirmation</title>
        <script language="JavaScript1.2">

            /*
             * Use two JavaScript functions to do the polling.
             * The startTimer function specifies that the
             * refresh function should be called every second.
             * When the refresh function is called, it requests
             * the viewResults.jsp page again, effectively
             * causing the Java code in the page to execute.
             * Because the code calls the isPurchaseComplete
             * method, the page will keep refreshing until
             * the method returns "true".
             *
             * Note that the page refresh happens because the
             * page's body onload event invokes the startTimer
             * function if isPurchaseComplete doesn't return
             * "true". If it the method returns "true", then
             * a different <body> tag is used -- one that does
             * not call the startTimer function.
             */
            function startTimer()
            {
                var refreshTimer = setTimeout("refresh()", 1000);
            }

            function refresh()
            {
                window.location.reload(false);
            }
        </script>
```

Continued

Listing 10-8 *(Continued)*

```
    </head>
<%
    /*
     * Call the web service's isPurchaseComplete method to
     * see if it has finished processing the purchase
     * request.
     */
    if(storeProxy.isPurchaseComplete(ch)) {
%>
    <body>
<%
        /*
         * If the purchase processing is complete, check to
         * see if any items were returned. If not, it means
         * that the customer's credit was denied, and an
         * appropriate message should be displayed. If the
         * collection was returned, then displayed the contents
         * of the array in a table.
         */
        Item[] items = storeProxy.getResults(ch);
        if (items != null) {
%>
        <h1>Widgets R Us Online Store</h1>
        <p>Thanks! Here are the results of your purchase.</p>
                <table width="401">
                  <tr>
                    <td width="120">
                       <div align="left"><b>Item Name</b></div>
                    </td>
                    <td width="80"><b>Item Price</b>
                       <div align="left"></div>
                    </td>
                    <td width="100">
                       <div align="left"><b>Item Code</b></div>
                    </td>
                  </tr>
                  <tr>
                    <td colspan=3>
                       <hr noshade size="1"/>
                    </td>
                  </tr>
<%
                for (int i = 0; i < items.length; i++){
                    Item currentItem = items[i];
```

Chapter 10: Calling Web Services from Outside WebLogic Workshop

```
%>
                        <tr>
                          <td width="120">
                            <div align="left">
                                <%= currentItem.getName() %>
                            </div>
                          </td>
                          <td width="80">
                            <div align="left">
                                <%= currentItem.getPrice() %>
                            </div>
                          </td>
                          <td width="100">
                            <div align="left">
                                Code: <%= currentItem.getCode() %>
                            </div>
                          .</td>
                        </tr>
<%
            }
%>
                </table>
<%
        } else {
        /*
         * If an array of items was not returned by the web
         * service, it means that the customer's credit
         * wasn't accepted.
         */
%>
        <h1>Widgets R Us Online Store</h1>
        <p>Sorry. It looks as though your credit has been
           declined.</p>
<%
        }
%>
    </body>
<%
    } else {
%>
    <!--
        The startTimer is called (in other words, polling begins)
        only if the isPurchaseComplete method returned "false".
    -->
```

Continued

Listing 10-8 *(Continued)*

```
    <body onload="startTimer()">
        <h1>Widgets R Us Online Store</h1>
        <p><b>Please wait while we process your order.</b></p>
    </body>
</html>
<%
    }
} catch ( java.rmi.RemoteException re )
{
    session.setAttribute( "errMsg", re.detail.getMessage() );
    response.sendRedirect( "errorPage.jsp" );
}
%>
```

Developing a Swing Client

In this section, I describe how you can use the proxy within a Swing application. Rather than describe how you might build a complete Swing application to use the OnlineStore Web service, I'll focus on the pieces related to WebLogic Workshop. The basics of a Swing application are the same for a Web service client as they are for any client that accesses some remote resource.

In particular, in this example I'll focus on how you might use the proxy to get the list of items in the catalog and display them in a table, as shown in Figure 10-6. Along the way, the example shows code for setting up the proxy and using the conversation.

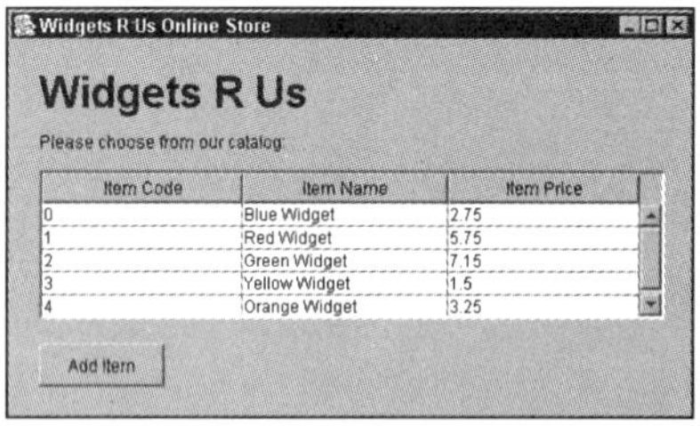

Figure 10-6: A simple Swing application displaying a list of items.

As with the JSP example, your application will need to import the classes and packages needed to use the proxy.

```
import weblogic.jws.proxies.*;
import org.openuri.www.Item;
import org.openuri.www.x2002.x04.soap.conversation.*;
```

Chapter 10: Calling Web Services from Outside WebLogic Workshop

In Listing 10-9, we'll declare the member variables for things we'll need in various parts of the application. This includes proxy classes, variables needed for the conversation, and variables for user interface components.

Listing 10-9: Declaring Proxy and Conversation Variables

```
/*
 * Declare variables to hold the proxy classes and the URL that
 * points to the web service. Of course, in a real application,
 * the URL's host name and port number would not likely belong to
 * the local server.
 */
OnlineStorePoll_Impl storeServiceProxy;
OnlineStorePollSoap storeProxy;
String serverURL =
"http://localhost:7001/bookproject/Chapter08/OnlineStorePoll.jws?WSDL";

/*
 * Variables needed when starting and maintaining a conversation.
 */
String convID;
StartHeader sh;
ContinueHeader ch;

/*
 * Variables to hold the Item array returned by the viewCatalog
 * method, and to represent the JTable and JScrollPane that we'll
 * use in the user interface.
 */
Item[] catalogItems;
javax.swing.JTable tblCatalog;
javax.swing.JScrollPane scrCatalog;
```

This simple example implements several methods designed to set up the Web service proxy, generate the conversation ID as a GUID, and create a JTable and fill it with items from the catalog.

The createProxy method assigns values to the proxy variables declared earlier. The code in Listing 10-10 should look similar to what you saw in the JSP example in Listing 10-5.

Listing 10-10: A Function to Initialize the Proxy Classes

```
private void createProxy()
{
```

Continued

Listing 10-10 *(Continued)*

```
    try
    {
        storeServiceProxy = new OnlineStorePoll_Impl(serverURL);
        storeProxy = storeServiceProxy.getOnlineStorePollSoap();
}
    catch (IOException ex)
    {
        System.out.println("Error creating proxy");
    }
}
```

The `generateConvID` method in Listing 10-11 merely creates a GUID that we can use when sending conversation headers. The code here was introduced earlier in this chapter.

Listing 10-11: A Function to Generate a GUID

```
public void generateConvID()
{
    java.rmi.server.UID uid = new java.rmi.server.UID();
    String iastr = null;
    try
    {
        java.net.InetAddress ia =
            java.net.InetAddress.getLocalHost();
        iastr = ia.getHostAddress();
    }
    catch(java.net.UnknownHostException uhe)
    {
        iastr = "uknownhost";
    }

    String guid = iastr + "-" + uid.toString();

    /*
     * Colons won't be accepted by the WebLogic
     * Workshop runtime.
     */
    guid = guid.replace(':', '.');
    guid = guid.replace('[', '(');
    guid = guid.replace(']', ')');
    convID = guid;
}
```

Chapter 10: Calling Web Services from Outside WebLogic Workshop

The `generateCatalogTable` method in Listing 10-12 does most of the interesting work in this example. It starts the conversation to get things going, then continues it when retrieving catalog information.

Listing 10-12: Generating a Table to Contain the List of Items

```
public TableModel generateCatalogTable () {
   try {
      /*
       * Call the startShopping method with a user name and
       * and customer number passed from a login dialog box
       * (that code is not shown here). This starts the
       * conversation by passing a StartHeader (initialized
       * in code later in this section).
       */
      String greeting = storeProxy.startShopping(userName,
         customerNumber, sh);
      /*
       * Call the viewCatalog method to retrieve the list of
       * items in the catalog. Notice that a ContinueHeader is
       * passed with the method call.
       */
      catalogItems = storeProxy.viewCatalog(ch);
   } catch (java.rmi.RemoteException re) {
      /*
       * Code to retrieve the contents of the error detail
       * and display an error message the user.
       */
   }

   /*
    * Declare an array of Object arrays to use for filling the
    * table with the list of items. We'll assign a value from a
    * method that converts the Item array returned by the web
    * service to the type we need here. Code for the method
    * follows.
    */
   final Object[][] itemsList = convertItems(catalogItems);

   /*
    * Create a new TableModel object that will be used to create a
    * JTable.
    */
   TableModel catalogTable = new AbstractTableModel() {
```

Continued

Listing 10-12 *(Continued)*

```
            /* Set the table's values to the contents of the array
             * of Object arrays.
             */
            Object[][] data = itemsList;
            /* Set the table's headers. */
            String[] headers = {"Item Code", "Item Name", "Item Price"};

            /* Implement methods of the AbstractTableModel interface
             * using the data and headers variables.
             */
            public int getRowCount() {
                return itemsList.length;
            }
            public int getColumnCount() {
                return headers.length;
            }
            public Object getValueAt( int row, int column ) {
                return data[row][column];
            }
            public String getColumnName( int column ) {
                return headers[column];
            }
        };
        return catalogTable;
    }
```

The convertItems method in Listing 10-13 is a utility method needed to convert the Item array returned by the viewCatalog method into a type that we can use to fill out the table. There are other ways to accomplish this task, such as creating a custom table model that accepts an array of Item objects, but this will do for our purposes.

Listing 10-13: Converting the Item Array to an Array of Object Arrays

```
public Object[][] convertItems (Item[] items) {

    /*
     * Declare an array of Object arrays, giving it values
     * corresponding to the number of items in the list (for
     * table rows) and the number of fields in the Item class
     * for table columns.
     */
    Object[][] itemsArray = new Object[items.length][3];

    /*
```

Chapter 10: Calling Web Services from Outside WebLogic Workshop

```java
     * Loop through the array of items, turning each one into
     * an array whose members are its code, name, and price fields.
     */
    for (int i = 0; i < items.length; i++) {
        Object[] itemArray = new Object[3];
        itemArray[0] = new Integer(items[i].getCode());
        itemArray[1] = items[i].getName();
        itemArray[2] = new Double(items[i].getPrice());
        itemsArray[i] = itemArray;
    }

    /* Return the new array of Object arrays. */
    return itemsArray;
}
```

Finally, the `initComponents` method in Listing 10-14 sets up all the pieces.

Listing 10-14: Setting Up the User Interface

```java
public void initComponents() throws Exception {

    /*
     * Call the createProxy and generateConvID methods to initialize
     * the proxy classes and conversation ID value.
     */
    createProxy();
    generateConvID();

    /*
     * Initialize variable for the start header and continue values.
     * These use the conversation ID assigned to a member variable
     * from generatedConvID.
     */
    sh = new StartHeader(convID,
        "http://localhost:7001/OnlineStorePoll.jws");
    ch = new ContinueHeader(convID);

    /*
     * Initialize the catalog table using the TableModel object
     * returned by the generateCatalogTable method. Insert the
     * new table into a JScrollPane.
     */
    tblCatalog = new javax.swing.JTable(generateCatalogTable());
    scrCatalog = new javax.swing.JScrollPane(tblCatalog);
```

Continued

Listing 10-14 *(Continued)*

```
/*
 * The remaining code sets up other user interface elements
 * used by the application, the pull it all together in the
 * window.
 */
tblCatalog.setVisible(true);
tblCatalog.setSize(new java.awt.Dimension(450, 103));
tblCatalog.setLocation(new java.awt.Point(20, 90));

scrCatalog.setSize(new java.awt.Dimension(450, 103));
scrCatalog.setLocation(new java.awt.Point(20, 90));
scrCatalog.setVisible(true);

lblCatalog.setSize(new java.awt.Dimension(240, 20));
lblCatalog.setLocation(new java.awt.Point(20, 60));
lblCatalog.setVisible(true);
lblCatalog.setText("Please choose from our catalog:");
lblCatalog.setForeground(java.awt.Color.black);
lblCatalog.setFont(new java.awt.Font("SansSerif", 0, 12));

btnAddItem.setSize(new java.awt.Dimension(90, 30));
btnAddItem.setLocation(new java.awt.Point(20, 210));
btnAddItem.setVisible(true);
btnAddItem.setText("Add Item");

lblWidgetsLogo.setSize(new java.awt.Dimension(220, 50));
lblWidgetsLogo.setLocation(new java.awt.Point(20, 10));
lblWidgetsLogo.setVisible(true);
lblWidgetsLogo.setText("Widgets R Us");
lblWidgetsLogo.setForeground(java.awt.Color.black);
lblWidgetsLogo.setFont(new java.awt.Font("Dialog", 1, 30));

setLocation(new java.awt.Point(0, 0));
setSize(new java.awt.Dimension(497, 285));
getContentPane().setLayout(null);
setTitle("Widgets R Us Online Store");
getContentPane().add(scrCatalog);
getContentPane().add(lblCatalog);
getContentPane().add(btnAddItem);
getContentPane().add(lblWidgetsLogo);

}
```

As you can see, the proxy-related code for interacting with a conversational Web service is essentially the same whether the client is a JSP page or a Swing application (although the code around it is obviously different). In both cases, you create instances of the proxy so you can communicate with the Web service. You also generate a conversation ID that the client can use to associate itself with its initial request. In both the JSP and Swing cases, the proxy does the work of packaging your client's requests into a form the Web service can understand, and unpackaging responses for your client.

Summary

Test View provides a great way to test your Web service while you're debugging it, but to really put it through its paces you need a client. WebLogic Workshop provides an easy way for you to generate the proxy components that clients need to send requests to Web services and receive corresponding responses. This chapter showed you how to get those components and how to use them from JSP pages and a Swing application.

- If the Web service returns its response with callbacks, it may need to provide an alternative means for clients to get results if it will be accessed by clients that aren't other WebLogic Workshop Web services. In this way, clients unable to handle callbacks can query for results themselves.

- One way to provide an alternative to callbacks is with a wrapper service. A wrapper service acts as an intermediary between the client and the original service, storing the request results and providing a synchronous method through which clients can retrieve the results.

- Clients access Web services via a proxy. Proxy components are available through a link in Test View. Client code accesses the Web service by calling methods of the proxy.

- Clients that interact with conversational Web services include a conversation ID with their requests. Through this unique identifier, WebLogic Server keeps track of the client's exchanges with a particular instance of the service. Client code sends the conversation ID as the last parameter of calls to Web service methods.

- Through a combination of scripting and HTML, JavaServer Pages provides a way to create a browser-based request-specific user interface. Server-side Java code enables the user interface to be based on data specific to the request. Through client-side code, you can add polling behavior that repeatedly asks the service for its results.

- Through code very similar to what you might use in a JSP, you can also use the proxy components from a Swing application.

Chapter 11

Using JavaScript in XML Maps

IN THIS CHAPTER

- Translating between XML and Java
- Understanding the JavaScript language
- Getting acquainted with the tools the JavaScript extensions provide
- Putting JavaScript to work with maps

As you discovered in Chapter 6, you can use XML maps to control how incoming XML messages are translated to Java, and how Java is translated into outgoing XML. XML maps offer a declarative approach through which they resemble the XML messages they are intended to translate. As a result, they're fairly easy to use.

For those times when the declarative approach alone isn't enough, WebLogic Workshop provides a way for you to incorporate JavaScript's procedural approach into your maps.

To ease XML handling, WebLogic Workshop includes a set of language extensions planned for future versions of ECMAScript, the international standard version of JavaScript. These extensions include enhancements to existing JavaScript operators and keywords, as well as several new functions specifically for use with XML.

Enhancing XML Maps with Script

Before getting into JavaScript, I'd like to add to what you already know about XML maps by giving a little information about how you connect script to them. You use JavaScript for mapping by "calling" a JavaScript function from within an XML map. You define this function in a JSX file, declaring it according to certain rules so that the run-time environment knows how to use it. At run time, when WebLogic Server checks the XML map for translation guidelines, it executes the script.

In Listing 11-1, a parameter XML map example, the code in curly braces is a reference to a JavaScript function in a file called POMaps.jsx. The JSX file is part of a WebLogic Workshop project called PurchaseOrder.

Listing 11-1: A Parameter Map with a Call to a JavaScript Function

```
/**
 * @jws:operation
 * @jws:parameter-xml xml-map::
 * <submitOrder>
 *     {PurchaseOrder.POMaps.translatePurchaseOrder(
 *         addr, items)}
 * </submitOrder>
 * ::
 */
public PurchaseOrder submitOrder(Address addr, Item[] items)
{...}
```

Connecting JavaScript with XML maps is an area that can be somewhat confusing at first glance. Later in this chapter, I more fully describe the relationship between XML maps and script. First, I'd like to give a bit of introductory information about JavaScript. If you're already familiar with JavaScript, you may want to skip on to the section of the chapter about WebLogic Workshop's JavaScript tools for XML.

A JavaScript Primer

If you've never used JavaScript, this section is for you. I'll give a brief overview of the language, focusing on the pieces that are most useful to get you started with writing script for your mapping needs. If you're a Java programmer, JavaScript will look, well, a little familiar. Despite its name, however, JavaScript isn't Java, or even a subset of Java. Yet, because they do have some syntax similarities, you probably won't need much time to get acquainted with it.

Variables

As with other programming languages, you use variables to store values your code will use. Typically, you declare a variable in JavaScript by using the `var` keyword.

```
/* Declaring a JavaScript variable and assign a value to it. */
var i = 42;
```

One of the most important distinctions between JavaScript and Java is that variables in JavaScript are dynamically typed. That is, in JavaScript you don't need to indicate a variable's type when you declare it; the JavaScript interpreter assigns a type based on the value you assign to the variable. As a result, you have a great deal of flexibility when working with JavaScript variables, as in the following example:

```
/* Declare a JavaScript variable and assign it a number value. */
var i = 42;

/* Assign a string value to the same variable. */
i = "A string value.";
```

You can also declare variables as objects of a specific type, as shown in Listing 11-2. This is useful in script for mapping because you'll want to use types from your Web service project's Java code in your JavaScript mapping code.

Listing 11-2: Declaring Object Variables

```
/*
 * Declare a variable to hold the current date using JavaScript's
 * Date object.
 */
var currentDate = new Date();

/*
 * Declare a variable to hold purchase order information. Use a
 * PurchaseOrder class defined in your web service project. Notice
 * that it is first necessary to import the class into the script.
 * The import statement used here is a part of JavaScript, not Java.
 */
import MyService.PurchaseOrder;
var purchaseOrder = new PurchaseOrder();
```

In JavaScript that you write for mapping, the interpreter supports new underlying data types designed specifically for XML. As you'll see in "JavaScript Tools for Handling XML," this type is used automatically when you assign an XML value to a variable.

Objects and object hierarchies

Through JavaScript, you can access an object's properties and navigate the hierarchies of which objects are often a part. For example, imagine that a `PurchaseOrder` object defined by your Web service defined an `orderNumber` field. You could set the field's value using the following code:

```
import MyService.PurchaseOrder;
var purchaseOrder = new PurchaseOrder();

/* Use the dot operator to specify the orderNumber field. */
purchaseOrder.orderNumber = "12-345-6789";
```

The dot operator is used here to access the `orderNumber` field. As you will see, this operator is similarly handy in accessing XML within WebLogic Workshop.

There's another way to get at the properties of objects in JavaScript as well. You can use square brackets instead of the dot operator. This is especially handy when the property name is available only at run time, and it's very useful with XML. In typical JavaScript, for example, the following lines are equivalent:

```
var propertyValue = objectVariable.objectProperty;
var propertyValue = objectVariable["objectProperty"];
```

I describe this in more detail in the section on working with XML hierarchies.

You can call functions exposed by objects. For example, you can use the `Math` object when writing script that makes calculations. The `Math` object's `ceil` function rounds a number to the closest integer that is greater than or equal to its argument.

```
var unroundedNumber = 5.2;

/* Round the unrounded number up. The result is 6.0. */
var roundedNumber = Math.ceil( unroundedNumber );
```

As you will see, JavaScript in WebLogic Workshop includes many functions useful for handling XML. For a summary of these functions, see Table 11-4 at the end of this chapter.

Arrays

As in Java, arrays in JavaScript are lists of numbered items. You access a given item by its number, or *index*. Listing 11-3 demonstrates this for you.

Listing 11-3: Creating and Accessing JavaScript Arrays

```
/* Declare an array variable. */
var myArray = new Array();

/*
 * Using the array's indices, set the values of the array's first
 * and second items. Note that the array index starts from 0.
 */
myArray[0] = "item1";
myArray[1] = "item2";

/*
 * Declare a variable with the value of the array's first member:
 * "item1".
 */
```

```
var item1String = myArray[0];
```

Notice that an array's index numbering begins at 0, rather than 1. So, the first item will be at index 0, the second at 1, and so on.

You can also create a new array simply by initializing a variable to a value enclosed in square brackets. The following code accomplishes the same result as the preceding array declaration and assignment examples.

```
var myArray = ["item1", "item2"];
```

The syntax of array use, particularly the square brackets, is an important part of handling lists of XML elements in WebLogic Workshop.

Declaring functions

As in Java, functions in JavaScript are a way to define a piece of code that you can use from other code. In your function's declaration, you can optionally specify parameters. You can also define the function's code so that it returns a value (see Listing 11-4).

Listing 11-4: Declaring a JavaScript Function

```
/* Declare a function designed to put two strings into an array. */
function namesArray( name1, name2 )
{
    /*
     * Create the array, put the two strings into it, and return it
     * to the caller.
     */
    return [name1, name2];
}

/*
 * Call the function, passing it two strings as arguments. The
 * result is that bothNames is an array whose first member is
 * "Joe", and whose second member is "Maxine".
 */
var bothNames = makeNamesArray( "Joe", "Maxine" );
```

In JavaScript functions, you call from XML maps, the function declaration and return value follow specific rules, as you'll see later in "Writing Script Functions for Mapping."

if, else if, and else

Through `if...else` structures, you can write code that executes based on a particular condition. The JavaScript interpreter tests to see whether the expression in parentheses following the `if` statement is true; if it is, the interpreter executes the code in curly braces. You can optionally include an `else if` statement to test for another condition, and an `else` statement to execute if all tests return false.

For an illustration, take a look at Listing 11-5. Imagine passing to it the `bothNames` array from the preceding array example.

Listing 11-5: Using if, else if, and else

```
function composeSalutation ( arrayOfFirstNames )
{
   /*
    * Declare a variable that may be set from multiple places in
    * code.
    */
   var salutation = null;

   /*
    * Use conditions to test for gender and set an appropriate
    * salutation.
    */
   if ( arrayOfFirstNames[0] == "Joe" )
   {
      salutation = "Dear Sir";
   }
   else if ( arrayOfFirstNames[0] == "Maxine" )
   {
      salutation = "Dear Madam";
   }
   else
   {
      salutation = "To Whom It May Concern";
   }

   /*
    * Combine the salutation with another string to make a complete
    * greeting.
    */
   return salutation;
}
```

for and for...in

JavaScript provides a few ways to write code that repeats an action for a set of variables. However, the `for` and `for...in` statements, which examine a list of items and perform an action for each one, may prove to be most useful in your mapping script. This is because code for mapping is often designed to interact with lists: XML elements, members of an array or collection defined in your Web service project, and so on.

The `for` statement loops through a list of numbered items, so it's a natural for use with arrays. The syntax of a `for` loop looks like the following:

```
for( set a variable ; test a condition ; change the variable )
    do something each time the test succeeds
```

Listing 11-6 shows how your code might loop through an array.

Listing 11-6: Using for and for...in

```
/* Declare a variable as an array with two members. */
var arrayOfNames = ["Joe", "Maxine"];

/*
 * Create a number to test by and set it to 0. Make the test "as
 * long as the number is less than the total number of items in the
 * arrayOfNames array" (in other words, 2). After each loop,
 * increment the test number by one.
 */
for( var i = 0; i < arrayOfNames.length; i++ )
{
    /* Print the current name to the console. */
    print ( arrayOfNames[i] );
}
```

Note the `print` statement in this example. In JavaScript that you write in a JSX file, this statement prints the specified text to the console (command prompt) window created when you start WebLogic Server.

Like a `for` loop, a `for...in` loop examines a list of items and executes code for each one. However, a `for...in` loop is designed to loop through an object by using a property of the object, rather than an index of its members. The following code accomplishes the same result as the preceding array example.

```
for( var name in arrayOfNames )
{
    /* Print the current name to the console. */
    print ( arrayOfNames[name] );
}
```

As you might imagine, this kind of loop is useful when the `for...in` statement specifies an XML element. I'll describe that approach in more detail later in this chapter.

JavaScript includes many other statements, including other loop structures, you may find useful. I've limited this primer to those most commonly used, but you may want to explore the others by reading a book that covers the subject in more depth, such as *JavaScript Bible*, by Danny Goodman and Brendan Eich.

Now, on to XML!

JavaScript Tools for Handling XML

As I've mentioned, WebLogic Workshop provides an extended version of JavaScript through which you can handle XML as you might handle similar containers for structured data, including objects and arrays. These extensions include native XML data types, as well as operators and functions designed specifically for use with the new types.

If you're familiar with other approaches to handling XML within a programming language, you've seen how awkward they can sometimes be. For example, working with a document object model (DOM) application programming interface (API) can mean writing a string of function calls to get to a nested element or attribute. WebLogic Workshop's JavaScript extensions simplify the process by building on conventions and concepts inherent in the JavaScript language.

Listing 11-7 is a simple example that you could write without importing or declaring any supporting types.

Listing 11-7: Using XML in JavaScript

```
/*
 * Declare an XML variable and assign values to its elements.
 * Note that the value on the right side of the assignment
 * is an XML literal. It begins with a < symbol. Note, too, that
 * enclosing the value in quotation marks would end up assigning a
 * string to myXML, rather than an XML value.
 */
var myXML = <name><first/><last/></name>;
myXML.name.first = "John";
myXML.name.last = "Doe";
```

This code builds the following XML:

```
<name>
    <first>John</first>
    <last>Doe</last>
</name>
```

Support for XML is built into the JavaScript interpreter available with WebLogic Workshop. In the remainder of this chapter, I'll describe the tools that WebLogic Workshop gives you for XML access. I'll also provide examples of those tools in use. Finally, I'll illustrate how you can connect the JavaScript you write with your Web service via XML maps.

Creating XML variables

As illustrated in the preceding examples, the JavaScript extensions that do the most to support XML handling in WebLogic Workshop are, as it turns out, pieces of technology you don't have to think much about. The extended JavaScript includes new data types to represent XML. Variables you declare as XML differ from other kinds of variables in that with them, you can use operators and functions specifically intended for use with XML.

However, in keeping with JavaScript's dynamically typed nature, the role of these new types is transparent. They're automatically used when you assign an XML value to a variable, as in Listing 11-8.

Listing 11-8: Declaring XML Variables

```
/* Create an integer variable. */
var i = 4;

/* Create a string variable. */
var s = "Joe";

/* Create an XML variable.
 * Note that the assignment is not enclosed in quotes
 */
var x = <name>
    <firstname>Joe</firstname>
    <lastname>Smith</lastname>
</name>;
```

Notice that the value on the right side of the XML variable assignment looks like it might be a string, but isn't enclosed in quotes. This is important. If the value were enclosed in quotation marks, the script interpreter would treat it just as any other string. By beginning the value with a bare < symbol, you're telling the interpreter that the value should be treated as XML. This is similar to declaring an array variable with a value that begins with a [symbol. Such a declaration might appear as follows: `var letters = ["a", "b", "c"];`

As I mentioned, there are two new data types in the extended JavaScript. The preceding example shows a simple XML assignment in which the root element is <name>. For those cases when you need a variable containing XML that isn't well-formed (in other words, doesn't have a root), you can make the assignment as in the following example:

```
/* Create an XML variable. */
var nameFragment = <>
    <firstname>Joe</firstname>
    <lastname>Smith</lastname>
</>;
```

Notice the use of <> and </> to enclose the value. These "anonymous" element tags represent a kind of false root — a sanctioned "cheat" through which you can assign values that aren't well formed. Still, you'll find anonymous tags invaluable in handling XML.

Working with hierarchies

One of XML's most recognizable and useful characteristics is its hierarchical nature. JavaScript in WebLogic Workshop provides several tools through which you can navigate hierarchically deep XML. These are the . (dot) operator, the .. (double-dot) operator, and the .@ (attribute) operator.

To illustrate these, I'll use the `purchaseOrderXML` variable defined in Listing 11-9.

Listing 11-9: An XML Variable Illustrating Hierarchy and Lists

```
var purchaseOrderXML = <purchaseOrder orderNumber = "12-345-6789">
  <shippingAddress>
    <name>
        <first>Bob</first>
        <last>Smith</last>
    </name>
    <street>1234 Somewhere Lane</street>
    <city>Someplace</city>
    <state>SW</state>
    <zip>12345</zip>
  </shippingAddress>
  <item>
    <name>Green Widget</name>
    <price>25.92</price>
    <quantity>3</quantity>
  </item>
  <item>
    <name>Blue Widget</name>
```

```
      <price>44.66</price>
      <quantity>6</quantity>
    </item>
    <item>
      <name>Yellow Widget</name>
      <price>22.16</price>
      <quantity>2</quantity>
    </item>
</purchaseOrder>;
```

For handling hierarchies, the dot operator is perhaps the most familiar. When used with objects, the dot operator accesses the value of the object property specified on the right side of the operator. The same is true with XML, in which an element's children are treated as properties of the element. The following example illustrates one way to retrieve the first name of the person whose shipping address is given on the purchase order:

```
/* Declare a variable set to "Bob". */
var firstName =
    purchaseOrderXML.purchaseOrder.shippingAddress.name.first;
```

Fortunately, there are easier ways to reach deeply nested children. WebLogic Workshop introduces a double-dot operator through which you can skip multiple levels of the hierarchy to get to the level you're interested in. The following example accomplishes the same goal as the preceding.

```
var firstName = purchaseOrderXML..first;
```

When using the double-dot operator to query for a list, keep in mind that the expression will return *all* matching elements (or attributes) nested within the XML represented by the left operand — regardless of where they are in the hierarchy. Looking back at the `purchaseOrderXML` variable, imagine an expression querying for <name> elements.

```
var names = purchaseOrderXML..name;
```

This expression will return the <name> elements nested in both the <shippingAddress> and <item> elements. And that may not be what you wanted. When you need to, you can reduce the ambiguity by specifying the parent of the element you're trying to reach.

```
/* Get all of the <name> elements nested within <item> elements. */
var names = purchaseOrderXML..item.name;
```

Incidentally, the extensions for XML also support using square brackets to access property values — in other words, accessing the XML as an associative array. In this way, you can write code that accesses a child element even when you don't know the element's name until run time. The following example returns the <first> element:

```
var childElementName = "first";
var firstName = purchaseOrderXML..name[childElementName];
```

Another new operator is the attribute operator. Like the dot and double-dot, its use is fairly straightforward:

```
/*
 * Declare a variable and assign to it the value of the
 * purchaseOrder element's orderNumber attribute.
 */
var orderNumber = purchaseOrderXML.purchaseOrder.@orderNumber;
```

Finally, the extensions to JavaScript for XML offer four functions through which you can access XML hierarchically. A few of them overlap with other, more intuitive means for handling XML described in this section. Also, because they bear a resemblance to somewhat awkward DOM-oriented APIs, you may find yourself gravitating away from them and toward using operators. However, some functions are useful when you won't know the value by which you're querying until run time. These functions are:

- attribute
- child
- childIndex
- children
- parent

The attribute function returns the value of the attribute specified as its argument. The attribute function is an alternative to the .@ operator. Because you may pass it a variable rather than a literal value, the attribute function is useful when the attribute in question is unknown until run time:

```
/*
 * Declare a variable and assign to it the value of the
 * purchaseOrder element's orderNumber attribute.
 */
var numberAttribute = "orderNumber";
var orderNumber =
```

```
                    purchaseOrderXML.purchaseOrder.attribute(numberAttribute);
```

The `child` function returns a child of an element based on the child's *index* (its place in the order of the element's children):

```
/* Declare a variable set to "Bob". */
var firstNameIndex = 1;
var firstName =
    purchaseOrderXML.purchaseOrder.shippingAddress.name.child(
        firstNameIndex);
```

The `childIndex` function returns the index of the child element specified in the function's argument:

```
/* Declare a variable set to the index of the <first> element: "1". */
var firstNameIndex =
    purchaseOrderXML.purchaseOrder.shippingAddress.name.first.childIndex();
```

The `children` function returns all of the children of the XML on which the function is called:

```
/*
 * Declare a variable set to the first and last name of the person
 * whose shipping address is given.
 */
var recipientName =
    purchaseOrderXML..shippingAddress.name.children();
```

The `parent` function returns, as you might expect, the parent of the XML on which the function is called. Note that the element returned is the entire element and its children.

```
/*
 * Declare a variable set to the <purchaseOrder> element -- in other
 * words, the entire XML.
 */
var rootElement =
    purchaseOrderXML..shippingAddress.parent();
```

Before moving on, I should point out something that may already have struck you as unusual. When accessing XML variables declared from literal XML values, such as the `purchaseOrderXML` variable, you interact with the variable itself as a container for the XML — not the top level of the hierarchy.

Working with lists

Many of the queries you make using the extensions described in this chapter will return an XML list. With lists, you can write code that accesses listed members iteratively, as with an array.

For the next several examples, I'll use the following XML variable shown in Listing 11-10.

Listing 11-10: An XML Variable Illustrating an XML List

```
var itemList = <items>
    <item number = "12-345-6789">
        <name>Green Widget</name>
        <price>25.92</price>
        <quantity>3</quantity>
    </item>
    <item number = "98-765-4321">
        <name>Blue Widget</name>
        <price>44.66</price>
        <quantity>6</quantity>
    </item>
    <item number = "22-333-4444">
        <name>Yellow Widget</name>
        <price>22.16</price>
        <quantity>2</quantity>
     </item>
</items>;
```

In the `itemList` variable, the set of `<item>` elements, along with their respective children, forms an XML list. The following code returns the complete list of the `<item>` elements and their children:

```
var itemElements = itemList..item;
```

You can access the siblings in this value by treating the value as if it were an array whose index starts at 0. For example, the following code changes the first `<item>` element's `<quantity>` value from 3 to 5:

```
itemElements[0].quantity = 5;
```

Filtering by value

Accessing XML list members by index is useful when your code must access all members in the list. When the XML's content drives the action, on the other hand, you'd be better off using a filtering predicate expression. With filtering predicates (a term borrowed from a query technology called XPath), you use parentheses to specify how XML returned from an expression should be filtered. Predicates are especially useful when the value you'll be filtering with won't be known until run time.

You might write the following code if you wanted to find out if the purchase order your service received requested certain quantities.

```
/*
 * Declare a variable holding the number of items that will serve as
 * a threshold, then use the variable in a predicate to find any
 * <item> whose <quantity> child elements contain values greater
 * than 5.
 */
var amountThreshold = 5;
var bigPurchase = itemList..item.(quantity > amountThreshold);
```

In another example, you may want to check to see if the purchaser requested an item with a particular number. You can use a predicate to filter attributes as well as elements. When filtering attributes, you must use the thisXML keyword. thisXML specifies that the action following it should be performed on the XML returned by the expression that precedes it. In the following example, thisXML represents the list of all <item> elements in itemList:

```
/*
 * Declare a variable holding the number to look for, then use
 * the variable in a predicate to find any <item> element whose
 * number attribute is "22-333-4444".
 */
var magicNumber = "22-333-4444";
var magicItem =
    itemList.items.item.(thisXML.@number == magicNumber);
```

Note that predicates can even contain expressions that evaluate to XML values, as in the following rather redundant example:

```
var bigPurchase =
    itemList..item.(quantity > itemList..item[0].quantity);
```

Xpath Syntax and JavaScript

I mentioned that the idea of predicates is borrowed from a technology called XPath. XPath is a syntax for identifying XML. Although its syntax is very different, what it does bears some resemblance to some of the JavaScript conventions described in this chapter. The extensions for JavaScript provide a way for you to use XPath expressions if that's a technology you're familiar with. The `xpath` function executes an XPath expression. The following example using the `xpath` function is equivalent to the preceding predicate example:

```
var bigPurchase =
    itemList.items.xpath("//item[quantity > '5']");
```

Combining, inserting, and deleting

Pruning and grafting the branches of XML trees can be a large part of script for mapping. In particular, within ToXML functions, where you may be assembling a large or complex XML structure for an outgoing message, you'll want the ability to combine separately created XML chunks. The JavaScript extensions for XML provide three operators that are useful for this kind of work: + (plus), += (plus-equals), and `delete`.

The `plus` operator combines pieces of XML. This is comparable to concatenating separate strings, except that you can access the distinct XML pieces within the combined unit. The plus-equals operator appends its right operand to the end of the list that includes the element represented by the left operand. The plus-equals operator can be a shortcut alternative to the plus operator.

Listing 11-11 uses both operators. First, it builds a list of two <item> elements, then it inserts the list at the end of the existing set of <item> elements.

Listing 11-11: Combining XML with the + and += Operators

```
/* Declare a variables to hold new <item> elements. */
var newItem1 = <item number = "66-564-5482">
        <name>Black Widget</name>
        <price>58.63</price>
        <quantity>1</quantity>
    </item>;

var newItem2 = <item number = "65-852-1596">
        <name>Red Widget</name>
        <price>49.95</price>
        <quantity>9</quantity>
    </item>;

/*
 * Use the plus operator to combine the new elements, and the
 * plus-equals operator to insert the newly combined
 * elements as children of the <items> element.
 */
itemList..items.item[1] += newItem1 + newItem2;
```

The result of the example in Listing 11-11 would be the following:

```
<items>
    <item number="12-345-6789">
        <name>Green Widget</name>
        <price>25.92</price>
        <quantity>3</quantity>
    </item>
    <item number="98-765-4321">
        <name>Blue Widget</name>
        <price>44.66</price>
        <quantity>6</quantity>
    </item>
    <item number="22-333-4444">
        <name>Yellow Widget</name>
        <price>22.16</price>
        <quantity>2</quantity>
    </item>
    <item number="66-564-5482">
        <name>Black Widget</name>
        <price>58.63</price>
        <quantity>1</quantity>
    </item>
    <item number="65-852-1596">
        <name>Red Widget</name>
        <price>49.95</price>
        <quantity>9</quantity>
    </item>
</items>
```

The `appendChild` function is similar to the plus-equals operator. However, `appendChild` inserts well-formed XML immediately after the element specified on the left side of the dot operator. The `combinedItems` variable in the preceding example holds two sibling `<item>` elements, so it isn't well-formed. However, you could write code such as the following to insert them using `appendChild`:

```
/*
 * Insert each new element separately using the appendChild
 * function.
 */
itemList..items.appendChild(newItem1);
itemList..items.appendChild(newItem2);
```

The `prependChild` function works in a similar fashion, inserting its argument immediately preceding the element specified on the left side of the dot operator.

Like `appendChild`, the `innerXML` function inserts its argument into XML. You can use `innerXML` when you want to replace all of an element's children (if any) with other XML. If the element on which you call `innerXML` does not have any children, the function inserts the XML from its argument. As in the following example, you could use `innerXML` to replace (rather than append) the three existing `<item>` elements with the two new ones:

```
/*
 * Replace the three <item> elements in itemList with the two new
 * ones.
 */
itemList..items.innerXML(combinedItems);
```

The `delete` operator removes the XML specified by the expression to its right. Having assembled the list of `<item>` elements, you could remove the second one using the following code:

```
delete itemList..items[1];
```

Embedding expressions

In JavaScript you may use { } (curly braces) in a way you may already have seen in XML maps. With the extensions for XML, you can use { } to hold an *embedded expression* (an expression that will be evaluated before the surrounding XML is acted on by the script). This is useful when an XML value or element name will only be known at run time. For example, you might embed a calculation expression or an expression resolving to the value of another chunk of XML. Embedding expressions also allows you to fully initialize an XML variable when you declare it, as in the following example:

```
/* Declare variables to insert as attribute and element values. */
var number = "66-564-5482";
var itemName = "Black Widget";
var itemPrice = "58.63";
var itemQuantity = 1;

/*
 * Declare a variable to hold a new <item> element. Use embedded
 * expressions to fill in attribute and element values.
 */
var newItem1 = <item number = {number}>
        <name>{itemName}</name>
        <price>{itemPrice}</price>
        <quantity>{itemQuantity}</quantity>
    </item>;
```

Using loop structures with XML

Whether the XML message you're handling contains information for a purchase order, a shipment, or an employee list, the ability to write code that loops through a list of items is as useful as anywhere else. JavaScript's `for` and `for...in` are supported in the extensions for XML as they are elsewhere.

As with JavaScript arrays, you can use `for` statements to loop through XML lists based on the index of each list member. The following example uses the index of each `<item>` element to access the element and its attribute. The value returned by specifying the `number` attribute is a string, so using the `+=` operator here simply concatenates it with the value in quotation marks, appending `-01` to the end of each `number` attribute's value.

```
for ( var i = 0; i < itemList..item.length; i++ )
{
    itemList..item[i].@number += "-01";
}
```

A `for...in` loop differs from a `for` loop in that it accesses an object by property, rather than by index number. In the context of XML, when the object you're accessing is XML, its properties are its child elements.

Note that Listing 11-12 uses an embedded expression to calculate a 25 percent discount based on the value of the current `<item>` element's `<price>` element.

Listing 11-12: Using a for...in Loop with XML

```
/*
 * Declare a variable x as the current <item> element in the
 * loop. The expression "itemList..item" returns a list of all
 * <item> elements in itemList.
 */
for ( x in itemList..item )
{
    /*
     * Append "-01" to the end of each number attribute's value.
     */
    x.@number += "-01";

    /*
     * Create a new <discountPrice> element to hold the price of the
     * item with a 25 percent discount applied. Use the += operator
     * to insert the new element as the last child of the current
     * <item>. Use {} to hold an embedded expression to
     * calculate the new element's value before it's inserted.
     */
```

Continued

Listing 11-12 *(Continued)*
```
    x.quantity +=
        <discountPrice>{x.price - (x.price * .25)}</discountPrice>;
}
```

The preceding example results in the following XML:

```
<items>
    <item number="12-345-6789-01">
        <name>Green Widget</name>
        <price>25.92</price>
        <quantity>3</quantity>
        <discountPrice>19.44</discountPrice>
    </item>
    <item number="98-765-4321-01">
        <name>Blue Widget</name>
        <price>44.66</price>
        <quantity>6</quantity>
        <discountPrice>33.495</discountPrice>
    </item>
    <item number="22-333-4444-01">
        <name>Yellow Widget</name>
        <price>22.16</price>
        <quantity>2</quantity>
        <discountPrice>16.62</discountPrice>
    </item>
</items>
```

Filtering by namespace

Given XML's flexibility (you can name elements and attributes pretty much anything) naming collisions are likely to happen. This is particularly true when XML documents from disparate sources are combined. For example, a single XML chunk describing books authored by employees of a company might include two kinds of <title> elements — one for the book title and another for the employee's job title.

XML namespaces serve to ensure uniqueness and to label XML as belonging to a particular application. The uniqueness of a namespace is determined by its Uniform Resource Identifier (URI). (A URL is an example of a URI.) The URI is in turn associated with a short prefix, and the prefix is prepended to element tag names and attribute names to indicate that the elements belong to the namespace.

To access an element belonging to a particular namespace, you declare a variable corresponding to the namespace, then use the variable as a prefix when referring to the element in code. To declare a namespace variable, use the `namespace` operator. The declaration syntax looks like this:

Chapter 11: Using JavaScript in XML Maps

```
namespace ns as "theNamespaceURI";
```

In code that accesses the namespace-qualified element, you prefix the element's name with the namespace variable, separating the prefix and element names with :: (double colon), as shown here:

```
var elementValue = xmlVariable.ns::elementName;
```

With all the dots in it, this syntax can be a little hard to parse at first. To illustrate namespace access, I've altered the purchase order XML example (see Listing 11-13) so that it mixes elements from two namespaces. It now contains information sent to a book publisher requesting a book. As it happens, this publisher has a division that publishes college textbooks. They use two namespaces: one for the company as a whole and one for the division. Both namespaces have a <PO> element. The code following the XML declaration declares namespace variables for each of the two, then uses the variables to select data from the XML.

Listing 11-13: Accessing Namespace-Qualified XML

```
var PO =
<wly:PO xmlns:wly="http://www.wiley.com/">
    <wly:purchaseOrder orderNumber = "12-345-6789">
        <whe:PO xmlns:whe="http://jws-edcv.wiley.com/college/">
            <whe:title id="0-471-04365-6">Classical
                Mechanics</whe:title>
            <whe:author>Tai L. Chow</whe:author>
            <whe:pubDate>1996</whe:pubDate>
            <whe:count>56</whe:count>
        </whe:PO>
    </wly:purchaseOrder>
</wly:PO>;

/*
 * Declare namespace variables to hold each of the two URIs. The
 * variables need not be the same as the namespace prefixes, but
 * it's convient to use them.
 */
namespace wly as "http://www.wiley.com/";
namespace whe as "http://jws-edcv.wiley.com/college/";

/*
 * Use the wly namespace variable to return the PO number for this
 * purchase order.
 */
```

Continued

Listing 11-13 *(Continued)*

```
var poNumber = PO..wly::purchaseOrder.@orderNumber;

/*
 * Use the whe namespace variable to ensure that the correct <PO>
 * element is used to reach the <title> element.
 */
var title = PO..whe::PO.whe::title;
```

While you're thinking about namespaces, I'd like to point out that the extensions for XML provide a function through which you can get the namespace with which a given chunk of XML is associated. The following code, for example, will return http://jws-edcv.wiley.com/college/:

```
var titleURI = title.namespaceURI();
```

Importing Java classes

When you write script to translate XML to Java, you must import the Java classes that define the types to which your code is translating. For example, if your code translates XML to a `PurchaseOrder` object defined in your Web service, you must import the `PurchaseOrder` class in order to use it in script. In fact, you may import any Java class just as you would for Java code.

There is an important difference between the Java `import` statement and the `import` statement available with JavaScript in WebLogic Workshop: the JavaScript `import` statement does not support importing packages — only classes. In other words you may not use a * symbol to import all classes within the specified package. Here is an example of the JavaScript `import` statement:

```
import BookProject.Chapter11.POTranslator.PurchaseOrder;
```

Debugging JavaScript

It may not look like it, but your JSX file in Source View *does* support debugging. The fact that the syntax isn't colored is pretty misleading. Still, you can set breakpoints and examine values just as you would with your Web service's Java code. Try it!

That concludes the roundup of JavaScript tools WebLogic Workshop provides for working with XML. In the next section I'll describe how you can connect your script functions to your Web service by calling the script from XML maps. The next section also includes a full example of script in use for translation both to and from XML.

Writing Script Functions for Mapping

As I described near the beginning of this chapter, JavaScript you write for mapping acts as an extension to an XML map. You put your JavaScript function code into a JSX file, then "call" the function from an XML map. You can design the map-and-script combination so that the script does all the translating between Java and XML, or does only part of it. In fact, your script need not handle XML at all. You might simply want to throw a last-minute calculation into an outgoing XML message (say, a sum or an average, or the current time). This is the kind of thing that XML maps simply can't do on their own.

I also suggested earlier that connecting your JavaScript to XML maps can be confusing at first glance. Let's take another look at the example I gave, shown in Listing 11-14. Remember that the code in curly braces is a reference to a JavaScript function in a file called POMaps.jsx. The JSX file is part of a WebLogic Workshop project called PurchaseOrder.

Listing 11-14: A Script Call in an XML Map

```
/**
 * @jws:operation
 * @jws:parameter-xml xml-map::
 *   <submitOrder>
 *       {PurchaseOrder.POMaps.translatePurchaseOrder(
 *           addr, items)}
 *   </submitOrder>
 * ::
 */
public PurchaseOrder submitOrder(Address addr, Item[] items)
{...}
```

Note that the function name in this call is `translatePurchaseOrder`. In the JSX file, however, the script function itself is declared as `translatePurchaseOrderFromXML`. That's correct; the function is not called `translatePurchaseOrder`. One of the things to keep in mind about calling a JavaScript function from within an XML map is that it's not like a typical function call.

Connecting function names with function calls

A JSX file can contain two kinds of functions that are callable from an XML map: a `FromXML` function and a `ToXML` function. WebLogic Workshop uses the context of the call to figure out which one to use. Here, the call is in the parameter map of a method on the left side of the service, facing the client. This means that the method's parameters will get their values from incoming XML, and that this map (including the script function called from it) will be used to translate *from XML* to

Java. As a result, WebLogic Workshop automatically appends `FromXML` to the function name used in the call and finds the function matching that name in the JSX file.

As you might imagine, a function reference in a return map on this method would end up calling a ToXML function — after all, for a return map data is moving in the other direction. In other words, the `translatePurchaseOrder` reference shown in the preceding example would call a `translatePurchaseOrderToXML` function if called from this method's return map.

To take this a little further, consider a function reference in a client-facing *callback's* XML map. Because the callback works in the opposite direction from a method — parameters are going out, return value is coming in — the translation works in the opposite way. On a client-facing callback, the parameters result in data on its way *out* of the service as an XML message. A parameter map applied there, including a function called from the map, would be intended to translate *to XML*. WebLogic Workshop would look for a ToXML function to use. As with the method, the reverse would be true for the callback's return map and function.

Finally, one more thing may seem a little odd about the function reference in the method example I gave. If it's designed to translate from XML to Java, shouldn't the function's parameter be the incoming XML? Well, as it turns out, the JavaScript declaration for the `translatePurchaseOrderFromXML` function does have as a single parameter the incoming XML. Parameters in the function *reference,* however, are the Java types the translation is acting on. In the preceding example, the `submitOrder` method's `addr` and `items` parameters are used as parameters for the script function call because they'll be receiving the incoming XML data.

One last note about the arguments of function references. If the `submitOrder` method example featured a return XML map with a function call, the call might look something like the following:

```
{PurchaseOrder.POMaps.translatePurchaseOrder(return)}
```

The standard argument for a function reference in a return map is simply "return". This call would prompt WebLogic Workshop to look in POMaps.jsx for a `translatePurchaseOrderToXML` function, then use the function to translate the return value to XML to send to the client.

How translation through functions works

As I've mentioned elsewhere in this chapter, a JavaScript function you call from an XML map conforms to certain rules. You declare these functions in a JSX file, then add code to do the appropriate translation between XML and Java. These functions differ slightly depending on whether the function maps from XML or to XML.

To create a JSX file in WebLogic Workshop, click the File menu, point to New, then click New JavaScript File. The Create New File dialog box will provide a place for you to name your JSX file. After you click OK, WebLogic Workshop will display Source View with a template for creating script functions you can use for mapping.

By looking at the template, you can see that a function that maps from XML to Java takes the incoming XML as a parameter and returns the Java types that will be used by your Web service. To illustrate this with a simple example, consider a script designed to map the following XML to Java:

```
<name>
    <first>John</first>
    <last>Doe</last>
</name>
```

The function designed for mapping this XML might look like the JavaScript defined in a file called AddressBookScript.jsx, as shown in Listing 11-15:

Listing 11-15: A JavaScript FromXML Function for Translating Name Data

```
/*
 * Declare a function for mapping from XML to Java. It's
 * parameter is the incoming XML.
 */
function translateNamesFromXML ( xml )
{
    /* Assign values from the XML to new script variables. */
    var firstName = xml..first;
    var lastName = xml..last;

    /*
     * Return the two script variables as an array with two
     * members.
     */
    return [ firstName, lastName ];
}
```

You could call this function from an XML map such as the one in Listing 11-16. Remember that the function call omits the FromXML suffix used in the function declaration. When the submitName method is called by a client, WebLogic Workshop will execute its XML map, using the script for translation. When the script has finished executing, WebLogic Workshop will extract the firstName and lastName values from the script's array return value, then pass them to the submitName method's first and last parameters.

Listing 11-16: Calling a FromXML Function from an XML Map

```
/**
 * @jws:operation
 * @jws:parameter-xml xml-map::
```

Continued

Listing 11-16 *(Continued)*

```
 * <submitName>
 *     {AddressBookService.AddressBookScript.translateNames(
 *         first, last)}
 * </submitName>
 * ::
 */
public String[] submitName (String first, String last)
{
    String[] arrayOfNames = new String[];
    arrayOfNames[0] = first;
    arrayOfNames[1] = last;

    return arrayOfNames;
}
```

Now let's examine the reverse scenario: using script to translate the return value sent back to the client. For simplicity's sake, let's assume that the client expects to get back the same XML they sent. In keeping with the actual order in which the code would execute, take a look first at the return XML map applied to the submitName method you saw in the preceding example. Notice in this map (Listing 11-17) that the script call takes as its argument the method's return value.

Listing 11-17: Calling a ToXML Function from an XML Map

```
/**
 * @jws:operation
 * @jws:return-xml xml-map::
 * <submitNameReturn>
 *     {AddressBookService.AddressBookScript.translateNames(return)}
 * </submitNameReturn>
 * ::
 */
public String[] submitName (String first, String last)
{
    String[] arrayOfNames = new String[];
    arrayOfNames[0] = first;
    arrayOfNames[1] = last;

    return arrayOfNames;
}
```

When the submitName method finishes executing, WebLogic Workshop passes its return value to the map for translation. The value is in turn passed to the JavaScript function. Because this map is translating Java to XML, WebLogic Workshop looks in AddressBookScript.jsx for a function called translateNames

ToXML, shown in Listing 11-18. The function translating Java to XML will take the service method's Java data as a parameter and return the XML that results from the translation.

Listing 11-18: A JavaScript ToXML Function for Translating Name Data

```
/*
 * Declare a function for mapping from Java to XML. It's
 * parameter is the incoming Java.
 */
function translateNamesToXML ( nameArray )
{
    /*
     * Declare an XML variable to return to the client. For its
     * first and last elements, insert values from the array of
     * names returned by the submitName method.
     */
    var nameXML = <name>
        <first>{nameArray[0]}</first>
        <last>{nameArray[1]}</last>
    </name>;

    /*
     * Return the newly constructed XML for return to the client.
     */
    return nameXML;
}
```

Of course, in an actual Web service, this parameter map and return map would both be in the source code immediately preceding the Java method. I've separated them here to make explaining it a little easier.

As you've noticed, there are several things to keep in mind about how script functions for mapping connect with XML maps. The following list summarizes these:

- ◆ A function intended to translate XML to Java takes the incoming XML as a parameter and returns an array containing the Java types needed by the Web service.

- ◆ A function intended to translate Java to XML takes the Web service's Java types as parameters and returns the outgoing XML.

- ◆ Function calls specify arguments specific to the needs of the XML map and script.

- ◆ A JavaScript function called from an XML map is stored in a JSX file.

- ◆ The function itself uses the name specified in the call, but with ToXML or FromXML appended, depending on its role.

Example: A FromXML function

The next few examples illustrate how you might write JavaScript to do the same kind of mapping that Chapter 6 illustrates with XML maps. Keep in mind that most of what these scripts do — primarily one-to-one mapping between XML values and Java values — can be accomplished with XML maps. However, these examples illustrate how you can manipulate XML with JavaScript.

Listing 11-19 shows what the `submitOrder` method would look like if it used the function calls instead of the XML maps you saw in Chapter 6.

Listing 11-19: A Parameter Map and Return Map for the submitOrder Method

```
    /**
     * @jws:operation
     * @jws:parameter-xml xml-map::
     *      <purchaseOrder xmlns="http://www.wiley.com/">
     *          {BookProject.Chapter11.POMaps.translatePurchaseOrder(
     *              shippingAddr, billingAddr, poNumber, items)}
     *      </purchaseOrder>
     * ::
     *
     * @jws:return-xml xml-map::
     *      <purchaseOrder xmlns="http://www.wiley.com/">
     *          {BookProject.Chapter11.POMaps.translatePurchaseOrder(
     *              return)}
     *      </purchaseOrder>
     * ::
     */
    public PurchaseOrder submitOrder(Address shippingAddr,
        Address billingAddr, String poNumber, Item[] items)
    {
        /*
         * Declare a PurchaseOrder variable and add the
         * data from incoming parameter values to it. Note
         * that the incoming data has been translated from
         * the XML message sent by the client. The parameter
         * XML map, along with the JavaScript function it
         * calls, has parsed values from the XML message
         * into the Java parameters of this method.
         */
        PurchaseOrder po = new PurchaseOrder();

        po.shippingAddr = shippingAddr;
        po.billingAddr = billingAddr;
        po.items = items;
        po.orderNumber = poNumber;
```

```
    /*
     * Return the new PurchaseOrder object. From here,
     * it will be translated via the return XML map and
     * the JavaScript function called by the map.
     */
    return po;
}
```

As you can see, the `submitOrder` method here simply takes purchase-related information submitted in separate pieces — addresses, items, PO number — and returns the information packaged into a `PurchaseOrder` object. The next example shows a JavaScript function designed to do approximately what an XML map might do. In reality, this script is not a substitute for an equivalent XML map; the map is a much more efficient approach in this case. But comparing the XML maps in Chapter 6 with Listing 11-20 and Listing 11-21 might help you see the potential for both XML maps and JavaScript in your own work.

Listing 11-20: A FromXML Function to Translate Purchase Order Data

```
/*
 * Import Java classes needed for translation. These
 * classes happen to be defined in the web service
 * itself. Note that the import statement available
 * with JavaScript in WebLogic Workshop does not support
 * importing entire packages with the * symbol. You must
 * specify classes by name.
 */
import BookProject.Chapter11.POTranslator.Address;
import BookProject.Chapter11.POTranslator.Item;
import BookProject.Chapter11.POTranslator.PurchaseOrder;

/*
 * Declare the function for translating from incoming
 * XML to Java. This kind of function's name must end with
 * the suffix "FromXML". Its parameter is the incoming
 * XML.
 */
function translatePurchaseOrderFromXML ( poXML )
{
    /*
     * Declare an array variable to later hold data
     * from <item> elements in the incoming XML
     * message. Also, declare Address variables to
     * hold the message's <shippingAddress> and
     * <billingAddress> values.
```

Continued

Listing 11-20 *(Continued)*

```
 */
var items = new Array();
var shippingAddr = new Address();
var billingAddr = new Address();

/*
 * Extract shipping and billing address information
 * from the XML message and assign them to separate
 * XML variables.
 */
var shippingAddressXML = poXML..shippingAddress;
var billingAddressXML = poXML..billingAddress;

/*
 * Assign values in the separate shipping and
 * billing address XML variables to fields of
 * separate the Address objects.
 */
shippingAddr.name = shippingAddressXML.name;
shippingAddr.street = shippingAddressXML.street;
shippingAddr.city = shippingAddressXML.city;
shippingAddr.state = shippingAddressXML.state;
shippingAddr.zip = shippingAddressXML.zip;

billingAddr.name = billingAddressXML.name;
billingAddr.street = billingAddressXML.street;
billingAddr.city = billingAddressXML.city;
billingAddr.state = billingAddressXML.state;
billingAddr.zip = billingAddressXML.zip;

/*
 * Collect XML for all of the <item> elements
 * into a single XML list that can be used in
 * a loop.
 */
var itemsXML = poXML..item;

/*
 * Create a new Item object for each of the elements
 * in the <item> element list. Assign each <item>
 * element's children's values to fields of the Item
 * object.
 */
var i = 0;
```

```
    for ( var itemXML in itemsXML )
    {
        var newItem = new Item();

        newItem.name = itemXML.name;
        newItem.price = itemXML.price;
        newItem.quantity = itemXML.quantity;

        items[i] = newItem;

        i++;
    }

    /*
     * Assign the PO number from the orderNumber attribute
     * to a variable.
     */
    var poNumber = poXML.@orderNumber;

    /*
     * Return the two Address objects and the Item
     * array for use as parameters of the submitOrder
     * method.
     */
    return [ shippingAddr, billingAddr, poNumber, items ]
}
```

Example: A ToXML function

But what about a function used to translate in the other direction – converting the return value to XML? It would differ in a couple of ways. One obvious difference is that the variable assignments would work in the opposite direction. Instead of assigning incoming XML values to Java types, your code would assign Java values to elements of outgoing XML.

Again, we'll borrow from the XML map example in Chapter 6. But to make things a little more interesting, let's have the return value be a little more complex than a string. In addition to formatting the outgoing XML from data in the return value, the ToXML function will add summary information to the message, including the total cost of the order and the averagePrice of the items ordered. See Listing 11-21.

Listing 11-21: A ToXML Function to Translate Purchase Order Data

```
/*
 * Declare the function for translating from the method's
```

Continued

Listing 11-21 *(Continued)*

```
 * Java return value to outgoing XML. This kind of function

 * must end with the suffix "ToXML". It may have multiple
 * parameters, depending on how the Java data it receives is
 * structured.
 */
function translatePurchaseOrderToXML ( purchaseOrder )
{
    /*
     * Declare an XML variable to serve as a root. The
     * remaining code in this function will build on this
     * variable to generate the outgoing XML message
     * from values in the submitOrder return value
     * captured in the purchaseOrder parameter of this
     * function.
     */
    var poXML = <purchaseOrder/>;

    /*
     * Declare XML variables to hold the XML for shipping and
     * billing address information.
     */
    var shippingAddressXML = <shippingAddress>
        <name/><street/><city/><state/><zip/></shippingAddress>;
    var billingAddressXML = <billingAddress>
        <name/><street/><city/><state/><zip/></billingAddress>;

    /*
     * Assign values from the Address objects contained by the
     * incoming PurchaseOrder object to corresponding XML.
     */
    shippingAddressXML..name = purchaseOrder.shippingAddr.name;
    shippingAddressXML..street = purchaseOrder.shippingAddr.street;
    shippingAddressXML..city = purchaseOrder.shippingAddr.city;
    shippingAddressXML..state = purchaseOrder.shippingAddr.state;
    shippingAddressXML..zip = purchaseOrder.shippingAddr.zip;

    billingAddressXML..name = purchaseOrder.billingAddr.name;
    billingAddressXML..street = purchaseOrder.billingAddr.street;
    billingAddressXML..city = purchaseOrder.billingAddr.city;
    billingAddressXML..state = purchaseOrder.billingAddr.state;
    billingAddressXML..zip = purchaseOrder.billingAddr.zip;

    /*
```

```
 * Append the new <shippingAddress> and <billingAddress>
 * elements (and their children) to the <purchaseOrder> root
 * element.
 */
poXML.purchaseOrder.appendChild(shippingAddressXML);
poXML.purchaseOrder.appendChild(billingAddressXML);

/*
 * For each Item object in the PurchaseOrder object returned
 * by the submitOrder method, declare a new XML variable.
 * The syntax used here is efficient in that it uses few
 * lines of code. In a single statement this code declares
 * a variable containing four elements and assigns a value
 * to each using embedded expressions.
 *
 * However, compressing so much into a single statement
 * can make it hard to debug. For example, the debugger
 * will only stop at a breakpoint set at the top of the
 * statement. If you were trying to track down an error
 * related to just one of the values, this could be
 * awkward. Still, it's useful to see what is possible.
 */
for ( var i in purchaseOrder.items )
{
    var elementItem = <item>
        <name>{purchaseOrder.items[i].name}</name>
        <price>{purchaseOrder.items[i].price}</price>
        <quantity>{purchaseOrder.items[i].quantity}</quantity>
    </item>;

    /* Append the newly created <item> element to the root. */
    poXML.purchaseOrder.appendChild(elementItem);
}

/* Assign the PO number submitted by the requestor. */
poXML.purchaseOrder.@orderNumber = purchaseOrder.orderNumber;

/*
 * Use the XML variable containing the <item> elements to
 * calculate the total cost of the purchase, as well as
 * the total quantity of items ordered.
 */
var sumOfPurchase = 0;
var sumOfQuantity = 0
```

Continued

Listing 11-21 *(Continued)*

```
    for ( item in poXML..item )
    {
        var itemTotal = item.price * item.quantity;
        sumOfPurchase += new Number(itemTotal);
        sumOfQuantity += new Number(item.quantity);
    }

    /*
     * Declare an XML variable to hold the information calculated
     * from item values. Note that this XML was not part of the
     * XML request message sent by the client.
     */
    var summaryXML = <summary><totalCost/><averagePrice/></summary>;
    summaryXML..totalCost = sumOfPurchase;
    summaryXML..averagePrice = sumOfPurchase / sumOfQuantity;

    /*
     * Append the <summary> element (with its children) to the
     * <purchaseOrder> root element.
     */
    poXML.purchaseOrder.shippingAddress += summaryXML;

    /* Return the newly generated XML for return to the client. */
    return poXML;
}
```

You've probably noticed that the two script functions in this section do approximately the same sort of thing, but in different directions. In actual practice, a more efficient approach would be to use XML maps for both the parameter and return mapping, and to use a script function on the return map simply to handle inserting the summary values.

Finally, you may remember from Chapter 6 that XML maps don't allow you to mix substitutions and literal values within the same element. The following is not legal in an XML map:

```
<aTag>Some text {param} more text</aTag>
```

But the result you'd be looking for is certainly possible through script, as in the ToXML example in Listing 11-22:

Listing 11-22: A ToXML Function to Mix Strings and Parameters into a Single Element

```
function combineMixedValuesToXML ( param )
{
    var myXML = <aTag/>;
```

```
    var firstValue = "Some text ";
    var lastValue = " more text";

    /*
     * Assume that "param" corresponds to a parameter
     * in a Java declaration.
     */
    myXML.aTag = firstValue + param + lastValue;

    return myXML;
}
```

Here is the result of this script:

`<aTag>Some text myParam more text</aTag>`

Summary of Extensions for Use with XML

The following Tables 11-1 through 11-4 summarize the JavaScript extensions discussed in this chapter.

TABLE 11-1 OPERATORS FOR USE WITH XML

Operator	Example	Description
<	a = <b></b>;	Assign the XML <b></b> to a.
.@	a = b.@c;	Assign the value of the c attribute to a.
[] element	a = b[1];	Assign the value of the second b to a.
::	namespace wly as "http"//www.wiley.com/";	

Continued

TABLE 11-1 OPERATORS FOR USE WITH XML *(Continued)*

Operator	Example	Description
a = b..wly::c;	Find any c elements whose namespace is http://www.wiley.com/", then assign those elements to a.	
{}	a = "b";	
c = <d>{a}</d>;	Assign "b" to a, then assign <d>b</d> to c.	
.	a = b.c;	Assign the c child element of b to a.
.. c	a = b..c;	Assign the c child element of b to a. The element may be many levels down, hierarchically, beneath the b element.
.()	a = b..c(d == 6);	Get the value of a c element that has a d child element whose value is 6, and assign the value to a.
+	a = b + c;	Assign a the combined XML values represented by b and c.
+=	a.b[1] += c;	Insert c as a child of the a element.
delete	delete a.b.c[1];	Delete the second c child of the b element.

TABLE 11-2 STATEMENTS FOR USE WITH XML

Statement	Example	Description
import	import java.util.ArrayList;	Make the ArrayList class available to script in a JSX file.
namespace	namespace myco as "http://openuri.org/";	Declare myco as a variable representing the namespace http://openuri.org/.

TABLE 11-3 PROPERTIES FOR USE WITH XML

Property	Example	Description
thisXML	a = b..c.(thisXML.@d == 6);	Find any c elements whose d attribute has a value of 6, then assign those elements to a.

TABLE 11-4 FUNCTIONS FOR USE WITH XML

Function	Description
appendChild(*newChild*)	Inserts a new child node after the existing children of the XML value.
attribute(*attributeName*)	Returns the value of the specified attribute.
attributes()	Returns a list of attributes for the specified element.
child(*childIndex*)	Returns the XML at the 0-based ordinal position specified by childIndex.
childIndex()	Returns the 0-based ordinal position of the XML value within its parent.
children()	Returns a list of the element's children.
copy()	Returns a copy of the specified element.
domNode()	Returns a org.w3c.dom.Node representation.
innerXML(*newContent*)	Replaces the entire contents of the XML value with new content.
length	Returns the length of a list XML elements.
namespaceURI()	Returns a string representing the namespace URI.
parent()	Returns the parent of the element.
prependChild(*newChild*)	Inserts a new child node before the existing children of the XML value.
tagName()	Returns the name of the element tag.
text()	Returns a string containing the value of all XML properties that are of type string.

Continued

TABLE 11-4 FUNCTIONS FOR USE WITH XML *(Continued)*

Function	Description
toString()	Returns the element and its content as a string.
-toXMLString()	Returns an XML encoded string representation.
xpath(*xPathExpression*)	Evaluates the XPath expression using the XML value as the context node.

Summary

Using JavaScript can greatly enhance the power of XML maps. WebLogic Workshop includes an extended version of JavaScript through which you can write code that accesses or constructs XML in a manner similar to handling other kinds of listed and hierarchical data. The extensions for XML, along with JavaScript's ease of use, make it possible to handle complex XML documents and to augment mapping with the kind of functionality a procedural language can provide.

- WebLogic Workshop provides an extended version of JavaScript that includes tools especially for manipulating XML.
- The extensions for XML are similar to existing JavaScript conventions for handling hierarchical data.
- Through the extensions, you can access XML in a manner similar to other structured data in JavaScript.
- Functions you write for translating XML are essentially enhancements to XML maps.

Appendix A: What's on the CD-ROM?

THIS APPENDIX DESCRIBES the contents of the CD accompanying this book. For the latest information about this CD, please refer to the ReadMe file located at the root of the CD. Here is what you will find:

- System Requirements
- How to install the BEA software from the CD
- What's on the CD
- Troubleshooting

System Requirements

Make sure that your computer meets the minimum system requirements listed in this section. If your computer doesn't match up to these requirements, you may have a problem using the contents of the CD.

- One of the following versions of Windows is required:
    - Microsoft Windows 2000 Professional Edition with Service Pack 2 or later
    - Microsoft Windows NT (Server) 4.0 with Service Pack 6 or later
- PC with 512 MB of total RAM installed on your computer (1 GB RAM recommended for full WebLogic Platform installation)
- Pentium II processor running at 400 Mhz or faster (Pentium III processor running 500 MHz or faster recommended for optimum performance)
- Ethernet network interface card (NIC) on TCP/IP network
- Approximately 231MB free storage space for the installed product and roughly 170 MB of temporary storage space required by the installer (525 MB free storage space is required for full WebLogic Platform installation)
- A CD-ROM drive
- JDK 1.4. This component is installed with the WebLogic Workshop IDE.

For the latest hardware requirements or additional operating system compatibility, you can check the BEA Web site for updated information at www.bea.com.

Appendix A: What's on the CD-ROM?

 The CD-ROM with this book only includes the Windows version of BEA WebLogic Platform. However, the code samples, procedures, and advice in this book are applicable to BEA WebLogic Workshop on any supported platform. You can download a copy of BEA WebLogic Platform for evaluation for Solaris or RedHat Linux from BEA's Web site at http://commerce.bea.com/downloads/weblogic_platform.jsp.

Installing BEA WebLogic Platform Trial Edition in Windows

Prior to installing the BEA software from this CD-ROM, you need to obtain a license key for the trial version from BEA from the following Web site:

www.bea.com/eval/christofferson

After you've registered, you will immediately be sent an e-mail with instructions for downloading your key. This license key will enable you to install the BEA WebLogic Platform 7 software, including BEA WebLogic Workshop and BEA WebLogic Server, and use it for up to 90 days with access for up to 20 client connections.

 Licenses for pre-7.0 versions of WebLogic Server will not work with WebLogic Server 7.0. If you already have a license for BEA WebLogic Server, please see the directions at http://e-docs.bea.com/wls/docs70/install/instlic.html#1036174 to update your license.

After you download the license key, rename the key "license.bea" and install in the Home directory (the default is c:\bea – see Step 6 in the following procedure). To install the BEA software from this CD, follow these steps:

1. Insert the CD into your computer's CD-ROM drive.

2. Open Windows Explorer and browse to the root of your CD-ROM.

3. Double-click BEAEVALCD.exe to begin the installation process for BEA WebLogic platform.

4. At the Welcome screen, click Next.

5. At the BEA License agreement screen, select Yes and click Next.
6. Specify the BEA Home directory. By default this is `c:\bea`.
7. Specify the install type, either Typical or Custom.

    If you choose a Custom installation, you will be prompted for which components to install.
8. Specify the product directory.

    By default this is `c:\bea\weblogic700`. When you click Next at this screen, the installer begins copying files to your computer.
9. If you choose the Custom installation method, you'll have the option to run the configuration Wizard to create an application domain.
10. When finished, click Done to exit the installer.

What's on the CD

The following sections provide a summary of the software and other materials you'll find on the CD.

Author-created materials

Sample code from the book is on the CD in the folder named "Author." These files are stored in ".zip" formatted archives, you'll need a special program to "unzip" them. We've included a trial copy of WinACE on the CD for your convenience. Extract zip files into the Workshop application directory. By default, this directory is `C:\bea\weblogic700\samples\workshop\applications`.

Applications

The CD-ROM contains a 90-day trial version of the BEA WebLogic Platform 7. BEA WebLogic Platform 7 includes BEA WebLogic Workshop and BEA WebLogic Server, as well as WebLogic Integration and WebLogic Portal.

Shareware programs are fully functional, trial versions of copyrighted programs. If you like particular programs, register with their authors for a nominal fee and receive licenses, enhanced versions, and technical support. *Freeware programs* are copyrighted games, applications, and utilities that are free for personal use. Unlike shareware, these programs do not require a fee or provide technical support. *GNU software* is governed by its own license, which is included inside the folder of the GNU product. See the GNU license for more details.

Trial, demo, or evaluation versions are usually limited either by time or functionality (such as being unable to save projects). Some trial versions are very sensitive to system date changes. If you alter your computer's date, the programs will "time out" and will no longer be functional.

eBook version of BEA WebLogic Workshop: Building Next Generation Web Services Visually

The complete text of this book is on the CD in Adobe's Portable Document Format (PDF). You can read and search through the file with the Adobe Acrobat Reader (also included on the CD).

Troubleshooting

If you have difficulty installing or using any of the materials on the companion CD, try the following solutions:

- **Turn off any antivirus software that you may have running.** Installers sometimes mimic virus activity and can make your computer incorrectly believe that it is being infected by a virus. (Be sure to turn the antivirus software back on later.)
- **Close all running programs.** The more programs you're running, the less memory is available to other programs. Installers also typically update files and programs; if you keep other programs running, installation may not work properly.
- **Reference the ReadMe.** Please refer to the ReadMe file located at the root of the CD-ROM for the latest product information at the time of publication.
- **Reference the BEA Web site.** If you're experiencing difficulty installing the BEA WebLogic Platform software, be sure to check the installation information and Dev2Dev newsgroups at www.bea.com.

If you still have trouble with the CD, please call the Customer Care phone number: (800) 762-2974. Outside the United States, call 1 (317) 572-3994. You can also contact Customer Service by e-mail at techsupdum@wiley.com. Wiley Publishing, Inc. will provide technical support only for installation and other general quality control items; for technical support on the applications themselves, consult the program's vendor or author.

Appendix B

A Java Primer

IN THIS APPENDIX

- ◆ The core Java language
- ◆ The Java libraries

THIS SECTION IS AIMED at readers who intend to get a quick understanding of the Java Programming language. It covers the basic Java programming syntax. If you have already programmed in Java, you are free to skip this section.

Java is a third-generation programming language like Fortran, C, Smalltalk, and many others.

The CPU of a computer performs actions specified by what are known as the *machine language* instructions. Programs written in a high-level language such as Java, C, Pascal, and others cannot be executed directly on a computer. These programs have to be converted into the machine language.

A Java compiler translates Java source code into Java byte codes. These byte codes serve as the machine language instructions for the Java Virtual Machine (JVM). These byte code instructions are then interpreted by the JVM and passed on to the CPU of a computer to perform actions. So, if there is an interpreter (JVM) for a platform, then a Java program can be executed on it. Every platform (Windows, Unix, Linux, and so on) can have its own JVM, thus making Java "write once, run anywhere". Figure B-1 illustrates this.

The Core Java Language

The Java programming language provides the basic rules with which Java programs can be written. In addition, it also provides a rich library of Application Programmer Interfaces (API).

A simple Java program

First let's write a simple Java program that prints out a message "Hello World." This is shown in Listing B-1.

Listing B-1: HelloWorld.java

```
public class HelloWorld
{
    public static void main(String[] args)
    {
        System.out.println("Hello World");
    }
}
```

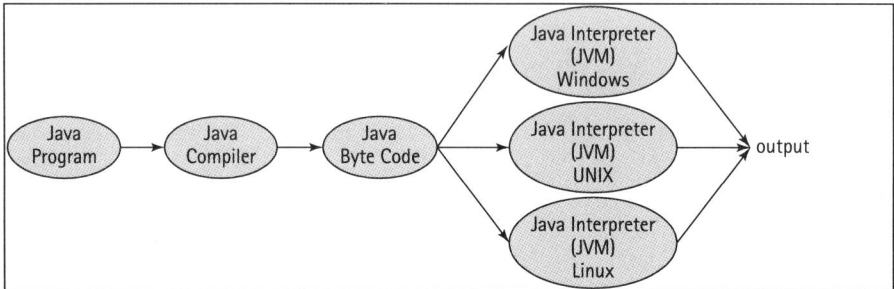

Figure B-1: Java Compiler and Interpreter (JVM).

In this example, we have a class named `HelloWorld`. (I talk more about classes later in this appendix.) It has a method called `main`, which is invoked by the JVM when the program is executed. For this we need to compile this program first using a Java compiler.

```
javac HelloWorld.java
```

The result of this compilation is a Java class file (HelloWorld.class), which is nothing but a set of Java byte codes. Now, let's tell the Java Interpreter (JVM) to run the program.

```
java HelloWorld
```

This will start the JVM, which in turn will invoke the `main` method of the HelloWorld Program. The set of statements inside the `main` method are then executed. The output of the program is as follows:

```
Hello World
```

Figure B-2 illustrates this entire process.

Now that we have gone through the basics of a Java program, let's now talk more about the Java language.

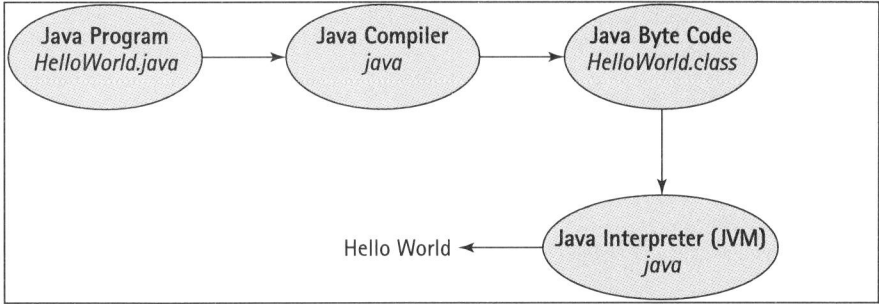

Figure B-2: The Java Compiler and Interpreter (JVM) for HelloWorld.

Identifiers

A Java identifier is a name that represents an item in a Java program.
Rules for creating Java Identifiers are as follows:

- It can be a sequence of Java letters and Java digits where Java letters include all letters (upper and lower case) of the English alphabet, the underscore (_) and the dollar ($) sign and Java Digits include the decimal digits 0 through 9.
- It should start with a Java letter.
- It should not be a Java-reserved keyword.
- It has no maximum length.
- It is case sensitive. This means that "XYZ" and "xyz" are considered to be two different Java identifiers.

Examples of valid Identifiers include `sample`, `Example`, `HelloWorld`, `s123`, `$usa`, `_amount`, and `_alto9`.

The following are Java-reserved keywords and cannot be used as identifiers:

abstract	double	Int
boolean	else	interface
break	extends	Long
byte	final	Native
case	finally	New
catch	float	package
char	for	Private
class	goto	protected
const	If	Public
continue	implements	Return
default	Import	Short
do	instanceof	Static

Strictfp	this	try
Super	throw	void
Switch	throws	volatile
synchronized	transient	while

The following are Java literals and cannot be used as identifiers:

true   false   Null

Variables

A Java variable represents a piece of data. In other words, it represents a memory location (or several locations treated as a single unit) where the data is stored.

Rules for creating Java Identifiers are as follows:

- The variable's name should be a Java identifier.
- The variable should be associated with a type.
- The variable should have a scope.

I discuss type in the next section. The section of code within a Java program where a variable can be used is called the *scope*. The general syntax for declaring a variable is as follows:

Scope Type Name

Let's add a few variables to our HelloWorld Java program (see Listing B-2).

Listing B-2: HelloWorld.java with Variables

```
public class HelloWorld
{
    private int age;
    public static void main(String[] args)
    {
        boolean isValid;
        System.out.println("Hello World");
    }
}
```

In the preceding example, `age` is a class-level variable that can be referenced from any method inside the HelloWorld class. The variable `isValid`, on the other hand, is a local variable and can be referenced only within the main method.

Types

Type represents the kind of data that can be stored in a variable. For example, in Listing B-2, `age` is a variable that can hold data of type integer (`int`), and `isValid` is another variable that can hold boolean data (true or false). The Java programming language has two categories of data types: *primitive* data types and *reference* data types.

PRIMITIVE DATA TYPES

There are eight primitive data types in Java. They contain a single value of a fixed size and are passed by value to methods. Table B-1 illustrates this.

TABLE B-1 JAVA PRIMITIVE DATA TYPES

Keyword	Description
Byte	8-bit integer
Short	16-bit integer
Int	32-bit integer
Long	64-bit integer
Float	32-bit floating point
Double	64-bit floating point
Char	16-bit single character
Boolean	1 bit - true or false

REFERENCE DATA TYPES

Reference data types are defined by Java classes and are passed by reference to methods. The Java programming language defines *wrapper classes* for every primitive data type. A wrapper class encapsulates the primitive data within it. Table B-2 illustrates these wrapper classes.

TABLE B-2 JAVA WRAPPER CLASSES FOR PRIMITIVE DATA TYPES

Wrapper Class	Java Primitive Data Type
Byte	byte

Continued

TABLE B-2 JAVA WRAPPER CLASSES FOR PRIMITIVE DATA TYPES *(Continued)*

Wrapper Class	Java Primitive Data Type
Short	short
Integer	int
Long	long
Float	float
Double	double
Char	char
Boolean	boolean

 In the Java programming language, reference data types start with an uppercase letter and primitive data types start with a lowercase letter.

Java also defines arrays, classes, and interfaces as reference data types.

ARRAYS *Arrays* are data structures that allow you to store a set of similar data, each in a unique position. In order to use arrays, you should declare an array variable, give it a dimension, and then initialize it.

```
int[] employeeNumbers;
employeeNumbers = new int[3];
employeeNumbers[0] = 101;
employeeNumbers[1] = 121;
employeeNumbers[2] = 145;
```

An array can also be initialized using curly brackets:

```
int[] employeeNumbers = {101, 121, 145};
```

Arrays can also be created by making use of the methods provided by the `java.lang.reflect.Array` class.

CLASSES A Java class represents a real-world entity. It's essentially a blueprint of a real-world entity. It can have attributes represented by variables and actions represented by methods. Listing B-3 illustrates this.

Listing B-3: The Employee Java Class

```java
public class Employee
{
    int employeeNumber;
    String employeeName;
    String employeeAddress;

    public int getEmployeeNumber()
    {
        //some business logic
    }

    public String getEmployeeName()
    {
        //some business logic
    }

    public void updateEmployeeAddress(String newAddress)
    {
        //some business logic
    }
}
```

In this example, we have a class called Employee, which can be accessed from outside this class, because its scope is public. It also has three member variables. An object is an instance of a class. An object is created or instantiated as shown here:

```java
Employee emp1 = new Employee();
```

Variables inside an object can be accessed using the dot "." operator.

```java
emp1.employeeNumber = 101;
```

INTERFACES An interface is a contract that has all the method definitions and constant values. A class later on implements the interface. Listing B-4 shows a BankAccount interface.

Listing B-4: The BankAccount Interface

```
public interface BankAccount
{
        double maximumWithdrawalAmount - 1000.0;

        public double getAccountBalance();
        public void deposit(double amount);
        public double withdraw();
}
```

In this example, we have a BankAccount interface with three methods and one constant value. They are just defined here. The actual implementation will be inside a class that implements this interface. For this, the class must use the `implements` keyword, as shown in Listing B-5.

Listing B-5: The Account Class Implementing the BankAccount Interface

```
public class Account implements BankAccount
{
        public double getAccountBalance()
        {
                //implement business logic
        }

        public void deposit(double amount)
        {
                //implement business logic
        }

        public double withdraw()
        {
                //implement business logic
        }
}
```

Essentially, when a class implements an interface, it inherits the method definitions and constant values of the interface. A class can also inherit from multiple interfaces. Let's assume we had three interfaces, each with a method, as shown in Listing B-6.

Listing B-6: The Three Interfaces

```
public interface interface1
{
        public void method1();
}
```

```
public interface interface2
{
      public void method2();
}

public interface interface3
{
      public void method3();
}
```

Now, let's write a class that inherits from all these three interfaces. This is done by using a comma "," separated list of interfaces as shown in Listing B-7.

Listing B-7: Multiple Inheritance

```
public class MyClass implements interface1, interface2, interface3
{
      public double method1()
      {
            //implement business logic
      }

      public void method2(double amount)
      {
            //implement business logic
      }

      public double method3()
      {
            //implement business logic
      }
}
```

In Java, implementing multiple interfaces as shown in Listing B-7, is how multiple inheritance is achieved.

ABSTRACT CLASSES *Abstract classes* represent an abstract model and they cannot be instantiated. They can only be sub-classed. *Abstract classes* serve as a base template for other classes to use. For example, a vehicle can be considered to be an *abstract class*. Then classes like car and truck can use this as a model. In this case you can instantiate a car or a truck class, but cannot instantiate a vehicle.

In order to define a class as abstract, use the keyword `abstract` in front as shown below.

```
abstract class Employee
```

```
{
      ...
}
```

Abstract classes in a way look similar to *interfaces*, but they are actually different. *Abstract classes* may have methods already implemented; whereas *interfaces* do not have the methods implemented in them, instead, the *class* that implements the *interface* implements the method.

Operators

An *operator* is a symbol that operates on one or more arguments to produce a result. These arguments are called *operands*. An operator that is used with one operand is called a *unary operator,* which supports both prefix and postfix notations.

```
operator operand1
operand1 operator
```

An operator that is used with two operands is called a *binary operator,* which supports the infix notation:

```
operand1 operator operand2
```

An operator that is used with three operands is called a *ternary operator,* which also supports the infix notation:

```
operand1?operand2:operand3
```

If operand1 is *true* then return operand1 or else return operand2.

Operators in the Java programming language can be grouped into different categories.

ARITHMETIC OPERATORS

There are four unary arithmetic operators defined in Java. Table B-3 lists them.

TABLE B-3 UNARY ARITHMETIC OPERATORS

Operator	Example	Description
+	+a	*A* will become an *int* if it is a byte, short, or char
-	-a	Negates a

Operator	Example	Description
++	++a	Increments the value of *a* by 1 before evaluating the value of *a*
	a++	Increments the value of *a* by 1 after evaluating the value of *a*
- -	- -a	Decrements the value of *a* by 1 before evaluating the value of *a*
	a- -	Decrements the value of *a* by 1 after evaluating the value of *a*

There are five binary Arithmetic Operators defined in Java. Table B-4 lists them.

TABLE B-4 BINARY ARITHMETIC OPERATORS

Operator	Example	Description
+	a + b	Addition: adds *a* and *b*
-	a - b	Subtraction: subtracts *b* from *a*
*	a * b	Multiplication: multiplies *a* and *b*
Operator	Example	Description
/	a / b	Division: divides *a* by *b*
%	a % b	Modulus: remainder of dividing *a* by *b*

RELATIONAL OPERATORS

The result of using a relational operator is a boolean (true or false). There are six binary relational operators in Java (see Table B-5).

TABLE B-5 BINARY RELATIONAL OPERATORS

Operator	Example	Description
==	a == b	Equal: evaluate to *true* if a and b are equal
!=	a != b	Not Equal: evaluate to *true* if a and b are not equal
<	a < b	Less than: evaluate to *true* if a is less than b
<=	a <= b	Less than or Equal to: evaluate to *true* if a is less than or equal to b
>	a > b	Greater than: evaluate to *true* if a is greater than b
>=	a >= b	Greater than or Equal to: evaluate to *true* if a is greater than or equal to b

CONDITIONAL OPERATORS

There is one unary conditional operator in Java (see Table B-6).

TABLE B-6 UNARY CONDITIONAL OPERATOR

Operator	Example	Description
!	! a	Not: evaluate to *true* if a is *false*

There are two binary conditional operators in Java (see Table B-7).

TABLE B-7 BINARY CONDITIONAL OPERATORS

Operator	Example	Description
&&	a && b	AND: evaluate to *true* if both a and b are true; and conditionally evaluate b
||	a || b	OR: evaluate to *true* if either a or b are true; and conditionally evaluate b

BITWISE-MANIPULATION OR SHIFT OPERATORS

Table B-8 shows the binary shift operators.

TABLE B-8 BINARY SHIFT OPERATORS

Operator	Example	Description
>>	a >> b	Right shift: Shift bits of a to the right by a distance of b
<<	a << b	Left shift: Shift bits of a to the left by a distance of b
>>>	a >>> b	Zero filled right shift: Shift bits of a to the right by a distance of b (unsigned)
&	a & b	Bitwise AND
|	a | b	Bitwise OR
^	a ^ b	Exclusive OR: evaluate to *true* if either a or b are true but not both
~	a ~ b	Bitwise complement

ASSIGNMENT OPERATORS

Table B-9 shows the binary assignment operators.

TABLE B-9 BINARY ASSIGNMENT OPERATORS

Operator	Example	Description
=	a = b	Assign b to a
+=	a += b	Add a and b and assign the result to a
-=	a -= b	Subtract b from a and assign the result to a
*=	a *= b	Multiply a and b and assign the result to a
/=	a /= b	Divide a by b and assign the result to a
%=	a %= b	Assign the remainder of a divided by b to a

Continued

328 Appendix B: A Java Primer

TABLE B-9 BINARY ASSIGNMENT OPERATORS *(Continued)*

Operator	Example	Description
&=	a &= b	Bitwise AND operation of a and b and assign the result to a
|=	a |= b	Bitwise OR operation of a and b and assign the result to a
^=	a ^= b	Bitwise XOR operation of a and b and assign the result to a
<<=	a <<= b	Shift bits of a to the left by a distance of b and assign the result to a
>>=	a >>= b	Shift bits of a to the right by a distance of b and assign the result to a
>>>=	a >>>= b	Shift bits of a to the right by a distance of b (unsigned) and assign the result to a

SELECTION OPERATOR

This is the only *ternary* operator in Java. See the selection operator in Table B-10.

TABLE B-10 SELECTION OPERATOR

Operator	Example	Description
?:	a ? b : c	If a is *true* then return b, else return c

ALLOCATION OPERATOR

The allocation operator is a special operator that is used to create a new Object of a class. For example, consider the Employee Java class in Listing B-3. To create a new Object for this Employee class, you should use the new allocation operator as follows:

```
Employee emp = new Employee();
```

In this example, `emp` is a variable that holds an object of the `Employee` Java class, which is a *reference data type*.

INSTANCE OPERATOR

Table B-11 shows the instance operator.

TABLE B-11 INSTANCE OPERATOR

Operator	Example	Description
instanceof	a instanceof B	Evaluates to true if a is an instance of the class B

In the previous example, we had created a new `Employee` Object called `emp`. It can be used with the `instanceof` operator as follows:

`emp instanceof Employee`

This will return *true*, because we know that `emp` is an instance of the `Employee` class as defined earlier.

Expressions, statements, and blocks

Expressions are part of a Java program that evaluate to a value. They help in assigning values to variables. Here's an example of a simple expression:

`a + 3`

In the previous expression, the value of *a* is incremented by 3. The result of an expression can be assigned to a variable using a statement as shown here:

`x = a + 3;`

This is called an *expression statement*. Here *a* is incremented by three and the resulting value is assigned to *x*.

 In the Java programming language, statements should always end with a semi-colon (;).

Smaller expressions can be grouped together to form compound expressions. The following example illustrates this:

```
x = a + b + c;
```

Here the result of adding *a*, *b*, and *c* is assigned to *x*. Expressions can also be grouped using the parentheses – (and).

```
x = a + (b * c);
```

In this case, *b* and *c* are first multiplied and the result is added to *a*. The final result is then assigned to *x*. If the parentheses are not specified, then the order in which the expression is evaluated is determined by the precedence of operators. The Java programming language specifies the order of precedence for all the operators that we saw earlier. Table B-12 illustrates this order from high to low.

TABLE B-12 ORDER OF PRECEDENCE FOR JAVA OPERATORS

Operator	Notation
Grouping and Postfix Unary	(), a++, a--
Unary	+a, -a, ++a, --a, ~a, !a
Allocation	New
Multiplication, Division, Modulus	a * b, a / b, a % b
Addition, Subtraction	a + b, a - b
Shift	<<, >>, >>>
Relational	<, <=, >, >=, instanceof
Equality	==, !=
Bitwise AND	&
Bitwise XOR	^
Bitwise OR	|
Logical AND	&&
Logical OR	||
Selection	?:
Assignment	=, +=, -=, *=, /=, %=, &=, ^=, |=, <<=, >>=, >>>=

In Table B-12, operators on the same line have equal precedence. When operators of equal precedence appear in an expression, they're all evaluated from right to left, except if they're assignment operators.

In the Java programming language, assignment operators are evaluated from left to right. All other operators are evaluated from right to left. Thus, a = 3 x 4 / 2 will evaluate to 6. First 4 / 2 is evaluated to 2 and then this is multiplied with 3. So, it evaluates from right to left. The final result 6 is assigned to a, which is evaluated from left to right.

In addition to the expression statements, the Java programming language provides two other statements – *declaration statements* and *control flow statements*. I discuss control flow statements in the next section. But first, let's take a look at the declaration statements.

A declaration statement declares a Java variable as shown:

```
int x = 100;
```

The preceding statement declares a variable called x, to be of type int and assigns it a value of 100.

When statements are grouped together they form a *block*. Blocks of statements should begin and end with curly braces {}. The following example lists a block of Java statements:

```
{
    int i = 21;
    i = i + 10;
    i++;
    System.out.println("The value of i is " + i);
}
```

As we shall see later, these blocks of Java statements will be used in conjunction with control flow statements.

Control flow statements

Control flow statements determine the order in which statements are executed in a Java program. The Java programming language supports a number of such statements.

IF-ELSE

The if statement allows for the execution of a statement or a block of statements based on a condition:

Appendix B: A Java Primer

Syntax

```
if (condition)
{
    Java Statement(s)
}
```

The `condition` is a java expression that will evaluate to a boolean value. The statements will be executed only if the condition is *true*.

 In the Java programming language, while using control flow statements, if there is only one Java statement in the block to be executed. Then the use of curly braces { } is optional.

Listing B-8 illustrates the use of the `if` statement.

Listing B-8: Use of if Statement

```
int a = 5;
int c = 2;
int b = 1;
if (a == 5)
{
    a++;
    b++;
}

if (b > c)
    c++;
```

In the preceding example, a and b are incremented by 1 only if a is equal to 5. Similarly, c is incremented by 1 only if b is greater than c.

The `else` statement can be used in conjunction with the `if` statement if you want to execute an alternate set of Java statements when the condition evaluates to *false*.

Syntax

```
if (condition)
{
    Java Statement(s)
}
else
{
```

```
   Java Statement(s)
}
```

Let's modify the example in Listing B-8 and add an `else` statement to it (see Listing B-9).

Listing B-9: Use of if-else Statement

```
int a = 5;
int b = 1;
if (a == 5)
{
   a++;
   b++;
}
else
{
   a--;
   b--;
}
```

In the preceding example, a and b are incremented by 1 only if a is equal to 5. Otherwise, they are decremented by 1.

SWITCH-CASE

The `switch` statement can be considered a variation of the `if-else` statement. It allows for the execution of a statement or a block of statements based on a condition.

Syntax

```
switch (condition)
{
   case value1: Java Statement(s)
             break;

   case value2: Java Statement(s)
             break;
   ...
   ...
   ...
   case valuen: Java Statement(s)
             break;

   default:   Java Statements(s)
             break;
}
```

The *condition* is a java expression that will evaluate to either an integer value or a character value. The Java statements will be executed based on this result. Every set of Java statements can have an optional break statement at the end. The break statement makes the program jump to the end of the switch statement block after a particular case is executed. If the break statement is not used, then the program will execute the next set of Java statements until it reaches the end of the switch statement. This might not be the usual expectation. Hence, the use of break statements is highly recommended. The default condition will be executed if none of the case values matches with the result of evaluating the switch condition. Use of this default case is optional, though.

 In the Java programming language, the use of the break statement will make the Java interpreter jump to the end of the control flow statement block.

The following example in Listing B-10 illustrates the use of the switch-case statement.

Listing B-10: Use of switch-case Statement

```
int a = 1;
int b = 5;
switch(b-2)
{
   case 1: a = a + 1;
           break;

   case 2: a = a + 2;
           break;

   case 3: a = a + 3;
           break;

   case 4: a = a + 4;
           break;
}
```

In the preceding listing, first the expression b-2 is computed, which will yield a result of 3. This will make the program jump to case 3 and the value of a will be incremented by 3. Then it will encounter the break statement, which will make the program jump to the end of the switch statement. If there were no break statement, then the next Java statement would be executed and the value of a would be incremented by 4. This would have finally resulted with a having a value of 8.

WHILE

A while statement is used to execute a set of Java statements repeatedly based on a boolean condition.

Syntax

```
while (condition)
{
   Java Statement(s)
}
```

The condition should evaluate to a boolean value – *true* or *false*. The Java statements will be executed again and again as long as the condition evaluates to be *true*. The example in Listing B-11 illustrates this.

Listing B-11: Use of while Statement

```
int a = 1;
while(a <= 5)
{
   System.out.println("Hello World");
   a = a + 1;
}
```

In the preceding example, the expression a <= 5 is first evaluated. This will result in a boolean *true* because the value of a is 1, which is less than 5. Because this is true, the Java statements will be executed and the condition evaluated again. Now the value of a is 2, because it was incremented by 1 in the previous run. This will go on until a reaches a value of 6, which is not less than or equal to 5. So, the output of this while loop will be that the text "Hello World" will be printed five times and the value of a at the end will be 6.

DO-WHILE

A do-while statement is similar to the while statement that I showed you in the previous "while" section. It's also used to execute a set of Java statements repeatedly based on a boolean condition. The only difference is that the Java statements are executed even before the condition is evaluated.

Syntax

```
do
{
   Java Statement(s)
}
while (condition);
```

Note the semi-colon at the end of the while statement. The following example in listing B-12 illustrates this.

Listing B-12: Use of do-while Statement

```
int a = 6;
do
{
   System.out.println("Hello World");
   a = a + 1;
}
while(a <= 5);
```

In the preceding example, the Java statements are executed first. Then the expression a <= 5 is evaluated. So, the value of a when the condition is evaluated will be 7. This will result in a boolean *false,* because 6 is not less than or equal to 5. So, the output of this while loop will be that the text "Hello World" will be printed one time and the value of a at the end will be 7. Note that the Java statements were executed initially even if the value of a was 6.

FOR

The for statement is also used to execute a set of Java statements for a fixed number of times, which can be specified by a condition.

Syntax

```
for (initialization; condition; update)
{
   Java Statement(s)
}
```

First a variable is initialized, then it is subject to a condition, the Java statements are then executed, and finally the variable is updated. The condition should evaluate to a boolean value – *true* or *false.* The Java statements will be executed again and again as long as the condition evaluates to be *true.* The example in Listing B-13 illustrates this.

Listing B-13: Use of for Statement

```
for(int a = 1; a <= 4; a+=2)
{
   System.out.println("Hello World");
}
```

In the preceding example, the variable a is first initialized to be an integer with a value of 1. Then the expression a <= 5 is evaluated. This will result in a boolean *true.* Hence, the Java statement will be executed and then the value of a is updated by the update statement a+=2. This will result in a being incremented by 2. Then the condition is evaluated again, which will result in a *true,* because 3 is less than 5. The Java statement is executed. Now when the update statement is executed, the value of a becomes 5, which is greater than 4. Hence, the condition will evaluate to a *false* and the loop will end. So, in this example, the text "Hello World" will be printed two times and the value of a at the end will be 5.

CONTINUE

A continue statement makes the Java interpreter quit the current iteration of a while, do-while, or for loop and start the next one.

Syntax

```
continue;
```

Consider the example in Listing B-14.

Listing B-14: Use of continue Statement

```
int sum = 0;
for(int counter = 1; counter <= 5; counter++)
{
   if(counter == 4)
       continue;

   sum = sum + counter;
}
```

In the preceding example, we have a for loop that adds all the numbers from 1 to 5. But as you can see, there is an if condition in the middle that checks to see if the value of the counter is 4 and if so, executes the continue statement. This will make the Java interpreter skip the remainder section (which is the summing part) and start the next iteration. Thus, we see that the final outcome of the above example is:

```
sum = 1 + 2 + 3 + 5 = 11
```

RETURN

The return statement makes the Java interpreter stop the execution of the current method and continue executing the Java statements in the calling method. The return statement can also have an argument, if the method has a return value.

Syntax

```
return expression;
```

The expression should be present only if the method has a return value. Moreover, the expression should evaluate to a value, which matches the return type of the method. To illustrate this, consider the example shown in Listing B-15.

Listing B-15: Use of a return Statement

```
int sum = 0;
int x = 1;
int y = 2;

sum = addNumbers(x, y);

System.out.println("Sum of Numbers is " + sum);

public int addNumbers(int a, int b)
{
   int total = 0;
   total = a + b;
   return total;
}
```

In the preceding example, the Java interpreter calls the `addNumbers` method and passes x and y as parameters. Then the `addNumbers` method is executed. As you can see, the `total` is returned. In this case, the type of the variable `total` and the return type of the method are the same. Also, as soon as the `return` statement is executed, the statement following the original calling statement is executed. So, finally, the text "Sum of Numbers is 3" is printed.

Sometimes, there may be methods that return nothing. This happens when we have the return type of a method as `void`. In such cases an explicit `return` statement is not required. As soon as the Java interpreter reaches the last statement of the method, it automatically returns the control of execution to the statement following the calling statement.

There could also be scenarios where the explicit mention of an empty `return` statement might be useful. Consider the example in Listing B-16.

Listing B-16: Use of an Empty return Statement

```
int sum = 0;
int x = 1;
int y = 2;

sum = printTotal(x, y);

// Other Java statements

public void printTotal(int a, int b)
{
   int total = 0;
   total = a + b;

   if(total < 0)
```

```
        return;

    System.out.println("Sum of Numbers is " + total);
}
```

In the listing, the `printTotal` method is invoked. This method has a return type of `void`. This method will print the total only if the sum is greater than or equal to zero. Otherwise, it would simply return.

TRY-CATCH-FINALLY

The `try-catch-finally` Java statement is used to handle exceptions in Java. This statement has three blocks – the `try` block, `catch` block and `finally` block. The `try` block can have a set of Java statements that can be tried for any Java exceptions. For every `try` block, there can be one or more `catch` blocks. Every `catch` block can have Java statements that can handle an `exception`. The `catch` block can be followed by an optional `finally` block, which can contain cleanup code that will be executed irrespective of what happens in the `try` block.

Syntax

```
try
{
        //Java Statements
}
catch (exception to be caught)
{
        //Exception handling statements
}
finally
{
        //Cleanup code
}
```

The `catch` block must have an argument, which is a valid Java `Exception`.

An exception indicates an abnormal condition. The Java programming Language defines an exception as an Object of type `java.lang.Throwable` or one of its subclasses – `java.lang.Error` or `java.lang.Exception`.

There are some well-defined exceptions and errors in Java:

```
IOException
RuntimeException
NullPointerException
ArrayIndexOutOfBoundsException
OutOfMemoryError
```

Appendix B: A Java Primer

Other than these well-defined exceptions, you can also have user-defined exceptions, which indicate business logic errors. In order to define an exception, we need extend from the Exception class, as shown below in Listing B-17.

Listing B-17: User-Defined Exception

```
public class NotEnoughFundsException extends java.lang.Exception
{
}
```

The preceding example defines an exception, which can indicate an error when a user tries to withdraw more money than is available from his or her account. Because every Java exception is an Object, it can contain data that indicates the error and methods that can operate on this data. A new Object of the preceding exception type can be created by making use of the new allocation operator as shown here:

```
NotEnoughFundsException xyz = new NotEnoughFundsException();
```

If the try block has any Java statement that is capable of *throwing* a Java exception, then that exception should be *caught* in the catch block. In the next section, I discuss more about how to throw exceptions. The following example in Listing B-18 shows the usage of a try-catch-finally statement.

Listing B-18: Use of try-catch-finally

```
int accountBalance = 0;
try
{
        //Get Account Balance
        //Withdraw funds
        //Java Statements
}
catch(NotEnoughFundsException nef)
{
        System.out.println("You don't have sufficient funds");
}
catch(NullPointerException npe)
{
        //Exception Handling Logic
}
finally
{
        System.out.println("Your Balance is " + accounttBalance);
}
```

In the preceding example, the `try` block is executed first. If there is an exception, the corresponding `catch` block is executed. The `finally` block is executed irrespective of whether an exception was thrown in the `try` block.

THROW
In the Java programming language, the `throw` statement is used to throw an exception. When a method encounters an abnormal condition that it can't handle by itself, then it can throw an exception.

Syntax

```
throw expression;
```

The expression will evaluate to an Object of the corresponding exception type. The example in Listing B-19 illustrates the use of a `throw` statement.

Listing B-19: Use of throw Statement
```
NotEnoughFundsException xyz = new NotEnoughFundsException();

throw xyz;
```

The Java Libraries

The Java programming language provides a rich set of Java class libraries. In this section, I discuss a few of these, which I consider as core. For a complete list of these libraries, you should refer to a textbook dedicated to the Java language.

package java.io

The `java.io` package provides for standard system input and output through the use of a few concepts like serialization, data streams, and file system. It provides the ability to read and write files as well as other advanced I/O functionality.

JAVA.IO.SERIALIZABLE INTERFACE
Serialization is the process by which a Java object or a primitive data type is converted into a byte stream that can be sent across a network or file system. All primitive data types implement this interface. It has no methods or constants defined. Any Java class that needs to be serialized should implement this interface as shown here:

```
public class EmployeeData implements java.io.Serializable
{
        //Java Statements related to this class
}
```

JAVA.IO.DATAOUTPUT INTERFACE

Java primitive data cannot be sent over a network in their raw form. They have to be converted into a stream of bytes. This interface has methods that will convert a Java primitive data type into a stream of bytes and write them to a binary stream. See a summary in Table B-13.

TABLE B-13 METHOD SUMMARY FOR JAVA.IO.DATAOUTPUT INTERFACE

Method	Description
void write(byte[] arr_val)	All the bytes in the array arr_val are written to the output stream.
void writeBoolean (boolean bool_val)	The boolean value bool_val is written to this output stream.
void writeByteA (int x_val)	Java primitive data type int is made of 8 bits. This method writes those 8 bits of int x_val to the output stream.
void writeBytes (String str_val)	The String value str_val is written to the output stream.
void writeChar (int ch_val)	The Character value ch_val, which is comprised of two bytes, is written to the output stream.
void writeChars (String str_val)	The String value str_val is written to the output stream, in order, two bytes per character.
void writeDouble (double d_val)	The double value d_val, which is comprised of eight bytes, is written to the output stream.
void writeFloat (float f_val)	The float value f_val, which is comprised of four bytes, is written to the output stream.
void writeInt (int i_val)	The int value I_val, which is comprised of four bytes, is written to the output stream.
void writeLong (long l_val)	The long value l_val, which is comprised of eight bytes, is written to the output stream.
void writeShort (int sh_val)	The short value sh_val, which is comprised of two bytes, is written to the output stream.

JAVA.IO.DATAINPUT INTERFACE

This interface has methods that will read bytes from a binary stream and reconstruct the corresponding primitive data. See Table B-14.

TABLE B-14 METHOD SUMMARY FOR JAVA.IO.DATAINPUT INTERFACE

Method	Description
`boolean readBoolean()`	Reads one byte from the input binary stream and returns true if that byte is nonzero, false if that byte is zero.
`byte readByte()`	Reads one byte from the input binary stream and returns that input byte.
`char readChar()`	Reads a char from the input binary stream and returns that char value.
`short readShort()`	Reads two bytes from the input binary stream and returns a short value (size of short is two bytes).
`float readFloat()`	Reads four bytes from the input binary stream and returns a float value (size of float is four bytes).
`int readInt()`	Reads four bytes from the input binary stream and returns an int value (size of int is four bytes).
`long readLong()`	Reads eight bytes from the input binary stream and returns a long value (size of long is eight bytes).
`double readDouble()`	Reads eight bytes from the input binary stream and returns a double value (size of double is eight bytes).
`String readLine()`	Reads the next line of text from the input stream and returns it as a String.

JAVA.IO.OBJECTOUTPUT INTERFACE

Just like Java primitive data, Java objects also cannot be sent over a network in their raw form. This interface has methods that will convert Java objects into a stream of bytes and write them to a binary stream. This interface extends from the DataOutput interface. See Table B-15.

TABLE B-15 METHOD SUMMARY FOR JAVA.IO.OBJECTOUTPUT INTERFACE

Method	Description
`void close()`	The output stream to which data is written is closed.
`void flush`	Data in the output stream are flushed.

Continued

TABLE B-15 METHOD SUMMARY FOR JAVA.IO.OBJECTOUTPUT INTERFACE
(Continued)

Method	Description
void write(byte[] arr_val)	The array of bytes, arr_val, is written to the output stream.
void write(byte[] arr_val, int x_val, int length)	A subset of the array, arr_val, is written to the output stream.
void writeObject (Object obj)	The object, obj, is written to the output stream.

JAVA.IO.OBJECTINPUT INTERFACE

This interface has methods that will read bytes from a binary stream and reconstruct the corresponding object. It extends from the DataInput interface. See Table B-16.

TABLE B-16 METHOD SUMMARY FOR JAVA.IO.OBJECTINPUT INTERFACE

Method	Description
int available()	Returns the number of bytes that can be read from the input stream without blocking.
void close()	Closes the input stream.
int read()	Reads a byte of data from the input stream.
int read(byte[] arr_val)	Reads data from the input stream into an array of bytes, arr_val.
int read(byte[] arr_val, int x, int length)	Reads data from the input stream into a subset of the byte array, arr_val.
Object readObject()	Reads and returns an Object from the input stream.

JAVA.IO.FILE CLASS

This class is used to represent a file. It has methods that can operate on the file. An Object of type `File` can be created using the following constructors shown in Table B-17. It implements `java.io.Comparable` and `java.io.Serializable` interfaces.

TABLE B-17 CONSTRUCTORS FOR JAVA.IO.FILE CLASS

Constructor	Description
`File(String path)`	Creates a new `File` object that represents the file referred to by the path.
`File(URI uri)`	Creates a new `File` object that represents the file referred to by the uri.

TABLE B-18 METHOD SUMMARY FOR JAVA.IO.FILE CLASS

Method	Description
`boolean delete()`	Deletes this file and returns true if the file was successfully deleted.
`String getName()`	Returns the name of the file.
`long lastModified()`	Returns the time when this file was last modified.
`long length()`	Returns the length of the file.
`boolean setReadOnly()`	Sets the Read Only attribute of this file to be true and returns true if it was successful.

JAVA.IO.PRINTWRITER CLASS

This class has methods that will format data and write them to an output stream. It takes either the `java.io.OutputStream` or the `java.io.Writer` objects as a parameter to its constructor. `java.io.PrintWriter` extends from the `java.io.Writer` class.

Table B-19 Constructors for java.io.PrintWriter Class

Constructor	Description
PrintWriter (OutputStream os)	Creates a new `PrintWriter` object, which writes to an `OutputStream` represented by `os`.
PrintWriter (Writer wr)	Creates a new `PrintWriter` Object, which writes to a `Writer` represented by `wr`.

Table B-20 Method Summary for java.io.PrintWriter Class

Method	Description
void close()	Closes the `OutputStream`.
void print (Type xyz)	Prints a value of the specified Type. Here Type could be one of `boolean`, `char`, `char[]`, `double`, `float`, `int`, `long`, `Object`, or `String`.
void println (Type xyz)	Prints a value of the specified Type and ends the current line by printing an end-of-line character at the end. Here Type could be one of `boolean`, `char`, `char[]`, `double`, `float`, `int`, `long`, `Object`, or `String`.

JAVA.IO.IOEXCEPTION CLASS

This exception class is used to indicate an error while performing some I/O operation. It extends from the `java.io.Exception` class.

Table B-21 Constructors for java.io.IOException Class

Constructor	Description
IOException()	Creates a new `IOException` Object with no detailed error message.
IOException (String msg)	Creates a new `IOException` Object with a detailed error message indicated by `msg`.

It has no specific method of its own. It inherits all the methods defined by `java.lang.Throwable` and `java.lang.Object`.

package java.lang

This package provides interfaces, classes, exceptions, and errors that together form the foundation of the Java programming language. It defines the `java.lang.Object` and the `java.lang.Class`. It also contains the definitions for all the wrapper classes for the Java primitive data types.

JAVA.LANG.OBJECT CLASS

This is the base class for all Java classes. This is the root of the Java class hierarchy.

TABLE B-22 CONSTRUCTORS FOR JAVA.LANG.OBJECT CLASS

Method	Description
`Object()`	Creates a new Object.

TABLE B-23 METHOD SUMMARY FOR `java.lang.Object` CLASS

Method	Description
`Boolean equals (Object obj)`	Compares this Object with the Object `obj` and returns the boolean true if they are equal.
`String toString()`	Converts this Object to a String and returns it.

JAVA.LANG.CLASS CLASS

This represents the basic block of the Java language. It extends from `java.lang.Object` class and implements `java.io.Serializable` interface. There are no constructors for this class. A class Object is created when the JVM or the Java Interpreter loads a class into memory.

TABLE B-24 METHOD SUMMARY FOR JAVA.LANG.CLASS

Method	Description
`static class forName (String name)`	Loads or returns the class represented by the `String`, name.

Continued

TABLE B-24 METHOD SUMMARY FOR JAVA.LANG.CLASS *(Continued)*

Method	Description
Field[] getField()	Returns the fields defined in this Class as an array of java.lang.Field.
Class[] getInterfaces()	Returns the interfaces implemented by this Class as an array of java.lang.Class.
Method[] getMethods()	Returns the methods defined in this Class as an array of java.lang.Method.
Object newInstance()	Creates and returns a new instance of this Class.
String toString()	Returns the String equivalent of this Class.

JAVA.LANG.RUNNABLE INTERFACE

This interface has one single method called run that will start the execution in a threaded environment. Any class that wants to be executed in a threaded environment should implement this interface.

TABLE B-25 METHOD SUMMARY FOR JAVA.LANG.RUNNABLE INTERFACE

Method	Description
void run()	This method will be called when a Thread is started.

JAVA.LANG.BOOLEAN CLASS

This class is the wrapper class for the Java primitive type boolean. It implements the java.io.Serializable interface.

TABLE B-26 CONSTRUCTORS FOR JAVA.LANG.BOOLEAN CLASS

Constructor	Description
Boolean(boolean bool)	Creates a new Boolean Object wrapping the boolean value represented by bool.

Constructor	Description
Boolean(String value)	Creates a new Boolean Object wrapping the boolean value true if the String value is not null and is equal to "true" case insensitive.

TABLE B-27 METHOD SUMMARY FOR JAVA.LANG.BOOLEAN CLASS

Method	Description
boolean booleanValue()	Returns the primitive boolean value represented by this Boolean Object.
String toString()	Returns the String Object equivalent of this Boolean Object.

JAVA.LANG.BYTE CLASS

This class is the wrapper class for the Java primitive type byte. It extends from java.lang.Number class and implements the java.io.Comparable interface.

TABLE B-28 CONSTRUCTORS FOR JAVA.LANG.BYTE CLASS

Constructor	Description
Byte(byte b_value)	Creates a new Byte Object wrapping the byte value represented by b_value.
Byte(String value)	Creates a new Byte Object wrapping the byte value represented by the String, value.

TABLE B-29 METHOD SUMMARY FOR JAVA.LANG.BYTE CLASS

Method	Description
byte byteValue()	Returns the byte equivalent of this Byte Object.
Double doubleValue()	Returns the double equivalent of this Byte Object.

Continued

Table B-29 Method Summary for Java.Lang.Byte Class *(Continued)*

Method	Description
float floatValue()	Returns the float equivalent of this Byte Object.
int intValue()	Returns the int equivalent of this Byte Object.
long longValue()	Returns the long equivalent of this Byte Object.
short shortValue()	Returns the short equivalent of this Byte Object.
String toString	Returns the String equivalent of this Byte Object.

JAVA.LANG.CHARACTER CLASS

This class is the wrapper class for the Java primitive type char. It implements the java.io.Serializable and java.io.Comparable interfaces.

Table B-30 Constructors for Java.Lang.Character Class

Constructor	Description
Character(char c_value)	Creates a new Character Object wrapping the char value represented by c_value.

Table B-31 Method Summary for Java.Lang.Character Class

Method	Description
char charValue()	Returns the char value equivalent of this Character Object.
static boolean isWhiteSpace(char ch_value)	Returns boolean true if the char ch_value is a valid Java white space.
static char toLowerCase(char ch_value)	Returns after converting the char ch_value to the corresponding lower case.
static char toUpperCase(char ch_value)	Returns after converting the char ch_value to the corresponding upper case.

JAVA.LANG.DOUBLE CLASS

This class is the wrapper class for the Java primitive type `double`. It extends from `java.lang.Number` class and implements the `java.io.Comparable` interface.

TABLE B-32 CONSTRUCTORS FOR JAVA.LANG.DOUBLE CLASS

Constructor	Description
`Double(double d_value)`	Creates a new `Double` Object wrapping the `double` value represented by `d_value`
`Double(String value)`	Creates a new `Double` Object wrapping the `double` value represented by the `String` Object value.

TABLE B-33 METHOD SUMMARY FOR JAVA.LANG.DOUBLE CLASS

Method	Description
`byte byteValue()`	Returns the `byte` equivalent of this `Double` Object
`double doubleValue()`	Returns the `double` equivalent of this `Double` Object.
`float floatValue()`	Returns the `float` equivalent of this `Double` Object.
`int intValue()`	Returns the `int` equivalent of this `Double` Object.
`long longValue()`	Returns the `long` equivalent of this `Double` Object.
`short shortValue()`	Returns the `short` equivalent of this `Double` Object.
`String toString`	Returns the `String` equivalent of this `Double` Object.

JAVA.LANG.FLOAT CLASS

This class is the wrapper class for the Java primitive type `float`. It extends from `java.lang.Number` class and implements the `java.io.Comparable` interface.

TABLE B-34 CONSTRUCTORS FOR JAVA.LANG.FLOAT CLASS

Constructor	Description
Float(float f_value)	Creates a new Float Object wrapping the float value represented by f_value.
Float(String value)	Creates a new Float Object wrapping the float value represented by the String Object value.

TABLE B-35 METHOD SUMMARY FOR JAVA.LANG.FLOAT CLASS

Method	Description
byte byteValue()	Returns the byte equivalent of this Float Object.
double doubleValue()	Returns the double equivalent of this Float Object.
float floatValue()	Returns the float equivalent of this Float Object.
int intValue()	Returns the int equivalent of this Float Object.
long longValue()	Returns the long equivalent of this Float Object.
short shortValue()	Returns the short equivalent of this Float Object.
String toString	Returns the String equivalent of this Float Object.

JAVA.LANG.INTEGER CLASS

This class is the wrapper class for the Java primitive type int. It extends from java.lang.Number class and implements the java.io.Comparable interface.

TABLE B-36 CONSTRUCTORS FOR JAVA.LANG.INTEGER CLASS

Constructor	Description
Integer(long i_value)	Creates a new Integer Object wrapping the int value represented by i_value.
Integer(String value)	Creates a new Integer Object wrapping the int value represented by the String Object value.

TABLE B-37 METHOD SUMMARY FOR JAVA.LANG.INTEGER CLASS

Method	Description
`byte byteValue()`	Returns the `byte` equivalent of this `Integer` Object.
`Double doubleValue()`	Returns the `double` equivalent of this `Integer` Object.
`float floatValue()`	Returns the `float` equivalent of this `Integer` Object.
`int intValue()`	Returns the `int` equivalent of this `Integer` Object.
`long longValue()`	Returns the `long` equivalent of this `Integer` Object.
`short shortValue()`	Returns the `short` equivalent of this `Integer` Object.
`String toString`	Returns the `String` equivalent of this `Integer` Object.

JAVA.LANG.LONG CLASS

This class is the wrapper class for the Java primitive type `long`. It extends from `java.lang.Number` class and implements the `java.io.Comparable` interface.

TABLE B-38 CONSTRUCTORS FOR JAVA.LANG.LONG CLASS

Constructor	Description
`Long(long l_value)`	Creates a new `Long` Object wrapping the `long` value represented by `l_value`.
`Long(String value)`	Creates a new `Long` Object wrapping the `long` value represented by the `String` Object value.

TABLE B-39 METHOD SUMMARY FOR JAVA.LANG.LONG CLASS

Method	Description
`byte byteValue()`	Returns the `byte` equivalent of this `Long` Object.
`Double doubleValue()`	Returns the `double` equivalent of this `Long` Object.

Continued

TABLE B-39 METHOD SUMMARY FOR JAVA.LANG.LONG CLASS *(Continued)*

Method	Description
float floatValue()	Returns the float equivalent of this Long Object.
int intValue()	Returns the int equivalent of this Long Object.
long longValue()	Returns the long equivalent of this Long Object.
short shortValue()	Returns the short equivalent of this Long Object.
String toString	Returns the String equivalent of this Long Object.

JAVA.LANG.SHORT CLASS

This class is the wrapper class for the Java primitive type short. It extends from java.lang.Number class and implements the java.io.Comparable interface.

TABLE B-40 CONSTRUCTORS FOR JAVA.LANG.SHORT CLASS

Constructor	Description
Short(short s_value)	Creates a new Short Object wrapping the short value represented by s_value.
Short(String value)	Creates a new Short Object wrapping the short value represented by the String Object value.

TABLE B-41 METHOD SUMMARY FOR JAVA.LANG.SHORT CLASS

Method	Description
byte byteValue()	Returns the byte equivalent of this Short Object.
Double doubleValue()	Returns the double equivalent of this Short Object.
float floatValue()	Returns the float equivalent of this Short Object.
int intValue()	Returns the int equivalent of this Short Object.
long longValue()	Returns the long equivalent of this Short Object.

Method	Description
short shortValue()	Returns the short equivalent of this Short Object.
String toString	Returns the String equivalent of this Short Object.

JAVA.LANG.STRING CLASS

This class represents a set of characters or a string of characters. It has methods that perform operations on this String. It implements the java.io.Serializable, java.io.Comparable, and java.lang.CharSequence interfaces.

TABLE B-42 CONSTRUCTORS FOR JAVA.LANG.STRING CLASS

Constructor	Description
String()	Creates a new String Object with an empty character.
String(char[] c_value)	Creates a new String Object with a sequence of characters represented by the array of characters c_value.
String(String str_value)	Creates a new String Object with a String represented by str_value.

TABLE B-43 METHOD SUMMARY FOR JAVA.LANG.STRING CLASS

Method	Description
char charAt(int pos)	Returns the character at the pos position of this String.
String concat (String app_str)	Returns the resulting String after appending the String app_str with this String.
int length()	Returns the length of this String.
String toLowerCase()	Returns the String after converting it into lower case.
String toUpplerCase()	Returns the String after converting it into upper case.
String trim()	Returns the String after deleting the white spaces at the end of this String.

JAVA.LANG.THREAD CLASS

The `java.lang.Thread` class encapsulates the properties and behavior of a thread of execution. It essentially represents a unit of work for the CPU. In a multitasking environment, you can have multiple threads running at the same time or multiple units of work being done simultaneously. This class implements the `java.lang.Runnable` interface.

TABLE B-44 CONSTRUCTORS FOR JAVA.LANG.THREAD CLASS

Constructors	Description
Thread()	Creates a new Thread Object. This Object is identified by a name, Thread-n, where n is an automatically generated integer.

TABLE B-45 METHOD SUMMARY FOR JAVA.LANG.THREAD CLASS

Method	Description
void destroy()	Destroys this thread of execution.
String getName()	Returns the name of this Thread of execution.
int getPriority()	Returns the priority level of this thread of execution.
boolean isAlive()	Returns a boolean true if this thread is still running.
void run()	This method is called when this Thread is started.
void setPriority(int priority)	Sets the priority level of this Thread to the specified value.
void setName(String name)	Sets the name of this Thread to the specified value.
void start()	Starts this Thread of execution and then calls the run method of this Thread.

JAVA.LANG.THROWABLE CLASS

The `java.lang.Throwable` class is the root of all exceptions and errors in the Java programming language. It implements the `java.io.Serializable` interface.

Table B-46 Constructors for Java.Lang.Throwable Class

Constructors	Description
Throwable()	Creates a new Throwable Object with no detailed error message.
Throwable (String s_message)	Creates a new Throwable Object with a detailed error message specified by s_message.

Table B-47 Method Summary for Java.Lang.Throwable Class

Method	Description
String getMessage()	Returns the detailed error message as a String value.
void printStackTrace()	Prints the stack trace for this Object to the output stream.

JAVA.LANG.EXCEPTION CLASS

The java.lang.Exception class indicates the occurrence of an abnormal condition. It extends from the java.lang.Throwable interface.

Table B-48 Constructors for Java.Lang.Exception Class

Constructors	Description
Exception()	Creates a new Exception Object with no detailed error message.
Exception (String s_message)	Creates a new Exception Object with a detailed error message specified by s_message.

It has no specific method of its own. It inherits all the methods defined by java.lang.Throwable and java.lang.Object.

package java.net

This package provides the required set of interfaces, classes, and exceptions that address networking functions. It has the `java.net.Socket` and `java.net.ServerSocket` among others that address the TCP client and server functions. It also has `java.net.DataGramSocket` to address UDP.

JAVA.NET.SOCKET CLASS

This class represents a client connection-oriented socket. A *socket* is one endpoint of a two-way communication link between two programs running on the network.

TABLE B-49 CONSTRUCTORS FOR JAVA.NET.SOCKET CLASS

Constructor	Description
Socket()	Creates a new Socket Object that does not specify any IP address or port number. Essentially, it is an unconnected socket.
Socket(String host_name, int port_num)	Creates a new Socket Object and connects it to the specified port number on the host, host_name.

TABLE B-50 METHOD SUMMARY FOR JAVA.NET.SOCKET CLASS

Method	Description
void close()	Closes this Socket connection.
InputStream getInputStream()	Returns the InputStream for this socket. This InputStream is later used to receive data.
OutputStream getOutputStream()	Returns the OutputStream for this socket. This OutputStream is later used to send data.

JAVA.NET.DATAGRAMSOCKET CLASS

This class implements the client and server sockets using the UDP protocol, which is a connectionless protocol. Pieces of data called *datagrams* are used for data exchange.

TABLE B-51 CONSTRUCTORS FOR JAVA.NET.DATAGRAMSOCKET CLASS

Constructor	Description
DatagramSocket()	Creates a new DatagramSocket Object and associates it with a freely available port on the local machine.
DatagramSocket (int port_number)	Creates a new DatagramSocket Object and associates it with the specified port number on the local machine.

TABLE B-52 METHOD SUMMARY FOR JAVA.NET.DATAGRAMSOCKET CLASS

Method	Description
void close()	Closes this datagram socket.
void connect(InetAddress addr, int port_num)	Connects to the remote IP address and port number as specified.
void disconnect()	Disconnects this datagram socket.
void receive(Datagram Packet dp)	Receives the incoming data and places them in the DatagramPacket, dp.
void send(Datagram Packet dp)	Sends the datagram packet, dp.

JAVA.NET.URL CLASS

This class represents the Universal Resource Locator (URL). It essentially encapsulates the URL address.

TABLE B-53 CONSTRUCTORS FOR JAVA.NET.URL CLASS

Constructor	Description
URL(String str)	Creates a new URL Object represented by the String, str.

Table B-54 Method Summary for Java.Net.URL Class

Method	Description
Object getContent()	Retrieves the content specified by this URL address and returns it as a Java Object.
String getHost() String	Returns the host name specified by this URL as a value.
int getPort() int	Returns the port number specified by this URL as an value.
String getProtocol()	Returns the protocol used by this URL for communication (for example, HTTP, FTP, and so on).
InputStream openStream()	Returns the input stream over which data is read.

JAVA.NET.SOCKETEXCEPTION CLASS

This class extends from `java.io.IOException` class.

Table B-55 Constructors for Java.Net.SocketException Class

Constructor	Description
SocketException()	Creates a new `SocketException` Object with no detailed error message.
SocketException (String msg)	Creates a new `SocketException` Object with a detailed error message specified by the `String msg`.

It has no specific method of its own. It inherits all the methods defined by `java.lang.Throwable` and `java.lang.Object`.

package java.util

This package has a set of utility interfaces, classes, and exceptions, which supplement the existing Java packages. They include `Collection`, `Iterator`, `ArrayList`, `Calendar`, `Hashtable`, `Vector`, and many more.

JAVA.UTIL.COLLECTION INTERFACE

A *collection* is a group of items or elements. Classes that implement this interface provide the functionality to store groups of data or elements.

TABLE B-56 METHOD SUMMARY FOR JAVA.UTIL.COLLECTION INTERFACE

Method	Description
`boolean add (Object obj)`	Adds the `Object obj` to the Collection and returns a boolean, true if the Collection was updated or changed. There can be collections that do not permit duplicate entries. In such cases, if the `Object obj` already exists, then the Collection is not updated and a boolean, false id is returned.
`void clear()`	Deletes all the elements of this Collection.
`Iterator iterator()`	Returns an iterator over this Collection. This iterator can then be used to retrieve each single element and perform an operation over them.
`boolean remove (Object obj)`	Deletes the element represented by the Object, `obj`, from the Collection and then returns a boolean, true if the Collection was updated, else it returns a boolean, false
`int size()`	Returns the number of elements in this Collection.

JAVA.UTIL.ITERATOR INTERFACE

This interface provides a means by which the elements inside a collection can be operated upon.

TABLE B-57 METHOD SUMMARY FOR JAVA.UTIL.ITERATOR INTERFACE

Method	Description
`boolean hasNext()`	Returns a boolean, true if the iteration has more elements.
`Object next()`	Retrieves the next element in the iteration and returns it as a Java Object.
`void remove()`	Removes from the Collection the last element retrieved by the iterator.

JAVA.UTIL.ARRAYLIST CLASS

The `java.util.ArrayList` class holds a set of Java Objects. It can grow its size dynamically as required. The `ArrayList` is not synchronized, which means that elements in an `ArrayList` are not thread-safe. It extends from `java.util.AbstractList` class and implements the `java.io.Serializable, java.lang.Cloneable, java.util.List,` and `java.util.RandomAccess` interfaces.

TABLE B-58 CONSTRUCTORS FOR JAVA.UTIL.ARRAYLIST CLASS

Constructor	Description
`ArrayList()`	Creates a new and empty `ArrayList` Object with an initial capacity of ten elements.
`ArrayList (Collection col)`	Creates a new `ArrayList` Object and fills it up with the elements retrieved from the Collection, `col`.
`ArrayList(int x)`	Creates a new `ArrayList` Object with an initial capacity that can hold *x* elements.

TABLE B-59 METHOD SUMMARY FOR JAVA.UTIL.ARRAYLIST CLASS

`void add(int pos, Object obj)`	Adds the Object, `obj`, to the position, `pos`, of the `ArrayList`.
`boolean add (Object obj)`	Adds the Object, `obj`, to the end of the `ArrayList` and returns a boolean, true if the `ArrayList` was updated.
`Object get (int pos)`	Retrieves the Object from the position, `pos`, of the `ArrayList` and returns it.
`Object remove (int pos)`	Removes the Object from the position, `pos`, and returns it.
`Object set(int position, Object obj)`	Replaces the Object at the position, `pos`, of the `ArrayList` with the new Object, `obj`, and returns the old Object.
`int size()`	Returns the number of elements in this `ArrayList`.

JAVA.UTIL.DATE CLASS

The `java.util.Date` class can be used to construct objects that represent a specific point in time, with millisecond accuracy. It implements the `java.lang.Cloneable, java.lang.Compareable,` and `java.io.Serializeable` interfaces.

TABLE B-60 CONSTRUCTORS FOR JAVA.UTIL.DATE CLASS

Constructor	Description
Date()	Creates a new Date Object and initializes it to the time when it was created.
Date(long l_time)	Creates a new Date Object and initializes it to the time specified by the long value l_time.

TABLE B-61 METHOD SUMMARY FOR JAVA.UTIL.DATE CLASS

Method	Description
long getTime()	Returns the time specified by this Date Object as a long value.
void setTime(long l_time)	Sets the time specified by this Date Object to the long value l_time since January 1, 1970, 00:00:00 GMT.

JAVA.UTIL.CALENDAR CLASS

java.util.Calendar is an abstract class that provides the basic functionality common to calendars, such as setting, getting, and comparing dates. This class helps in interpreting the java.util.Date Object according to a specific Calendar. It implements the java.lang.Cloneable and java.io.Serializeable interfaces.

TABLE B-62 CONSTRUCTORS FOR JAVA.UTIL.CALENDAR CLASS

Constructor	Description
Calendar()	Creates a new Calendar Object with the default time zone and locale.
Calendar(TimeZone tz, Locale, lo)	Creates a new Calendar Object with the specified time zone, tz, and locale, lo.

TABLE B-63 METHOD SUMMARY FOR JAVA.UTIL.CALENDAR CLASS

Method	Description
void clear	Clears all the fields in this Calendar Object.
long getTime()	Returns the time specified by this Calendar Object in milliseconds.
TimeZone getTimeZone()	Returns the time zone specified by this Calendar Object as a TimeZone Object.
void roll(int field, int amount)	Rolls the specified field in this Calendar Object by the specified time.
void setTime(long l_time)	Sets the time in this Calendar Object to the specified time, l_time.
void setTimeZone (TimeZone tz)	Sets the time zone in this Calendar Object to the specified TimeZone, tz.

JAVA.UTIL.HASHTABLE CLASS

Hashtable is an extremely useful mechanism for storing data. It works by mapping a key to a value, which is stored in an in-memory data structure. Instead of searching through all elements of the hashtable for a matching key, a hashing function analyzes a key, and returns an index number. This index matches a stored value, and the data is then accessed. It extends from java.util.Dictionary and implements the java.util.Map, java.lang.Cloneable, and java.io.Serializable interfaces.

TABLE B-64 CONSTRUCTORS FOR JAVA.UTIL.HASHTABLE CLASS

Constructor	Description
Hashtable()	Creates a new Hashtable Object with an initial capacity of 11.
Hashtable(int i_capacity)	Creates a new Hashtable Object with an initial capacity specified by i_capacity.

TABLE B-65 METHOD SUMMARY FOR JAVA.UTIL.HASHTABLE CLASS

Method	Description
void clear()	Removes all keys from this Hashtable.
Object get(Object key)	Returns the Object specified by the key.
Object put(Object key, Object newValue)	Replaces the old value pointed by the key with the Object newValue and returns the old value if any.
Object remove (Object key)	Removes the Object pointed by this key and returns it.
int size()	Returns the number of key-value pairs in this Hashtable.

JAVA.UTIL.VECTOR CLASS

A vector is similar to an array in that it can store lists of values. But it can store only references to objects and not primitive data types like int, char, Boolean, and so on. It can change its size as needed. It extends from java.util.AbstractList class and implements the java.util.List, java.util.RandomAccess, java.lang.Cloneable, and java.io.Serializable interfaces.

TABLE B-66 CONSTRUCTORS FOR JAVA.UTIL.VECTOR CLASS

Constructor	Description
Vector()	Creates a new Vector Object that is empty and has an initial capacity to store 10 elements.
Vector(int i_capacity)	Creates a new Vector Object with an initial capacity to store i_capacity elements.
Vector(Collection col)	Creates a new Vector Object and fills it with the elements iterated out of the Collection, col.

TABLE B-67 METHOD SUMMARY FOR JAVA.UTIL.VECTOR CLASS

Method	Description
void add(int position, Object obj)	Adds a new Object, obj, to the specified position of this Vector Object.
void addElement (Object obj)	Adds a new Object, obj, to the end of this Vector Object.
void clear()	Removes all elements from this Vector Object.
Object elementAt (int position)	Returns the Object stored at the specified position in this Vector Object.
Object get(int position)	Returns the Object stored at the specified position in this Vector Object.
Object remove (int position)	Deletes the Object stored at the specified position in this Vector Object and returns it.
Object set(int position,Object obj)	Stores the Object, obj, at the specified position in this Vector Object and returns the Object, if any, that was previously stored there.
int size()	Returns the number of elements in this Vector Object.

package java.math

This is a very small package that provides two classes—BigDecimal and BigInteger. These classes allow operations to be performed on arbitrary-size and arbitrary-precision integers and floating-point values.

JAVA.MATH.BIGDECIMAL CLASS

The BigDecimal class provides immutable, arbitrary-precision decimal numbers. The methods of the BigDecimal class provide operations for fixed and floating-point arithmetic, comparison, format conversions, and hashing. It extends from java.lang.Number class and implements the java.io.Comparable interface.

TABLE B-68 CONSTRUCTORS FOR JAVA.MATH.BIGDECIMAL CLASS

Constructor	Description
BigDecimal (double d_val)	Creates a new BigDecimal Object by wrapping the double value represented by d_val.
BigDecimal (String s_val)	Creates a new BigDecimal Object by wrapping the String value represented by s_val.
BigDecimal(BigInteger b_val)	Creates a new BigDecimal Object by wrapping the BigInteger value represented by b_val.

TABLE B-69 METHOD SUMMARY FOR JAVA.MATH.BIGDECIMAL CLASS

Method	Description
BigDecimal abs()	Returns the absolute value of this BigDecimal Object.
double doubleValue()	Returns the double value equivalent of this BigDecimal Object.
float floatValue()	Returns the float value equivalent of this BigDecimal Object.
int intValue()	Returns the int value equivalent of this BigDecimal Object.
short shortValue()	Returns the short value equivalent of this BigDecimal Object.
String toString()	Returns the string value equivalent of this BigDecimal Object.
BigInteger to BigInteger()	Returns the BigInteger value equivalent of this BigDecimal Object.

JAVA.MATH.BIGINTEGER CLASS

The java.math.BigInteger class represents integers that are arbitrarily larger than eight bytes (Java primitive long). It extends from java.lang.Number class and implements the java.io.Comparable interface.

Appendix B: A Java Primer

TABLE B-70 CONSTRUCTORS FOR JAVA.MATH.BIGINTEGER CLASS

Constructor	Description
BigInteger(byte[] val)	Creates a new BigInteger Object by wrapping the byte array represented by val. It translates the byte array into the two's complement binary representation of the BigInteger.
BigInteger(String s_val)	Creates a new BigInteger Object by wrapping the String value represented by the String Object s_val.

TABLE B-71 METHOD SUMMARY FOR JAVA.MATH.BIGINTEGER CLASS

Method	Description
BigInteger abs()	Returns the absolute value of this BigInteger Object.
double doubleValue()	Returns the double value equivalent of this BigInteger Object.
float floatValue()	Returns the float value equivalent of this BigInteger Object.
int intValue()	Returns the int value equivalent of this BigInteger Object.
short shortValue()	Returns the short value equivalent of this BigInteger Object.
String toString()	Returns the String value equivalent of this BigInteger Object.
BigInteger add (BigInteger val)	Adds the BigInteger, val, to this BigInteger object and returns the resulting BigInteger.

Summary

This Java appendix is only an introduction to the Java programming language and not an exhaustive Java textbook. It covers some of the basics that you will require while working with WebLogic Workshop.

In the first section, I showed you the basics of the core language – variables, expressions, data types, statements, and control flow statements. In the second section, I showed you some of the interfaces, classes, and exceptions available in the Java class library.

Index

Symbols

@ (at sign)
  @jws:context annotation, 32
  @jws:control annotation, 141
  @jws:conversation annotation, 82, 83
  @jws:conversation-lifetime annotation, 93
  @jws:jms annotation, 179
  @jws:message-buffer annotation, 99
  @jws:operation annotation, 24–25, 33, 35
  @jws:parameter-xml annotation, 123
  @jws:protocol annotation, 226
  @jws:return-xml annotation, 123
. (dot) operator in JavaScript, 276
/ (slash) for comments, 15, 33
[] (square brackets) for JavaScript arrays, 277
* (star) for comments, 15, 33

A

abstract classes (Java), 323–324
actions (JSP), 248
Add Control drop-down (Design View), 139
Add Database Control dialog box, 153
Add EJB Control dialog box, 169
Add JMS Control dialog box
  connection-factory option, 178
  JMS destination type option, 178
  JMS message option, 183
  Message type options, 181–187
  Object option, 183
  overview, 177–178
  receive-jndi-name option, 178
  send-jndi-name option, 178
  Text option, 182
  XML map option, 182–183
Add Method command, 22, 23
Add Operation drop-down list, 22, 23
Add Service Control dialog box, 139–140
Add Timer Control dialog box, 144–145
addItem method, 86, 89, 259
addItem.jsp page, 259
allocation operator (Java), 328–329
alphabetical order
  in Design View, 80
  in Structure Pane, 56
annotations. *See* Javadoc annotations

APIs (Application Programming Interfaces), 4, 280
appendChild function (JavaScript), 289
application object (JSP), 249
applications on the CD, 313–314
arithmetic operators (Java), 324–325
arrays
  converting item array to array of object arrays, 268–269
  defined, 276, 320
  Java, 320
  JavaScript arrays, 276–277
  JavaScript for and for..in statements for, 279
  JavaScript if...else structures for, 278
assignment operators (Java), 327–328
asterisk (*) for comments, 15, 33
asynchronous model, 97–98, 217
asynchronous Web services. *See also* buffering; callbacks
  buffering, 98–103
  callbacks, 99, 103–113
  Caller example, 109–110, 111–112
  CreditReport example, 106–107
  Listener example, 110–111, 112
  mechanisms, 98–99
  SimpleBuffer example, 99–102
at sign (@)
  for Javadoc tags, 33
  @jws:context annotation, 32
  @jws:control annotation, 141
  @jws:conversation annotation, 82, 83
  @jws:conversation-lifetime annotation, 93
  @jws:jms annotation, 179
  @jws:message-buffer annotation, 99
  @jws:operation annotation, 24–25, 33, 35
  @jws:parameter-xml annotation, 123
  @jws:protocol annotation, 226
  @jws:return-xml annotation, 123
attributes
  changing values, 79
  conversation-lifetime, 93
  default values, 82–83
  defined, 78

continued

attributes *continued*
    descriptions in Property Editor, 83
    mapping to and from, 121
    for message formats, 226-227
    of message-buffer tag, 99, 102
    specifying for tags, 82

B

backing up, .Workshop file, 51
BEA WebLogic Server Bible (Zuffoletto, Joe), 7
BEA WebLogic Workshop eBook version on CD
    (Christofferson, Sean and Jayanthi,
    Srinivas and Traut, Steven and
    Pradjinata, Wira), 314
binary operators (Java)
    arithmetic, 325
    assignment, 327-328
    bitwise-manipulation or shift, 327
    conditional, 326
    relational, 325-326
bitwise-manipulation operators (Java), 327
BookProject project (on the CD), 19-20
breakpoints, 67
buffering
    defined, 98-99
    function of, 103
    icon for buffered methods, 99
    @jws:message-buffer annotation, 99
    message-buffer tag, 99, 102
    SimpleBuffer Web service, 99-102
business processes, session beans and, 167
BytesMessage type (JMS), 185-186

C

Call Stack Pane (Debugger), 70-71
Callback interface, 104-105
<CallbackHeader> SOAP header, 228, 233
callbacks. *See also* operations
    Caller Web service example, 109-110,
        111-112
    control factory, 205-206
    controlling with Context object, 108-113
    conversations and, 106
    creating in Design View, 103
    CreditReport Web service example, 106-107
    defined, 22, 99
    handlers in CreditCheck JMS control,
        195-197, 203-204
    instances, 105
    interface for, 104-105
    Listener Web service example, 110-111, 112
    in Message Log, 107-108
    methods versus, 103
    NewSubService Web service, 152
    sending to many listeners, 112-113
    source code, 103-104
    Timer control, 145-146, 148
    viewing in Test View, 107-108
    wrapper service as alternative to, 238-242
Caller Web service, 109-110, 111-112
callListener method, 111
CD-ROM with this book
    author-created materials on, 19, 313
    contents, 313-314
    installing WebLogic Workshop platform trial
        edition in Windows, 312-313
    non-Windows versions of WebLogic
        Workshop and, 312
    system requirements, 311
    troubleshooting, 314
changeSubscription method, 152
checkout method, 87
classes. *See also specific classes*
    abstract (Java), 323-324
    automatic name changes, 46
    importing, 31
    importing with JavaScript, 294
    initializing proxy classes, 265-266
    inner, with conversations, 87-88
    Java, 321
    Java proxy, 60
    java.io.File, 345
    java.io.IOException, 346
    java.io.PrintWriter, 345-346
    java.lang.Boolean, 348-349
    java.lang.Byte, 349-350
    java.lang.Character, 350
    java.lang.Class, 347-348
    java.lang.Double, 351
    java.lang.Exception, 357
    java.lang.Float, 351-352
    java.lang.Integer, 352-353
    java.lang.Long, 353-354
    java.lang.Object, 347
    java.lang.Short, 354-355
    java.lang.String, 355
    java.lang.Thread, 456
    java.lang.Throwable, 356-357

Index 373

java.math.BigDecimal, 366–367
java.math.BigInteger, 367–368
java.net.DatagramSocket, 358–359
java.net.Socket, 358
java.net.SocketException, 360
java.net.URL, 359–360
java.util.ArrayList, 361–362
java.util.Calendar, 363–364
java.util.Date, 362–363
java.util.Hashtable, 364–365
java.util.Vector, 365–366
for JSP client support, 252
member variables, 32
for Swing client support, 264
wrapper classes for primitive data types (Java), 319–320
Clear All State persistence setting, 62
clearing. *See* deleting
client-jar, 167–168
clients for Web services. *See also* JSP clients; Swing clients
design questions, 237–238
in Design View, 21
developing JSP clients, 245–264
developing Swing clients, 264–271
generating a conversation ID, 243–244
generating proxies, 242–243
planning for client support, 237–242
sending a conversation ID, 245
WebLogic Workshop test client, 26–29
wrapper service for, 238–242
clients (JMS), 176, 177, 219–221
code completion, 51–53
code order
in Design View, 80
in Structure Pane, 56
<code> tag (Javadoc), 36
Color Picker dialog box, 50
Color Preferences dialog box, 50
colors
breakpoints, 67
selecting objects in Design View and, 78
syntax coloring, 49–51
comments. *See also* Javadoc annotations
Convert method example, 35–36
Javadoc, 33–34
separating text from tags, 34
in Web services source code, 15

compiler
Java, 315, 316
Test View auto-compilation, 66
Warnings page (Test View), 65
Complete WSDL link (Test View Overview page), 60
conditional operators (Java), 326
config.xml file, 9, 155. *See also* WebLogic Server
Console page (Test View), 60–62
constructors
default for inner classes, 88
java.io.File class, 345
java.io.IOException class, 346
java.io.PrintWriter class, 346
java.lang.Boolean class, 348–349
java.lang.Byte class, 349
java.lang.Character class, 350
java.lang.Double class, 351
java.lang.Exception class, 357
java.lang.Float class, 352
java.lang.Integer class, 352
java.lang.Long class, 353
java.lang.Object class, 347
java.lang.Short class, 354
java.lang.String class, 355
java.lang.Thread class, 456
java.lang.Throwable class, 357
java.math.BigDecimal class, 367
java.math.BigInteger class, 368
java.net.DatagramSocket class, 359
java.net.Socket class, 358
java.net.SocketException class, 360
java.net.URL class, 359
java.util.ArrayList class, 362
java.util.Calendar class, 363
java.util.Date class, 363
java.util.Hashtable class, 364
java.util.Vector class, 365
consumer, 176
Context object
automatic addition of, 32
callback-related methods, 109
controlling callbacks with, 108–113
controlling conversations with, 93–96
conversation-related methods, 94
CurrencyCalc Web service, 32, 55
declaration, 137–138
Design View and, 138

continued

Context object *continued*
   instances, 32
   `onException` method, 55
   `onFinish` method, 55
Continue (debugging command), 68
continue methods of conversations
   indicator, 79
   `@jws:conversation` annotation for, 82
   overview, 77
   setting for tags, 79
   terminology, 76
   Test View and, 90, 91
`continue` statement (Java), 337
`<ContinueHeader>` SOAP header, 228, 230-232, 245
control factories, 140, 204-207
control flow statements (Java)
   `continue`, 337
   defined, 331
   `do-while`, 335-336
   `else`, 332-333
   `for`, 336-337
   `if`, 331-333
   `return`, 337-339
   `switch`, 333-334
   `switch-case`, 334
   `throw`, 341
   `try-catch-finally`, 339-341
   `while`, 335
controls. *See also* Context object; *specific controls*
   control factories, 140, 204-207
   Database, 152-163
   declaration for, 137-138
   defined, 55
   in Design View, 22, 138
   EJB, 165-172
   icons for, 55
   initialization and, 105, 139
   JMS, 165-166, 173-192
   J2EE components and, 165-166
   `@jws:control` annotation, 141
   OnlineStore Web service example, 192-204
   overview, 137-139
   Service, 139-144
   in Structure Pane, 55
   Test View Overview page link for, 60
   Timer, 144-152
`conversation` tag, 79
ConversationAge Web service, 95-96

conversational states
   clearing stored states, 62
   defined, 75
   excluding fields from, 89
   maintaining, 76, 88-89
   OnlineStore Web service example, 88-89
   persistence of, 76, 89
   rules for adding, 89
   sorting methods in Design View by, 81
   storage of, 76
conversation-lifetime property, 92-93
conversations
   callbacks and, 106
   clearing stored state, 62
   continue methods, 76, 77
   controlling with `Context` object, 93-96
   conversation key, 77-78
   ConversationAge Web service example, 95-96
   in Design View, 78-81
   finish methods, 76, 77-78
   IDs, 243-245, 266
   importance of, 75
   indicators for phases, 79
   inner classes with, 87-88
   JSP clients for, 245-264
   `@jws:conversation` annotation for, 82
   lifetimes, 92-93
   loan application example, 75
   OnlineStore Web service example, 83-91
   overview, 75-76
   phases, 76-78
   setting phase of, 79
   SimpleConversation Web service example, 81-82
   SOAP headers for, 228-233, 245
   start methods, 76, 77
   Swing clients for, 264-271
   testing conversational Web services, 89-91
   Web service with control factory, 207
   workflows, 76
conversion calculator. *See* CurrencyCalc Web service
`Convert` method
   adding to Web service, 22-23
   commented example, 35-36
   `@jws:operation` annotation, 24-25, 33, 35
   SOAP body text box, 63-64
   source code, 24, 25, 26, 32, 35

in Structure Pane, 55
test client after invoking, 28, 29
writing business logic for, 24–26
`convertItems` method, 268–269
copying files or folders, 46–47
`create` method, 171, 194
CreditCheck JMS control, 194–197, 203–204
CreditReport Web service, 106–107
CTRL files
    for CurrencyCalcControl Web service, 142–143
    for Database control, 156–157
    for EJB control, 169–170
    generating in Project Tree, 143–144
    for JMS control, 178–179
    naming conventions, 144
    for Service control, 140, 142–143
`CurrencyCalc` class, 31–32
CurrencyCalc Web service
    class declaration, 31–32
    `Context` object, 32, 55
    `Convert` method, 22–26, 32–33, 55
    creating a new service, 20–22
    creating project for, 18–20
    import statement, 31
    Navigation Bar for, 58
    scenario, 17–18
    source code, 29–33
    Structure Pane for, 55
    testing, 26–29
CurrencyCalcControl Web service
    CTRL file, 142–143
    interface, 142–143
    `@jws:control` annotation, 141
    overview, 140
    source code, 141
    type definition, 142
customizing WebLogic Workshop, 50–51

D

data types. *See* types (Java)
Database controls
    adding methods, 154
    adding to Web service, 153
    CTRL file for, 156–157
    database connection for, 155
    icons for methods, 154
    interface, 157
    LibraryCatalog Web service example, 159–163
    overview, 152

for queries that return a row, 157–158
for queries that return multiple rows, 158–159
Query Editor for, 154–155
Debug menu
    Start and Debug command, 68
    Start command, 27
Debugger
    Call Stack Pane, 70–71
    debugging commands, 68
    debugging interface, 68–71
    described, 41, 66
    Locals Pane, 68–69
    setting breakpoints, 67
    stepping through Web services, 67–68
    Watch Pane, 70
debugging
    commands for, 68
    JavaScript, 294
declaring
    `Context` object, 137–138
    control factory variables, 205
    functions in JavaScript, 277
    JSP declarations, 247
    object variables in JavaScript, 275
    proxy and conversation variables for Swing clients, 264–265
    variable instances in JSPs, 247
    XML variables in JavaScript, 281–282
`delete` operator (JavaScript), 288, 290
deleting
    clearing conversation stored state, 62
    files or folders, 47
Design View
    Add Control drop-down, 139
    adding methods in, 22–23
    alphabetical order, 80
    code order, 80
    `Context` object and, 138
    controls in, 22, 138
    conversations in, 78–81
    creating callbacks, 103
    display preferences, 79–81
    EJB control in, 169
    Map Editor, 117–119
    message format settings, 224–227
    for new Web service, 21
    overview, 21–22
    selecting objects in, 78

continued

Design View *continued*
   sorting methods in, 79–81
   switching with Source View, 30
   type order, 81
   as Web-service specific, 42
   XML maps in, 1117–1119
directives (JSP), 246–247
directories. *See* folders or directories
displayCatalog.jsp page, 255–259
DOM (Document Object Model), 132, 280
dot (.) operator in JavaScript, 276
`do-while` statement (Java), 335–336
Duplicate dialog box, 46
duplicating files or folders, 46–47

E

editing files in projects, 48
Eich, Brendan (*JavaScript Bible*), 280
EJB control
   accessing EJBs, 166–167, 171–172
   adding to Web service, 166, 168–170
   benefits of, 165–166
   CTRL source code, 169–170
   in Design View, 169
   EJB types accessed by, 166–167
   entity beans and, 171
   Inventory control example, 193–194
   JAR or client-jar for, 167–168
   JNDI name, 168
   OnlineStore Web service example, 192–204
   session beans and, 170–171
   using, 170–172
EJBs (Enterprise Java Beans)
   accessing through EJB control, 166–167, 171–172
   entity beans, 166–167, 171–172
   message-driven beans (MDBs), 167, 177
   methods for, 167
   overview, 8
   redeploying, 62
   session beans, 166–167, 170–172
   specification, 166
elements (JMS), 218
`else` statement (Java), 332–333
embedding expressions in JavaScript, 290
`Enable` attribute, 99
Enterprise Java Beans. *See* EJBs
entity beans, 166–167, 171–172. *See also* EJBs (Enterprise Java Beans)

error messages
   compiler warnings (Test View Warnings page), 65
   for JSP pages, 249, 251
   Map Editor error highlighting, 119
   in Message window, 54–55
   for SOAP messages, 227–228
   Source View error highlighting, 54
`exception` object (JSP), 249
executing. *See* starting
expressions
   embedding in JavaScript, 290
   Java, 329–331
   JSP, 247–248
external address XML maps, 130–132

F

fields
   excluding from conversational state, 89
   finding in Structure Pane, 56
   member list for, 51–52
   transient, 89
File menu, New Project command, 19
files. *See also* folders or directories; *specific kinds*
   adding to projects, 20–21
   copying, 46–47
   creating, 43
   for custom settings, 51
   deleting, 47
   editing in projects, 48
   moving, 46
   renaming, 47
   WebLogic Workshop file types, 45
filtering
   messages with JMS control, 191–192
   XML list members by value in JavaScript, 286–287
   by XML namespace in JavaScript, 292–294
`find` method (entity beans), 171
finish methods of conversations
   indicator, 79
   `@jws:conversation` annotation for, 82
   overview, 77–78
   setting for tags, 79
   terminology, 76
   Test View and, 90, 91
`finishConversation` method, 94

folders or directories. *See also* Project Tree
  copying, 46–47
  creating, 43–44
  deleting, 47
  installation default, 42
  for JAR files, 24
  moving, 45–46
  for projects, 19
  renaming, 47
  WEB-INF, 19
for and for..in statements (JavaScript), 279–280, 291–292
for statement (Java), 336–337
form-get message format, 225
form-post message format, 224
FromXML function (JavaScript), 297–298, 301–302
functions. *See also* methods
  declaring in JavaScript, 277
  to initialize proxy classes, 265–266
  JavaScript function call in XML map, 295, 297–298
  stack frame for calls, 70–71
  for XML (JavaScript), 309–310

G

generateCatalogTable method, 266–268
generateConvID method, 244, 266
getApproval method, 195
getCallbackLocation method, 109
getCallbackPassword method, 109
getCallbackUsername method, 109
getCoalesceEvents method, 146
getConversationAge method, 95–96
getConversationID method, 96
getCurrencyName method, 55
getCurrencyTypeCode method, 55
getCurrentAge method, 94
getCurrentIdleTime method, 94
getMaxAge method, 94
getMaxIdleTime method, 94
getRepeatsEvery method, 146
getResults method, 238
getService method, 96
getTimeout method, 146
getTimeoutAt method, 146, 147
getX naming convention, 102
Goodman, Danny (*JavaScript Bible*), 280

Group by Title option (Structure Pane), 56
GUIDs (globally unique identifiers), 243–245, 266

H

headers
  JMS, 175, 188, 219
  SOAP, 210, 227–233
  XML maps with TextMessage headers, 188
Hello World Web service
  description of, 13, 14
  modifying to use name as parameter, 15–17
  running, 13
  WebLogic Workshop source code, 15
  WSDL source code, 38–41
HelloWorld.java program, 315–317, 318
Help system, 20
HTML-based service disadvantages, 6–7
HTTP (Hypertext Transport Protocol)
  asynchronous messaging and, 217
  body of SOAP message request, 210–211
  invoking Web services using, 209–217
  overview, 209–210
  request overview, 210–211
  request payload example, 211
  response message example, 212
  SOAP header, 210
  SOAP message example, 210–211
  viewing message flow in Test View, 212–217
http-soap message format, 225–226
http-xml message format, 225

I

icons
  for buffered methods, 99
  for controls, 55
  for Database control methods, 154
  in Project Tree, 42
IDE
  advantages of, 37
  manual coding versus use of, 38–41
  primary features, 41–42
identifiers (Java), 317–318
if...else structures (JavaScript), 278
if statement (Java), 331–333
implicit objects (JSP), 248–249
import statements
  CurrencyCalc Web service, 31
  member list for completing, 53

378 Index

in scope variables, 68
index of JavaScript arrays, 276, 277
`initComponents` method, 269-270
initializing
    `Callback` interface, 105
    controls and, 105, 138
    proxy classes, 265-266
inner classes, 87-88
installing WebLogic Workshop platform trial edition from CD, 312-313
instances
    for callbacks, 105
    `Context` object, 32
    declaring for variables in JSPs, 247
    Java operator, 329
    session beans, 171
interfaces
    `Callback`, 104-105
    Database control, 157
    for entity beans versus session beans, 167
    Java, 321-323
    `java.io.DataInput`, 342-343
    `java.io.DataOutput`, 342
    `java.io.ObjectInput`, 344
    `java.io.ObjectOutput`, 343-344
    `java.io.Serializable`, 88, 341
    `java.lang.Runnable`, 348
    `java.util.Collection`, 360-361
    `java.util.Iterator`, 361
    polling, 238
    Service control, 142-143
interpreter, Java, 315, 316
Inventory EJB control, 193-194
invoking. *See* starting
`isComplete` method, 101-102
`isFinished` method, 94
`isPurchaseComplete` method, 260
`isX` naming convention, 102

J

JAR (Java Archive) files
    for EJB control, 167-168
    folder for, 24
    for Java proxy, 60, 243
    for OnlineStore Web service, 192
Java. *See also* control flow statements (Java); Java libraries
    abstract classes, 323-324
    arrays, 320
    classes, 321
    compiler, 315, 316
    control flow statements, 331-340
    expressions, statements, and blocks, 329-331
    file type, 45
    Hello World program, 315-317, 318
    identifiers, 317-318
    interfaces, 321-323
    interpreter, 315, 316
    for JSPs, 246
    JWS and, 29
    naming conventions for methods, 102
    naming rules, 43
    operators, 324-329
    order of precedence for operators, 330
    primitive data types, 319
    reference data types, 319-320
    scoping rules, 68
    as third-generation language, 315
    types, 319-324
    variables, 318
    wrapper classes for primitive data types, 319-320
Java Archive files. *See* JAR files
JAVA files, 45
Java libraries. *See also specific packages*
    `java.io` package, 341-346
    `java.lang` package, 347-357
    `java.math` package, 366-368
    `java.net` package, 358-360
    `java.util` package, 360-366
    member list for, 52
Java methods. *See* methods
Java Naming and Directory Service (JNDI), 166, 168
Java Proxy link (Test View Overview page), 60
Java Server Pages. *See* JSP clients; JSPs
Java 2 Enterprise Edition. *See* J2EE
Java Virtual Machine (JVM), 315, 316
Java Web Services files. *See* JWS files
Javadoc annotations. *See also* comments; properties
    `<code>` tag, 36
    commented `Convert` method example, 35-36
    comments, 33-34
    defined, 32
    `jws` prefix, 35
    `@jws:context`, 32
    `@jws:control`, 141

Index

@jws:conversation, 82, 83
@jws:conversation-lifetime, 93
@jws:jms, 179
@jws:message-buffer, 99
@jws:operation, 24–25, 33, 35
@jws:parameter-xml, 123
@jws:protocol, 226
@jws:return-xml, 123
Property Editor and, 81
separating text from tags, 34
tags, 33–34
Web site, 34
java.io package
   java.io.DataInput interface, 342–343
   java.io.DataOutput interface, 342
   java.io.File class, 345
   java.io.IOException class, 346
   java.io.ObjectInput interface, 344
   java.io.ObjectOutput interface, 343–344
   java.io.PrintWriter class, 345–346
   java.io.Serializable interface, 88, 341
   overview, 341
java.lang package
   java.lang.Boolean class, 348–349
   java.lang.Byte class, 349–350
   java.lang.Character class, 350
   java.lang.Class class, 347–348
   java.lang.Double class, 351
   java.lang.Exception class, 357
   java.lang.Float class, 351–352
   java.lang.Integer class, 352–353
   java.lang.Long class, 353–354
   java.lang.Object class, 347
   java.lang.Runnable interface, 348
   java.lang.Short class, 354–355
   java.lang.String class, 355
   java.lang.Thread class, 356
   java.lang.Throwable class, 356–357
   overview, 347
java.math package
   java.math.BigDecimal class, 366–367
   java.math.BigInteger class, 367–368
   overview, 366
java.net package
   java.net.DatagramSocket class, 358–359
   java.net.Socket class, 358
   java.net.SocketException class, 360
   java.net.URL class, 359–360
   overview, 358
JavaScript
   appendChild function, 289
   arrays, 276–277
   calling FromXML function from XML map, 297–298
   calling ToXML function from XML map, 298
   comments, 15
   connecting function names with function calls, 295–296
   connecting functions for mapping with XML maps, 299
   debugging, 294
   declaring functions, 277
   declaring object variables, 275
   declaring XML variables, 281–282
   delete operator, 288, 290
   dot operator, 276
   embedding expressions, 290
   enhancing XML maps with, 273–274
   file type, 45
   filtering by XML namespace in, 292–294
   filtering XML list members by value, 286–287
   for and for..in statements, 279–280, 291–292
   FromXML function examples, 297, 300–303
   function call in XML map, 295, 297–298
   functions for XML, 309–310
   further information, 280
   if...else structures, 278
   importing Java classes, 294
   knowledge required, 9
   objects and object hierarchies, 275–276
   operators for XML, 307–308
   overview, 9
   plus operator, 288–289
   plus-equals operator, 288–289
   prependChild function, 289–290
   primer, 274–280
   properties for XML, 309
   statements for XML, 308
   tools for handling XML, 280–294
   ToXML function examples, 298–299, 303–307
   for translating XML name data, 297, 298–299

continued

JavaScript *continued*
    using XML in, 280–281
    variables, 274–275
    writing functions for mapping, 295–307
    XML hierarchies in, 282–285
    XML lists in, 286
    XML loop structures in, 291–292
    for XML mapping, 132
    XML translation through functions, 296–299
    XML tree management, 288–290
    XPath syntax and, 287–288
JavaScript Bible (Goodman, Danny and Eich, Brendan), 280
`java.util` package
    `java.util.ArrayList` class, 361–362
    `java.util.Calendar` class, 363–364
    `java.util.Collection` interface, 360–361
    `java.util.Date` class, 362–363
    `java.util.Hashtable` class, 364–365
    `java.util.Iterator` interface, 361
    `java.util.Vector` class, 365–366
    overview, 360
JDBC Connection Pool, 155
JMS control. *See also* Add JMS Control dialog box; messages (JMS)
    adding methods, 187–188
    adding to Web service, 166, 177–181
    benefits of, 165–166
    correlating received messages, 190–191
    CreditCheck control example, 194–197, 203–204
    CTRL file for, 178–179
    default method and callback with XML maps applied, 179–181
    filtering messages, 191–192
    JMS primer, 173–177
    `@jws:jms` annotation, 179
    for `MapMessage` type, 185–187
    message types exposed by, 182–183
    message-driven beans and, 167
    for `ObjectMessage` type, 185
    OnlineStore Web service example, 192–204
    for `TextMessage` type, 183–185, 188–190
    using message types, 181–187
    XML maps with `TextMessage` headers, 188
    XML maps with `TextMessage` properties, 188–190

JMS (Java Message Service). *See also* messages (JMS)
    clients, 176, 177, 219–221
    elements, 218
    invoking Web services using, 221–224
    message body, 219
    message headers, 175, 188, 218–219
    message properties, 175, 188–190, 219
    message sections, 218
    message types, 176, 181–187
    messages, 174–176
    primer, 173–177
    queues, 173–174, 176
    terminology, 176
    topics, 174, 176
    writing a client, 219–221
`jms-soap` message format, 225–226
`jms-xml` message format, 225
JNDI (Java Naming and Directory Service), 166, 168
JSP clients
    addItem.jsp page, 259
    conversations using, 252–264
    displayCatalog.jsp page, 255–259
    importing classes and packages, 252
    JSP primer, 246–249
    login page, 250–251
    startShopping.jsp page, 253–255
    suitability of, 245–246
    testing setup, 250
    using the proxy from JSP code, 249
    viewResults.jsp page, 259–264
JSPs (Java Server Pages)
    actions, 248
    addItem.jsp example, 259
    declarations, 247
    developing clients, 245–264
    directives, 246–247
    displayCatalog.jsp example, 255–259
    expressions, 247–248
    implicit objects, 248–249
    JWS files versus, 21
    overview, 245–246
    primer, 246–249
    scriptlets, 247
    startShopping.jsp example, 253–255
    viewResults.jsp example, 259–264

JSX files, described, 45
J2EE (Java 2 Enterprise Edition)
    application servers, 7
    applications, 8
    distributed applications and, 166
    EJB specification, 166
    JNDI name for resources, 166
    overview, 7–8
    Web service roles and, 166
    WebLogic Workshop and, 8
JVM (Java Virtual Machine), 315, 316
JWS (Java Web Services) files
    creating, 20–21
    CTRL and WSDL files and children of, 144
    Java and, 29
    JSPs versus, 21
    overview, 21, 29, 45
jws prefix for WebLogic Workshop tags, 35
JWS tags. *See* tags
@jws:context annotation, 32
JwsContext class, automatic import of, 31
@jws:control annotation, 141
@jws:conversation annotation, 82, 83
@jws:conversation-lifetime
    annotation, 93
@jws:jms annotation, 179
@jws:message-buffer annotation, 99
@jws:operation annotation, 24–25, 33, 35
@jws:parameter-xml annotation, 123
@jws:protocol annotation, 226
@jws:return-xml annotation, 123

L

launching. *See* starting
libraries. *See* Java libraries
LibraryCatalog Web service, 159–163
licenses for WebLogic Server, 312
Listener Web service, 110–111, 112
listItems method, 194
localhost machine name, 66
Locals Pane (Debugger), 68–69
Log all messages option, 62
Log Settings (Test View Console page), 60, 62
login page for JSP clients, 250–251

M

machine language, 315
makeName method, 119–122

Map Editor. *See also* XML maps
    changing XML maps using, 119–120
    default map method, 117
    Map Type button, 118–119
    Parameter XML tab, 118
    Return XML tab, 118, 121
    signature of method in, 118
    starting, 117
    text boxes, 118
MapMessage type (JMS), 185–187
max-age attribute, 93, 94
max-idle-time attribute, 93, 94
MDBs (message-driven beans), 167, 177. *See also* EJBs (Enterprise Java Beans)
member list
    bold methods in, 52
    choosing members from, 51–52
    for field and method names, 51–52
    for method parameters, 52–53
    in Navigation Bar, 58–59
    for packages in import statements, 53
member variables, 32
message formats
    attributes, 226–227
    setting in Design View, 224–225
    setting in Source View, 226
Message Log
    callbacks in, 107–108
    HTTP message flow in, 214–217
Message window, 54–55
message-buffer tag, 99, 102
messages (JMS). *See also* JMS control
    body, 219
    BytesMessage type, 185–186
    correlating received messages, 190–191
    exposed by JMS control, 182–183
    filtering using receive-selector property, 191–192
    headers, 175, 188, 218–219
    MapMessage type, 185–187
    ObjectMessage type, 185
    overview, 174–175
    payload, 175
    properties, 175, 188–190, 219
    StreamMessage type, 185–186
    TextMessage type, 183–185, 188–190
    types, 176, 181–187
    XML maps for, 175, 188–190

methods. *See also* conversations; Java methods; nonexposed methods; *specific methods*
   adding from member list, 52–53
   adding in Design View, 22–23
   adding to Database control, 154
   adding to JMS control, 187–188
   API documentation, 34
   bold in member list, 52
   callbacks versus, 103
   code completion for parameters, 53
   Context object, callback-related, 109
   Context object, conversation-related, 94
   conversational, 76–78, 79
   default XML map for, 117
   defined, 22
   for EJBs, 167
   finding in Structure Pane, 56
   GUID generation, 244
   icon for buffered methods, 99
   Java naming conventions, 102
   java.io.DataInput interface, 343
   java.io.DataOutput interface, 342
   java.io.File class, 345
   java.io.ObjectInput interface, 344
   java.io.ObjectOutput interface, 343–344
   java.io.PrintWriter class, 346
   java.lang.Boolean class, 349
   java.lang.Byte class, 349–350
   java.lang.Character class, 350
   java.lang.Class class, 347–348
   java.lang.Double class, 351
   java.lang.Float class, 352
   java.lang.Integer class, 353
   java.lang.Long class, 353–354
   java.lang.Object class, 347
   java.lang.Runnable interface, 348
   java.lang.Short class, 354–355
   java.lang.String class, 355
   java.lang.Thread class, 456
   java.lang.Throwable class, 357
   java.math.BigDecimal class, 367
   java.math.BigInteger class, 368
   java.net.DatagramSocket class, 359
   java.net.Socket class, 358
   java.net.URL class, 360
   java.util.Calendar class, 364
   java.util.Collection interface, 361
   java.util.Date class, 363
   java.util.Hashtable class, 365
   java.util.Iterator interface, 361
   java.util.Vector class, 366
   @jws:operation annotation, 24–25, 33, 35
   member list for, 51–53
   in Navigation Bar, 58
   OnlineStore Web service example, 86–87, 192–204
   signature of, 118, 154, 155
   sorting in Design View, 79–81
   Timer control, 145–147
   Web service versus Java class methods, 22, 25
   wrapper service exposure of, 238
   writing business logic for, 24–26
moving, files or folders, 45–46
mustUnderstand SOAP header attribute, 227

N

naming
   automatic class name changes, 46
   controls, 140
   CTRL file conventions, 144
   Java conventions for methods, 102
   Java naming rules, 43
   JNDI names, 166
   machine running WebLogic Server, 66
   methods, 22
   renaming files or folders, 47
   WSDL file conventions, 144
Navigation Bar, 41, 57–59
New File dialog box, 20–21
New Folder dialog box, 43
New Project command (File menu), 19
New Project dialog box, 20
NewSubService Web service, 148–152
nonexposed methods, 22. *See also* methods

O

object variables, 275
ObjectMessage type (JMS), 185
onException method, 55
onFinish method, 55
OnlineStore Web service
   checkout method, 203
   CreditCheck JMS control, 194–197
   with EJB and JMS controls, 192–204
   exceptions, 202
   important features, 86
   inner classes, 87–88

Inventory EJB control, 193-194
    JAR file for, 192
    maintaining conversational state, 88-89
    methods, 86-87
    source code, 83-86, 197-201
    testing, 89-91
    viewCatalog method, 87, 90, 202-203, 255
    wrapper service for, 239-242
opening. *See* starting
operations. *See also* callbacks; methods
    defined, 22
    @jws:operation annotation, 24-25, 33, 35
    in Structure Pane, 55
    types of, 22
operators for XML (JavaScript), 307-308
operators (Java)
    allocation, 328-329
    arithmetic, 324-325
    assignment, 327-328
    bitwise-manipulation or shift, 327
    conditional, 326
    defined, 324
    instance, 329
    order of precedence, 330
    relational, 325-326
    selection, 328
Oracle, database connection to, 155
order of precedence for Java operators, 330
out object (JSP), 249
Overview page (Test View), 59-60, 243

P

package statements, 44, 46
packages. *See also specific packages*
    java.io, 341-346
    java.lang, 347-357
    java.math, 366-368
    java.net, 358-360
    java.util, 360-366
    for JSP client support, 252
    member list for, 53
    member list for completing, 53
    for new Web services, 44
    for Swing client support, 264
    WebLogic Workshop project structure and, 19
Persistence Settings (Test View Console page), 62
phase attribute, 79

plus operator (JavaScript), 288-289
plus-equals operator (JavaScript), 288-289
point-to-point messaging model, 176
polling interfaces, 238
POTranslator XML map, 124-126
Preferences command (Tools menu), 50, 79
Preferences dialog box, 50-51, 79-81
prependChild function (JavaScript), 289-290
primitive data types (Java), 319-320
print statement (JavaScript), 279
producer, 176
Project Browser. *See* Project Tree
Project Tree. *See also* folders or directories
    copying files or folders, 46-47
    creating files, 43
    creating folders, 43-44
    deleting files or folders, 47
    editing files in projects, 48
    generate options, 48
    generating CTRL files, 143-144
    generating WSDL files, 143-144
    icons, 42
    managing projects, 43-47
    moving files, 46
    moving folders, 45-46
    overview, 18-19, 41, 42
    renaming files or folders, 47
projects. *See also* Project Tree
    adding files to, 20-21
    creating a new project, 19-20
    described, 18
    editing files in, 48
    folders for, 19
    Java package system and structure of, 19
    managing, 43-47
    WEB-INF folder, 19
properties. *See also* Javadoc annotations; tags
    attributes, 78-79
    conversation-lifetime, 92-93
    getting for JavaScript objects, 275-276
    Javadoc annotations and, 81
    in source code, 81-83
    structure of, 78-79
    tags, 78-79
    for XML (JavaScript), 309
Property Editor
    Javadoc annotations and, 81
    overview, 78
    structure of properties in, 78-79
    tag or attribute descriptions in, 83
    as Web-service specific, 42

proxies. *See also* clients for Web services
    generating, 242–243
    initializing proxy classes, 265–266
    Java proxy class, 60
    Java Proxy link, 60
    Proxy Support JAR link, 60, 243
    using from JSP code, 249
publish-and-subscribe model, 176
purchase order translator XML map, 124–126
PurchaseOrder Web service, 127–130, 301–306

Q

Query Editor, 154–155
queues (JMS), 173–174, 176

R

`receive-correlation-property` attribute, 191
receive-selector property, 191–192
Redeploy Beans persistence setting, 62
reference data types (Java), 319–320
relational operators (Java), 325–326
Remote Method Invocation (RMI), 167
`removeItem` method, 86
Rename dialog box, 47
renaming. *See* naming
Repeats-every option (Timer control), 145
`request` method, 206–207
`request` object (JSP), 249, 251
`requestScore` method, 107
`resetIdleTime` method, 94
`response` object (JSP), 249
`restart` method, 146
restoring default WebLogic Workshop settings, 51
`retry-count` attribute, 102
`retry-delay` attribute, 102
`return` statement (Java), 337–339
`returnScore` callback, 107
reusing XML maps, 130–132
RMI (Remote Method Invocation), 167
running. *See* starting

S

scoping rules, 68
scriptlets, 247
selection operator (Java), 328
`send` method, 195–196
`sendCallback` method, 112

`send-correlation-property` attribute, 191
sending a conversation ID, 245
`sendTimer` control, 152
Server Progress dialog box, 26–27
Service controls
    adding to Web service, 139–140
    control factories, 140, 204–207
    CTRL file format for, 140
    CurrencyCalcControl example, 140–144
    function of, 140–144
    naming, 140
    overview, 139
    WSDL format for, 140
`ServiceHandle` object, 96
session beans, 166–167, 170–172. *See also* EJBs (Enterprise Java Beans)
`session` object (JSP), 249
`setAttribute` method, 251
`setCallbackLocation` method, 109
`setCallbackPassword` method, 109
`setCallbackUsername` methods, 109
`setCoalesceEvents` method, 146
`setMaxAge` methods, 94
`setMaxIdleTime` methods, 94
`setRepeatsEvery` methods, 146
`setSubscriptionStatus` method, 152
`setTimeout` methods, 146
`setTimeoutAt` method, 147
`setX` naming convention, 102
shift operators (Java), 327
signature of methods, 118, 154, 155
SimpleBuffer Web service, 99–102
SimpleConversation Web service, 81–82
single-shot timers, 145
slash (/) for comments, 15, 33
SOAP (Simple Object Access Protocol)
    controlling headers, 227–233
    `Convert` method and, 63–64
    defined, 5
    error messages, 227–228
    headers for conversations, 228–233, 245
    HTTP body for messages, 210–211
    HTTP header for messages, 210
    message example, 210–211
    `mustUnderstand` header attribute, 227
    overview, 5
    Web site for standard, 5
`soap-style` attribute, 225, 226–227
sorting methods in Design View, 79–81

Index

source code
    `<code>` tag (Javadoc), 36
    comments in, 15
    properties in, 81–83
    viewing for stack frame entries, 71
    XML maps in, 122–123
Source View
    code completion, 51–53
    described, 29–30, 41
    error messages, 54–55
    message format settings, 226
    switching with Design View, 30
    syntax coloring, 49–51
    text editor, 49
    using, 15
spring icon, 99
square brackets ([]) for JavaScript arrays, 277
stack frames, 70–71. *See also* Call Stack Pane
star (*) for comments, 15, 33
Start and Debug command (Debug menu), 68
Start command (Debug menu), 27
`start` method, 147
start methods of conversations
    indicator, 79
    `@jws:conversation` annotation for, 82
    overview, 77
    setting for tags, 79
    terminology, 76
    Test View and, 90, 91
Start WebLogic Server command
    (Tools menu), 26
`startConversation` method, 95
`<StartHeader>` SOAP header, 228, 229, 232,
    233, 245
starting
    Hello World Web service, 13
    Help system, 20
    invoking Web services using HTTP, 209–217
    invoking Web services using JMS, 221–224
    Map Editor, 117
    Test View directly, 66
    WebLogic console, 9
    WebLogic Server, 26, 27
    WebLogic Workshop, 12
`startProcessing` method, 101–102
`startShopping` method, 86, 89, 90
startShopping.jsp page, 253–255
Step Into (debugging command), described, 68
Step Out (debugging command), described, 68
Step Over (debugging command). described, 68
`stop` method, 147

`StreamMessage` type (JMS), 185–186
Structure Pane, 41, 55–57
Structure Pane Ordering dialog box, 56, 57
`submitOrder` method, 128, 300–301
`Subscribe` method, 151
substitution directives
    for attributes, 121
    changing, 119–120
    defined, 119
    mixed content and, 122
    Return maps, 121
Swing clients
    converting item array to array of object
        arrays, 268–269
    declaring proxy and conversation variables,
        264–265
    generating conversation IDs, 266
    generating table for list of items, 266–268
    importing packages and classes, 264
    initializing proxy classes, 265–266
    setting up user interface, 269–271
    Swing application example, 264
`switch` statement (Java), 333–334
`switch-case` statement (Java), 334
synchronous model, 97–98, 167, 209–210
syntax coloring, 49–51
system requirements for the CD, 311

T

tags. *See also* Javadoc annotations; properties
    attributes, 78–79, 82
    defined, 78
    descriptions in Property Editor, 83
    JSP actions, 248
    mapping to and from attributes, 121
    message-buffer, 99, 102
    specifying attributes for, 82
ternary selection operator (Java), 328
Test Form page (Test View), 62–63
Test View. *See also specific pages*
    accessing directly, 66
    auto-compilation, 66
    callbacks in, 107–108
    Console page, 60–62
    for conversational Web services, 89–91
    described, 41, 59
    HTTP message flow in, 212–217
    for OnlineStore Web service, 89–91
    Overview page, 59–60, 243

continued

Test View *continued*
    tabs for switching pages, 59
    Test Form page, 62–63
    Test XML page, 63–65
    Warnings page, 65
    XML Map text box, 120
Test XML page (Test View), 63–65
testing Web services
    conversational Web services, 89–91
    CurrencyCalc example, 26–29
    JSP clients, 250
text editor. *See* Source View
TextMessage type (JMS), 183–185, 188–190
throw statement (Java), 341
Timeout option (Timer control), 145
Timer control
    adding to Web service, 144–145
    callbacks, 145–146, 148
    methods, 145–147
    NewSubService Web service example, 148–152
    overview, 144
    Repeats-every option, 145
    single-shot timers, 145
    Timeout option, 145
Tools menu
    Preferences command, 50, 79
    Start WebLogic Server command, 26
topics (JMS), 174, 176
ToXML function (JavaScript), 298–299, 303–307
transient fields, 89
trial edition of WebLogic Workshop (on the CD), 312–313
troubleshooting companion CD materials, 314
try-catch-finally statement (Java), 339–341
type order in Design view, 81
types (Java)
    arrays, 320
    classes, 321
    defined, 319
    interfaces, 321–323
    primitive data types, 319
    reference data types, 319–320
    wrapper classes for primitive data types, 319–320

U

UDDI (Universal Description, Discovery, and Integration), 6
unary operators (Java)
    arithmetic, 324–325
    conditional, 326
user interface for Swing clients, 269–271

V

ValidateCredit EJB, 169, 171–172
variables
    changing values, 68, 70
    declaring for control factories, 205
    declaring for Swing clients, 264–265
    declaring instances in JSPs, 247
    declaring object variables in JavaScript, 275
    declaring XML variables in JavaScript, 281–282
    in scope, 68
    Java, 318
    JavaScript, 274–275
    in Locals Pane, 70
    scoping rules, 68
    to support control factories, 205
    in Watch Pane, 70
viewCart method, 86, 259
viewCatalog method, 87, 90, 202–203, 255
viewResults.jsp page, 259–264

W

WAR files, 19
Warnings page (Test View), 65
Watch Pane (Debugger), 70
Web service Description Language. *See* WSDL
Web services. *See also* clients for Web services
    adding Database control, 153
    adding EJB control, 166, 168–170
    adding JMS control, 166, 177–181
    adding methods, 22–26
    adding Service control, 139–140
    adding Timer control, 144–145
    Caller example, 109–110, 111–112
    comments, 15
    controlling SOAP headers, 227–233
    ConversationAge example, 95–96
    conversational, with control factory, 207
    creating, 17–29, 43–44
    CreditReport example, 106–107

Index

CurrencyCalc example, 17–29
CurrencyCalcControl example, 140–144
defined, 4
file type, 45
future of computer industry and, 4
generating proxies for, 242–243
Hello World example, 13–17
importance of, 6–7
invoking using HTTP, 209–217
invoking using JMS, 221–224
LibraryCatalog example, 159–163
Listener example, 110–111, 112
message formats, 224–227
modifying, 15–17
NewSubService example, 148–152
OnlineStore example, 83–91, 192–204, 239–242
overview, 4–7, 10
PurchaseOrder example, 127–130, 301–306
SimpleBuffer example, 99–102
SimpleConversation example, 81–82
standards, 4–6
stepping through, 67–68
testing, 26–29
Web sites
   Java naming rules, 43
   Javadoc, 34
   SOAP standard, 5
   UDDI standard, 6
   WebLogic Workshop documentation, 12
   WSDL standard, 6
WEB-INF folder, 19
WebLogic console, starting, 9
WebLogic Server. *See also* `config.xml` file
   on the CD, 313–314
   configuration knowledge required for, 9
   further information, 7
   licenses, 312
   starting, 26, 27
   as WebLogic Workshop requirement, 8
WebLogic Workshop
   adding methods to Web services, 22–26
   creating a new project, 18–20
   creating a new Web service, 20–22
   described, 7
   documentation site, 12
   file types, 45
   first time using, 12–13
   Help system, 20
   installing trial edition from CD, 312–313

   J2EE world and, 8
   knowledge not required for, 8
   knowledge required for, 9
   restoring default settings, 51
   Source View tab, 15
   starting, 12
   testing Web services, 26–29
   WebLogic Server required for, 8
`while` statement (Java), 335
WinAce on the CD, 313
workflows, 76
Workshop Control link (Test View Overview page), 60
.Workshop file, 51
wrapper classes for primitive data types (Java), 319–320
wrapper service
   as alternative to callbacks, 238
   for OnlineStore Web service, 239–242
   process for creating, 239
WSDL (Web service Description Language)
   defined, 5
   file naming conventions, 144
   generating files in Project Tree, 143–144
   overview, 5–6
   Service control format, 140
   source code for Hello World, 38–41
   Test View Overview page link for, 60
   Web site for standard, 6
w3C standards, 5, 6

X

XML
   JMS `TextMessage` containing, 184–185
   messages, 115–116
   for SOAP messages, 63–64
XML maps. *See also* Map Editor
   attributes and, 121
   calling a JavaScript FromXML function, 297–298
   calling a JavaScript ToXML function, 28
   changing, 119–120
   connecting JavaScript function names with function calls, 295–296
   connecting JavaScript functions for mapping with, 299
   default for method, 117
   in Design View, 1117–1119
   DOM for, 132
   enhancing with JavaScript, 273–274

continued

XML maps *continued*
    external address maps, 130–132
    JavaScript for, 132
    JavaScript FromXML function examples, 297, 300–303
    JavaScript function call in, 295, 297–298
    JavaScript ToXML function examples, 298–299, 303–307
    JMS control and, 175, 179–181, 182–183, 188–190
    `makeName` method examples, 119–122
    overview, 116–117
    POTranslator example, 124–126
    repetitive elements and, 126–130
    reusing, 130–132
    in source code, 122–123
    substitution directives, 119–122
    syntax, 119–122
    in Test View, 120
    with `TextMessage` headers, 188
    with `TextMessage` properties, 188–190
    translation through JavaScript functions, 296–299
    writing JavaScript functions for, 295–307
    `xm:multiple` attribute, 129–130

XML with JavaScript
    declaring variables, 281–282
    filtering by namespace, 292–293
    filtering list members by value, 286–287
    hierarchies, 282–285
    importing Java classes, 294
    JavaScript functions, 309–310
    JavaScript operators, 307–308
    JavaScript properties, 309
    JavaScript statements, 308
    lists, 286
    loop structures, 291–292
    tools, 280–294
    using, 280–281
    XML tree management, 288–290
    XPath syntax and, 287–288

`xml-map` attribute, 123
`xml-map` tag, 131
`<xm:map-file>` tag, 130
`xm:multiple` attribute, 129–130
XPath syntax, JavaScript and, 287–288

Z

Zuffoletto, Joe (*BEA WebLogic Server Bible*), 7

Wiley Publishing, Inc.
End-User License Agreement

READ THIS. You should carefully read these terms and conditions before opening the software packet(s) included with this book "Book". This is a license agreement "Agreement" between you and Wiley Publishing, Inc."WPI". By opening the accompanying software packet(s), you acknowledge that you have read and accept the following terms and conditions. If you do not agree and do not want to be bound by such terms and conditions, promptly return the Book and the unopened software packet(s) to the place you obtained them for a full refund.

1. **License Grant.** WPI grants to you (either an individual or entity) a nonexclusive license to use one copy of the enclosed software program(s) (collectively, the "Software" solely for your own personal or business purposes on a single computer (whether a standard computer or a workstation component of a multi-user network). The Software is in use on a computer when it is loaded into temporary memory (RAM) or installed into permanent memory (hard disk, CD-ROM, or other storage device). WPI reserves all rights not expressly granted herein.

2. **Ownership.** WPI is the owner of all right, title, and interest, including copyright, in and to the compilation of the Software recorded on the disk(s) or CD-ROM "Software Media". Copyright to the individual programs recorded on the Software Media is owned by the author or other authorized copyright owner of each program. Ownership of the Software and all proprietary rights relating thereto remain with WPI and its licensers.

3. **Restrictions On Use and Transfer.**
   (a) You may only (i) make one copy of the Software for backup or archival purposes, or (ii) transfer the Software to a single hard disk, provided that you keep the original for backup or archival purposes. You may not (i) rent or lease the Software, (ii) copy or reproduce the Software through a LAN or other network system or through any computer subscriber system or bulletin- board system, or (iii) modify, adapt, or create derivative works based on the Software.
   (b) You may not reverse engineer, decompile, or disassemble the Software. You may transfer the Software and user documentation on a permanent basis, provided that the transferee agrees to accept the terms and conditions of this Agreement and you retain no copies. If the Software is an update or has been updated, any transfer must include the most recent update and all prior versions.

4. **Restrictions on Use of Individual Programs.** You must follow the individual requirements and restrictions detailed for each individual program in the About the CD-ROM appendix of this Book. These limitations are also contained in the individual license agreements recorded on the Software Media. These limitations may include a requirement that after using the program for a specified period of time, the user must pay a registration fee or discontinue use. By opening the Software packet(s), you will be agreeing to abide by the licenses and restrictions for these individual programs that are detailed in the About the CD-ROM appendix and on the Software Media. None of the material on this Software Media or listed in this Book may ever be redistributed, in original or modified form, for commercial purposes.

5. **Limited Warranty.**

    (a) WPI warrants that the Software and Software Media are free from defects in materials and workmanship under normal use for a period of sixty (60) days from the date of purchase of this Book. If WPI receives notification within the warranty period of defects in materials or workmanship, WPI will replace the defective Software Media.

    (b) WPI AND THE AUTHOR OF THE BOOK DISCLAIM ALL OTHER WARRANTIES, EXPRESS OR IMPLIED, INCLUDING WITHOUT LIMITATION IMPLIED WARRANTIES OF MERCHANTABILITY AND FITNESS FOR A PARTICULAR PURPOSE, WITH RESPECT TO THE SOFTWARE, THE PROGRAMS, THE SOURCE CODE CONTAINED THEREIN, AND/OR THE TECHNIQUES DESCRIBED IN THIS BOOK. WPI DOES NOT WARRANT THAT THE FUNCTIONS CONTAINED IN THE SOFTWARE WILL MEET YOUR REQUIREMENTS OR THAT THE OPERATION OF THE SOFTWARE WILL BE ERROR FREE.

    (c) This limited warranty gives you specific legal rights, and you may have other rights that vary from jurisdiction to jurisdiction.

6. **Remedies.**

    (a) WPI's entire liability and your exclusive remedy for defects in materials and workmanship shall be limited to replacement of the Software Media, which may be returned to WPI with a copy of your receipt at the following address: Software Media Fulfillment Department, Attn.: BEA Weblogic Workshop: Building Next Generation Web Services Visually, Wiley Publishing, Inc., 10475 Crosspoint Blvd., Indianapolis, IN 46256, or call 1-800-762-2974. Please allow four to six weeks for delivery. This Limited Warranty is void if failure of the Software Media has resulted from accident, abuse, or misapplication. Any replacement Software Media will be warranted for the remainder of the original warranty period or thirty (30) days, whichever is longer.

    (b) In no event shall WPI or the author be liable for any damages whatsoever (including without limitation damages for loss of business profits, business interruption, loss of business information, or any other pecuniary loss) arising from the use of or inability to use the Book or the Software, even if WPI has been advised of the possibility of such damages.

    (c) Because some jurisdictions do not allow the exclusion or limitation of liability for consequential or incidental damages, the above limitation or exclusion may not apply to you.

7. **U.S. Government Restricted Rights.** Use, duplication, or disclosure of the Software for or on behalf of the United States of America, its agencies and/or instrumentalities "U.S. Government" is subject to restrictions as stated in paragraph (c)(1)(ii) of the Rights in Technical Data and Computer Software clause of DFARS 252.227-7013, or subparagraphs (c) (1) and (2) of the Commercial Computer Software - Restricted Rights clause at FAR 52.227-19, and in similar clauses in the NASA FAR supplement, as applicable.

8. **General.** This Agreement constitutes the entire understanding of the parties and revokes and supersedes all prior agreements, oral or written, between them and may not be modified or amended except in a writing signed by both parties hereto that specifically refers to this Agreement. This Agreement shall take precedence over any other documents that may be in conflict herewith. If any one or more provisions contained in this Agreement are held by any court or tribunal to be invalid, illegal, or otherwise unenforceable, each and every other provision shall remain in full force and effect.